Strategies for Generating E-Business Returns on Investment

Namchul Shin
Pace University, USA

IDEA GROUP PUBLISHING
Hershey • London • Melbourne • Singapore

Acquisitions Editor:	Mehdi Khosrow-Pour
Senior Managing Editor:	Jan Travers
Managing Editor:	Amanda Appicello
Development Editor:	Michele Rossi
Copy Editor:	Maria Boyer
Typesetter:	Amanda Appicello
Cover Design:	Lisa Tosheff
Printed at:	Yurchak Printing Inc.

Published in the United States of America by
    Idea Group Publishing (an imprint of Idea Group Inc.)
    701 E. Chocolate Avenue, Suite 200
    Hershey PA 17033
    Tel: 717-533-8845
    Fax: 717-533-8661
    E-mail: cust@idea-group.com
    Web site: http://www.idea-group.com

and in the United Kingdom by
    Idea Group Publishing (an imprint of Idea Group Inc.)
    3 Henrietta Street
    Covent Garden
    London WC2E 8LU
    Tel: 44 20 7240 0856
    Fax: 44 20 7379 3313
    Web site: http://www.eurospan.co.uk

Library of Congress Cataloging-in-Publication Data

Strategies for generating e-business returns on investment / Namchul Shin, editor.
    p. cm.
  Includes bibliographical references and index.
  ISBN 1-59140-417-7 (hardcover) -- ISBN 1-59140-418-5 (pbk.) -- ISBN 1-59140-419-3 (ebook)
 1. Electronic commerce--Technological innovations. 2. Electronic commerce--Technological innovations--Cost effectiveness. 3. Electronic commerce--Information technology. I. Shin, Namchul, 1962-
  HF5548.32.S782 2004
  658.8'72--dc22

                               2004003757

British Cataloguing in Publication Data
A Cataloguing in Publication record for this book is available from the British Library.

All work contributed to this book is new, previously-unpublished material. The views expressed in this book are those of the authors, but not necessarily of the publisher.

Strategies for Generating E-Business Returns on Investment

Table of Contents

Preface vi

Chapter I
Customer Relationship Management – A Strategy for Success in
Electronic Commerce 1
> *Nils Madeja, WHU, Germany*
> *Detlef Schoder, WHU, Germany*

Chapter II
Customer-centric Internet Strategies: Achieving Competitive
Advantage through CRM 21
> *Călin Gurău, Heriot-Watt University, UK*

Chapter III
eCRM Integration in E-Business: First Line of Offense to
Competitive Advantage 50
> *Cain Evans, University of Central England in Birmingham, UK*

Chapter IV
The Effects of IT on Supply Chain Management in the
Automobile Industry 86
> *Ki Chan Kim, The Catholic University of Korea, Korea*
> *Il Im, New Jersey Institute of Technology, USA*
> *Myung Soo Kang, Hansung University, Korea*

Chapter V
The Potential of B2B Commerce for Competitive Advantage 102
> *Ronan McIvor, University of Ulster, N. Ireland*
> *Paul Humphreys, University of Ulster, N. Ireland*

Chapter VI
**Know Your Why's and How's – Towards a Contingency Model
for Industrial E-Procurement** 125
    Jakob Rehme, University of Linköping, Sweden
    Daniel Kindström, University of Linköping, Sweden
    Staffan Brege, University of Linköping, Sweden

Chapter VII
**A Framework for Addressing Minority Suppliers as an E-Business
Strategy** 143
    Dale Young, Georgia College and State University, USA

Chapter VIII
Alaska's Embrace of Digital Opportunities 163
    Ping Lan, University of Alaska Fairbanks, USA
    David C. Yen, Miami University, USA

Chapter IX
**Strategic Success Factors for Selling Content Online:
Which Success Factors will make Internet Content a
Sustainable and Profitable Business?** 187
    Stephan A. Butscher, Simon, Kucher & Partners, UK
    Frank Luby, Simon, Kucher & Partners, USA
    Markus B. Hofer, Simon, Kucher & Partners, Germany

Chapter X
**Past Purchasing Behavior in E-Commerce: The Impact on
Intentions to Shop Online** 209
    TerryAnn Glandon, University of Texas at El Paso, USA
    Christine M. Haynes, University of Texas at El Paso, USA

Chapter XI
**Identifying Purchase Perceptions that Affect Consumers'
Internet Buying** 235
    Thomas W. Dillon, James Madison University, USA
    Harry L. Reif, James Madison University, USA

Chapter XII
**Strategic E-Commerce Aspects of the E-Banking/E-Lending
Industry** 254
    William T. Rupp, University of Montevallo, USA
    Alan D. Smith, Robert Morris University, USA

Chapter XIII
An E-Business System Development and Modernization Model to
Improve the Profitability of Investment Decisions 286
    Bahador Ghahramani, University of Nebraska at Omaha, USA

Chapter XIV
A Complementary Tele-Working Platform for Data and Voice
Networks 317
    Philip Sotiriades, University of Patras, Greece
    G.-P. K. Economou, University of Patras, Greece

About the Editor 339

About the Authors 340

Index 347

Preface

Companies invest in e-business and its supporting technology for their e-business initiatives. E-business applications such as supply chain management and customer relationship management improve transaction efficiency and scope economies, as well as promote new product and service offerings and close customer relationships. However, it is difficult for companies to capture these benefits as economic value or profits. Many companies launching e-businesses have not been successful at creating economic value. A survey done by AMR Research Inc. (2001) showed that companies would increase their e-business spending even during an economic downturn. However, the return on these investments has been mixed at best.

According to DMR Consulting Group Inc. (2002), 62% of companies that have implemented customer relationship management (CRM) products are not getting much benefit from their investments, which can run into millions of dollars. To justify continued expenditures, it may be necessary for IT managers to move beyond simply demonstrating the benefits of technology and objectively demonstrate the increase in economic value these technologies can produce. To create value from e-business, companies may have to develop appropriate strategies or unique value propositions to complement their e-business investments. This book presents a group of studies that yield significant new insights into the creation of e-business value.

The first chapter, by Madeja and Schoder, investigates empirically the impact of CRM on corporate success in e-commerce at the firm level. The authors find that a skill-set based on accumulating and exploiting customer knowledge for e-commerce is a critical success factor in e-commerce. This is especially true for B2C and small companies. The study is based on 469 companies in the German-speaking area of Europe, specifically Germany, Austria, and Switzerland.

Gurău's chapter analyzes the implementation process of a customer relationship management (CRM) system in online retailing and the challenges of transforming a product-focused business into a customer-centric organization. The author argues that the implementation of CRM systems in online organizations determines a complex restructuring of the organizational elements and processes to adapt to new customer-centric procedures.

The chapter by Evans presents Customer Relationship Operational Systems Integrated Technologies (CROSIT) and Customer Process Reference (CPR) models to assist e-businesses in articulating eCRM through a combination of system, application, and process activities. According to the author, the CROSIT model provides a five-layered approach to integrate technologies, resources, strategy, and manageability of an eCRM system. The CPR model is an extension of CROSIT, which is used to gauge the readiness of the eCRM system, including its applications, interrelated processes and sub-systems, and their integration into the e-business environment.

Kim, Im, and Kang's chapter introduces the concept of electronic supply chain design (eSCD) and develops a model that shows the effects of eSCD on the customization capability of companies. The model identifies three major effects of eSCD—electronic linkage effect, supply chain coordination effect, and co-engineering effect. The authors empirically test the model using data collected from the automobile industry in Korea.

The chapter by McIvor and Humphreys examines the strategic implications of B2B commerce for the buyer-supplier interface. The authors identify a number of areas where Internet technologies can make a contribution to the creation of competitive advantage. They argue that closed-network problems and the nature of buyer-supplier relations present major impediments to companies achieving the full strategic potential of Internet technologies at the buyer-supplier interface.

Analyzing the relationship between purchasing strategies and e-procurement solutions in handling different steps in the purchasing processes, Rehme, Kindström, and Brege propose a model based on purchasing strategies that identify appropriate e-procurement solutions to be considered for different types of purchased items. They argue that the model can be used to evaluate purchasing initiatives from both academic and practical perspectives.

Recognizing that minority-owned firms are excellent trading partners that offer competitive prices and high-quality products and services, Young examines how large corporations use their public websites to communicate with small, minority-owned, and women-owned businesses. Based on findings from a large-scale study of publicly available corporate websites, the author identifies common practices for Web-based supplier diversity efforts and proposes a framework for using the Web to initiate minority supplier contacts.

Lan and Yen's chapter investigates the impacts of the digital transition process in Alaska by systematically examining Internet usage in the state. The authors find that Alaska is very committed to taking advantage of digital opportunities and that the transition to digital technologies is at various stages of implementation throughout the state. This research can help policy makers and enterprises within Alaska to realize the potential of the current digital revolution and enterprises outside Alaska to target this market more effectively.

Based on the practical experience gained from numerous e-commerce consulting projects in Europe and the United States, Butscher, Luby, and Hofer provide an overview of strategic success factors for sustainable and profitable businesses with online content. The authors explore the practical implications of the strategic success factors they identify through a case study of a business selling music online. This leads them to a set of concrete action guidelines to be considered when starting a content-selling business on the Internet.

The chapter by Glandon and Haynes uses a modified form of the theory of planned behavior to examine the impact of past online purchasing behavior on intentions to purchase online in the future. The authors find that in addition to the theory's original constructs such as attitude, subjective norm, and perceived behavioral control, past purchasing behavior is directly related to intentions to shop online in the future. Their results indicate that the challenge to Web vendors is to entice potential customers to try online shopping, since they quickly gain control and confidence from the experience.

Dillon and Reif's chapter examines empirically how consumers' perception of purchases influences their Internet buying practices. Building upon existing knowledge of pre-Internet buying motivations, the authors identify 16 factors. These can be divided into four general categories: product perception, shopping experience, customer service, and consumer risk. The authors argue that successful e-businesses and e-commerce system developers must understand and acknowledge that consumers' perceptions about the marketplace in general, and about each vendor's website in particular, affect consumers' decisions to buy.

The chapter by Rupp and Smith examines strategic aspects of e-commerce that have a direct bearing on the complexities of the e-banking/e-lending industry. They argue that management must understand these complexities in order to leverage the power of the Internet and achieve sustainable competitive advantage. The authors use diffusion theory to help understand the practitioner's viewpoint of the many changes within the e-banking/e-lending industry.

Ghahramani's chapter proposes an Internet-based systems development and modernization model (SDMM) that can be used to develop new systems, to modernize legacy systems, and to increase the net present worth of current systems. The model uses online modules to develop products that are fully capable of bridging the design to the system development lifecycle phases. It is a structured approach through which system designers and developers can interact with users before the system is designed.

The chapter by Sotiriades and Economou introduces the premises, the implementation, and performance evaluation of a tele-working platform that was put into operation in the Public Bureaus of Thessaly's rural county in Hellas. According to the authors, this platform complies with various telecommunications service providers' specifications and is built on a distributed computing basis.

Acknowledgments

I would like to acknowledge the help of all those involved for the editing process for this book. Without their support the project could not have been satisfactorily completed. Deep appreciation and gratitude is due to Susan Merritt, Dean of the School of Computer Science and Information Systems, Pace University, for her generous allocation of summer research grants and editorial support services for this project.

I wish to thank all of the authors for their insights and excellent contributions. Most of these writers also served as referees for articles written by other authors, making this a truly collaborative project. Thanks go to all those who provided constructive and comprehensive reviews.

Special thanks also go to the publishing team at Idea Group Publishing. This book would not have been possible without their ongoing professional support. Particular recognition is due to Michele Rossi and Jan Travers, whose continual prodding via e-mail helped keep the project on schedule, and to Mehdi Khosrow-Pour, whose enthusiasm motivated me to accept his invitation to work with him on this undertaking.

Finally, I want to thank my wife, Joy, for her love and support throughout this project, and my son, Philip, the ultimate reason for all my work.

Namchul Shin, PhD
New York, NY, USA
January 2004

Chapter I

Customer Relationship Management –
A Strategy for Success in Electronic Commerce[*]

Nils Madeja
WHU, Germany

Detlef Schoder
WHU, Germany

Abstract

Customer relationship management (CRM) is a concept for increasing companies' profitability by enabling them to identify and concentrate on their profitable customers. The term "electronic commerce customer relationship management" (ECCRM) refers to the application of CRM in electronic commerce, i.e., when business relationships are maintained via the Internet or World Wide Web. Previous studies on the effectiveness of ECCRM have often focused on the process level, technical aspects, or on marketing issues. Yet only little evidence has been reported for the impact of ECCRM on the company level. In this chapter we present the results from a large-scale empirical study investigating the impact of ECCRM on corporate success in electronic commerce. The study comprises 469 cases of general companies in the German-speaking market. We find that ECCRM is a critical success factor in electronic commerce, independent of companies' time on the Web. It is especially critical for B2C and small companies.

Introduction

Customer relationship management (CRM) is a strategic concept enabling companies to systematically build up and extend the knowledge of their customers, thus empowering companies to actively conduct, i.e., manage, the business relationships with their customers. CRM can be understood as a revolving process during which companies interact with their customers, thereby generating, aggregating, and analyzing customer data obtained from all channels, and employing the results for service and marketing activities (Seybold, 2001; Strauß & Schoder, 2002, p. 81f).

Companies may pursue several goals when employing CRM to manage their customer relationships. An economic goal which companies seek to achieve by the use of CRM is to increase profitability by concentrating on the economically valuable customers, thus increasing revenue ("share of wallet") from them, while possibly "de-marketing" and discontinuing the business relationship with non-profitable customers. Strategic considerations represent another motivation for companies to employ CRM: By providing customized products and services to them, companies can increase their customer satisfaction, which is likely to lead to higher customer loyalty and longer customer retention. This, in turn, makes it less probable that their customers will defect to other companies (i.e., it lowers the churn rate).

Electronic commerce customer relationship management or ECCRM (Kundisch, Wofersberger, Calamis, & Kloeper, 2001; Romano & Fjermestad, 2001a) strongly relies on Internet or Web-based interaction of companies with their customers, yet also includes customer data obtained through the other channels (such as phone or fax). As the term suggests, ECCRM is a key element of CRM by specifically aiming at supporting electronic commerce, which we understand as the activities related to initiating, negotiating, and executing business transactions online. Since the beginning of the commercial use of the Web, ECCRM has received increasing attention from both practitioners (Adams, 2000; Holden, 2001; Malis, 2000; Orr, 2001) and researchers (Romano & Fjermestad, 2001b).

The same as for conventional CRM, companies have invested large sums in ECCRM implementations, lured by the prospect of higher profitability. Yet, it seems that the resulting business value or benefit often fails to emerge, putting managers under high pressure to justify their investments. AMR Research (2002) finds disastrous evidence for the lacking effectiveness of CRM implementations in practice, stating that only "16% of [all CRM] projects reach the promised land and measurably influence business performance," while a fraction 12% of implementations already "fail to go live," and business change and adoption fail in another 47%.

So far, research has not been able to contribute much guidance for managerial practice on this issue (Malis, 2000). Especially, the question of central interest to decision makers—If and to what extent do the high investments in ECCRM translate into bottom-line benefits at the corporate level, such as increased profitability or a better competitive standing?—has received only little attention (Tan, Yen, & Fang, 2002). As can be seen from a recent overview of existing ECCRM research (Romano & Fjermestad, 2001b), previous studies have frequently focused on technical aspects of corporate Web presences (e.g., design, usability, features, and the acceptance of Web pages) or on marketing issues (e.g., customer behavior, satisfaction, and retention, as well as trust). Further, past ECCRM studies have often concentrated on specific industries (e.g., the financial industry) or business models (e.g., Web-centric business models). Additionally, to the best of the authors' knowledge, there have been no comprehensive studies comparing the effectiveness of ECCRM for business-to-business (B2B) and business-to-consumer (B2C) companies or for different company sizes.

The objective of this chapter is to present broad empirical evidence on the effectiveness of ECCRM at the corporate level, thus addressing the gap in existing research and providing guidance for managerial practice at the same time. We summarize and discuss the results of an empirical study based on 469 cases from a representative survey comprising 1,308 cases in the German-speaking market, one of the key international electronic commerce markets.

The remainder of this chapter is structured as follows: We begin the next section by discussing the relevant aspects of ECCRM, i.e., its instruments and some of the related issues. Then, we explain the research approach and, reviewing related literature, show the development of hypotheses leading to the research model. In the following section, the survey is presented and the results of the statistical analysis are summarized and discussed. We then sketch future research opportunities and derive some implications for practice. Finally, the key findings of this chapter are summarized in the conclusion.

Background

The Concept of ECCRM—Instruments and Issues

In order to enable the revolving (EC)CRM process as defined in the introduction, a number of instruments must be implemented. They comprise a technical infrastructure as a base, as well as a number of business processes conducted on top. The instruments can be grouped into the following categories, each representing a step in the revolving process:

1. *Data Collection.* To generate customer information, customer data should first be collected across all available channels. In electronic commerce, these are typically a company's website, but also email, interaction with the (Web) call center, and the offline channels. Customer data can be collected either actively, i.e., with the knowledge of the customers, e.g., through interactive questionnaires on the Web, or passively, i.e., without the knowledge of the customers, e.g., through clickstream analyses or by otherwise logging customers' surfing behavior while on the company's website. Correspondingly, the type of the data collected may range from personal information, preferences, or purchase histories, to rather intimate behavioral data which the customers themselves might even be unconscious of.

2. *Data Aggregation.* In this step, customer data is first pooled from all sources (channels) and then "distilled" (i.e., concentrated) to customer information. Depending on the industry and customer type, a considerable amount of business intelligence is necessary in order to recognize certain patterns within the customer information, i.e., typical profiles. While collecting all kinds of customer data may be relatively simple, condensing it and making proper sense of it, i.e., as the final consequence, drawing the right conclusion with respect to the profitability of a customer, is a lot more difficult. Over the Internet and World Wide Web, most competitors in a market (segment) may have access to the same customer base, especially as search and switching costs tend to be very low. Therefore it is the quality of customer information and its evaluation with which companies can secure their competitive advantage.

3. *Customer Interaction.* With this step, one cycle of the revolving ECCRM process is closed. Companies can react to their customers based on the customer information they have. They can provide positive feedback to, i.e., actively market to their customers, thus intensifying the revolving

ECCRM process, or they can provide negative feedback to their customers, i.e., de-market and terminate the business relationship with them.

For example, they can make individualized product and service offerings with respect to the price in order to fully capture a customer's individual valuation. Typically, related e-business concepts such as mass customization or one-to-one marketing can be employed in this step. Yet companies can also maintain the dialogue with their customers if they offer certain features designed to affect customer retention. Also, they can offer individualized information services on their websites ("my-xyz.com") or via email (newsletters), or they can offer other value-added services (e.g., stock quotes or small applications like a currency converter). All of these features are designed to keep the customer interacting with the company, thus providing new customer data, leading to the next data collection step and to the next revolution of the ECCRM cycle.

Ideally, an ECCRM system constitutes an information system with which the instruments from all of these three categories can be managed and which constitutes a single interface to all relevant customer data. An ideal ECCRM system can be characterized as an intraorganizational knowledge management platform: It should allow all employees in a company with customer contact and who are involved in the sales process—comprising the sales force, the marketing department, the billing department, the customer service department, and others—to access and contribute to the customer database. Yet, the functionalities and the view of the customer data which an ECCRM system provides to its users usually depend on the role the users fulfill inside the company. For example, salesmen are most involved in gathering and accessing data that is relevant "in the field"—a customer's contact information, personal information, preferences, order history, etc. On the other hand, marketers are concerned with analyzing customer data, profiling customers, and determining their value for the company. Therefore, to users from the marketing department, the system should offer data analysis tools such as a rule engine that allows one to define and implement a set of rules, with which patterns in the customer database can be identified and individual customers can be classified. Further, an ECCRM system should enable marketers to run campaigns based on the customer data (e.g., newsletters, email) and control the instruments for interacting with the customers individually (e.g., through personalized Web pages).

Companies that master the revolving (EC)CRM process and have already accumulated a sufficient base of customer information can judge their customers according to economic criteria. They know who of their customers are profitable and who are not. Consequently, these companies can classify the customers that are important to them and provide economically efficient individual service. We summarize companies' skill sets resulting from all of these abilities into one central concept that we term "companies' ECCRM-capability." As a positive side effect, by collecting and aggregating customer data across different departments, companies can also capture a considerable amount of tacit or implicit customer knowledge from its employees and retain it within the organization, which may reduce their dependence on certain individuals (e.g., highly paid star salesmen).

For initializing the (EC)CRM cycle and keeping it in motion, a certain extent of process knowledge or process competence is necessary, as a number of issues may arise, spanning the following multiple dimensions:

1. *Technical Issues.* The right ECCRM software package that fits specific company needs may be hard to choose. Even if it is eventually found, its functionalities might not be sufficient to meet the respective company requirements, and additional development may become necessary.

2. *Integration Issues.* The existing IT infrastructure of the respective company may fit the system requirements of ECCRM software only very poorly. For example, customer data might be distributed across different information systems, not allowing for a unified view of the customer. Therefore, the integration of ECCRM software might be very costly and might even require additional reorganization. In addition, external service providers for ECCRM systems might be able to provide only limited assistance.

3. *Organizational Issues.* The implementation of an ECCRM system may require considerable effort for training affected staff. An additional effort may become necessary to persuade those who resist the accompanying process and organizational changes.

4. *Management Issues.* Once implemented after all, how can the benefits arising from the ECCRM implementation be measured adequately?

The Research Approach

As the objective of the empirical study is to find firm-level evidence for the effectiveness of ECCRM, an integrated perspective must be assumed. For example, the corporate level is chosen as the level of analysis and the whole company as the object under study. For the same reason, we must also take a comprehensive view of the dependent factors, not only concentrating on single facets such as customer loyalty, retention, and brand awareness. We therefore employ the broad concept of corporate success in electronic commerce as the dependent construct.

Further, we concentrate on the business benefit from ECCRM as a specific concept. Consequently, we use only directly ECCRM-related concepts as independent constructs in our model and obtain a partial, rather than a total model for corporate success in electronic commerce. The model structure consisting of independent constructs, their interrelations, and their impact on the dependent construct is obtained from formalizing the above discussion on the concept of ECCRM, as developed in the following.

Literature Review and Derivation of Model Hypotheses

The central hypothesis follows directly from the introductory literature and from numerous case studies (e.g., Kannan, Tan, Handfield, & Ghosh, 1998; Strau², 2002, p. 79ff). Companies that are able to manage their customer relationships and, thus, focus mainly on profitable customers are more successful than companies which, in an economic sense, waste their resources serving unprofitable customers:

Hypothesis H_1: Corporate success in electronic commerce increases with increasing ECCRM-capability.

It is evident from our initial definition that companies that strive to actively manage the relationships with their customers must first of all know their customers and therefore need to collect customer data. As shown in studies of website usability and user interaction, the most effective way of collecting customer data is online, in an interactive, feature-rich environment, in order to meet customers' expectations of a company's website, thereby increasing their convenience and loyalty (Breitenbach & Van Doren, 1998; Jutla, Craig, & Bodoik, 2001; Kuk & Yeung, 2002). In 2000, Adams recommends subsidized electronic commerce functionalities (online trading in the case of the banking industry) as a measure for retaining customers. As an intermediate step between interacting with customers and analyzing customer data based on individual profiles, a company should attain a unified view of its customers. This is achieved by aggregating and condensing customer data (Yu, 2001). To summarize these considerations, the collection of indicator variables representing ECCRM instruments in our model should comprise the collection and aggregation of customer data, as well as website features designed for increasing customer loyalty.

As with every other electronic commerce concept, ECCRM may not be suitable for every company, and there may be many companies that resist the implementation of ECCRM. Some companies might resist simply because of the necessary up-front investment. Yet, particularly in the B2C segment, some companies may resist the implementation of ECCRM because they might fear, for example, that certain legal issues concerning customers' privacy may not have been resolved yet, which would make the collection and aggregation of customer data for ECCRM a legal risk. Also, typically, consumers are very sensitive to infringements on their privacy and are concerned that profiles based on their personal data, surfing habits, and shopping behavior may be abused. If they feel that a company violates their personal rights, they are likely to turn away from that company and take their business elsewhere. Or, in an even worse scenario, they might raise protests, causing other consumers to turn away from that company, too.

On the one hand, it is obvious that companies which opt against implementing ECCRM will have a lower ability to address and serve their customers individually than companies which decide in favor of implementing ECCRM. On the other hand, if companies have made an active and informed decision against the implementation of ECCRM, we propose that the expertise gained during the underlying process of information gathering and analysis may save them from making a futile investment in ECCRM and should be a driver for corporate success in electronic commerce:

Hypothesis H$_{2a}$: Companies' refusal to implement ECCRM based on an active and informed decision negatively impacts their ECCRM-capability.

Hypothesis H$_{2b}$: Companies' refusal to implement ECCRM based on an active and informed decision positively impacts their success in electronic commerce.

The issues and difficulties in planning and implementing ECCRM have become the subject of numerous articles in scientific research (Gefen & Ridings, 2002; Wilson, Daniel, & McDonald, 2002) and practitioners' literature (Holden, 2001; Malis, 2000; Orr, 2001). As explained above, an ECCRM system must be selected (or built), configured, and integrated with existing systems. Moreover, it must be implemented into the business processes of the respective company, i.e., the employees need to be able to use the system and be motivated to actually do so (Davis, 2002). Therefore, decision makers competent in managing these issues and difficulties are key factors in determining their company's success in ECCRM. As these executives should also be able successfully to manage other electronic commerce or electronic business initiatives, they can be regarded as a key factor for their company's success in electronic commerce in general. This leads us to our final pair of hypotheses:

Hypothesis H$_{3a}$: The more managerial competence in planning and implementing ECCRM is present in a company, the more its ECCRM-capability increases.

Hypothesis H$_{3b}$: The more managerial competence in planning and implementing ECCRM is present in a company, the more its success in electronic commerce increases.

Conceptualizing Corporate Success in Electronic Commerce

We choose to focus our view of the concept of corporate success in electronic commerce on the shareholders' perspective. The concept is viewed and implemented as a complex construct comprising several theoretical subdimensions so as to accommodate the major theories on competitive advantage, value creation, and firm performance (Amit & Zott, 2001). Further, corresponding to the research hypotheses derived above, a potential positive impact on every subdimension can be motivated from companies' use of ECCRM:

1. *Hard Factors.* This reflects economic performance indicated by economic quantities or coefficients, e.g., revenue and profit growth. Companies that have achieved a certain ECCRM-capability can concentrate their activities on serving their profitable customers. As they no longer incur losses from wasting resources on their non-profitable customers, their profit increases. Further, when a company intensifies its sales efforts, e.g., cross-selling, up-selling, and repeat selling, towards its valuable customers, its sales figures, revenues, and, depending on the competition, its market share are also likely to rise.

2. *Soft Factors.* This accounts for a company's achievement(s) in relation to, or by perception of, its customers, e.g., increased loyalty, improvement of the corporate image, or increased customer satisfaction. As a company actively manages the business relationships with its customers and, especially, discontinues the relationships with its non-profitable customers, the service level experienced by their remaining valuable customers will probably increase. Consequently, their satisfaction with and loyalty towards that company will probably also increase.

3. *Cost Reduction.* This indicates a company's improvement(s) in process efficiency as well as procurement conditions, e.g., reduced purchasing or marketing costs, therefore covering firm performance from a transaction-cost economical perspective. As a company implements ECCRM and

develops a certain ECCRM-capability, customer knowledge can be captured and exchanged more easily inside its own organization, which is likely to make the sales process more efficient.

4. *Innovation.* This measures the extent by which a company has strengthened its competitive position from the perspective of Schumpeterian theory, i.e., by being innovative—by offering new services and by developing new markets. A company's ECCRM-capability also reflects its level of individual understanding of its customers' needs and preferences. As this understanding increases, the company's ability to successfully develop and offer new products and services can be expected to rise as well.

5. *Corporate Value.* A company's valuation not only depends on its economic or overall performance, but also (mostly) on the way it is perceived by third parties, such as investors. Therefore, this final subdimension is the

Figure 1. Research model

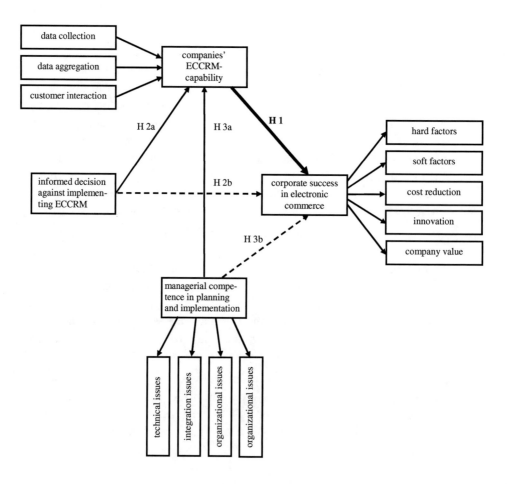

broadest and most susceptible to external influential factors (micro and macroeconomic, psychological, etc.). As a company improves its performance in the other subdimensions of corporate success in electronic commerce due to the use of ECCRM, the valuation it receives from its investors, analysts, and customers is likely to increase.

The Resulting Model Structure

Figure 1 illustrates the structure of the resulting research model. Companies' ECCRM-capability is the central construct. It serves as a moderating construct, aggregating the effect that several ECCRM instruments, the decision against implementing ECCRM, and managerial competence in planning and implementing ECCRM have on corporate success in electronic commerce, which is the dependent construct. The paths between the central constructs depicted in Figure 1 represent the research hypotheses derived above. Further, the instruments constituting companies' ECCRM-capability, the issues requiring managerial competence during planning and implementation, as well as the dimensions reflecting corporate success in electronic commerce have been integrated into the research model.

Empirical Investigation and Statistical Analysis

The research model is implemented as a structural equation model (SEM) or, more specifically, as a covariance structure model (also known as a LISREL model). This model is tested with numerical data obtained from a large-scale survey. The numerical results are summarized and evaluated to establish if they give support to the research hypotheses.

The Survey

The numerical data used in the statistical analysis of this model were collected in a large survey that was conducted from May to June 2000, and which was published as the "e-Reality 2000 Study" in September 2000, including an extensive descriptive analysis (Strauß & Schoder, 2000). This survey was targeted at decision makers of companies in the German-speaking area of Europe, specifically Germany, Austria, and Switzerland. All data was gathered in personal interviews, which market research professionals conducted with upper- to top-level executives from 1,308 companies.

The executives were questioned about the implementation of ECCRM in their companies, among other e-business concepts and initiatives. Specifically, they were asked to assess the success that their companies had achieved with their electronic commerce activities, using a broad set of measures. Thereby, all of the data collected in our survey was recorded with self-reported measures. Although the data is thereby subject to information and response biases, self-reported measures have been employed for two important reasons: First, the concepts of interest, namely companies' internal activities and resources as well as the success of their electronic commerce activities, can hardly be measured, if not by self-reported measures, because the desired information may not be available from external sources (outsiders). Second, in order to limit the administrative effort for conducting a large-scale survey, it is desirable to obtain all relevant information for each company from one interviewee as a single source of information.

Aggregation of Survey Data

Prior to the statistical analysis, the gathered raw data is reduced and condensed to an essential subset as follows: First, the data from companies that were not actively participating in electronic commerce at the time of the survey and that were not planning to enter electronic commerce within six months, are eliminated, reducing the original data set to 901 cases. Second, we reject those respondents who specified that they had not yet gained sufficient online experience to provide information on the success of their company's electronic commerce activities, leaving a total of 469 valid cases as the base for our numerical analyses.

Descriptive Analysis

As in the original survey, the remaining cases constitute a heterogeneous selection of companies from all industry backgrounds, company sizes, and business models. Grouped according to the U.S. Standard Industrial Classification (SIC), the 469 companies in our numerical base are structured as follows: 23.1% (108, as an absolute figure) of the remaining companies operate in the manufacturing sector; 5.8% (27) in transportation, communication, and utilities; and 9.8% (46) in construction. A large percentage (25.3%/119) are active in the trade sector, and 12% (56) are in finance, insurance, or real estate. Further, 18%

(89) belong to the service industry. Finally, 1.1% (5) of businesses are in the public administration segment.

Of the 469 companies examined in our study, 215 (45.8%) mainly serve businesses, and thus operate in the B2B segment, while 224 (47.8%) consider themselves belonging to the B2C segment. (Possibly remaining cases or fractions in this subsection cannot be classified due to missing values in the respective structural variable.) There are 101 companies (21.5%) with 50 or more employees, 203 companies (43.3%) with between 20 and 49 employees, and 142 companies (30.3%) with fewer than 20 employees. These latter three groups of companies are referred to as large, medium or medium-sized, and small companies, respectively, in the following analysis. To conclude the grouping of the companies, 225 (48.0%) had up to two years of experience on the Web at the time of the survey, while 241 (51.4%) had been on the Web for two years or more.

Concerning the use of ECCRM techniques, 23% (108) of the companies either actively or passively collect and 28% (131) aggregate customer data. A total of 46.1% (216) feel that, on the basis of their customer data, they can either economically provide individual service to their customers or classify their most important customers. Finally, 64 companies (13.6%) refuse to use ECCRM techniques because they fear that either legal issues or consumer protests might arise.

Statistical Analysis

The numerical estimation is performed simultaneously for several analyses, each consisting of the same structural model, but differing in the numerical base. Thereby, model validity is tested for the general case as well as for the case of specific categories of companies, and the interrelations between the hypothesized constructs (i.e., model parameters) can be compared between different categories of companies. A full discussion of the statistical analysis, including the operationalization of constructs, the wording and scaling of the indicator variables, typical fit measures for the numerical estimation, as well as the numerical results, can be found in Schoder and Madeja (2004). The numerical estimation is conducted as follows:

1. In the first analysis, the general set of all 469 companies is employed.

2. As an extension of previous studies (Romano & Fjermestad, 2001a), and as an issue which has been raised for further research (Madeja & Schoder, 2003), the second and third analyses are performed on the subsets of 215 B2B and 224 B2C companies only.

3.   The fourth through sixth analyses are based on the subsets of 101 large, 202 medium-sized, and 142 small companies, and are intended to provide control for company size. In the case of the subset of 101 large companies, the construct for rejecting ECCRM (H_{2a} and H_{2b}) must be excluded from the numerical analysis, since it causes convergence problems. A look at the data set reveals that only six (5.9%) of the 101 large companies refuse to implement ECCRM, rendering this construct irrelevant for the group of large companies.

4.   The seventh and eighth analyses use the group of 225 companies with up to two years and the group of 241 companies with more than two years of experience on the Web at the time of the survey. With this step, we intend to control for the effect that companies' experience on the Web may have on their ability to benefit from ECCRM, which can also be understood as controling for lag effects (Madeja & Schoder, 2003). Companies that were new to the Web (and, thus, to ECCRM) at the time of the survey may have been employing ECCRM already, but may have been unable to increase their corporate success in electronic commerce.

Summary and Discussion of the Results

The numerical results for our research model are summarized in Table 1. While we have obtained empirical evidence backing some of our hypotheses, some of the findings need to be discussed.

First of all, our central hypothesis has been that companies' ECCRM-capability, defined as companies' ability to identify their important customers and to economically provide individual service, is a success factor in electronic commerce. Our analyses have provided strong numerical support for this hypothesis in the general case, as well as for all subsets obtained from different cross-sections through a broad base of companies.

Second, the numerical results of our analyses suggest that, in general and for all subsets of companies (except for the medium-sized companies), the active decision not to implement ECCRM does not significantly reduce companies' ECCRM-capability, yet tends to increase corporate success in electronic commerce, as we have hypothesized. The second half of this statement is not surprising; it corresponds to our research hypothesis H_{2b}. The first half, however, is: Why is it that the active decision not to implement ECCRM has no significant negative impact on companies' ECCRM-capability? Maybe those companies which stated that they refuse to implement ECCRM already have a sufficient understanding of their customers? Or maybe they are just better at avoiding legal issues and adverse consumer reactions (increasing their success), while they still implement the ECCRM instruments to a certain extent?

Table 1. Numerical results for the research hypotheses

Hypo-thesis	General Case	Main Customer Segment		Company Size			Years of Experience on the Web	
		B2B	B2C	large	medium	small	up to 2	more than 2
H₁	+ +	+ +	+ +	+ +	+ +	+ +	+ +	+ +
H₂ₐ	•	•	•	n. a.	+	•	•	•
H₂ᵦ	+	•	+	n. a.	•	+	•	+
H₃ₐ	+ +	•	+	•	•	+ +	•	+
H₃ᵦ	•	•	−	•	•	− −	•	•

'+ +' *indicates strong support,* '+' *indicates support,* '•' *indicates no support,*
'−' *indicates no support, empirical evidence suggesting the opposite,*
'− −' *indicates no support, empirical evidence strongly suggesting the opposite*

Third, managerial competence in planning and implementing ECCRM has been found to increase their companies' ECCRM-capability (in the general case and for some of the subsets of companies), while it does not increase their companies' success in electronic commerce. Seemingly, companies are unable to leverage their managers' competence in ECCRM in order to increase their success in electronic commerce. This may be due to the fact that usually, the managerial competence in ECCRM that is built up inside a company is not used in the planning and implementation of other electronic business concepts, e.g., because different teams work on different electronic business projects or even external consultants are involved who take their competence with them once the implementation is finished. Or maybe the managerial competence in ECCRM is just not transferable to other electronic business concepts or management areas.

Our separate analyses for companies operating in the B2B and B2C segments provide evidence that the ECCRM concept—its instruments and accompanying know-how—is a significantly more important success factor for B2C than it is for B2B companies. This finding can be understood from comparing the customer structure in each segment. First of all, in the B2C segment, the customer is always an individual consumer, whereas a B2B customer is usually an organization comprising several persons. Therefore, a B2B company typically has to interact with several persons on every customer's site. Secondly, corporate buyers are usually subjected to purchasing guidelines determined by their organization and are less flexible in their buying decisions than B2C customers. Thirdly, B2B companies use a variety of selling mechanisms that may include, for example, participation in auctions and marketplaces, making it impossible to interact directly and personally with customers as can be done via a Web storefront. For all of these reasons, a typical B2B customer may be more difficult to target individually than a B2C customer. Consequently, the benefits arising from the use of the ECCRM concept are probably more difficult for the seller to achieve. For the same reasons, privacy issues and potential consumer protests can be expected to be an issue far more critical to success in electronic commerce when selling to consumers than when selling to businesses. The findings for H_{3a} and H_{3b} may be interpreted as reflecting a learning process. Companies build up their ECCRM-competence, which increases their ECCRM-capability. However, this involves making mistakes, to a certain extent, resulting in a negative impact on success in electronic commerce. As success in the B2C segment is more sensitively linked to the ECCRM concept than in the B2B segment, the support for H_{3a} and H_{3b} can be found in the analysis of the group of B2C companies only.

Our three model analyses controlling for company size show great differences between the results for large and medium-sized companies on the one hand and small companies on the other hand. The construct for rejecting ECCRM (corresponding to H_{2a} and H_{2b}) cannot be included in the analysis for large companies, which means that rejecting ECCRM is just not an issue for large companies (cf. above). For medium companies, rejecting ECCRM clearly diminishes ECCRM-capability (i.e., medium companies strongly depend on ECCRM in order to have an understanding of their customers) and does not contribute to their success in electronic commerce (i.e., the savings from refusing to implement ECCRM lead to no net benefit for medium companies). These results hint at the fact that ECCRM is also a "must" for medium companies. Then why is it that for large and medium-sized companies, managerial ECCRM-competence has no significant effect either on ECCRM-capability or on corporate success in electronic commerce? Maybe large and medium-sized companies rely on external consultants and system vendors for their ECCRM implementations so that their internal competence becomes relatively unimportant. On the contrary, our findings for small companies suggest that their success is very dependent on ECCRM issues: ECCRM-capability is found to be a very strong success driver for small companies. Yet, while rejecting ECCRM has no effect on their ECCRM-capability (i.e., does not diminish their understanding of their customers), it obviously leads to great benefits (e.g., by saving the costs of the ECCRM implementation or by avoiding legal issues and conflicts with their customers). In addition, small companies significantly increase their ECCRM-capability from building up internal ECCRM competence, while the necessary expenses for building up this competence decreases their success in electronic commerce.

Our last two analyses for companies with up to and more than two years of Web experience, respectively, reveal only minor differences between these groups. In particular, the impact of companies' ECCRM-capability on corporate success in electronic commerce is almost the same for both groups. This observation suggests that the effect of the ECCRM concept does not depend on the length of a company's time on the Web. In both cases, companies do not significantly decrease their ECCRM-capability by refusing to implement ECCRM, and they cannot leverage their ECCRM-specific managerial competence in order to increase their success in electronic commerce. Yet, only companies with more than two years of Web experience can increase their success in electronic commerce by refusing to implement ECCRM and increase their ECCRM-capability by building up internal ECCRM competence. Perhaps the companies with longer Web experience have reached a certain state of maturity, such that the deliberate decision not to implement ECCRM becomes a differentiating criterion for success in electronic commerce? Similarly, it may take a certain experience before managerial ECCRM competence significantly improves companies' ECCRM-capability.

Future Trends

Research Opportunities

Although our study produces some useful insights, it leaves a number of issues open for future empirical research. Some suggestions are as follows:

1. The survey should be repeated in a similar manner in order to eliminate possible lag problems and assess how the identified interrelations change with time, as the integrated business concept ECCRM and the market environment mature.

2. It should be investigated whether the findings vary in different markets or industries.

3. Data aggregation and analysis in ECCRM implementations, as well as how the knowledge that companies have gained about their customers translates into action, should be studied in more detail.

4.   Finally, one more issue for future research should be the role of ECCRM as an enabler for other integrated electronic commerce concepts, such as one-to-one-marketing and mass customization.

Implications for Practice

Companies' ECCRM-capability, which we have described as their ability to identify important customers and economically provide individual service, has proved to be a key success factor in electronic commerce. Although companies must usually employ a set of instruments in order to achieve this capability, decision makers should also consider the option not to implement the integrated electronic commerce concept of ECCRM. Thereby, they might save their companies a major investment for achieving a level of understanding of their customers which they already have. Furthermore, as integrating the concept of ECCRM implies operating on customers' personal data and profiles, managers should consider the risk that their customer relationships might actually deteriorate or result in legal claims or protests from a feeling that their privacy has been infringed upon. Moreover, decision makers should build up competence in planning and implementing ECCRM in order to increase their companies' ECCRM-capability, although apparently, this effect takes time to achieve, because it requires a certain experience on the Web. All of these considerations are especially important for companies with very close customer or consumer interaction, with typically few customers and with limited financial resources, as is often the case with B2C or small companies.

Conclusion

In this chapter, we have presented broad empirical evidence on the general effectiveness of ECCRM at the corporate level. We have thus contributed to closing a gap in existing research, and we were able to derive relevant implications for practice at the same time. The central message of this chapter is that a skill set based on accumulating and exploiting customer knowledge, which we term companies' ECCRM-capability, is a key success factor in electronic commerce. Yet for the time being, it must be left up to every company to decide *how* they can attain a sufficient level of ECCRM-capability. While some companies may have already built up their ECCRM-capability through their regular business processes, others might require the implementation of an ECCRM system.

Endnote

* An earlier version of this book chapter was accepted for publication in the *Journal of Electronic Commerce Research, 5*(1).

References

Adams, J. (2000). The hidden opportunity of e-commerce: e-CRM. *Future Banker, 4*(11), 41.

Amit, R., & Zott, C. (2001). Value creation in e-business. *Strategic Management Journal, 22,* 493-520.

AMR Research (2002). *CRM: Inflicting pain or profit.* Accessed September 15, 2003, from: http://www.amrresearch.com.

Breitenbach, C.S., & Van Doren, D.C. (1998). Value-added marketing in the digital domain: Enhancing the utility of the Internet. *Journal of Consumer Marketing, 15*(6), 558.

Davis, R. (2002). The Wizard of Oz in CRM-land: CRM's need for business process management. *Information Systems Management, 19*(4), 43-48.

Gefen, D., & Ridings, C.M. (2002). Implementation team responsiveness and user evaluation of customer relationship management: A quasi-experimental design study of social exchange theory. *Journal of Management Information Systems, 19*(1), 47-69.

Holden, J. (2001). CRM shouldn't hurt. *Sales & Marketing Management, 153*(2), 29-30.

Jutla, D., Craig, J., & Bodorik, P. (2001). Enabling and measuring electronic customer relationship management readiness. *Proceedings of the 34ᵗʰ Hawaii International Conference on System Sciences,* Hawaii.

Kannan, V.R., Tan, K.C., Handfield, R.B., & Ghosh, S. (1998). Managing competition, quality, customer relations, and the supply base, and its impact on firm performance. In K.B.P. (Coordinator), *Proceedings of the 29ᵗʰ Annual Meeting of the Decision Sciences Institute* (pp. 1259-1261), Las Vegas, Nevada.

Kuk, G., & Yeung, F.T. (2002). Interactivity in e-commerce. *Quarterly Journal of Electronic Commerce, 3*(3), 223-234.

Kundisch, D., Wolfersberger, P., Calaminus, D., & Kloepfer, E. (2001). Enabling eCCRM: Content model and management for financial services.

Proceedings of the 34th Hawaii International Conference on System Sciences, Hawaii.

Madeja, N., & Schoder, D. (2003). Impact of electronic commerce customer relationship management on corporate success—results from an empirical investigation. *Proceedings of the 36th Hawaii International Conference on System Sciences,* Big Island, Hawaii.

Malis, E. (2000). The CRM buzz. *Manufacturing Systems,* (May), 54.

Orr, J. (2001). Strategic options for CRM: Which way off the roundabout? *Vital Speeches of the Day, 67*(20), 615-618.

Romano, N.C. Jr., & Fjermestad, J. (2001a). Introduction to the special section: Electronic commerce customer relationship management (ECCRM). *International Journal of Electronic Commerce, 6*(2), 7f.

Romano, N.C. Jr., & Fjermestad, J. (2001b). Electronic commerce customer relationship management: An assessment of research. *International Journal of Electronic Commerce, 6*(2), 61-113.

Schoder, D., & Madeja, N. (2004). Is customer relationship management a success factor in electronic commerce? *Journal of Electronic Commerce Research, 5*(1).

Seybold, P.B. (2001). *The customer revolution.* New York: Crown Publishers.

Strauß, R., & Schoder, D. (2000). *e-Reality 2000—electronic commerce from vision to reality: Status, development, problems, success factors, and management implications of electronic commerce* (in German). Frankfurt: Consulting Partner Group.

Strauß, R., & Schoder, D. (2002). *e-Reality 2000—a modular concept for e-business management* (in German). Frankfurt: F.A.Z.-Institut für Management-, Markt- und Medieninformationen.

Tan, X., Yen, D.C., & Fang, X. (2002). Internet-integrated customer relationship management—a key success factor for companies in the e-commerce arena. *Journal of Computer Information Systems,* 42 (Spring), 77-86.

Wilson, H., Daniel, E., & McDonald, M. (2002). Factors for success in customer relationship management (CRM) systems. *Journal of Marketing Management, 18*(1/2), 193-219.

Yu, L. (2001). Successful customer relationship management. *MIT Sloan Management Review,* 42(4), 18f.

Chapter II

Customer-centric Internet Strategies:
Achieving Competitive Advantage through CRM

Călin Gurău
Heriot-Watt University, UK

Abstract

This chapter analyzes the implementation process of a CRM system in online retailing and the challenges of transforming a product-focused business into a customer-centric organization. Customer relationship management (CRM) is increasingly found at the top of corporate agendas. Online companies in particular are embracing CRM as a major element of corporate strategy, because online technological applications permit a precise segmentation, profiling, and targeting of customers, and the competitive pressures of the digital markets require a customer-centric corporate culture. The chapter argues that the implementation of CRM systems in online organization determines a complex restructuring of the organizational elements and processes to adapt to new customer-centric procedures. The proper understanding of the benefits and challenges of implementing an online CRM system may help professional organizations to plan, design, and manage more effectively this major organizational restructuring.

Introduction

The World Wide Web has allowed companies to reach customers in previously inaccessible markets, and to compete efficiently with the traditional store-based retailers (De Kare-Silver, 1998). However, the low entry barriers, the market size, and the relatively low costs of online business activities have created a situation of intense competition. An effective answer to this situation is to build a strong brand name and to enhance customers' long-term loyalty (Novo, 2001a). The strategic planning process needs to adapt to the challenges of this new marketing channel, in which the customer is no more a target, but a partner (Chaffey, Mayer, Johnston, & Ellis-Chadwick, 2000).

The adoption of a customer-oriented strategy is referred to as customer relationship management (CRM). Companies are increasingly embracing CRM as a major element of corporate strategy for two important reasons: New technologies now enable companies to target chosen market segments, micro-segments, or individual customers more precisely; and new marketing thinking has recognized the limitations of traditional marketing and the potential of more customer-focused, process-oriented perspectives (Payne, 2002).

Table 1. A new business organization (Adapted from Pétrissans, 1999)

Organizational Elements	Before 2000	After 2000
Enterprise Vision	Short-term Product-focused	Long-term Customer-focused
Organization	Hierarchical structure	New business processes and organization to take advantage of IT opportunities
Sales	Little customer knowledge Face-to-face selling	High customer knowledge Mass-customization Multiple channel selling E-commerce
After sales and services	Reactive Separate processes and organization Slow	Proactive Integrated processes and organization High responsiveness

The value chain of the customer-focused enterprise now follows the 'sell-build-redesign' principle in contrast with the former one of 'design-build-sell'. In other terms, the enterprise has to be organized with a customer-focused vision rather than a product-centered one (Pétrissans, 1999).

In the online environment the introduction and maintenance of CRM requires a complex process of planning, analysis, strategy design, and implementation. This conceptual chapter presents a model for the implementation of a customer-centric approach in online retail businesses, discussing the advantages and the challenges of this new system, and comparing it with a product-oriented model. After considering the present importance of the customer relationship management in online markets, the chapter presents the main stages of implementing a customer-centric approach: (1) implementing the tools of the CRM system within the operational structure of the firm, and (2) introducing customer-centric values, objectives, and procedures in the organizational culture. The differences between product-focused and customer-centric organization are discussed, and the conclusions summarize the advantages of the customer-centric approach in the new e-business environment.

Customer Relationship Management in Online Markets

CRM is a comprehensive business and marketing strategy that integrates technology, process, and all business activities around the customer (Anton, 1996; Anton & Hoeck, 2002). It is mostly defined in terms of the acquisition and retention of customers, and the resulting profitability (Menconi, 2000; Nykamp, 2001). Effective CRM is assumed to lead to bottom-line benefits for the organization (Anton & Hoeck, 2002; Cusack, 1998; Rust & Zahorik, 1993; Swift, 2001; Tschohl, 2001). According to Bain and Company (Feinberg & Kadam, 2002), profits increase by 25-80% when customer retention rates increase by five points. The Internet has provided a platform to deliver CRM functions on the Web (eCRM), thus as business moves to the Web, eCRM will move to center stage.

The Internet represents a new media, with specific characteristics (see Table 2). The Internet is characterized by (Chaston, 2001):

1.   quick access and transfer of information;
2.   lack of space and time barriers;

3. ease of comparison between various objects, events, or organizations;
4. interactivity and flexibility.

Also, it has to be taken into consideration that in most cases, the e-service represents a one-to-one experience (company-customer).

Table 2. An interpretation of the differences between the old communication channels and the Internet (Adapted from Chaffey et al., 2000)

Old Media	Internet	Comment
One-to-many communication model	One-to-one or many-to-many communication model	Theoretically the Internet is a many-to-many medium, but for company-to-customers communication, it is best considered as one-to-one
Mass marketing	Individualized marketing or marketing customization	Personalization possible because of technology to monitor preferences and tailor content
Monologue	Dialogue	Indicates the interactive nature of the World Wide Web, with the facility for feedback
Branding	Communication	Increased involvement of customer in defining brand characteristics Opportunities for adding value to brand
Supply-side thinking	Demand-side thinking	Customer pull becomes more important
Customer as a target	Customer as a partner	Customer provides more input into products and services required
Segmentation	Communities	Aggregation of like-minded consumers rather than arbitrarily defined target markets

In this specific environment, the customer will therefore be able to access the company's website from any place in the world (as long as it has a working Internet connection), to compare the company's offer and to interact with the organization on a one-to-one basis. On the other hand, the company is capable of attracting and developing relationships with customers located anywhere in the world, to make an ongoing competitors' analysis, and to personalize its interaction with the customer.

Balancing the two sides of the experience (company/customer), an online service provider will have to define and select its target customers (focus) to analyze the specific competition for that particular market segment (competitive analysis), and to design its long-term interaction with the customer in order to achieve sustained customer satisfaction (strategic planning and implementation).

eCRM can be therefore defined as an interactive, content-centered, and Internet-based customer process, driven by the customer and integrated with related organizational customer support processes and technologies, with the goal of strengthening the customer-service provider relationship.

The Internet empowers the customer (Chaston, 2001). The Internet user has the opportunity to switch the suppliers with several mouse clicks, to compare price and products on a worldwide basis, and to select without external pressure the best available offer. The winning combination of low-price/high-quality product does not work properly on the Internet because the same offer may be available to hundreds of other online retailers (Wundermann, 2001). The only possibility to increase the competitive advantage of online retailing is to create not only product-related satisfaction, but also customer-firm relationship satisfaction.

The eLoyalty Matrix (Figure 1), an economic model developed at eLoyalty (Conway & Fitzpatrick, 1999), shows that turnover is greatest with customers who are dissatisfied with the relationship they have with the company. By coupling relationship and product strategies, organizations can effectively create customer loyalty (Lindström & Andersen, 2000).

- **Customer A** was satisfied with the product purchased, but dissatisfied with his relationship with the company. This customer type is vulnerable to switching. The customer/company relationship profoundly affects how a product or company is viewed and affects customer behavior. Properly managed and serviced, this category of customer can become a significant source of future transactions and move into the loyalty quadrant.

- **Customer B** is the type of customer every company desires: very satisfied with the product and the relationship with the company. The company can count on his repeat purchase, and will most likely benefit from referral business via positive word-of-mouth.

- **Customer C** is most undesirable, being seen as a saboteur to the organization. A bad experience with the product and the relationship with the company guarantees that he/she will never buy from the company again. This category of customer will bad-mouth the company because they feel wronged, which compounds the problem, as they tell others about their bad experience and discourage potential customers from ever interacting with the company.

- **Customer D** was not satisfied with the product, but is hopeful that the next purchase will be satisfactory. A good relationship creates a reservoir of goodwill upon which the customer is willing to give the company or product another chance.

The eLoyalty Matrix provides a framework for better understanding the problem of customer turnover and shows direction about where to look for opportunities for improvement. The key is to focus on the customer's relationship with the company. Even though Customers C and D both had poor product experiences, Customer D's willingness to continue a relationship with the company dramatically differs from the behavior of the saboteur.

Figure 1. The eLoyalty matrix (Adapted from Conway & Fitzpatrick, 1999)

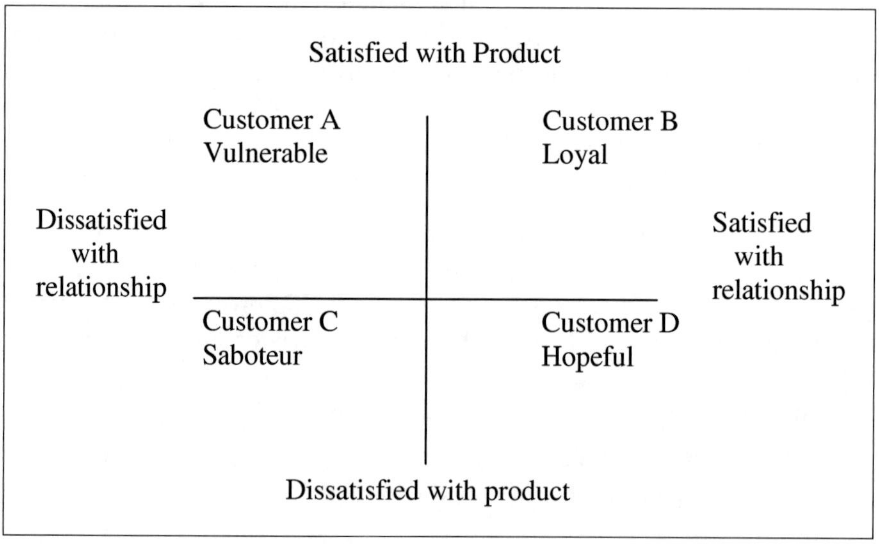

Satisfied with Product

Customer A
Vulnerable

Customer B
Loyal

Dissatisfied with relationship

Satisfied with relationship

Customer C
Saboteur

Customer D
Hopeful

Dissatisfied with product

The implementation of customer relationship management (CRM) represents the key to increasing customer loyalty in the digital environment. Despite widespread agreement that CRM and eCRM have a direct and indirect impact on customer satisfaction, sales, profit, and loyalty (Anton & Hoeck, 2002; Cusack, 1998; Rust & Zahorik, 1993; Sterne, 1996; Swift, 2001; Tschohl, 2001), 70% of online retailers lack operational strategies for cultivating their customer relationships. This was the finding of a "Customer Development Survey" conducted among a cross-section of online retailers by FollowUp.Net (1999). The study found that 26% of online retailers have no customer relationship development plan. Almost half (45%) perform their customer development programs on an ad-hoc basis. That leaves 29% that are actively pursuing consistent, multi-step programs for developing customer relationships. "Virtual stores have a significant opportunity to develop targeted customer communications," said FollowUp.Net CEO Chris Woods (Pastore, 1999). "Those online retailers who swiftly integrate segmentation and targeting capabilities into their day-to-day operations will enjoy a strategic advantage versus their competitors."

Besides the necessity of CRM systems in online businesses, the Internet also offers the possibility of implementing effective customer management operations through the use of complex IT applications (e.g., database software, customer management applications). For the first time in marketing history, it is now possible to track some end-user activities (Mabley, 2000) and use this data to maximize customer's profitability and loyalty throughout the entire lifecycle, from customer acquisition to retention (Cody, 2000).

The ultimate purpose of eCRM products and services is to help firms build better customer relationships and maximize a customer's lifetime value (Taylor & Hunter, 2002). In fact, Kalakota and Robinson (2001, p. 171) state that within the context of eCRM, "the timely delivery of excellent service is customer relationship management." The growing focus on eCRM underscores the relationship marketing foundations of e-service practices, an important area of recent academic inquiry. Parvatiyar and Sheth (2000, p. 9) review the literature to date and conclude with an overall definition of relationship marketing as: "...the ongoing process of engaging in cooperative and collaborative activities and programs with immediate end-user customers to create or enhance mutual economic value at a reduced cost." At present, a relationship-based behavioral model can be assessed within the eCRM industry that focuses on the customer-centric long-term orientation.

In order to implement and use successfully eCRM systems and procedures, the strategic planning process and the architecture of an e-business organization need to be adjusted to the needs of a customer-centric culture (Kotorov, 2002). This adjustment has two major stages:

1. Implementing the tools of the CRM system within the operational structure of the firm.

2. Introducing customer-centric values, objectives, and procedures in the organizational culture.

Recent studies (Taylor & Hunter, 2002; Adebanjo, 2003) have pointed out the danger of considering the implementation of an eCRM system as only a problem of finding and buying the most efficient eCRM software applications. In an analysis of CRM failures, Trembly (2002) noted that many organizations foster a false expectation that simply buying a piece of software will lead to CRM benefits. With the availability of hundreds of commercial software applications, the selection of the appropriate application can pose a major challenge. This difficulty is facilitated by the fact that CRM means different things to different people, with a scope ranging from direct emails to mass customization to call centers (Winer, 2001).

April and Harreld (2002) found that most large companies tend to have five to 10 CRM applications running concurrently. They also found that these applications tend to be diverse in functionality and therefore create the need for integration. Bradshaw and Brash (2001) further noted that CRM applications must not only integrate functionally at the front office, but also integrate with back office functions such as manufacturing and billing.

Consequently, the selection of CRM applications needs to be strategic and based on relevant criteria for implementation to stand a chance of success. These criteria will include functionality, company strategy, legacy back office systems, and application architecture. Current classification of CRM applications identifies three groupings (Karimi, Somers, & Gupta, 2001):

1. *Operational CRM products*—for improving customer service, online marketing, automating sales force, etc.

2. *Analytical CRM products*—for building data warehouses, improving relationships, analyzing data, etc.

3. *Collaborative CRM products*—for building online communities, developing business-to-business customer exchanges, personalizing services, etc.

The implementation of an efficient CRM strategy requires the introduction of a customer-focused organizational culture (Kotorov, 2002). According to Levy (2000), customer-centric organizations are defined as being very committed to raising customer satisfaction levels, using customer data to increase sales, improving customer data quality, gaining a deeper knowledge of customers, and implementing customer-management systems. The key operations for building an effective CRM strategy include (Conway & Fitzpatrick, 1999):

* identifying unique characteristics of each customer within the targeted customer segments;
* modeling the current and the potential value of each customer;
* creating proactive strategies and operational plans, or business rules that will support the desired experience for the customer, starting with the highest value customers;
* redesigning the organization, processes, technology, and reward system to implement the relationship strategies.

Implementing the Tools of the CRM System

Before the strategic planning process can be applied to customer-centric procedures, the firm needs to put in place the tools and procedures to collect relevant information about its customers, to process efficiently this information, and to segment the market.

Organizations that adopt eCRM solutions would expect that the applications improve their operational effectiveness and therefore deliver value to the organization. Value can be gained in a number of ways including (Adebanjo, 2003):

a) Reducing the cost of contacting customers—by making customer details readily available, customer contact personnel have better opportunities to resolve customer enquiries in less time, thereby freeing them for other productive work.

b) Transferring some responsibility to the customer (e.g., product configuration, order tracking, online customer details collection) reduces administrative and operational costs for the organization and, therefore, increases the value that an eCRM solution will deliver to the organization.

c) Integration of eCRM applications with back office systems such as production, finance, and supply chains can improve workflow and, consequently, the efficiency of the organization, thereby delivering cost savings. For example, field salespeople could use handheld devices to initiate orders, check stock, track orders, request invoices, and check production status with minimal effort and cost.

d)   eCRM applications have the potential to improve sales by customer profiling, automated campaign management, email marketing, etc., thereby improving the bottom line for the organization. Improving the overall interaction with customers would lead to better service and improve customer satisfaction and loyalty, and ultimately customer lifetime value. The importance of loyalty to commercial success has been identified by many researchers (Reichheld & Schefter, 2000).

The implementation of customer-centric systems comprises a number of essential stages:

- collect information about customers;
- calculate the customer lifetime value;
- segment the customers in terms of value (profitability) and establish the priority segments;
- establish operational procedures for day-to-day company-customer interaction, which can be supported and powered by automated campaign management applications.

Each of these stages will be further discussed in detail.

Collecting Customer Information

As the CRM system is based on a customer's profile and transaction history, the company needs to collect information about its customers. The implementation of CRM procedures requires the existence of historical data that is used to identify the main market segments and create an accurate customer profile. This data is available either though online automated systems that register the history of customer-firm interaction (historical data) and/or buying the necessary data from a third party (usually a specialized market research agency).

The implementation of an efficient profiling/segmentation methodology has to address the following issues (Thearling, 1999; Wundermann, 2001):

1.   robust transaction data, properly collected and updated;

2. data warehousing capabilities for capturing and storing the data (data-bases);

3. an associated retrieval and data delivery system;

4. data mining tools that reflect the unique nature of the business;

5. detailed costing information, including the process cost, as well as the physical product or service cost;

6. a meaningful business model that represents clearly the company-customer interaction and the fluctuation of customers' and business' lifecycle.

The collected data is stored in databases, and then accessed for processing.

Calculating the Customer Lifetime Value (CLV)

The CLV consists of taking into account the total financial contribution—i.e., revenues minus costs—of a customer over his or her entire life of a business relationship with the company. Despite its simplicity, the measurement of CLV requires great care. The cash flows involved in the process have to be identified and measured on a very detailed level, and allocated precisely to each customer or type of customer. The diagram in Figure 2 represents a concise seven-step approach to measure CLV (Bacuvier, 2001).

The calculation of the Customer Lifetime Value is not problem-free. However, most of these problems can be successfully solved, taking into consideration two main issues:

Figure 2. Seven-step process to measure customer lifetime value (Adapted from Bacuvier, 2001)

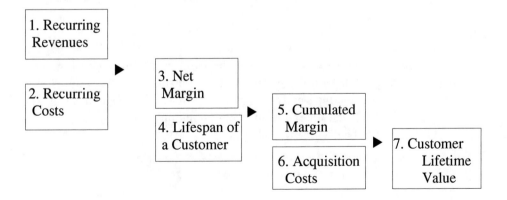

- the company applying this method has to clearly define from the beginning the purpose of using Customer Lifetime Value analysis and the expected benefits;

- the problems raised by the Customer Lifetime Value analysis are often industry and company specific, and as a result the company has to select the most appropriate way to apply this concept in its particular situation.

Defining a 'Customer'

The first challenge is to define the customer unit (Ness, Schroeck, Letendre, & Willmar, 2001). Is it an individual, an account, a household, or a business address? A second challenge is linking customer information into a single customer record when they leave and return multiple times during their lifetime.

The answer to these questions is industry specific. The business organization has to identify the characteristics of its customer relationship, and, on this basis, define the customer unit and the customer lifetime cycle. In the present marketplace, a company can be confronted with various situations determined by the number of customers, number and frequency of transactions, and level of customer-company involvement. For example, a company with a small number of customers, which makes a small number of transactions that require a high level of company-customer involvement, will probably define the customer unit as being single customers (individuals or organizations), and the customer lifecycle depending on the business cycles specific for the industry (production cycle, investment cycles, consumption cycles). On the other hand, for a company dealing with a large number of clients, with a large number of transactions and low involvement, it might be more appropriate to aggregate the individual customers into particular segments with homogeneous profiles and behavior.

Evaluating Costs

The measurement of cost to the customer level poses the greatest challenge to customer lifetime value measurement (Smith & Dikolli, 1995). While revenue can usually be collected by customer from the appropriate billing system, cost information is aggregated into general ledger departments and accounts, and requires a good deal of analysis and disaggregation before it can meaningfully be attached to individual customers or customer segments. The indirect costs are especially difficult to be divided and allocated.

In solving these problems, three key principles about costing should be applied by the company (Connolly & Ashworth, 1994):

- customer costs must be related to the revenues they generate;
- not all costs within the organization should be attributed down to a customer level;
- it should be made absolutely clear who can influence different types of cost and revenues.

Predicting the Business Lifetime of the Customer

One of the most difficult elements of CRM systems is to predict the business lifetime of the customer (Forsyth, 2001). In order to obtain an accurate estimation, a thorough analysis of existing and past customers' behavior needs to be conducted. Comparing the behavioral profile of the new customer with the profile of the main targeted segments, the client can be integrated from the beginning into the appropriate market segment.

Value Segmentation

Segmentation is the key to understanding the lifetime value of a specific customer, and to apply the most appropriate customer management strategy (Bacuvier, 2001). As a result of the Customer Lifetime Value calculation, the company's clients can be segmented in terms of profitability. E-business organizations should select segmentation dimensions that are discriminating either on the revenue side (e.g., usage intensity and behavior), or on the cost side (e.g., products purchased, channel used, intensity of customer care usage, and service levels). Using this analysis, the company can have a complete mapping of the "wells" of value creation and "pits" of value destruction of the business, and an understanding of why they are such.

The segmentation is performed, creating customer profiles. Profiles can be **demographically** or **behaviorally** based, and both these types of profiles are important in their own ways (Novo, 2001b).

The specific culture of the Internet encourages diversity and anonymity (Chaston, 2001). The customers of a digital retail shop can be located in various geographical regions, with different cultural backgrounds. In these conditions the demographic data about a customer has to be interpreted in a specific cultural context that is often difficult to define and understand. There is the risk that customers with a similar demographic profile will have different needs and wants, determined by their cultural values. On the other hand, in a digital relationship, the Internet user is usually reluctant to provide detailed and accurate personal information that is absolutely necessary to create a demographic profile.

However, the interactive behavior between the customer and the website of the company can be thoroughly registered and analyzed with specialized automatic software (data mining), providing a detailed behavioral profile (Mabley, 2000; Peacock, 2001).

The identification and definition of customers' profiles is important not only for the existing market of the firm, but also for its future clients. Once the main customer segments have been identified and their behavioral profiles defined, the online behavior of any new customer can be compared with the existing profiles. The new customer is integrated into the most appropriate customer segment, and focused, effective marketing strategies are applied from the very beginning of firm-customer interaction.

To be effective, customer behavior profiling needs to be connected with the segmentation of customers on different value categories using CLV (Ness et al., 2001). The connection between the Customer Value and the Customer Behavior can be highlighted creating a Relationship Equity Matrix (Conway & Fitzpatrick, 1999).

Analyzing the segments represented in the matrix, the strategic priority of each segment is easily identifiable:

- **Customer E**, high value but disloyal, represents a group that deserves the greatest amount of attention. The company is at risk of losing profitable, influential customers.

Figure 3. The relationship equity matrix (Adapted from Conway & Fitzpatrick, 1999)

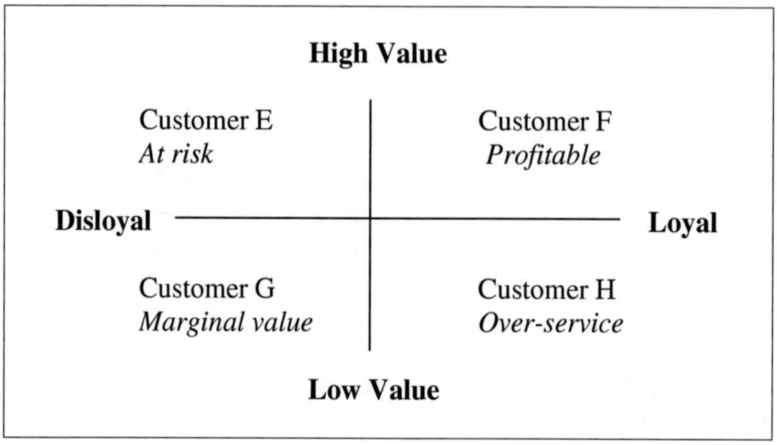

- **Customer F** is what makes the company successful at present. Companies must pay great attention to this group as a way of expressing appreciation for their ongoing business and recognizing their importance.

- **Customer G**, low value and disloyal, does not represent a group with long-term potential. If they choose to switch suppliers, the economic loss will be minimal for the company. This customer is usually opportunistic and price oriented.

- **Customer H**, low value but loyal, can be over-serviced, and therefore unprofitable for the company in the long term.

The analysis and the definition of each customer segment in terms of profitability will depend on the firm's profile and strategic objectives. The customer lifecycle also needs to be taken into consideration. Sometimes the low value/loyal customers can become in the future highly profitable customers for the company, either through increased purchase or through positive referrals.

Strategies for Profit Maximization

Considering the procedure of CLV calculation, in any business there are essentially five levels of customer value creation (Bacuvier, 2001):

1. *Conquer:* Acquire new customers with positive customer values or who contribute to spread the fixed costs over a wider basis, thus increasing the value of existing customers as well.

2. *Increase Revenues:* Stimulate the usage of existing customers in order to generate more revenues from them at each transaction.

3. *Retain:* Increase the loyalty of customers in order to extend their individual lifetime with the company.

4. *Reduce Recurring Costs:* Improve the efficiency of operations in order to reduce the cost of serving each customer.

5. *Reduce Acquisition Costs:* Improve the process of attracting new customers.

Table 3 shows the main customer-oriented strategies, with the corresponding tactics and operational procedures.

These five strategies should be used differently for each customer segment, in order to optimize the potential of value creation. Table 4 proposes differentiated

Table 3. The main customer-oriented strategies based on customer lifetime value analysis (Adapted from Gurău & Ranchhod, 2002)

Strategy	Tactics	Operation
Conquer—increase the number of customers	- improve the existing offer in order to attract the potential customers close to the existing customer segments	- improve: - product - price - distribution - promotion
	- diversify the offer in order to attract new segments of customers	- diversify the product/service portfolio
Increase recurring revenues	- increase the volume of sales	- diversification - stimulate the demand
	- increase the value of sales	- upgrade the offer
	- increase both the volume and the value of sales	- diversification - stimulate the demand - upgrade the offer
Reduce recurring costs	- reduce general costs (administration, maintenance, etc.)	- increased efficiency
	- reduce cost of: - product/service - distribution - communication	- cheaper supplies - cheaper outsourcing - increased efficiency
Retain—increase lifetime	- increase customers' loyalty maintaining and/or increasing customer satisfaction:	- improve present offer - better targeting - score better than competition
Reduce—acquisition costs	- better targeting of potential customers	- improve offer - improve targeting - use the same resources more efficiently

combinations of strategic approach for the four customer segments defined in the Relationship Equity Matrix.

The main goal of this stage in the strategic planning process is to understand the characteristics of customer segments and to identify the correct mix of operational activities, capable to optimize the value of each customer segment.

Table 4. Differentiated combinations of strategic approach for various customer segments

Value/Loyalty	High Value	Low Value
Loyal	Retain	Conquer Increase revenues Reduce recurring costs Reduce acquisition costs
Disloyal	Retain Reduce acquisition costs	Increase revenues Reduce recurring costs

Implementing a Customer-Centric Corporate Culture

Once the customer segments have been identified and prioritized in terms of profitability, it is possible to redesign the corporate culture of the business organization around a customer-centric approach. Considering the complexity of this transition process, there are many possible problems encountered by the organizations implementing CRM systems.

A study conducted by the Gartner Group evidenced that approximately 55% of companies implementing CRM applications fail to achieve their ROI goals on schedule (M. Polo Group, 2002). Typical challenges include:

- organizations' lack of consistent executive support, and clarity on expectations from staff;
- organizations' lack of resolve to change company culture and revise internal processes;
- shifting organizational culture from a product focus to a customer focus, where essential changes to day-to-day operations often determine success or failure of CRM strategies (adequate change management support is critical);
- inadequate strategic marketing planning and tactical execution;
- stalled implementation due to budget or other reasons, resulting in insufficient data integration to support CRM processes;

- unrealistic expectations of the time required to begin implementation, to achieve some small-scale successes, and then to continue incremental implementation.

Moreover, deficiency in organizations' value proposition to customers (what the customer gets for what the customer pays, relative to competition) diminishes overall business success, which can be confused with a failure of CRM to meet expectations.

Therefore, the redesign of the corporate culture as customer-centric needs to simultaneously transform and adjust: (1) the technological systems and procedures used to deal with customers (information collection systems, customer databases, customer segmentation, customer relationship strategies and their implementation); (2) the internal operations and processes within the organization (hierarchical structure, links and collaboration between different organizational departments, structure of managerial functions and responsibilities); and (3) the values and the objectives of the organization (application of the customer lifetime value concept, mass customization, pursuing an increase of customer satisfaction in order to retain and increase the return value of each client, differentiation through consistent customer service). On the other hand, the implementation of a customer-centric culture will also transform the relationship of the firm with its suppliers, requiring flexibility and consistent quality.

Considering the dynamism of customer segments and the level of details involved, this process needs to be done at a very concrete and operational level (Bacuvier, 2001). It is therefore important to create effective multi-functional teams that are intimately involved in the day-to-day operations of the business. The main success factors for the redesign of the corporate culture are project management capabilities, a high level of involvement of key operational staff, and the ability to measure the impact of the action plans on value creation at the customer segment level, or even for every individual customer.

The multi-functional teams will work on plans to achieve value-creation objectives, using the customer value measuring tools to analyze the financial impact of their action plans. A good example of a customer value creation plan is the alignment of customer servicing costs to the level of customer lifetime value. Using the value/behavior profiling of the existing customers, specific objectives can be established for each targeted segment, and then specific strategies can be designed and applied in order to reach these objectives.

Day-to-Day Management of Customer-Company Interaction

In light of their professional experience, the marketing managers will delegate to operational managers the responsibility to implement and coordinate the marketing strategies on a day-to-day basis. In order to satisfy customers' demands, the operational manager must get involved in the resource management process. The necessary resources can be varied, including core products and services, as well as supporting operations such as logistics, distribution, payment processing, and servicing. These resources may be available internally or need to be outsourced from external suppliers. Often the virtual company represents only the integrative interface between customers' demands and specialized suppliers, most resources and assets being outsourced. In this case the business relationship with these partners represents another complex process that has to be integrated in the CRM system, since the availability of these resources has a direct impact on customers' satisfaction.

The profiling of customer behavior does not have to stop at the level of main customer segments. The capacity of specialized Internet applications to register and process large amounts of data in real-time procedures has created the possibility to target specifically each individual customer and to automate the customer-company interaction.

Integrating Data Mining and Campaign Management Software

Data mining software permits the automatic detection of relevant patters in a database. Integrated at an IT level, with the organized databases containing a customer-firm transaction history, data mining tools will identify effectively the main customer segments using the segmentation criteria defined by top management.

The company's resources need to be differently allocated considering the established marketing strategy for each customer segment. This is usually coordinated on a day-to-day basis by the operational manager. Using Campaign Management software, the process can be almost fully automated, the operational manager preserving a supervision role (Thearling, 1999).

Campaign Management software automates and integrates the planning, execution, assessment, and refinement of a large number of highly segmented campaigns running continuously or intermittently. This software can also run campaigns that are triggered in response to customer behavior or milestones—

Table 5. The alignment of corporate functions with eCRM software applications (Adapted from Adebanjo, 2003)

Function	CRM application type	Comments
Sales	Collaborative, analytical	Sales analysis, customer contact, field sales, call centers, task allocation team management, etc.
Marketing	Collaborative, analytical	eMarketing, campaign analysis, historical analysis, enquiries, task allocation, team management, etc.
Finance	Analytical	Customer sales history, cashflow management, etc.
Logistics/Supply chain	Collaborative, operational	Order management, customer order tracking, customer contact, delivery management, etc.
Customer services/Desk support	Collaborative, operational	Call centers, order management, order tracking, troubleshooting, customer contact, etc.
Business unit directors	Analytical	Sales analysis, campaign analysis, employee productivity analysis, etc.
Operations	Operational	Order management
Product development	Collaborative, analytical	Collaborative development, market analysis, product analysis, project management, etc.

which is an essential skill in online CRM. Finally, the information about customer-firm interaction will be automatically registered by specific online applications, representing an input into the historical data archive of the firm.

The added value of automated eCRM systems cannot be achieved without the proper alignment between the corporate functions and the eCRM applications (see Table 5). This alignment can ultimately be facilitated by the multi-functional teams created to implement and supervise the eCRM strategy, which will have to identify possible problems related with compatibility of systems and fluidity of information flows, and design appropriate solutions to these challenges (Kotorov, 2002).

Comparing Product-Oriented and Customer-Centric Organizations

The design and implementation of a customer-oriented strategy, having as a central concept the Customer Lifetime Value (CLV), represents a very good example of a complex operation which necessitates a radical reorganization of the company. Such reorganization is not necessarily in terms of physical structure, but rather in terms of philosophy and process management.

In a product-oriented organization, the firm studies the market and its own resources, attempting to create a better marketing-mix offer than the competitors. The company's knowledge about its customers is often vague and general. Customers' segmentation is not very precise, the company taking advantage of the low cost of Internet communication to publish the offer online or to send promotional messages to its existing customers. The strategic objectives of the firm are also vague, since the company cannot predict accurately the customers' behavior. The results of the marketing campaign are usually measured calculating the ratio between the number of website visitors and the number of transactions concluded, or in the case of direct marketing, the number of offers per number of transactions. The management supervises the process, attempting to improve the offer in time and to stay ahead of competitors.

In the case of customer-centric online organizations, the integration of CRM tools within the business operational structure offers the possibility to identify, assess, and define precisely the main customer segments in terms of profitability, and to build predictive customer profiles. The strategic planning process involves the collaboration of various specialists, who try to establish realistic strategic objectives for each customer segment and to select the most appropriate marketing strategy to achieve these objective. The planning process incorporates both the strategic and operational perspectives, creating continuity and consistency among various strategic levels. The implementation process becomes more flexible, offering the possibility of a quick adjustment at the level of individual customer campaign. The integration of customer databases with data mining tools and customer management software permits the effective management of customer interaction at an individual level. The customer-firm interac-

Figure 4. Comparison between a product-oriented online firm and a consumer-centric online business in terms of business procedures

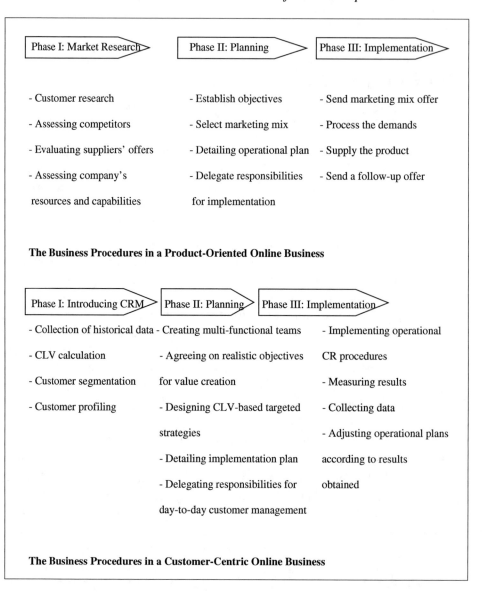

Phase I: Market Research   Phase II: Planning   Phase III: Implementation

- Customer research   - Establish objectives   - Send marketing mix offer

- Assessing competitors   - Select marketing mix   - Process the demands

- Evaluating suppliers' offers - Detailing operational plan - Supply the product

- Assessing company's   - Delegate responsibilities   - Send a follow-up offer

  resources and capabilities   for implementation

The Business Procedures in a Product-Oriented Online Business

Phase I: Introducing CRM   Phase II: Planning   Phase III: Implementation

- Collection of historical data - Creating multi-functional teams - Implementing operational

- CLV calculation   - Agreeing on realistic objectives CR procedures

- Customer segmentation   for value creation   - Measuring results

- Customer profiling   - Designing CLV-based targeted - Collecting data

                             strategies   - Adjusting operational plans

                             - Detailing implementation plan according to results

                             - Delegating responsibilities for obtained

                             day-to-day customer management

The Business Procedures in a Customer-Centric Online Business

tion is registered in the transaction history, creating the basis for the refinement of customer targeting in future marketing campaigns.

As a result of implementing the CRM system, the firm-customer interaction will be more effective, resulting in increased customer satisfaction, increased customer loyalty, and increased profitability for the firm.

Conclusion

The flexible and interactive nature of the Internet offers the possibility to collect a vast amount of data about online customers and their interaction with the company. Processing this data provides a good basis to segment the market precisely, to predict the behavior of customers, and to implement one-to-one marketing campaigns.

On the other hand, the volatility of online markets requires an increased focus on customer relationship and customer loyalty. Research shows that a 5% increase in customer retention can increase the company profits by 20-100% (Reichheld, Markey, & Hopton, 2000). The loyalty-based model effectively explains success and failure in the digital business world.

In this situation, CRM processes become a major element of corporate strategy for many digital organizations. The adoption of CRM is being fuelled by the recognition that long-term relationships with customers are one of the most important assets of an organization and that information-enabled systems must be developed to retain 'customer ownership'.

The applicability of the traditional approach to marketing in the online business environment has been increasingly questioned and criticized in recent years. This approach emphasized management of key marketing mix elements such as product, price, promotion, and place within the functional context of the marketing department in order to create a winning offer. The new CRM approach, while recognizing the importance of the marketing mix elements, reflects the need to create an integrated cross-functional focus on customer-firm interaction.

The implementation of the CRM model will re-structure the entire enterprise, creating new procedures for market research, strategic planning, operational implementation, and managerial control. Considering the magnitude of change, an organization needs to assess its core business and consider the form of CRM that is more appropriate for its structure and market. Then, having identified the present and the future focus of CRM, the organization has to access and implement the appropriate information architecture to enable its CRM strategy (see Figure 5).

The implementation of a CRM system requires changes at organizational, managerial, marketing, sales, and technical levels (Table 6). In comparison with the business process in a product-focused organization, the operational and managerial procedures in a CRM environment need to preserve flexibility, responsiveness, and adaptability to the requirements of customers. An appropriate policy is designed specifically for each targeted customer segment, requiring consistency and continuity between organizational strategic goals and marketing campaign operational objectives.

Table 6. The key changes triggered by CRM implementation (Adapted from Forsyth, 1999)

Organizational	Managing Change	Sales and Marketing	Technical
Incorporating 'customer' into the business planning cycle	Changing the boundaries of marketing, sales, and communication channels	Incorporating 'customer' into marketing decision and sales operations	Providing an evolving, user-friendly CRM-system
Setting customer-related objectives	Changing the company's culture to be customer-oriented rather than product-focused	Centralizing control of the sales and marketing process	Building the CRM database from the operational or 'legacy' systems
Multi-function teams required to implement customer relationship programs	Implementing a process of 'continuous change'	Learning the new skills of CRM-based marketing	Providing a cost-effective environment with good performance

This chapter attempted to present, analyze, and assess the advantages and the challenges of CRM system implementation, and to propose a model to redesign the organizational structure in this context. This model can provide beneficial information both for academics and practitioners:

1. On the basis of this theoretical framework, future research projects can be initiated to analyze the specific procedure of introducing a customer-centric culture in various CRM-based online organizations.

2. The model can be used by managers and business practitioners to reflect on the advantages/problems of implementing a CRM system in their organization, and to identify the main aspects regarding the adaptation of the business process to the new organizational structure.

Figure 5. The CRM journey—Realizing full value (Adapted from Forsyth, 1999)

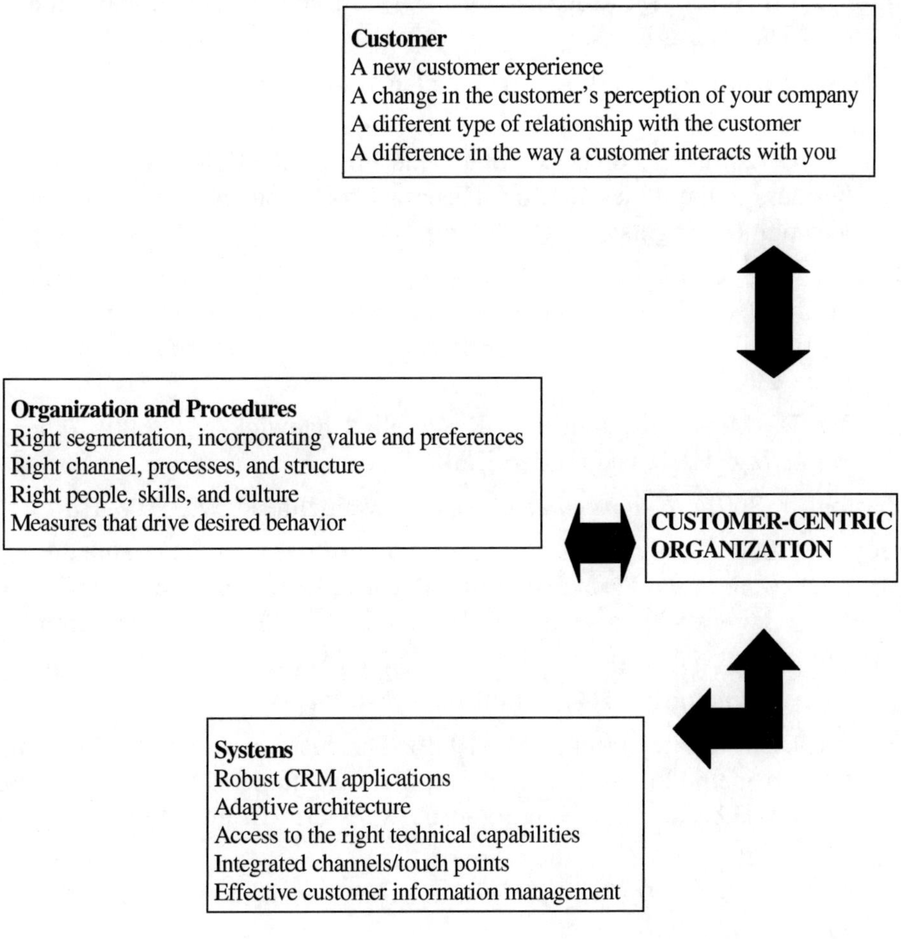

Customer
A new customer experience
A change in the customer's perception of your company
A different type of relationship with the customer
A difference in the way a customer interacts with you

Organization and Procedures
Right segmentation, incorporating value and preferences
Right channel, processes, and structure
Right people, skills, and culture
Measures that drive desired behavior

CUSTOMER-CENTRIC ORGANIZATION

Systems
Robust CRM applications
Adaptive architecture
Access to the right technical capabilities
Integrated channels/touch points
Effective customer information management

Ultimately, the organization's success in CRM will involve creating an appropriate strategic vision of the future, making the appropriate choice of applications, creatively using appropriate analytical techniques to exploit the data, and finally, incorporating the customer-centric procedures into a flexible organizational process at the corporate level (Payne, 2001).

References

Adebanjo, D. (2003). Classifying and selecting eCRM applications: An analysis-based proposal. *Management Decision, 41*(6), 570-577.

Anton, J. (1996). *Customer relationship management.* New York: Prentice-Hall.

Anton, J., & Hoeck, M. (2002). *e-Business customer service.* Santa Monica, CA: The Anton Press.

April, C., & Harreld, H. (2002). Seeking CRM integration. *Infoworld, 24*(35), 35.

Bacuvier, G. (2001). Customer Lifetime Value: Powerful insights into a company's business and activities. Retrieved February 2003 from: http://www.bah.com/viewpoints/insights/cmt_clv_2.html.

Bradshaw, D., & Brash, C. (2001). Managing customer relationships in the e-business world: How to personalize computer relationships for increased profitability. *International Journal of Retail and Distribution Management, 29*(12), 520-530.

Chaffey, D., Mayer, R., Johnston, K.,& Ellis-Chadwick, F. (2000). *Internet marketing.* Harlow: Prentice-Hall.

Chaston, I. (2001). *E-marketing strategies.* Maidenhead: McGraw-Hill.

Cody, D. (2000). Analytical CRM: Increasing lifetime customer value through prediction. *ServeWorld Magazine.* Retrieved February 2003 from: http://www.serveworldmagazine.com/sunserver/2/2000/12/analytical.shtml?

Connolly, T., & Ashworth, G. (1994). Managing customer for profit. *Management Accounting, 72*(4), 34-40.

Conway, D.K., & Fitzpatrick, J.M. (1999). The customer relationship revolution—a methodology for creating golden customers. *CRM-Forum.* Retrieved February 2003 from: http://www.crm-forum.com/crm_vp/crr/sld01.htm.

Cusack, M. (1998). *Online customer care.* Milwaukee, WI: ASQ Quality Press.

De Kare-Silver, M. (1998). *E-shock.* London: Macmillan Business.

Feinberg, R., & Kadam, R. (2002). eCRM Web service attributes as determinants of customer satisfaction with retail websites. *International Journal of Service Industry Management, 13*(5), 432-451.

FollowUp.Net. (1999). *Customer development survey.* Available online at: http://www.followup.net/press/press.html.

Forsyth, R. (1999). Implementing a successful marketing strategy based on CRM. *CRM-Forum.* Retrieved February 2003 from: http://www.crm-forum.com/library/pre/pre-007/brandframe.html.

Forsyth, R. (2001). Re-evaluating CRM clichés: Customer Lifetime Value. *CRM-Forum.* Retrieved February 2003 from: http://www.crm-forum.com/cgi-bin/framemaker.cgi?url=/ppv/crmlibrary/ed/cliches/index.html.

Gur ău, C., & Ranchhod, A. (2002). Measuring customer satisfaction: A platform for calculating, predicting and increasing customer profitability. *Journal of Targeting, Measurement and Analysis for Marketing, 10*(3), 203-219.

Kalakota, R., & Robinson, M. (2001). *E-business 2.0: Roadmap for success.* Boston, MA: Addison-Wesley.

Karimi, J., Somers, T.M., & Gupta, Y. (2001). Impact of information technology management practices on customer services. *Journal of Management Information Systems, 17*(4), 125-158.

Kotorov, R.P. (2002). Ubiquitous organization: Organizational design for eCRM. *Business Process Management Journal, 8*(3), 218-232.

Levy, M. (2000). Trend predictions: Customer-centric corporate restructuring. *Worldwide E-Commerce Developments, 2*(4). Retrieved February 2003 from: http://ecmgt.com/Apr2000/management.perspective.htm.

Lindström, M., & Andersen, T.F. (2000). *Brand building on the Internet.* London: Kogan Page.

M. Polo Group. (2002). Customer relationship management. Problems companies face. Retrieved February 2003 from: http://www.mpologroup.com/CRM%20Files/CRM%20Challenges.html.

Mabley, K. (2000). Privacy vs. personalization. *Cyber Dialogue.* Retrieved February 2003 from: http://www.cyberdialogue.com/library/pdfs/wp-cd-2000-privacy.pdf.

Menconi, P. (2000). CRM 101: Building a great customer relationship management strategy. In D.H. Renner (Ed.), *Defying the limits: Reaching new heights in customer relationship management* (pp. 31-33). San Francisco, CA: Montgomery Research.

Ness, A.J., Schroeck, J.M., Letendre, A.R., & Willmar, J.D. (2001). The role of ABM in measuring customer value. *Strategic Finance.* Retrieved February 2003 from: http://www.mamag.com/strategicfinance/2001/03f.htm.

Novo, J. (2001a). Customer loyalty. Retrieved February 2003 from: http://www.jimnovo.com/Customer-Loyalty-more.htm.

Novo, J. (2001b). A model of future customer value. Retrieved February 2003 from: http://www.digitrends.net/ebiz/13644_14931.html.

Nykamp, M. (2001). *The customer differential: The complete guide to implementing customer relationship management.* Chicago: American Management Association.

Pastore, M. (1999). E-tailers lack customer relationship plans. Retrieved February 2003 from: http://cyberatlas.internet.com/markets/retailing/print/0,,6061_153571,00.html.

Payne, A. (2001). CRM: Delivering improved customer profitability. *Journal of Customer Loyalty*. Retrieved February 2003 from: http://www.eloyaltyco.com/journal/Issue15Article6.htm.

Payne, A. (2002). A strategic framework for customer relationship management. BT Insight Interactive. Retrieved February 2003 from: http://www.bt.com/insight-interactive/browse/ii_content.jsp?contentKey=00352.

Parvatiyar, A., & Sheth, J. (2000). The domain and conceptual foundations of relationship marketing. In J. Sheth & A. Parvatiyar (Eds.), *Handbook of relationship marketing* (pp. 3-38). London: Sage Publications.

Peacock, P.R. (2001). Data mining in marketing. In J.N. Shath, A. Eshghi, & B.C. Krishnan (Eds.), *Internet marketing* (pp. 163-190). Fort Worth, TX: Harcourt College Publishers.

Pétrissans, A. (1999). *Customer relationship management: The changing economics of customer relationship*. White Paper prepared jointly by Cap Gemini and International Data Corporation. Retrieved February 2003 from: http://www.ie.cgey.com/services/crm_reports.html.

Reichheld, F.F., & Schefter, P. (2000). E-loyalty—your secret weapon on the Web. *Harvard Business Review, 78*(4), 105-113.

Reichheld, F.F., Markey, R.G. Jr., & Hopton, C. (2000). The loyalty effect—the relationship between loyalty and profits. *European Business Journal, 12*(3), 134-141.

Rust, R., & Zahorik, A. (1993). Customer satisfaction, customer retention and market share. *Journal of Retailing, 69*(2), 193-215.

Smith, M., & Dikolli, S. (1995). Customer profitability analysis: An activity-based costing approach. *Managerial Auditing Journal, 10*(7), 3-7.

Sterne, J. (1996). *Customer service on the Internet: Building relationships, increasing loyalty, and staying competitive*. New York: John Wiley & Sons.

Swift, R.S. (2001). *Accelerating customer relationships using CRM and relationship technologies*. Englewood Cliffs, NJ: Prentice-Hall.

Taylor, S.A., & Hunter, G.L. (2002). The impact of loyalty with eCRM software and e-services, *International Journal of Service Industry Management, 13*(5), 452-474.

Thearling, K. (1999). Increasing customer value by integrating data mining and campaign management software. Retrieved February 2003 from: http://www3primushost.com/~kht/text/integration/integration.htm.

Trembly, A. (2002). Why has CRM failed in insurance? *National Underwriter, 106*(26), 25.

Tschohl, J. (2001). *E-service.* Minneapolis, MN: Best Sellers Publishing.

Winer, R.S. (2001). A framework for customer relationship management. *California Management Review, 43*(4), 89-105.

Wundermann, C.J. (2001). Unlocking the true value of customer relationship management. *CRM-Forum.* Retrieved February 2003 from: http://www.crm-forum.com/crm_vp/utv/sld01.htm.

Chapter III

eCRM Integration in E-Business:
First Line of Offense to Competitive Advantage

Cain Evans
University of Central England in Birmingham, UK

Abstract

Integrating an eCRM system in today's business world is increasingly becoming the standard setting to the successful building of robust customer retention programs. However, integrating eCRM systems requires not only a technological perspective but a process perspective too. Developed in this work are several key phases that are integrated into the development of the CROSIT and CPR models. These two distinct models are developed to assist e-businesses in articulating eCRM through a combination of system, application, and process activities. The CROSIT model encompasses two central themes, with the centrifugal being the engine of the model. These attributes relate to the input and output of information flows: the customer and the e-business's response to the eCustomer or traditional customer. The CROSIT model encapsulates a five-layered dimensional approach to integrating technologies, resources, strategy, and manageability of an eCRM system. The extension of CROSIT is the CPR model is used to gauge the readiness of the eCRM system, its applications, interrelated processes, and sub-systems and their integration into the e-business environment.

Background

E-business success in today's economic climate is becoming more dependent upon customer retention programs than on achieving fully aligned business systems. E-businesses are continuing to endeavor to compete in the new, rich, and vibrant electronic markets, only to find that their CRM systems do not always match the expectations of online customers. Achieving competitive advantage requires a strong focus on internal value chains and the sustainability of an e-business' information technologies (Porter, 1980, 1985, 2001).

Success in today's customer-driven markets is based upon the realization that e-businesses require a methodological approach to handling customer information and data. Once an e-business has acquired customer data from its channels, there is a need to process it. The question is what information needs to be processed and how is it to be done (Ward, Griffiths, & Whitmore, 1993).

Operations within an e-business rely heavily on information technologies (ITs), so it is valuable to understand exactly what IT is. Information technologies invariably include hardware, software, database systems, and telecommunication systems (Turban, McLean, & Wetherbe, 2001). Furthermore, as highlighted by Evans (2001), e-businesses require a structure to develop IT and the peripheral services needed to operate an e-business: this structure is known as the E-Business InfoNet. The E-Business InfoNet is a flexible approach to integrating various types of technologies with one another, either physical or organic components being expanded as and when the e-business demands changes. The need e-business has for information systems (ISs), initially, is with the capture, transmission, retrieval, and manipulation of information used by an e-business, with one or more processes taking part in the transaction (Alter, 2002).

eCRM/CRM System Interactions

E-businesses today require eCRM/CRM systems to be interactive not only with a company's field engineers and salesmen, but more importantly with customers, both those coming through traditional routes and those coming through the World Wide Web (WWW). Online customers need to be focused upon without the firm having to extend itself beyond its capabilities and investment opportunities. So, then, what should an interactive eCRM/CRM system do?

There are a myriad of methods that can be used by managers to ascertain customer intelligence or improve retention ratios. For instance, mail campaigns are a great way to inform long-standing customers, as well as new and potential customers, of the great offers that are available. Mail campaigns are a great way to reach a wide audience without a huge outlay: technology provides a simple but effective method of targeting specific customers with information about particular products and brands.

The integration of front-end and back-office technologies has created a wealth of customer information that is available to be analyzed and formulated into data that is readily understood by managers and salesmen alike. Front-end systems invariably include a robust website that has a high impact visually, as well as dynamic content that attracts new and existing online customers to either purchase products or to acquire pertinent information. Websites are a great way to understand your customers better by improving the communication channels used and extending existing channels.

eCRM integration invariably includes Computer Telephony Integration (CTI) technologies which aim to improve the customer experience and processual efficiency. However, managing and using CTI is not always an easy task, given the complexity and continuing investment needed to keep the technology up to date. It is important to e-businesses to understand that to use an eCRM system without thinking about customer drivers will not create the harmonious environment needed to sustain customer-retention programs developed by either marketing or sales managers. Customer drivers invariably include the need for an eCRM/CRM system to be made available at any time and anywhere to its valued customer base. Failure to create conditions whereby online customers can reliably login or search an e-business' products or literature is not creating the best environment at all, and may even be pushing away potential online customers. Another key point with online CRM systems is that they do need to be made available without any latency affecting the services offered, or online customers will buy from a competitor. As regards this issue of service efficiency and zero latency, an e-business needs to make sure that its services are of a high standard, with expediency given top priority when dealing with individual customers.

E-business and their eCRM system(s) require constant updating to ensure that seamless service is guaranteed to online customers, even if this means that managers need to extend budgets or cut 'other' expenditures so that customers are given a priority, i.e., that the organization is focused purely on customer-centricity.

Implementing eCRM/CRM Programs

Any form of e-business implementation of eCRM requires a determined approach to ensure that there are no misadventures with either the budget being over-stretched or the management system not being fully integrated with ongoing organizational-wide office systems. There is a need for a formal approach to any type of eCRM/CRM implementation, given the considerable expense of human capital and the need to ensure that customer information is accurate and timely when managers need it.

Although there are many aspects to a CRM/eCRM implementation, the following factors could be seen as generic in nature. They are:

- Human Capital
- Customer Information [data]
- Financial Constraints
- E-Business Infrastructure

A CRM/eCRM project rollout needs to be successful, and human capital is a very important aspect of that success. The humanistic need for a CRM project is greatest when there is an organizational-wide fusion of disparate systems. It is important that a corporate stakeholder accepts overall responsibility for the whole project and not just for one aspect of it: the latter approach will only result in a project either failing or going over budget and outside project milestones. What is needed to facilitate vision, direction, and the completion of a successful project? Judging by the experiences of many project managers and marketing managers, it is clear that there is a distinct need for a senior executive to get involved from day one, rather than leave the project management to operational-level supervisors, who may not always have a visionary perspective of the organization's actual needs.

Specialist resources that are very familiar with both the technology and the processes involved with CRM/eCRM are also essential. Why is this an important feature of a project rollout and implementation? There are several reasons. Firstly, given the special nature of eCRM and the need an e-business has for storing, manipulating, and propagating sensible information about its customers, there is a need to utilize human resources who actually have first-hand knowledge and experience of such systems. Such resources will usually be well versed in eCRM management and online customer interfacing.

More importantly, as well as the need for specialist resources, there is a more demanding need for a dedicated project manager who will oversee the day-today operations of the project and who will be able to coordinate as well as interface with clients successfully, and motivate project staff to complete the implementation on time and within budget.

Data and Online Customer Systems

E-businesses need to hold and store accurate and up-to-date information, both for themselves and for their online customer, otherwise marketing campaigns will be carried out with information that is unusable. The need to store accurate information is paramount, and any manager requiring customer data needs to be able to have complete faith in the data they are provided with. It is useless for any manager to operate campaigns with inadequate and redundant data that is retrieved from the World Wide Web. The e-business frontline, the website, is present for a purpose, and this is to offer a trading portal and at the same time to collect customer information.

Online data needs to be consistent and needs to be complete: incomplete and inconsistent data will not help e-businesses and their management to gain a true picture of what is going on with their online interfacing site.

Implementation and Budgetary Control

The project manager of an eCRM/CRM rollout needs to ensure that the parameters to which the organization adheres are observed, or project and system failure may result. Key variables that are important ingredients are milestones. Why do milestones always need to be observed? One explanation is that without keeping to, for instance, the first milestone, then any other milestone will never be attained. It is necessary to reign in budgetary constraints early on so as not to debilitate the project at a later stage.

There is also a need for consideration when discussing return on investment (ROI), given that the CRM/eCRM initiative is to improve both the organizational structure and the customer experience. At the end of the project, the client will ask for some return for the investment that is made at the beginning of the project lifecycle. Failure to bear this in mind will create in the long run poor decision making on the part of the senior executive management, as well as create a condition whereby the organizational-wide systems are neither aligned nor efficient.

eCRM/CRM and Synchronized Implementation

The implementation of eCRM/CRM rollouts does require some form of method as opposed to leaving it to ad-hoc decision-making processes. According to Forrester the following are seen as key components of a successful eCRM/CRM implementation (Temkin et al., 2003):

- Define a strategy
- Set objectives
- Select the best technology
- Implement the acquired technology
- Define new business processes
- Drive adoption

Most difficulties arise when a CRM/eCRM project is initiated. At the beginning of a new project, there is a distinct need to ensure that the client requirements are included and adhered to meticulously.

Barriers to Successful eCRM/CRM Implementations

According to a research study by Pushkala in January 2002, a range of issues was raised that affected the successful implementation of an eCRM/CRM rollout:

- Inter-departmental conflict
- System functionality
- Resources

Organizations included in the survey said that the number of disparate systems created a condition whereby there were issues with aligning and integrating customer data effectively. Systems that are classed either as sub-systems or back-end systems do need to be comprehensively aligned and integrated, or there is little to be gained from organizing eCRM/CRM systems.

Sharing of Customer Data

Some organizations in the survey carried out by Pushkala (2002) felt that there was already an emerging problem of sharing customer data with other departments. The question of boundaries being placed at each end of a department creates a lot of redundancy and management issues, such as the cost of creating entirely new customer systems and databases to store customers' data that is, in effect, already in place in another department.

The business case for sharing customer data and distributing it internally is unquestionable, both in terms of economics and of business sense. Inter-departmental cooperation and inter-departmental facilitation of information is a necessary ingredient to successfully aligning and integrating departmental systems—eCRM/CRM systems. Failure to share data and customer information will only, in the long run, create serious problems for an e-business, especially when forming campaigns and mail-shots.

System Functionality and Customer Data

Where eCRM/CRM rollouts are decidedly late and poor performance is the result of a lack of control, then this will hit the budget significantly. Allowing milestones to be missed, allowing implementations to run over on costs, and not communicating changes to all concerned will create a complete project failure and, more importantly, the 'client' will lose out in terms of the lateness of the implementation and the manageability of its internal systems and data.

Important to a successful implementation and a successful eCRM/CRM project is the accuracy of the data that is truncated to respective managers. Data quality is of paramount importance when using a system that is seen as the engine of the organization. E-businesses in today's global markets depend not only upon the accuracy of front-end systems, but also on the quality and accuracy of customer data. Quality of data is important, but integrity should not be downgraded against efficiency drives. Data integrity supports the business value assigned to customer data and, without integrity of data and information, the value of the information diminishes and is less useful to management in either their marketing campaigns or online targeting of customers (Pushkala, 2002).

eCRM Implementation and Performance

E-businesses and their eCRM/CRM system(s) are implemented with one single goal—to serve their customer base (Gronroo & Powell, 2000). Rather than provide an eCRM/CRM system to support the optimization of a department, eCRM is a tool that encompasses the functionality required to permeate the whole organization. The interesting point with eCRM implementations is that only a third of them are attributed to a successful project implementation (Dickie, 1988). Many eCRM/CRM implementations have been shown to have been poorly carried out, only 25-30% of implementations being wholly successful.

Steps to eCRM Success

Initiating an eCRM project requires not only financial investment, but also a mixture of people skills, software selection, and an attention to detail. Without any of these key drivers, an implementation will not be as successful as it ought to be, given the extent of damage that can be done by not clearly defining project and management goals. The extent to which success is achieved could be measured by the eCRM/CRM's ability to add value to the already systems-oriented e-business. The concept behind eCRM/CRM is not just about interacting with customers online, but about improving the method and effectiveness of managing customer data.

It is suggested that there are four implementation steps that affect the viability of a project (Lee, 2003):

- Developing customer-centric strategies
- Redesigning workflow management systems
- Re-engineering work processes
- Supporting with the right technologies

However, Kimberley Hill of CRMDaily.com suggests that deploying eCRM modules one at a time is more productive and financially sound where businesses have strict budgets (Hill, 2003). Barton Goldenburg (2003) of eWeek.com suggests that to reduce costs, it is not always prudent to engage external implementation experts without qualifying the expense involved. Delivering internal implementations with support from an external specialist is better than completely outsourcing a project, saving sometimes more than 70% of costs, according to Goldenburg.

CROSIT and Alignment Issues

The CROSIT (Customer Relationship Operational Systems Integrated Technologies) model is developed based on previous works by Henderson and Venkatraman (1999) and their Strategic Alignment Model. Also, as a reference, the developments made by Curtin (1996), Alter (2002), and Earl (1992) have each played an important role in the development of the CROSIT and CPR (Customer Process Reference) models.

The CROSIT model is based on various models that relate to businesses either aligning systems or applications, or integrating processes across the organization. In particular, Henderson's (1999) model revolved around internal and external domains within the business context. The CROSIT model includes several different business perspectives, domains, and needs of an e-business' eCRM function. The CROSIT model is layered with five key elements that enable successful integration of eCRM processes and application technologies.

The CROSIT model is based on the generic input, process, and output model to keep the complexity to a minimum. The only input to the model is the online customer, also known as the eCustomer, whose actions require processing by the e-business. The online customer may be ordering products or possibly just 'browsing' a business' website. The response made by the e-business will entirely depend upon the efficiency of its eCRM function and the inter-organizational systems (IOSs) that are needed to support the online experience.

The intention with the CPR model, on the other hand, is to apply the model after the CROSIT model has matured. The CPR model is a mechanism for measuring the progression of the eCRM system and its cross-functional integration within the e-business.

The phases are illustrated as:

- Initial Phase: E-businesses to quantify the state of play

- Metrics: Process proficiency

- System Integration: Competency of the eCRM and organizational-wide systems

- CPR: Encapsulates all known states and competencies

The CPR model, as suggested, is applied once the CROSIT model has had sufficient time to mature and develop into a fully integrated eCRM enterprise-wide system. eCRM is not meant to be a stand-alone customer management system, but one that is fully integrated, with enterprise-wide systems that cross all aspects of the value chain (Porter, 1985).The CPR model is not appropriate for use before all efforts have been afforded to the CROSIT model, i.e., before a satisfactory conclusion has been achieved with the integration and alignment of eCRM systems and applications.

eCRM/CRM and Market Developments

The growth of the Internet over the last few years has afforded businesses a tremendous opportunity to adopt new technology and to integrate it with their internal functions. The Internet has swept across all types of businesses, brick and mortar as well as newly established dot.com firms, and with it brought forward the need to focus on providing the most efficient method of service, delivery, and performance of internal functional systems. This technological development has led CEOs, CIOs, CTOs, and managers to become more aware of the needs of the business and of both its traditional and its online customers. Businesses seem to be finding particular difficulties with integrating Internet-enabled technologies and are concerned about how to best apply new-wave technology to real business solutions (Grove, 1996; Porter, 1985).

The growth of the Internet has opened up opportunities to enable more and more traditional customers to access online services and products. CyberAtlas estimated in 2002 that the worldwide population of Internet users was 580 million, whereas eMarketer estimated total worldwide population with access to online services and products to be approximately 709 million users (CyberAtlas, 2003). Global trends, with the growth of Internet users becoming more interested in accessing services and products online, has increased significantly in most parts of the world today. Nielsen NetRating in their study found that Germany has achieved, so far, 35.6 million users online, whereas the UK has achieved 29 million Internet users, and Italy, 22.7 million (Nielsen, 2003). Nielsen's study also highlighted that the most matured markets are:

1.   Sweden
2.   Hong Kong
3.   The Netherlands
4.   Australia

Further, the global Internet market is currently being led by America, with 29% of the total Internet market, followed by Europe (23%), Asia (13%), and Latin America (2%) (Hill, 2003).

As the increase in Internet users becomes greater, the need for businesses to improve their Internet-enabled systems becomes more and more apparent. Increasing the scope of online services is only part of the solution to business demands from Internet users (Mougayer, 1998). Developing new commerce channels is available to every business. This can be an advantage if the business looks to integrate and align internal systems with Internet-enabled technologies (Jones & Kochtanek, 2002; Granger, 1994). However, creating advantage with the Internet is not necessarily based on improving front-end systems alone, and on providing an opportunity for new customer channels to flourish (Porter, 1980, 1985, 2001). As highlighted by Porter's (2001) paper on Internet strategy, business activities are being linked together through tools like CRM to improve efficiency, control, and customer servicing. However, businesses cannot afford to integrate Internet-enabled technologies without the complete support of senior managers, CEOs, and CIOs alike. Supporting new wave technologies is a requirement of the whole business and not just of individual business functions that are a part of the value chain mechanism (Porter, 1985). The opportunity provided for businesses to integrate front-end and back-end technologies with the Internet is one that can only be attained with the full support of management and where appropriate, with restructuring.

Since the dot.com 'boom 'n bust' several years ago, businesses have been quietly planning what to do next with Internet-enabled technologies and considering how best to absorb their power. Businesses have, although slowly, made concerted efforts to embrace the Internet by integrating internal functional systems with traditional and newly created channels, using the Internet to supplement traditional channels of commerce and servicing of its customers (Steinfield et al., 2002).

A new wave of commerce has evolved, and businesses have seen fit to re-focus attention from the business-centric view of commerce towards customer-centric models and tools. With this new wave of commerce, the need has grown for businesses to be more conscious of high-tech customers and their preference for online servicing, rather than for traditional channels. Biz Report (2002) found in their study that two-thirds of customer servicing is conducted online or via email.

This phenomenon, whereby customers are choosing online servicing in preference to traditional channels, has made it more important that businesses ensure that their internal systems, whether front/back-end, are both integrated and aligned inter-organizationally (IOS). More than half of businesses in the UK have embarked on a journey to integrate Internet technologies to enable their customers to either order products online or be serviced online (DTI, 2002).

There are many definitions of e-business to-date. To help with the understanding of e-business and the integration of new wave technologies, several of these definitions are presented. IBM (2003) defines e-business as:

"...The transformation of key business processes through the use of Internet technologies...."

The Department of Trade and Industry (DTI-UK) describes e-business as:

"...Fully integrated information and integrated communications technologies (ICTs) into its operations...integration of all these activities with internal processes of a business through ICT." (DTI, 2000)

Weill and Vitale (2001), in their book *Place to Space*, define e-business as:

"Marketing, buying, selling, delivering, servicing, and paying for products, services, and information across networks linking an enterprise and its prospects, customers, agents, suppliers, competitors, allies, and complementors."

And, finally:

"E-business is a cluster of features and techniques which are needed to support the business engagement in commerce as well as e-commerce with online and offline customers. Further, this engagement includes the interaction between other businesses and organizations that utilize computers, the Internet, and networking generally. Encompassing this business format are the rules and processes that combine many functions such as eCRM, eBRM, eERM, eSCM, eERP, eMRPII, and EAI." (Evans, 2001)

eCRM: What is it?

eCustomer Relationship Management, simply stated, is a new strategy to assist businesses in providing highly effective and efficient customer service by utilizing management to concentrate on customers in order to acquire, develop, and retain the company's most valuable asset—its customers. The potential market for eCRM/CRM products is estimated to grow to $10 billion by 2005 (Pastore, 2003).

eCRM, based on the utilization of the Internet (Daniel & Wilson, 2002), is an information industry term for methodologies, software, and capabilities that help a business manage eCustomers' relationships in a structured and methodical way. For example, businesses invariably need to collate, dissect, manipulate, and disseminate customer information that usually requires the use of a formal approach to storing raw data. This raw data, known as click-stream data, is truncated downstream through various processes until the data reaches a storing location that is normally a large database—RDBMS. In most cases, managers invariably need up-to-date customer information to make a decision and therefore retrieve the relevant information, using techniques such as slicing and dicing to make the most appropriate decision for the business. Online customers now have the ability to access products and services anywhere and at anytime. Nowadays, businesses are able to keep customers informed of new services, products, and promotions in real time.

Today, businesses are required to, initially, understand the new dynamics of the electronic markets and more importantly to learn how to adapt to and acquire this new technology for business advantage.

E-businesses are investigating methods of improving the business and customer relationship by building streamlined techniques and tools. One of the most prominent tools to date is the use of personalization technologies. Personalization technologies enable businesses to personalize the ongoing relationship on a 1:1 basis. The philosophy behind businesses utilizing personalization technologies includes concerns with improving business efficiencies, but also a desire to improve customer satisfaction and retention programs. However, none of these new approaches are viable unless e-businesses take advantage of the new and extremely pervasive technology. However, harnessing this technology does have some drawbacks. Some examples of the perils of implementing eCRM with the business are: not creating a comprehensive customer strategy, rolling out CRM before organizational changes have been made, thinking that an increase in CRM technology is good in itself, and poor investment in customers (Rigby et al., 2002).

Internet. World Wide Web. Electronic commerce. eCRM. These terms and technologies encapsulate the possibility of improved relationships between a business and its most important asset—its customers. Nevertheless, management of these technologies is only a small part of the complete eCRM system (Cox, 2000).

Even when the technology is in place, there is also a need for complete integration, both in terms of IS/IT and the platforms in which these systems will operate. With the advent of global integration and cooperation between alliances, competition between markets has increased and products have had to differentiate between one another (Porter, 1989).

Further, e-businesses have understood that business-centricity is no longer sustainable and a shift in business practice has moved towards customer-centricity (Evans, 2001).

In addition, technology has evolved to the point where a business has the opportunity to store details of customers in a single location, thereby enabling centralization to be adopted to ensure efficiency, data updates, data integrity, and the added ability to create data markets from data warehousing systems.

Given this, what are the benefits?

- the ability to provide faster responses to customer enquiries,
- increased efficiency through automation and acquiring a deeper knowledge of customers,
- attaining more marketing or cross-selling opportunities,
- identifying the most profitable customers, and
- obtaining information that can be shared among both internal functions and external alliances (Winer, 2001).

As with data-warehousing systems, the eCRM/CRM system within a business environment is a combination of various sub-systems that amalgamate to form a concise, effective, and more importantly from the business perspective, an efficient means to collate, communicate, analyze, store, and disperse pertinent information about a business customer. Karapetrovic (2002) suggests that a system is a composite of inter-linked processes that function harmoniously and share the same resources that come together to achieve a set of business goals or objectives.

In today's dynamic business environment, an eCRM/CRM system cannot solely partake on its own in a disjointed way, but must interrelate with 'other' systems that are in operation within the business environment. Whether they are systems or functions, the business relies upon the cohesiveness of its internal systems.

Businesses in today's developing and dynamic markets rely heavily on the supply of market-driven information, which encapsulates numerous dimensions relating to spatial customer information (SCI) needed by businesses to drive eCRM/CRM sub-systems, either within the marketing function or related business functions. Rigby (2002) suggests that a successful eCRM/CRM system depends more on strategy than on the amount a business invests on its technologies. Kalakota (1999) defines CRM as an integrated sales, marketing, and services strategy that depends on coordinated enterprise-wide activities. Furthermore, CRM aligns business processes with customer strategies to build customer loyalty and thus increases revenue, albeit over time (Rigby et al., 2002).

Figure 1. eCRM and its functional neighbors

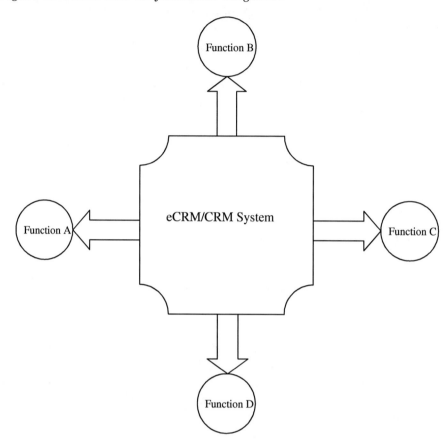

By extrapolating this trend whereby eCRM/CRM is not purely a sole function alone in its marketing environment, businesses can see that eCRM/CRM is a wholly integrated system linked, but not exclusively, to accounting, production, sales, marketing, and manufacturing. Figure 1 illustrates the integration issue of eCRM/CRM with neighboring functions within an e-business.

Integrating eCRM

Nowadays, e-businesses are frequently using customer relationship tools to improve the overall performance handling of each online/offline customer. In the past, customers were restricted to traditional channels such as contacting customer call centers or using the postal service. The days of 'snail-mail' have long since dissipated and been replaced by efficient, effective CRM tools like personalization. Personalization technologies have seen a dramatic rise in demand during the last few years, as they have become more and more important in handling customers with their individual needs (DataMonitor, 2001; Peppers & Rogers, 1993). Furthermore, according to DataMonitor (2001), personalization technology is to reach a peak of $2.1 billion by 2006. E-businesses have fully grasped the need to improve their internal CRM systems with 'other' inter-organizational systems such as supply chain management (SCM) and enterprise application integration (EAI). The Meta Group (2001) conducted a study of B2C and B2B firms, and found that there was an increase in online businesses using CRM and its technologies. Furthermore, IDC Research highlighted in its study that more than 50% of European businesses agreed that CRM/eCRM and its tools were critical to business operations (IDC, 2001). However, integrating CRM tools and applications is not always an easy option to choose, according to the Gartner Group (2001), which found that e-businesses were more likely to underestimate the costs of CRM/eCRM integration by as much as 40-50% by 2006 (Winer, 2001). The expected market share of CRM/eCRM-related technologies could reach as much as $16.5 billion by 2006, according to Jupiter Research (2002). The study by Jupiter Research expects the markets in the retail and financial industries to be as much as:

- Retail Sector, $3.2 billion by 2006
- Financial Sector, $5.4 billion by 2006

The driving force behind e-businesses and their eCustomers pursuing the readjustment of their approach to online business is the development of new eMarketing technologies such as personalization and integrated customer management systems.

Within eMarketing, a number of definitions have evolved, for instance that of Chaffey, Mayer, Johnston, and Ellis-Chadwich (2001):

"...The application of the internet and related digital technologies to achieve marketing objectives...."

Dibb, Simkin, Pride, and Ferrell (2000) write that eMarketing:

"...consists of individual and organizational activities that facilitate and expedite...exchange relationships...in a dynamic environment...."

In particular, meeting customer needs, either 1:1 or otherwise, requires coordinated activities to ensure that they are content with their individual service either online or offline (Jaworski & Kohli, 1993).

Nevertheless, although it is all well and good that e-businesses are asked to implement new eCRM/CRM paradigms, one aspect will be at the center of the CEO's as well as the CTO and CIO's mind, and that is cost. Acquiring eCustomers is not, in the short term, inexpensive (Reicheld & Schefter, 2000). E-businesses need to be reminded that there is a method involved in acquiring customers and that improving retention rates requires financial support for the acquisition, retention, and extension programs (O'Malley & Tynan, 2001).

Internet-enabled technologies have driven the need for e-business functions to work closer together to meet the needs of their customers. Furthermore, with the drive for integration of front/back-end technologies and the upstream/downstream processes, marketing and IT functions need to 'pull-together' to enable e-businesses to maximize impact in the electronic markets (Wells et al., 1999).

Utilizing eCRM systems has enabled managers to make clear decisions on market segmentations, channels, demographics, and process efficiencies within the customer center management (Nasi, 1999). Also, the development of eCRM and integrated customer management systems has enabled inter-organizational systems to share information about specific target groups, as well as products' share of the market (Papazoglou, Ribbers, & Tsalgatidou, 2000).

Slicing and dicing data, as is often required by key decision makers, is invaluable, especially when deciding on which services to offer to 'selected' customers and markets (Feelders, Daniels, & Holsheimer, 2000). Generally, data mining and data warehousing have become key tools in the demand for quality information that has been derived from integrating eCRM systems within an e-business enterprise-wide environment.

eCRM/CRM and Integration in a Horizontal Organization

Businesses have traditionally been founded upon turn-of-the-century principles, with the Taylorist approach to the management of a business. The pillars that businesses were built on, until recently, embodied division of labor, functional processes, structure, and span of control.

However, these traditional methods of work do not tally with the new working environment nor with business needs. There is a growing trend in business today to shift from a vertical organizational structure to a much more pervasive organic structure that is flattened—horizontally.

A horizontal organization is primarily structured around a number of key business processes or workflows that 'link' activities and capabilities together to improve business and operational performances. Where businesses continue down the vertical organization path, it is argued that performance will only be negligible (Ostrof & Smith, 1992).

The attributes of a typical horizontal organization are characterized by Ostrof and Smith (1992) as follows:

- organized around processes, not tasks;
- a flattened hierarchical structure;
- assigned ownership of processes and process performance.

Furthermore, there are several instances where e-businesses have moved away from the traditional Theory X style of management that has been pervasive for most of the twentieth century. Nevertheless, e-businesses these days are less concerned with traditional power bases, and more focused on horizontal processes and applications (EAI and EIS) and on creating a pervasive organizational structure.

For instance, Fed Ex adapted its internal business systems for more than 20 years using a centralized computer system called COSMOS (Farhoomand et al., 2000). The function that COSMOS carried out was to track all packages handled by the business. When a Fed Ex Corporation customer/e-customer entered new information via FedEx's website, internal systems were updated with the new information in real time.

By reviewing current business practices of functional units, to being less paramatized and becoming more 'trans-zontal', businesses would have a greater leverage of enabling the integration process to take place. The fallacy lies in the fact that businesses view eCRM/CRM as a stand-alone set of systems—it is an interrelated system made up of complex channeling and processes.

eCRM/CRM Integration with E-Business Systems

In the new Internet business age, technology has driven the need for businesses to re-focus their philosophies towards satisfying customers and shifting centricity from business-centricity to customer-centricity.

There have been instances where businesses have not had a successful eCRM/CRM integration program (Curtin, 1996). Where there has been a 'lack of understanding' with the eCRM/CRM system relating to architecture, system integration, infrastructure requirements, effective program management, or following a well-defined life cycle, the business has suffered poor performance and poor investment in business technology and customer retention.

With any new challenge, like the implementation of eCRM/CRM, there is a distinct need for leadership. However, at the operational and the strategic level, literature suggests that one reason for the failure of eCRM/CRM initiatives is poor judgment on the part of senior management and executives.

Furthermore, the desire businesses have to move from the planning phase directly to the implementation phase has proven to drive the proposed system off the rails. One further point that requires highlighting is the need a business has to align technologies, whether front-end or back-end, with customer-driven systems that can affect the relationship with online customers or traditional customers alike (Rigby et al., 2002).

This relationship that is either nurtured or attained through different opportunity channels requires substance and meaning. This 'substance' encapsulates five facets of workable and, more importantly, sustainable customer relationship management (Peppers & Rogers, 1997):

- *Identification:* Learn as much as you can about the customer.
- *Individualization:* Tailor the approach to each customer.
- *Interaction:* Continue to learn more about the customer.
- *Integration:* Extend the relationship with the customer throughout the organization.
- *Integrity:* Maintain the trust of the customer.

Two key aspects of Peppers and Rogers' (1997) work integration and integrity highlight the significance of an organizational-wide eCRM/CRM system. Proposed here is that business cannot have one without the other: Businesses must integrate their customer systems and must ingrain integrity at every phase of the eCRM/CRM system or sub-system, regardless of the function or stakeholder of the process.

Historically, businesses often felt that customer services were part of the back-end processes and tied-up loose ends that had not been dealt with by the sales process. In essence, customer service requires integration at the front end of the business, but not as a last resort to attainment of the company's customer base. The relationship that a business nurtures needs to be treated accordingly, not by sales people alone, but by a responsive, integrated, efficient eCRM/CRM system (Kotler & Stonich, 1991).

Retooling eCRM/CRM Implementations

Implementation is not only concerned with working with current business practices and current business processes; consideration should also be given to redefining and retooling businesses with the best technologies and efficient processes that actually improve performance.

One example in which processes and legacy systems were fully aligned can be seen with the AlliedSignal Aerospace company, now a division of Honeywell International. AlliedSignal had four distinct business units that had difficulties with sharing information about sales opportunities, the status of maintenance requests, or the products customers had on their aircraft (CIO.Com, 2002).

A new system was implemented to counteract the number of complaints AlliedSignal received from its customers by introducing an entirely new CRM system. Atlas included a Sales Force Automation (SFA) tool from Siebel, although there were some difficulties in getting employees of AlliedSignal to use the new tool. In the end, AlliedSignal assigned a new manager of business processes to implement the new CRM tool and to work with each sales unit to develop a new, single sales process tied into Atlas.

AlliedSignal overcame its difficulties of legacy loyalty by transferring data from existing databases into Atlas and then closing down old databases that its salespeople had used previously. Today, Atlas is widely used at AlliedSignal, and efficiency has increased and been attributed to the doubling of aftermarket sales (CIO.Com, 2002).

DHL is another international company that has improved its CRM processes by introducing a planning strategy to improve its efficiency drive and workflow practices (Wrenden, 2003). However, as with any new organizational-wide system, there is resistance to change, and DHL was no different. The company's planning initiatives encountered some resistance from sales forces as they felt that they were being undermined. This scenario typifies the growing canyon between what is best for the company and what the sales forces expect. Although sales forces are experienced in dealing with customers on a daily basis, this does not and cannot imply that sales forces can operate independently of an organizational system that is in place to improve customers' experiences.

It is interesting to see that the need for change is always met with resistance from one foe or another. However, in the end it is evident that change is inevitable, given the demands that are made upon all businesses every day of every month of every year.

eCRM/CRM Integrated Technologies

The traditional forms of coordinating customer services, relationships, and the development of a heavy reliance on disparate processes and applications have created an incomplete system view of eCRM.

Furthermore, the technologies used to support the customer experience failed to justify the means by which a business operated, i.e., a lack of integration and integrity with the eCRM/CRM systems throughout the organization.

The technologies that support the internal infrastructure and architecture require alignment with functions and their respective systems. The alignment factor is generally where businesses fail to appreciate the initial complexity associated with the planning and implementation of an interoperable, scalable eCRM/CRM program.

As proposed in Figure 2, to leverage an advantage over a competitor and leverage internal systems with the retention and attainment of customers, each component must be solidly, coherently, and seamlessly integrated with all business functions.

This seamless integration is not to be misunderstood in the sense that it relates purely to marketing or sales, but should become a part of a wholesale overhaul of the business offerings.

It's worth noting that businesses that fail to counteract their deficiencies will find, if not in the immediate future, that the task of maintaining and maximizing their leverage in the market will become more demanding than first realized or understood.

For businesses, quickly integrating components of eCRM/CRM should not be a priority. The priority should be to integrate sub-systems that are essentially mission-critical, e.g., customer services and support (CSS) and call centers. This form of business philosophy to implementation programming of staging the rollout will provide investment returns by reducing overheads and by shifting practices online in relation to business needs.

Figure 2. eCRM component technologies

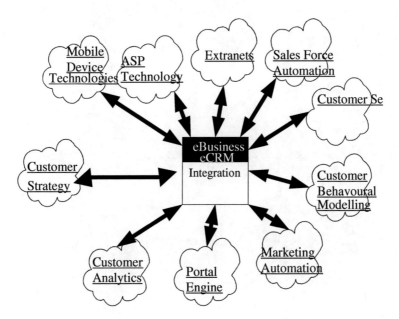

Where the overall business investment required is seen as 'worthwhile', and where the integral components are indeed integrated with existing or newly created processes, eCRM could be seen as integrated. Figure 3 illustrates the interrelatedness of eCRM/CRM and business functions throughout the organization.

As can be seen in Figure 3, there are two streams that require interoperability within the organization. The high-level posture of the eCRM/CRM system, with its indispensable sub-systems (low-level posture) and their interrelatedness towards other aspects of an e-business, requires the support of the business as a whole and leadership by the CEO to make the eCRM system a success.

Functions A, B, and C highlight the necessity of managing integration of one system and its particular sub-systems to functions within the business that require comprehensive integration with eCRM/CRM. However, this concept of interrelating sub-systems with each other must not be seen as an excuse to overload business with next-generation technologies and applications. Nevertheless, to introduce layering of sub-systems upon sub-systems without the proper coordination, i.e., with the interrelation activity not being fulfilled, would mean that there was no real advantage to implementing such a program. Why? The benefit of layering technologies, applications, and transactions will not

Figure 3. eCRM/CRM sub-system interrelatedness

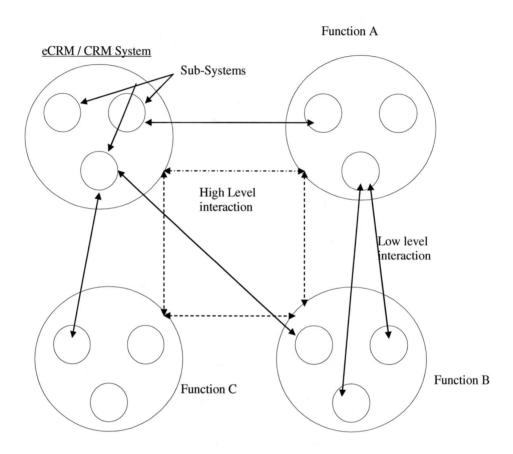

create the environment needed to nurture either the high-level posture of a system interface or the low-level sub-system interface with different systems that e-businesses have.

Alignment and Integration of eCRM/CRM with the E-Business Environment

The issues surrounding eCRM and alignment are more to do with a lack of understanding of how to manage customer information and the relationship of online/offline customer interaction. For instance, online customers require access to online business services, i.e., front-end systems, to browse through an electronic catalog of products that is available to Internet and traditional users alike. Now, if online users are experiencing or seem to be experiencing difficulties in getting access to such information, then it is reasonable to assume that there is some difficulty with the internal mechanisms that support this aspect of the business operation. Furthermore, let's say a customer has browsed a list of products on offer, and chooses a selection and then performs operations that generate payment transactions, but instead of taking the online customer to the rightful conclusion, the customer is taken to an error screen or worse still, to "…sorry, we do not have stock at the moment…'; that customer will inevitably look elsewhere.

Figure 4 illustrates an example eCRM workflow for online customers with both internal and external processes and associations with internal components of the system—used to illustrate process and functional integration. Further, the eCRM workflow diagram will be of interest to those who will face the inevitable question, "What can we do to compete in the highly changeable environment?" The simple answer, although not so simple in practice, is to integrate all business processes at a micro-level, and at the macro-level all functions of the business. Although the focus is eCRM/CRM, nevertheless, there is still a need to develop an overall model integrating the eCRM function into the business operation.

eCRM/CRM and its effectiveness within an e-business environment is dependent upon the clarification of the desire and need to fully align an integrated and organizational-wide customer system. E-businesses have the opportunity to receive from operational convergence of eCRM—with traditional business functional systems—and will not only achieve a leverage of internal efficiencies, but advantage in the marketplace by aligning customer-related systems together. However, successfully implementing customer services is not a haphazard mechanism for fashionable change, which could leave open the possibility that the change could be more detrimental to the e-business and its success.

These experiences by some dot.coms should be seen as caveats rather than a hindrance to successful customer relationship integration (Pinker et al., 2002). For example, with the online grocer marketplace, it isn't the dot.com e-business that is spearheading successful integration of Internet technologies, but solid businesses—traditional brick-and-mortar businesses like Tesco.com which are actually leading the way forward by integrating systems holistically.

In cases where e-businesses have neither anticipated customer needs and requirements nor integrated eCRM/CRM synergistically with the application backbone of the organization, efficiency losses reduce operational efficiency and more importantly customer retention. Twenty-first century business is not to

Figure 4. An eCRM workflow for online customers

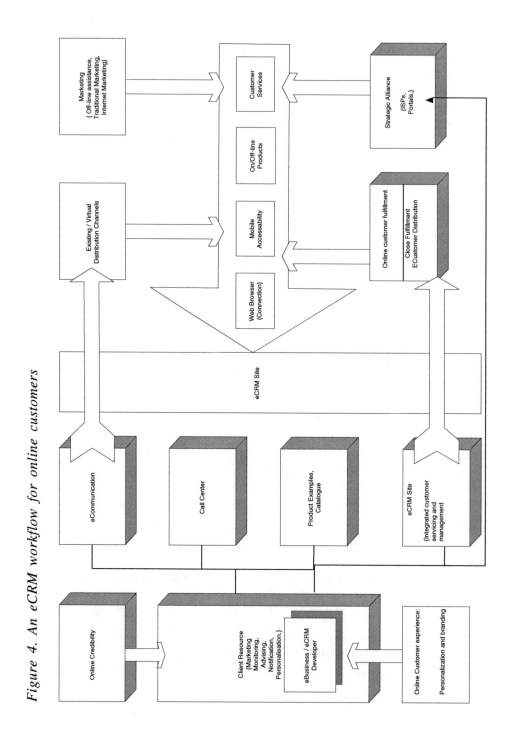

be paralleled with twentieth century ideologies and philosophies, given the complexities that are bound by carrying out restructuring of business today. E-businesses must be able to adapt and be more responsive, as well as to develop the ability to anticipate and act upon customer needs (Rowley, 2002).

The diffusion of functional boundaries provides opportunities for eCRM/CRM to be an integrated and fully aligned system that is coupled together with Web-based information systems (WBIS) and back-end processes (Jones & Kochtanek, 2002). The need e-businesses have to ensure suitability of eCRM is to adapt current systems and sub-systems, by coupling with eCRM/CRM as part of the backbone information system (BBIS) to business operations. An integrated eCRM/CRM system must capitalize on the capabilities provided by the e-business' sub-systems with organizational-wide functions (Mejabi, 1994).

Customer Process Reference (CPR) Model

E-businesses, in their pursuit of excellence and efficiency drives, need to adopt an approach that enables managers to qualify each stage of the implementation, as well as to assess the effectiveness of its eCRM/CRM system. The CPR model is developed on the basis that e-businesses need a way to measure the performance and state of an implementation, not only during the implementation, but afterwards as well. The model could be used as a way of evaluating the success of an eCRM/CRM implementation against a set of criteria that highlights the added value of the system.

The CPR model, as shown in Figure 5, is used as a tool associated with eCRM's state of play with the e-business. The customer process relates to the transition from one process to another and the value attached to each process of the end-to-end cycle, whereas the customer metric aspect of the process is qualified by a set of fixed benchmarks so that added value can be assessed or monitored against targets—whatever is attributed to the e-business needs of the eCRM system. The system integration aspect of the CPR model directly refers to the competencies attributed to system operations of eCRM in the e-business.

The CPR model illustrates the significance of aligning eCRM with related e-business systems, and ascertaining their 'state of play' and the challenges that are faced when dealing with an integrated eCRM system. Although an eCRM program can take up to 18-24 months to produce any real results, the two distinct

Figure 5. CPR model

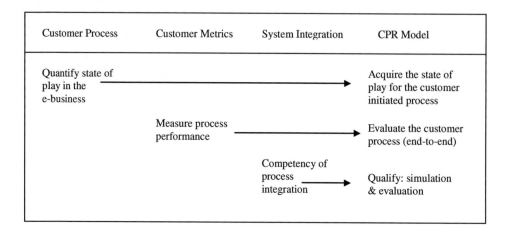

models (CROSIT and CPR) are developed to assist the evolution of a wholly integrated eCRM program to extend the rationale for a comprehensive cross-functional and process-integrated customer system.

As indicated in the model, the four distinct areas are customer processes, customer metrics, systems integration, and the final variable—the overall model behavior. At each stage of the implementation, the benchmark can be applied to measure overall effectiveness of the CRM system and whether or not it is meeting the objectives that had been set at the beginning of the rollout.

CPR and eCRM

Developing and implementing an efficient eCRM system does require a phased approach to fulfilling a comprehensive customer relationship management program that aligns itself with inter-organizational systems (IOSs). Formalizing and adopting a phased approach is less problematic than switching or adapting a complete specification using current norms and systems. Why? Given the need to re-assess front-end and back-end office technologies and applications, a business should look to re-scope its needs with internal business processes, systems, and functions, and external demands made by the online customer. However, the balance between integration and performance, and external demands for efficient, timely, and responsive customer management is one that continues to create much debate. In support of this debate, the CPR model extends the implementation and performance issues by defining a set of metrics ranging from a low-level posture (process) to a high-level posture—complete inter-organizational integration with cross-functional application, processes, and systems.

CROSIT and the E-Business Environment

The Customer Relationship Operational Systems Integrated Technology model, brings together the essential building blocks that are important to eCRM/CRM becoming not just a viable leverage, but a way of providing the balance needed in a business to improve the response times to customers as well as e-business' own internal demands that are made upon its systems. CROSIT's five interrelated building blocks provide a backbone enabling eCRM/CRM to become entwined with cross-functional processes.

Figure 6. E-business eCRM environment—CROSIT model

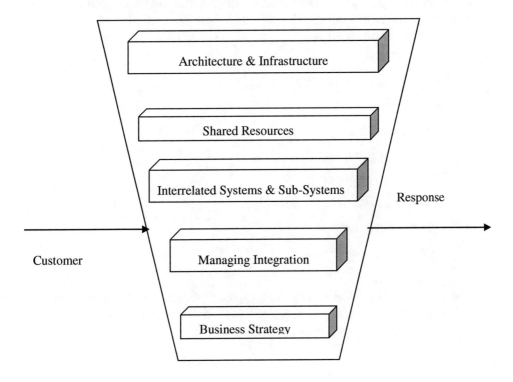

Architecture and Infrastructure

E-businesses in their endeavor to sustain their online operations; cross-functional demands on eCRM; service portfolio and competitiveness, need to encompass integrity, not to mention timeliness of each business system. There are two configured aspects that play a prominent role in the fusion of services, organic and physical components of an e-business—known as the e-business InfoNet (Evans, 2001).

An e-business' architecture and infrastructure rely almost entirely on organic and physical components of a business, and when these components are applied across the organization, they support the operations needed to perform not only eCRM/CRM, but a multitude of invaluable support systems too. Technical infrastructure such as intranets, extranets, and the World Wide Web (WWW) are requirements to supporting organic components such as ERP, ERM, MRP, SCM, and so forth.

Shared Resources

eCRM/CRM in an e-business environment is not about retaining data and monitoring customer behavior; it's also about business continuity and the dissemination of data across the spectrum of systems and functions that operate within the business environment, given that there are a number of sub-systems involved with eCRM, such as:

- Customer services and support (CSS)
- Customer billing
- Loyalty programs
- Sales force automation (SFA)
- Field sales and service
- Marketing and fulfillment campaigns
- Contact management
- Online management

These components of eCRM/CRM are not the complete spectrum of the system and its capabilities. Extending eCRM/CRM is in the interests of e-businesses in order to become more aware of the leverages that are available to develop competitiveness progressively in the marketplace. These cross-function systems include, but not exclusively:

- Manufacturing—demand to order
- Accounting—billing and account management
- Logistics—distribution

To what end will coupling eCRM/CRM with sub-systems within the organization be an advantage? In e-business today, more so than with the bricks-and-mortar era, the hybrid nature of business mixing electronic information and processes with traditional methods of work has found a place in the twenty-first century. This hybrid approach produces a need to decentralize resources so that Business Intelligence (BI) and Business Continuity (BC) are at the forefront of supporting the needs of both the business and its customer base.

Interrelated Systems and Sub-Systems

As illustrated in Figure 6, the interrelatedness of one system or sub-system with another is achievable through planning and transitioning. However, the question arises as to how this is to be carried out. There is little benefit to e-businesses in committing half-heartily to becoming an integrated business, if only half of the operations are interoperable. The purpose of businesses transitioning towards e-business is that all of the transactions, processes, systems, and sub-systems are interchangeable, interrelated, interoperable, and—more importantly—invested in.

Managing Integration and Business Strategy

Integration is a precarious entity, although when dealt with correctly, it will provide an abundance of positive returns. When e-businesses become fully aware of the intricacies of eCRM/CRM, for example, coupling sub-systems and channels together, then the customer experience will achieve the desired results. Furthermore, customer information provided by a Web presence must be fully integrated with 'other' databases of customer information, regardless of where the database is located.

To begin any form of integration or transitioning, a solid strategy needs to be in place that works alongside business strategy to accommodate the changes that are necessary to integrate eCRM into the business environment. The ability of the e-business to adapt and respond is just as important as is the ability the business has in formulating a strategy. It is proposed here that eCRM impacts upon business strategy to such an extent that a revision is needed to re-focus the attention toward customer-centricity.

However, this does not mean that business strategy alone can do this: There is significant attention required by the corporate strategy, marketing strategy, IS/IT strategy, and operations strategy to make eCRM a success (Papazoglou et al., 2000).

As highlighted by the AlliedSignal and DHL case studies, the need to share customer data and the need to integrate across an organization holistically is far too important to not appreciate. The CROSIT model's aim is to bring together the necessary components that will help managers to think carefully about what needs to be done rather than to see eCRM as a stand-alone application deployed only in one department. It is clear that to deploy eCRM/CRM without aligning an organizational-wide system will not invoke the performance and efficiency gains needed to sustain competitive advantage.

CROSIT and eCRM Component Technologies

Creating a seamless alignment and integrated eCRM system cannot occur without systems and applications being managed to support the online customer experience. Nowadays, customer relationship management tools and technologies have developed to an extent where they can be seen as ubiquitous and holistic, depending on the technologies and program to be implemented within a business. The broad range of technologies on the market encompasses: Sales Force Automation (SFA) tools, Customer Analytical tools, personalization technologies, customer behavior applications, and module extensions for specific business needs.

The layering and integration of components represent integral elements of CROSIT, as the model is designed in a way that enables a horizontal approach to complete system alignment and integration. Furthermore, the need businesses have to access data from different areas of business has raised the stakes between one function and another as regards sharing data, information, and knowledge about customers.

Sharing has become a key milestone in whether or not an e-business has evolved to a stage where there are no barriers, or formalized departmental structures and cross-functional applications, as with Enterprise Application Integration (EAI) and Enterprise Information Systems (EISs).

It is essential in today's business climate that customers and the needs of customers are taken on board when evaluating the best method of bringing together front-end and back-end technologies. There is no real advantage to an e-business developing, or purchasing, a front-end website that fails to integrate with back-end technologies and processes: no advantage and leverage is gained.

Conclusion

Arriving at an integrated and robust eCRM system cannot be seen purely as a trial-and-error approach to business performance, but a systematic endeavor to committing to re-defining the approach to integrating eCRM's systems in an e-business environment. For example, connecting the information flows from one eCRM sub-system to an e-business' functional sub-system will increase the effectiveness of customer relationships and eCRM program expansions.

Integrating a fully aligned eCRM system can have its drawbacks, as discussed, but there are also many positive aspects to integrating eCRM with organiza-tional-wide systems. Adapting new technologies to e-business needs will, in the long run, produce benefits for both the online customer and business by streamlining and improving performance of response times to online transactions and enquiries.

Competitiveness in today's economic climate requires e-businesses to embark on a journey into unknown territories. However, once e-businesses have acclimatized to the need to integrate and align disparate CRM systems within the organization, then the foundation will be laid down for future expansion and retention programs.

Finally, the application of CROSIT and CPR models is to be seen as a holistic approach to redefining the relationship between eCRM and its neighboring inter-organizational systems (IOSs) to enhance the customer experience.

Future Work

A case-based study is needed to assess the appropriateness of the CROSIT and CPR models with an e-business environment.

The aim of the study is to clarify and compare the needs of the customer relationship management system with the components of each model to evaluate where improvements to the metrics and IS/IT at each stage of the model can be refined, enabling businesses to integrate and align eCRM systems more effi-ciently and in a more timely way.

References

Alter, S. (2002). *Information systems: The foundation of e-business*. NJ: Pearson Education Ltd.

BizReport. (2002). High-tech customers prefer online service. Accessed August 16, 2003, from: http://www.nua.ie/surveys.

Chaffrey, D., Mayer, R., Johnston, K., & Ellis-Chadwich, initial. (2000). Internet marketing: Strategy, implementation and practice. *Financial Times*. Harlow, UK: Prentice-Hall.

CIO.com. (year). Available online at: http://www.cio.com/archive/040102/takeoff.html.

Cox, B. (2000). The law of averages: CRM on the Web. Accessed May 27, 2003, from: http://ecomerce.internet.com/news/insights/trends/print/010417_435911,00.html.

Curtin, T.E. (1996). IT alignment: New ideas for an old concept. IBM Advanced Business Institute, Paper 1 of 3, pp. 1-3. Accessed April 2003 from: http://www.ibm.com/ibm/palisades/assets/pdf/it_tc.pdf.

CyberAtlas. (2003). Population explosion. Accessed June 23, 2003, from: http://www.nua.ie/surveys.

Daniel, E., & Wilson, H. (2002). Adoption intentions and benefits realized: A study of e-commerce in UK SMEs. *Journal of Small Business Enterprise Development, 9*(4), 331-348.

DataMonitor. (2001). Personalization technology market. Accessed September 10, 2003, from: http://www.nua.ie/surveys.

Dibb, S., Simkin, L., Pride, W., & Ferrell, O. (2000). *Marketing. Concepts and strategies* (4th edition). Boston, MA: Houghton, Mifflin.

Dickie, R.J. (1988). *Customer relationship management. State-of-the-market review*. Boulder, CO: Insight Technology Group.

DTI. (2000). Business in the information age—international benchmarking study 2000. UK Department of Trade and Industry. Accessed March 2003 from: http://www.ukonlineforbusiness.gov.uk.

DTI. (2002). UK companies embrace e-business. Accessed December 3, 2002, from: http://www.nua.ie/surveys.

Earl, M.J. (1992). Putting IT in its place: A polemic of the nineties. *Journal of Information Technology,* 100-108.

Evans, C. (2001). An e-strategy for online e-business. *Information Systems Management Journal, 18*(4), 8-21.

Farhoomand, A., et al. (2000). *FedEx Corp: Structural transformation through e-business. Center for Asian Business Cases.* University of Hong Kong.

Feelders, A., Daniels, H., & Holsheimer, M. (2000). Methodological and practical aspects of data mining. *Information and Management, 37,* 271-281.

Gartner Group. (2001). Firms may underestimate CRM costs. Accessed September 11, 2003, from: http://www.nua.ie/surveys.

Goldenburg, B. (2003). Putting a lid on CRM implementation costs. Accessed September 11, 2003, from: http://www.eWeek.com.

Granger, M.J. (1994). Integrating the Internet into the business environment. *Industrial Management & Data Systems, 94*(8), 37-40.

Gronroo, C., & Powell, S. (2000). *Spotlight on Dr. Christopher Gronroos.* City: Emerald Now.

Grove, A. (1996). *Only the paranoid survive.* Doubleday.

Henderson, J., & Venkatraman, N. (1999). Strategic alignment: Leveraging IT for transformational organizations. *IBM Systems Journal, 38*(2/3), 472-484.

Hill, K. (2003). Sneaking up on CRM implementation. Accessed July 22, 2003, from: http://www.CRMGuru.com.

IBM. (year). Available online at: http://www.ibm.com/e-business.

IDC. (2001). Half of European firms use CRM. Accessed June 5, 2003, from: http://www.nua.ie/surveys.

Jaworksi, B., & Kohli, A. (1993). Market orientation: Antecedents and consequences. *Journal of Marketing,* (7), 53-70.

Jones, N., & Kochtanek, T. (2002). Consequences of Web-based technology usage. *Online Information Review, 26*(4), 256-264.

Jupiter Research. (2002). CRM spending growing in the U.S. Accessed February 27, 2003, from: http://www.nua.ie/surveys.

Kalakotam, R., & Robinson, M. (1999). *E-business roadmap to success.* New York: Addison-Wesley.

Karapetrovic, S. (2002). Strategies for the integration of management systems and standards. *The TQM Magazine, 14*(1), 61-67.

Kotler, P., & Stonich, P.J. (1991). Turbo marketing through time compression. *Journal of Business Strategy,* (910), 24-29.

Lee, D. (2003). Four steps to CRM success. Accessed September 21, 2003, from: http://www.CRMGuru.com.

Mejabi, O. (1994). An exploration of concepts and systems integration. *Integrated Manufacturing Systems, 5*(4/5), 5-12.

MetaGroup. (2001). Online firms increasingly using CRM. Accessed October 10, 2002, from: http://www.nua.ie/surveys.

Mougayer, M. (1998). E-commerce? E-business? Who cares? Accessed November 2, 2003, from: http://www.computerworld.com.

Nasi, J. (1999). Information systems and strategy design—the knowledge creation function in three modes of strategy-making. *Decision Support Systems, 26,* 137-149.

Nielsen NetRating. (2003) Global net population. Accessed February 23, 2003, from: http://www.nua.ie/surveys.

O'Malley, L., & Tynan, C. (2001). Reframing relationship marketing for consumer markets. *Interactive Marketing, 2*(3), 240-246.

Ostrof, F., & Smith, D. (1992). The horizontal organization. *The McKinsey Quarterly, 1,* 149-168.

Papazoglou, M.P., Ribbers, P., & Tsalgatidou, initial. (2000). Integrated value chains and their implications from a business and technology standpoint. *Decision Support Systems, 29,* 323.

Pastore, M. (2003). *Cyberatlas.com.* Accessed January 7, 2003, from: http://cyberatlas.internet.com/big_picture/hardware/print/0,,5921_502171, 00.html.

Peppers, D., & Rogers, M. (1993). *The one to one future.* New York: Doubleday.

Peppers, D., & Rogers, M. (1997). *Enterprise one to one.* New York: Doubleday.

Pinker, E.J. et al. (2002). Strategies for transitioning "old economy" firms to E-Business. *Communications of the ACM, 45*(5), 77-83.

Porter, M. (1989). How competitive forces shape strategy. In Ash, D., & Bowman, C. (Eds.), *Readings in strategic management* (pp. 133-143). Macmillian Press.

Porter, M.E. (1980). *Competitive strategy: Techniques for analyzing industries and competitors.* New York: The Free Press.

Porter, M.E. (1985). *Competitive advantage: Creating and sustaining superior performance.* New York: The Free Press.

Porter, M.E. (2001). Strategy and the Internet. *Harvard Business Review,* (3), 63-78.

Pushkala, R. (2002). Trends in customer relationship management. Accessed January 2003 from: http://www.CRMGuru.com.

Reicheld, F., & Schefter, P. (2000). E-loyalty, your secret weapon on the Web. *Harvard Business Review,* (7-8), 105-113.

Rigby, D.K. et al. (2002). Avoid the four perils of CRM. *Harvard Business Review,* (February).

Rowley, J. (2002). Synergy and strategy in e-business. *Marketing Intelligence and Planning, 20*(4), 215-22.

Steinfield, C. et al. (2002). Integrating bricks-and-mortar locations with e-commerce: Understanding synergy opportunities. *Proceedings of the Hawaii International Conference on System Sciences,* January 7-10.

Temkin, B. et al. (2003, April). *Choosing the right CRM consultant.* Forrester Research.

Turban, E., McLean, E., & Wetherbe, J. (2001). *Information technology for management, transforming business in the digital word* (3rd edition). New York: John Wiley & Sons.

Ward, J., Griffiths, P., & Whitmore, P. (1993). *Strategy planning for information systems.* Chichester, UK: John Wiley & Sons Ltd.

Weill, P., & Vitale, M.R. (2001). *Place to space: Migrating to e-business models* (pp. 5-6). Boston, MA: Harvard Business School Press.

Winer, R.S. (2001). A framework for CRM. *California Management Review, 43*(4), 89-105.

Wrenden, N. (2003). DHL increases profitability with customer planning. Accessed September 11, 2003, from: http://www.CRMGuru.com.

Chapter IV

The Effects of IT on Supply Chain Management in the Automobile Industry

Ki Chan Kim
The Catholic University of Korea, Korea

Il Im
New Jersey Institute of Technology, USA

Myung Soo Kang
Hansung University, Korea

Abstract

This chapter introduces the concept of electronic supply chain design (eSCD) and empirically examines the impacts of eSCD on supply chain management. eSCD is a supply chain design that integrates and coordinates suppliers, manufacturers, logistic channels, and customers using information technology (IT). In this chapter, a model that shows the effects of eSCD on the customization capability of companies was developed. From previous studies, the model identifies three major effects of eSCD—electronic linkage effect, supply chain coordination effect, and co-engineering effect. The model also shows a process through which an electronic supply chain network is transformed from a simple infrastructure for data exchange into a knowledge-sharing network for fast response and customization. The model was tested using the data collected from the automobile industry in Korea. It was shown that eSCD has significant effects on the supply chain coordination and co-engineering. It was also shown that eSCD affects the customization capability.

Introduction

The use of information technology in supply chains is becoming more important than in the past. One of the reasons is because business environments are moving from mass-production to customization. Supply chain combined with IT or Electronic Supply Chain (eSC) is a supply chain that integrates and coordinates suppliers, manufacturers, logistic channels, and customers using information technology (IT) (Briant, 2000; Kim & Im, 2002). The e-supply chain makes it easier and less costly to manage suppliers (Briant, 2000). IT can link all activities in a supply chain into an integrated and coordinated system that is fast, responsive, flexible, and able to produce a high volume of customized products at low cost.

eSCs are making a lot of impacts on the performance of supply chains in various industries (Fine, 1998). Moreover, eSCs are expected to bring more fundamental effects—from a simple network for information exchange to a network for knowledge creation and sharing (Kim & Im, 2002). However, not many studies have conceptualized various effects of eSC or empirically measured those effects. In this chapter, a new model is proposed to explain how an electronic network evolves from a network for simple data exchange into a space for knowledge creation and supply chain coordination. This model is empirically tested using the data collected from the companies in the Korean automobile industry.

Background

Electronic supply chain design (eSCD) is a process to build an electronic information network for transactions among supplier-manufacturer-retailer-customer in virtual space using IT (Kim & Im, 2002). eSCD has several aspects that are distinguished from traditional supply chain management and information systems for individual firms.

First, as Pine (1993) pointed out, customization cannot be achieved at an individual firm level. Every company in a large supply chain or distribution chain is dependent on each other. Thus, the unit of value creation has shifted from individual firms to value-networks that consist of partner firms and their close collaboration (El Sawy, Malhotra, & Gosain, 1999).

Second, supply chain design (SCD) focuses more on dynamic flow and interactions. SCD consists of choosing what work to outsource to suppliers (make vs. buy), selecting suppliers to use and negotiating contracts—both the legalities and the culture of the supply chain relationships. Fine (1998) noted that more emphases had been on the "static" material inventory management than on the "dynamic" flow within a supply chain. In the 1990s, many companies in competitive high-technology industries such as automobile, semiconductor, computer, and software failed even though they had high level of capabilities. On the other hand, some companies such as Dell Corporation accomplished competitive advantages based on a new supply chain design that enabled the partners in a supply chain to dynamically adapt themselves to changing technologies and markets. These successes and failures imply that the "dynamic capability"—the capability to rapidly integrate, design, and coordinate internal and external capabilities in response to the changes in technology and market environments—is becoming more critical in competition (Eisenhardt & Martin, 2000; Galunic & Eisenhardt, 2001; Teece, Pisano, & Shuen, 1997).

Third, for the optimization of a supply chain, it is critical to coordinate and integrate the whole supply chain in virtual space through information exchange, sharing, and integration. Gurbaxani and Whang (1991) posit that IT can facilitate the coordination necessary between business partners by nurturing cooperative relationships, which reduce market transaction costs. eSCD integrates physical supply chain with information systems, and optimizes the activities of participants to overcome physical and geographical constraints. It has become possible because IT enables information exchange and interaction simultaneously.

eSCD in the Automobile Industry

A car is a system product that on average consists of 20,000 parts. Thus, the automobile industry has a long and hierarchical supply chain. A hierarchical supply chain is one that has several levels of suppliers—the manufacturer outsources part modules (e.g., dashboard, seat, etc.) from primary suppliers who outsource the sub-parts from secondary suppliers, and so forth. In a hierarchical supply chain, information exchange takes a long time and causes frequent errors if it is done through fax or paper documents. Moreover, the hierarchical structure has the "bull-whip" effect—the fluctuation in inventory level is amplified along the supply chain (Fine, 1998; Lee, Padmanabhan, & Whang, 1997). As a result, the long and hierarchical supply chain in the automobile industry causes inefficiencies in various areas—design, development, procurement, manufacturing, and logistics—throughout the supply chain.

Thus, the automobile industry has a high potential for business-to-business (B2B) electronic business (e-business). In the U.S., the automobile industry was one of the first industries to adopt B2B electronic supply chain networks. We define electronic supply chain network (here called eSCN) as "a network structure that enables, using ITs, electronic transactions and information exchange between manufacturers and suppliers in a virtual space." Through B2B eSCNs, the participants of a supply chain can exchange and share information that is critical for the efficiencies of the supply chain.

B2B Network Infrastructure in the Automobile Industry

For a certain type of eSCNs, new e-business infrastructure is necessary because of the security and reliability problems of the Internet, and the compatibility and accessibility problem of proprietary networks. In the U.S., a new B2B e-business infrastructure, ANX (Automotive Network exchange), is being built for the electronic marketplace, for procurement and part supply. ANX is a TCP/IP-based e-business network infrastructure that has high security, reliability, and stability. Since January 1999, US ANX has initiated a Global ANX (GNX) project that would be a global standard network in the automobile industry.

Table 1. B2B electronic supply chain networks in automobile industry

Country	Name	Year Project Started	Service Start
U.S.	ANX (Automotive Network eXchange)	1994	November 1998 (about 500 suppliers)
EU (Germany, France, England, Spain)	ENX (European ANX)	1999	August 1999 in Germany
Japan	JNX (Japan ANX)	1998	November 2000
Korea	KNX (Korean ANX)	1999	2001

Similar regional networks are also emerging—for example, ENX in Europe, JNX in Japan, and KNX in Korea (KAMA, 2000).

B2B E-Business in the Automobile Industry

In 1999, General Motors and Ford built their e-marketplace separately on their own Internet-based procurement networks. GM, allied with Commerce One, developed TradeXchange, and Ford, partnered with Oracle, developed Auto-Xchange. However, their suppliers had problems because of the incompatibility between the two e-marketplaces. In February 2000, the Big Three—GM, Ford, and Chrysler—agreed to build a unified e-marketplace based on ANX. The result was Covisint, the biggest e-marketplace in the world. In Covisint, various types of services—auction, quoting, demand forecasting, production planning, automated transaction, financial services, payment, and logistics—are provided. The transaction volume by the Big Three is expected to be about $240 billion a year.

The Effects of IT in the Supply Chain

Gurbaxani and Whang (1991) argue that IT in an organization has multiple roles: a) it increases scale efficiencies of the firm's operations; b) it processes basic business transactions; c) it collects and provides information relevant to managerial decisions and even makes decisions; d) it monitors and records the performance of employees and function units; e) it maintains records of status of and changes in the fundamental business functions within the organization and maintains communication channels. Although these roles are in the context of organization, it is expected that IT will also affect supply chains in a similar fashion. From the work by Gurbaxani and Whang (1991), the effects of IT in eSCs can be conceptualized along three dimensions—linkage effect, brokerage effect, and integration effect as shown in Figure 1.

These effects are expected to change the capability and performance of a supply chain. In the figure, 'customization' is shown as the eSC performance because the focus of the empirical study at the end of this chapter is customization. However there are other important aspects of eSC performance such as speed and cost that are affected by IT.

The three effects of IT—linkage, brokerage, and integration effects—and also corresponding knowledge creation processes by Nonaka (1994)—externalization, combination, internalization/socialization—create competencies of supply chains.

Figure 1. A conceptual model for the impact of IT on supply chain performance

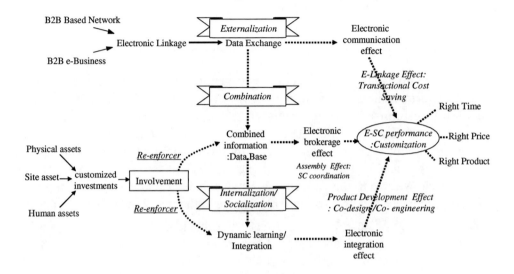

If those processes do not take place in a supply chain for some reason, a low level of involvement for example, the supply chain will not be able to create competencies. It may remain as a network just for data exchange. Once those processes are performed well, the supply chain will be able to create competencies through the three effects—electronic linkage effect, supply chain coordination effect, and co-engineering effect. Through these three effects, the competences created in the 'competence creation process' are realized.

In the following sections, the three effects of eSC are discussed further, and we explore how they are related to the framework for knowledge creation.

Linkage Effect of eSCD

The linkage effect of eSC is an instant gain due to the electronic transaction and electronic information sharing. Once a network for B2B transactions takes place, the efficiencies between manufacturers and suppliers increase instantly because they can exchange information and process transactions electronically. The cost savings by direct linkage such as EDI have been shown in past studies (Mukhopadhyay, Kekre, & Kalathur, 1995). Another short-term effect is the new competition among the suppliers. The network will enable the manufacturer to search for alternatives to current suppliers, which will intensify the competition among the suppliers. The competition will press down the procurement costs of the manufacturer in the short term.

Involvement of Suppliers

Customized investments of the suppliers transform the eSC from a network for simple information exchange into a network for customized product development. The customized investment means the customization in site, physical, and human assets (Dyer, 1996b). The customized investment is an indicator of involvement. Involvement refers to "the implicit or explicit pledge to continue the relationship between the transaction parties" (Heide & John, 1992). Dyer (1996a) showed that the customized investments of Japanese automobile suppliers increased their involvement because of the increased switching costs.

The importance of 'site asset specification' (physical location) has generally decreased due to the advancement of communication technologies. However, the physical location is still important for customized product design and production process engineering. Especially, when the product is a system product that requires continuous coordination in design phase, it is most efficient when engineers are collocated (Fine, 1998; Iansiti, 1993). An empirical study (Clark & Fujimoto, 1991) found that information distortion was decreased when the engineers from manufacturers and suppliers design the product together, increasing the quality of the product. As the customized investment and suppliers' involvement increases, the eSCs will evolve from a network for electronic data exchange into a network for information sharing and integration. The latter was referred to as "knowledge-sharing network" by Dyer and Nobeoka (2000). The knowledge-sharing network enables the coordination of the network at a whole supply chain level.

From a Network for Data Exchange to a Space for Knowledge Creation

eSCD will have more profound effects in the mid to long term. The more an eSCD is utilized, the more the participants invest and get involved in the supply chain, sharing more knowledge and coordinating more of their activities to optimize the whole supply chain. This will have more fundamental effects in those industries—such as the automobile industry—where 'tightly coupled' product development and manufacturing among the firms in the supply chain is critical for success.

Knowledge Creation Cycle in Supply Chains

The electronic linkage makes it possible to overcome time, space, and relationship limitations in a network through electronic communication and electronic information integration. Malone, Yates, and Benjamin (1987) suggest that there are three main effects of electronic market—electronic communication, brokerage, and integration. *Electronic communication effect* refers to the fact that IT allows faster and cheaper communication. *Electronic brokerage effect* means that electronic markets play, by connecting electronically many different potential suppliers quickly, the role of broker—reducing the need for buyers and suppliers to contact a large number of alternative partners individually. *Electronic integration effect* refers to tighter coupling of the processes of information creation and use. In other words, buyers and suppliers can create common information or common interpretation of data (Malone et al., 1987).

In another stream of research, Nonaka (1994) coined the concept of "knowledge creation cycle," which shows how information transfer in an organization evolves into information sharing/integration and ultimately into knowledge for coordinating value chain activities. They posit that there are two types of knowledge—knowledge that can be explained and documented (explicit knowledge) and knowledge that is difficult to explain or document (tacit knowledge). According to Nonaka's knowledge-creation cycle, people in an organization make their tacit knowledge explicit (*externalization*), combine tacit knowledge to create new knowledge (*combination*), learn and acquire knowledge (*internalization*), and sometimes they acquire tacit knowledge directly from the person who has it by hanging around with him/her (*socialization*) (Nonaka, 1994). Nonaka's framework implies that the knowledge in an organization can be effectively transferred and leveraged when those four types of knowledge-transfer processes are actively taking place.

- *Information exchange*—Malone et al.'s three main effects of electronic market have similarities with Nonaka's four processes of knowledge creation. Networking provides a mechanism for transferring information, knowledge, and technology (Hagedoom & Schakenraad, 1994). The electronic communication effect refers to easier information exchange due to IT. Easier information exchange will enable people in an eSCN to codify more information in order to communicate with others. For example, as companies utilize the Internet more and more, probably they will have to convert more and more information into electronic files or databases to share it with people outside their organizations. In this case, eSCN promotes codification and documentation of the information that has been considered as 'tacit' in the past. This process is similar to Nonaka's *'externalization.'*

- *Information brokerage*—The information transferred through eSCNs is stored in databases and becomes available to the participants of the supply chain. As more information is available, people in organizations will be able to combine and merge it to create more value. This is the "electronic brokerage effect" (Malone et al., 1987) and also Nonaka's *"combination"* process through which explicit knowledge is combined with other explicit knowledge (Nonaka, 1994).

- *Information integration*—In the network, the transferred/combined information is integrated through dynamic learning processes. This is the "electronic integration" and also Nonaka's *"internalization"* and *"socialization"* processes (Nonaka, 1994). Internalization refers to the process through which explicit knowledge is transmitted to others and they learn it to create their own tacit knowledge. Socialization is the process through which tacit knowledge is transmitted to others and becomes their own tacit knowledge. In the information integration process, some "data mining" is usually done on the collected data to find and create valuable information, which is a process of converting information into knowledge. As Malone et al. (1987) argued, buyers and suppliers work together in the 'integration' process to create common understandings or interpretations on the data.

The Effect of a "Knowledge-Sharing Network" on Supply Chain Coordination

Toyota has a system to increase its suppliers' involvement, share valuable knowledge, and prevent free riders in its supply chain (Dyer & Nobeoka, 2000). It was found that in the Toyota system, the suppliers were developing a "dynamic learning capability" that improved their competitive capabilities. This type of network—a network where manufacturers and suppliers are highly involved in the interactions and learning—is referred to as a "knowledge-sharing network." The effects of a knowledge-sharing network on the coordination of a supply chain and product customization are as follows.

- *Savings in procurement and transaction costs*—Technology, know-how, and human resources integrated through eSCNs increase efficiency (alignment effect). The alignment effect is the efficiency increase by aligning material specification, low-cost suppliers, and leveraged volume scale. The information integration effect also saves costs of information search, evaluation, transaction, and administration (Malone et al., 1987). Despite the required investment in specialized assets for B2B eSCNs (Williamson, 1985), savings in transaction cost can be obtained. Studies on the U.S. and Japanese automobile companies found that Japanese companies had lower transaction costs in spite of their higher relationship-specific investments (Dyer, 1997). The lower transaction costs of Japanese companies were because of the economies of scale and economies of scope due to the repeated transactions with a small number of suppliers, wide range of information exchange/sharing to reduce the information asymmetry, long-term performance orientation, and investments in the co-specialized assets. Therefore, if eSCNs lead to a similar transaction relationship, transaction cost savings will be possible.

- *Alleviation of the "bull-whip effect" and lower inventory*—The "bull-whip effect" occurs due to the time lag between demand and order, and the differences of the demand and order amount (Lee et al., 1997). The bull-whip effect is amplified as it goes upstream of the supply chain farther from the market (Fine, 1998). Electronic information integration can reduce the "bull-whip effect" because the participants can access demand information faster, and information distortion or delay is reduced.

- *The effect of R&D support and co-engineering*—As e-businesses in eSCNs evolve, co-engineering for modularization and customized product development advances, and the cost savings become larger. Specialized investment and involvement will push co-design and co-engineering further in the network. The co-engineering infrastructures enable the firms in the supply chain to provide customized products, without significant sacrifice of costs and efficiency, based on customers' characteristics, needs, and requests.

A Case—The Korean Automobile Industry

The conceptual model in Figure 1 is a comprehensive model for long-term research. To test the entire model, however, would take a huge dataset and a series of studies. In this chapter, we'd rather explore if the conceptual model in Figure 1 is correct in general and how much effect the three effects of IT in the figure have on eSC performance, 'customization' in particular. Thus, the model in Figure 1 was simplified for empirical test as shown in Figure 2.

Figure 2. A test model for the impact of IT on supply chain performance

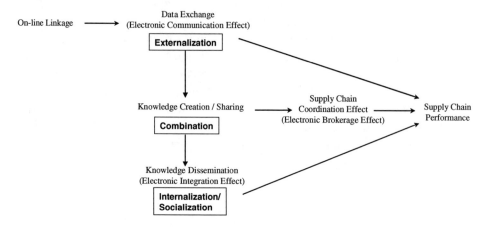

The model in Figure 2 was tested using data collected from suppliers in the automobile industry in Korea. A questionnaire was developed based on previous studies and in-depth interviews with 10 experts in the Korean automobile industry. The developed questionnaire was validated through a pilot test with 50 respondents.

Data Collection

The data were collected from major suppliers of five automobile companies in Korea. A total of 250 questionnaires were mailed out and some responses were collected through face-to-face interviews. The number of final responses was 177 (response rate = 70.8%). The researchers checked the collected questionnaires to filter out any invalid responses. A total of 150 responses were used in the final data analysis after discarding questionnaires containing invalid responses. The respondents' primary client companies are summarized in Table 2.

Table 2. Respondents' primary client automobile companies

Primary Client	Frequency	%
Hyundai	65	36.7
Kia	21	11.9
GM-Daewoo	55	31.0
SsangYong	15	8.5
Renault-Samsung	21	11.9
Total	**177**	**100**

Methodology

The operational variables for the constructs of the model in Figure 2 were developed based on the previous studies (Kim & Im, 2002) and after in-depth interviews with experts. A '1 to 7' Likert-type scale system was used for the operational variables. The reliability of the operational variables was tested by Cronbach's alpha (a) coefficients. The final operational variables of the constructs are shown in Table 3.

Although supply chain performance can be defined and measured in numerous ways, the main interest of this study is 'customization.' Although customization is not easy to measure, how much the parts are modularized and systemized is a good indicator of customization capability. Product 'modularization' refers to the extent to which suppliers assemble the products before they supply them. Product modularization is an important indicator of how much an automobile manufacturer is ready for customization. If the products of an automobile manufacturer are not modularized enough, customization will require a significant increase in cost and delivery time. If highly modularized, the automobile manufacturer can easily customize the final products by simply changing the assembled parts from its suppliers—e.g., a large engine instead of a small engine.

Table 3. Operational variables of the model

Constructs	Operational Variables	Cronbach's α
Electronic Communication Effect	Extent of information exchange on sales	0.814
	Extent of information exchange on inventory	
	Extent of information exchange on new product	
Electronic Information Sharing	Improved material flow using the shared information	0.906
	Improved coordination of activities in supply chain	
	Faster response to emergencies	
Electronic Integration Effect	Documentation of knowledge and experience during project	0.866
	Documentation of knowledge and experience after project	
	Sharing knowledge with other departments	
Electronic Brokerage Effect	Coordination of product spec/design	0.867
	Coordination of transaction conditions	
	Coordination of customer service	
Supply Chain Performance (Customization)	Modularization of product	0.878
	Systemization of product	

Product 'systemization' is similar to modularization, but it is about product design. Product systemization refers to the extent to which the suppliers independently design their products (parts). Higher systemization means that the suppliers design a larger module independently when a new car is developed. Systemization usually requires supplier empowerment and suppliers' high level of involvement in the earlier stages of new car development. High level of systemization means that the suppliers designed larger modules and tested different configurations within a module to make sure everything works fine. Like modularization, it is very likely that a higher level of systemization will lead to an easier customization. Therefore, supply chain performance was measured by modularization and systemization of product.

A structural equation modeling method was employed to test the model presented in Figure 2. The statistical package used for the analysis was AMOS 4.0 from SPSS Inc.

Analysis Results

After several rounds of model identification and fitting, the final model in Figure 3 was identified. In general, a structural equation model is considered adequate

Figure 3. Summary of test results

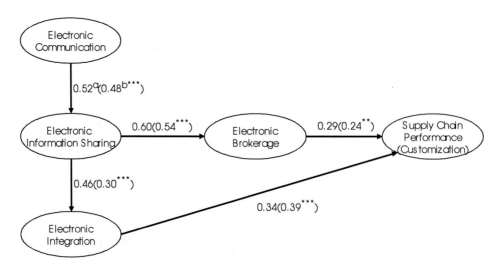

[a] Standardized parameter; [b] Unstandardized parameter; [*] $p < .05$, [**] $p < .01$, [***] $p < .001$
$\chi^2 = 89.805$ *(p=0.076, df=72), GFI = 0.903, AGFI=0.858, NFI=0.911, CFI = 0.981, RMSEA = 0.047*

if the p value for χ^2 is greater than 0.05, RMSEA is smaller than 0.05, and GFI, AGFI, NFI, and CFI are greater than 0.9. As shown in the figure, most indices, except for AGFI which is slightly below 0.9, are acceptable.

The results show that once the players in a supply chain are connected using IT, they use it for more electronic communication and that, in turn, it affects electronic information sharing. No direct effect from electronic communication and supply chain performance was found. Electronic information sharing increases electronic integration and supply chain coordination (electronic brokerage). Electronic brokerage and electronic integration together improve supply chain performance in customization.

Conclusions

This study provides a theoretical framework and empirical evidence of the impacts of IT on supply chain. From a theoretical point of view, this study integrated two theories from different research streams—impact of IT and knowledge creation—to explain how IT affect the performance of supply chains. Those theories imply that IT, if implemented and used properly, helps the partners in a supply chain share information and create knowledge. There are several necessary conditions such as involvement and shared database to make this happen. The integration of two theories provides a better theoretical foundation for understanding the impacts of IT in supply chain. For researchers, it would be interesting to further refine and test this integrated theory in supply chain and other contexts.

From practical point of view, this study showed that eSCD has significant effects on supply chain coordination and performance. This implies that eSCD can be an effective management tool to deliver customized products with the right timing and price. The result of this study has two main implications for future electronic supply chain research. First, the impact of IT on supply chain is more on knowledge sharing and supply chain coordination rather than on cost savings through electronic data exchange. This implies that the real impact of IT on supply chain performance is realized when the electronic supply chain network (eSCN) evolves from a network for data exchange into a knowledge-sharing space. When making decisions on IT for supply chain, managers will have to consider more indirect but fundamental effects such as knowledge sharing and coordination rather than direct cost savings. Second, electronic supply chain network affects supply chain performance in modularization and systemization capability. Although modularization and systemization are just two of the bases for customization in the automobile industry, it was shown that IT increases modularization and systemization capability of an automobile supply chain. It is therefore expected that IT will play a critical role in realizing customized automobiles, which would become common in the near future.

References

Briant, J. (2000). Making sense of the e-supply chain. *Machine Design, 17*(19), 62-66.

Clark, K.B., & Fujimoto, T. (1991). *Product development performance.* Boston, MA: Harvard Business School Press.

Dyer, J.H. (1996a). Does governance matter? Keiretsu alliances and asset specificity as source of Japanese competitive advantage. *Organization Science, 7*(6), 649-666.

Dyer, J.H. (1996b). Specialized supplier networks as a source of competitive advantage: Evidence from the auto industry. *Strategic Management Journal, 17*(4), 271-292.

Dyer, J.H. (1997). Effective interfirm collaboration: How firms minimize transaction costs and maximize transaction value. *Strategic Management Journal, 18*(7), 535-556.

Dyer, J.H., & Nobeoka, K. (2000). Creating and managing a high-performance knowledge sharing network: The Toyota case. *Strategic Management Journal, 21*, 345-367.

Eisenhardt, K.M., & Martin, J.A. (2000). Dynamic capabilities: What are they? *Strategic Management Journal, 21*(10/11), 1105.

El Sawy, O.A., Malhotra, A., & Gosain, S. (1999). IT-intensive value innovation in the electronic economy: Insights from Marshall Industries. *MIS Quarterly, 23*(3), 305-335.

Fine, C. (1998). *Clockspeed—winning industry control in the age of temporary advantage.* Perseus Books.

Galunic, D.C., & Eisenhardt, K.M. (2001). Architectural innovation and modular corporate forms. *Academy of Management Journal, 44*(6), 1229-1249.

Gurbaxani, V., & Whang, S. (1991). The impact of information systems on organizations and markets. *Communications of the ACM, 34*(1), 61-73.

Hagedoom, J., & Schakenraad, J. (1994). The effect of strategic technology alliances on company performance. *Strategic Management Journal, 15*, 291-309.

Heide, J.B., & John, G. (1992). Do norms matter in marketing relationship? *Journal of Marketing, 56*(2), 32-44.

Iansiti, M. (1993). Real-world R&D: Jumping the product generation gap. *Harvard Business Review, 75*(3), 138-147.

KAMA. (2000). *Implementation of CALS.* Seoul: KAMA (Korea Automobile Manufacturers' Association).

Kim, K.-C., & Im, I. (2002). The effects of electronic supply chain design (eSCD) on coordination and knowledge sharing: An empirical investigation. Paper presented at the *Hawaii International Conference on System Sciences,* Big Island, Hawaii, January.

Lee, H.L., Padmanabhan, V., & Whang, S. (1997). The bullwhip effect in supply chains. *Sloan Management Review, 38*(3), 93-102.

Malone, T.W., Yates, J., & Benjamin, R.I. (1987). Electronic markets and electronic hierarchies. *Communications of the ACM, 30*(6), 484-497.

Mukhopadhyay, T., Kekre, S., & Kalathur, S. (1995). Business value of information technology: A study of Electronic Data Interchange. *MIS Quarterly, 19*(2), 137-156.

Nonaka, I. (1994). A dynamic theory of organizational knowledge creation. *Organization Science, 5*, 14-37.

Pine, B.J.I. (1993). *Mass customization: The new frontier in business competition.* Boston, MA: Harvard Business School Press.

Teece, D.J., Pisano, G., & Shuen, A. (1997). Dynamic capabilities and strategic management. *Strategic Management Journal, 18*(7), 509.

Williamson, O.E. (1985). *The economic institute of capitalism.* New York: The Free Press.

Chapter V

The Potential of B2B Commerce for Competitive Advantage

Ronan McIvor
University of Ulster, N. Ireland

Paul Humphreys
University of Ulster, N. Ireland

Abstract

This chapter examines the implications of business-to-business (B2B) commerce for the buyer-supplier interface. Innovations in electronic commerce have a key role to play in managing inter-organizational networks of supply chain members. The evidence presented in this chapter illustrates that the Internet represents a powerful technology for commerce and communication at the buyer-supplier interface. Internet technologies are having a considerable impact on the communication patterns at the buyer-supplier interface. It is shown how electronic commerce technologies. have the potential to create competitive advantage through radically changing the structure and interaction patterns at the buyer-supplier interface. The chapter identifies a number of areas where electronic commerce technologies can make a contribution to the creation of competitive advantage. While the Internet offers ways for organizations to communicate and trade more effectively with their suppliers, and gives consumers higher levels of service and sophistication, it also poses major challenges to those within organizations who have to manage it. It is argued that closed network problems and the nature of buyer-supplier relations present major impediments to electronic commerce achieving its full strategic potential at the buyer-supplier interface.

Introduction

The objective of this chapter is to examine the strategic implications of business-to-business (B2B) commerce for the buyer-supplier interface. In the past few decades, ICTs have deeply affected the way business is performed and the way that organizations compete (Porter, 2001). In the business-to-business environment, inter-organizational information systems (IOSs) have been used since the 1970s to link one or more organizations to their customers or suppliers through private value added networks such as Electronic Data Interchange (EDI) (Archer & Yuan, 2000). Significant interest has grown in the potential use of the Internet at the buyer-supplier interface due to the potential benefits associated with the open systems protocol. By bringing together large numbers of buyers and suppliers and automating transactions, Internet-enabled markets expand the choices available to buyers, give suppliers access to new customers, and reduce transaction costs for all participants (Kaplan & Sawhney, 2000). Goldman Sachs estimates that online purchasing could save firms anything from 2% in the coal industry to perhaps 40% in electronic components. As a result of such cost savings, Goldman Sachs estimates, B2B commerce could increase the level of output in the developed economies by an average of 5% over time. More than half of that increase would come through within 10 years, an increase of 0.25% a year in the rate of growth over the next decade. Therefore, the importance of B2B commerce is increasing dramatically, either as private networks connecting cooperating organizations, or as networks linked through the Internet (Segev, Porra, & Roldan, 1997).

Innovations in electronic commerce have a key role to play in managing inter-organizational networks of supply chain members. The evolution of electronic commerce technologies is having a considerable impact on the communication patterns in supplier networks in many industries. Electronic commerce can reduce the costs of closely integrating buyers and suppliers, and through electronic networks firms can achieve an integration effect by tightly coupling processes at the interface between stages of the value chain (Benjamin, Malone, & Yates, 1986). Business-to-business e-commerce can reduce an organization's costs in a number of ways. It reduces procurement costs, both by making it easier to find the lowest priced supplier and through efficiency gains. It is much less costly to place an order online, and there are likely to be fewer errors in orders and invoicing. Cisco Systems reports that a quarter of its orders used to have to be reworked because of errors in telephone and fax ordering systems. When it switched to online ordering, the error rate fell to 2%, saving the company $500 million. Research carried out by Aberdeen (1999) has shown that B2B e-commerce can lead to average 5-10% price reductions for products and services through lower material and service costs, reductions in acquisition and order fulfillment cycle times of 50-70%, reductions in requisition processing costs of 70% per order, and improved inventory management practices. Much of the early literature on management information systems has examined the link between information technology and competitive advantage (Weill, 1992; Porter & Millar, 1985; McFarlan, 1984). This article focuses on how Internet technologies represent a powerful force in the evolution of the development of inter-organizational communication and trading. It is shown how electronic commerce technologies radically change the interaction patterns at the buyer-supplier interface by identifying a number of areas where Internet technologies can act as a source of competitive advantage. The effectiveness of electronic commerce implementations at the buyer-supplier interface is assessed. It is argued that closed network problems and the nature of buyer-supplier relations present major impediments to companies achieving the full potential of Internet technologies at the buyer-supplier interface.

The Evolution of B2B Commerce

Electronic business-to-business commerce has progressed through a number of phases of development based upon a series of changes in technology: Electronic Data Interchange, area networks (Value Added Networks), and the Internet (Croom, 2000). In the 1960s and 1970s, mainframe solutions focused initially on internal automation and proprietary EDI links with suppliers. EDI has been primarily used in the subcontracting area and has been proven most effective in supporting operational-level applications, mainly due to its limited technical capabilities and the existence of multiple technical standards (Li & Williams, 2000). In order to support more complex and strategically more important applications and processes, some organizations have maintained dedicated data links between their computer systems by themselves, using various interfaces and communication protocols capable of handling more sophisticated forms of information exchange (Borman & Williams, 1996). While considerable benefits were achieved by those companies that implemented EDI effectively, it tended to be only large companies and their suppliers that applied EDI due to the significant costs associated with implementation. EDI requires significant investments in systems and organizational infrastructure, as well as a large volume of transactions to justify the level of investment. In the 1980s to the mid-1990s, client-server solutions broadened the scope of participants in the supply chain by focusing on applications, such as supply chain management, enterprise resource planning (ERP), and customer relationship management (CRM). These approaches were often very expensive to purchase, difficult to implement, complex to use, and costly to maintain (Perry, 2000). Also, these approaches only improved the company's internal processes while not addressing the needs of the entire supply chain.

In the categories already discussed, all parties involved are predetermined and have agreed to trade or exchange other information electronically. However, in the mid-1990s the advent of the Internet has led to an explosion in connectivity that allows companies of different sizes and resource bases to interact. The Internet is a public network that is connected and routed over gateways. The Internet evolved from a software convention for computer networking developed by the U.S. Army's Advanced Research Projects Agency—termed the Transmission Control/Internet Protocol (TCP/IP). This open standard was adopted by a wide range of research, education, and public sector organizations. In the late '80s, a point-and-click hypertext interface was developed for the Internet which was called the World Wide Web. This development led to the explosion in interest in Internet usage, with organizations and individuals being able to easily access and use the Internet. The Internet has led to the redefinition of economies of scale and scope, and the reduction of transaction costs leading to the emergence of virtual markets (Rayport & Sviokla, 1995). Virtual markets refer to business transactions that are conduced over open networks based on fixed and wireless Internet infrastructure. These markets are characterized by high levels of connectivity (Dutta & Segev, 1999), the importance of information products and networks (Shapiro & Varian, 1999), and high reach and richness of information (Evans & Wurster, 1999). Reach refers to the number of products and services that are reachable in virtual markets, while richness refers to the depth and detail of information that can be collected, exchanged, and analyzed by the market participants. In fact, information itself becomes a source of competitive advantage in virtual markets (Weiber & Kollmann, 1998).

The connectivity associated with the Internet has the potential to bring an industry's customers and suppliers in a unified and economically perfect marketplace. For example, an organization offering a range of products and services can now create an electronic catalog on its website in order to achieve global reach. With the advent of Internet-enabled communications, it is now possible for an organization to establish links with other organizations at significantly lower costs than with previous technologies. The emergence of virtual markets clearly provides ways for organizations to create value for customers (Amit & Zott, 2001). Zahra (1999) argues that an organization's routines and processes are unique capabilities that allow organizations to make strategic changes that give them the flexibility to operate in dynamic markets. For example, a significant development from innovations in Internet technologies has been the growth of electronic intermediaries. It is now possible to offer an intermediary service, developed around a sophisticated IT platform. The intermediary has a Web front-end, allowing buyers to order from supplier catalogs, participate in auctions, or conduct tendering online (John, 2000). This is significantly different from EDI, which tended to be based on a 'hub and spoke' arrangement—with one large company acting as a hub and suppliers trading electronically. In contrast, an electronic intermediary can act as a single gateway to a range of products or services that are provided by a number of suppliers. It is designed to allow a number of suppliers to interact with a number of buyers through one connection.

Models of B2B Commerce

Although the exploitation of Internet technologies at the business-to-business level is in its infancy, a number of models have begun to emerge that manage transactions between buyers and suppliers:

1. Established Buyer-Supplier Relationship

This is a pre-determined one-to-one relationship between a buyer and supplier that is supported by electronic commerce technologies. Due to the aforementioned limitations associated with EDI, companies have now turned their attention towards the Internet to support these types of buyer-supplier relationships. Companies are now pursuing a more intensive and interactive relationship with their suppliers, impacting upon the buyer-supplier relationship in a number of areas, including the integration of manufacturing systems and supplier involvement in new product development. Exchanging information via extranets costs less and is more effective than through older traditional methods such as faxes and voicemail. For example, NEC has developed an advanced information system to carry out a large part of its procurement activities, ranging from procurement notices to settlement on the Internet (Nakamoto, 1997).

2. Supplier-Oriented Marketplace

In this model, both organizations and consumers use the supplier-provided marketplace. This is the most common type of B2B model. In this model, both business buyers and individual consumers use the same supplier-provided marketplace. An example of this model is RS Components (*rswww.com*). RS Components is a leading distributor of electronic, electrical, and mechanical components, instruments, and tools in Europe. The marketplace provides fast search and retrieval of 100,000 products, combined with personalized customer promotions based on the buying profiles of its major customers. A supplier-oriented marketplace may also provide an auctioning facility to offload surplus inventory or offer discounts to customers.

3. Buyer-Oriented Marketplace

Under this model, a buyer opens an electronic market on its own server and invites potential suppliers to bid on the announced Requests for Quotation (RFQs) (Turban, Lee, King, & Chung, 2000). One company that has successfully exploited this model is GE Lighting. The purchasing department receives electronic requisitions from internal customers that are then sent to potential suppliers over the Internet. Within two hours of the purchasing department starting the process, suppliers are notified of incoming RFQs and are given seven days to prepare bids and send them back over the extranet to GE. With the transaction handled electronically, the procurement function has been able to concentrate on more strategic activities rather than clerical and administration tasks.

4. Business-to-Business Intermediary

This model is sometimes referred to as a 'hub' or 'exchange'. It is established by an electronic intermediary that runs a marketplace where suppliers and buyers have a central point to come together. These B2B hubs tend to focus mainly on non-core items that may range from stationery and computers to catering services and travel. There are two types of hubs:

- *Vertical*—focus on an industry and provide content that is specific to the industry's value system of buyers and suppliers (Afuah & Tucci, 2001). Examples include e-Steel that acts as an intermediary between steelmakers and customers, and VerticalNet that provides intermediaries for many industries including electronics, process, telecommunications, and utilities.

- *Horizontal*—provide the same function for a variety of industries. An example is iMark.com, which acts as an intermediary between buyers and suppliers of used capital equipment in different industries.

An intermediary may be closed—where members and trading partners are vetted for legal and financial probity—or open to all-comers, with the marketplace itself acting as a trusted intermediary. It is important to note that intermediaries may be biased towards either buyers or suppliers. Supply-side intermediaries may be run by consortia of manufacturers such as Chemdex that acts as an intermediary for suppliers to the life sciences industry. Similarly, buy-side intermediaries may be run by a consortia of customers such as Covisint for car makers or by independent organizations such as Achilles for utilities (Bray, 2000). These intermediaries may attempt to aggregate demand for buyers in order to obtain reduced prices and more favorable terms from suppliers. In relation to payment, some intermediaries may charge a flat fee per transaction to both the buyer and suppliers. Alternatively, a percentage may be charged in

Figure 1. Customer-supplier life cycle (C-SLC): Following the e-touchpoints (Hackbarth & Kettinger, 2000)

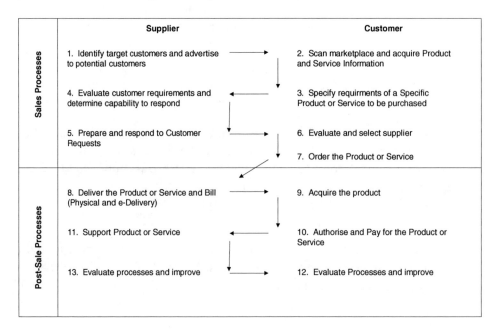

the case of value-added services such as auctions. In the case of large, repetitive transactions, to achieve maximum benefit the intermediary should be linked seamlessly to the buyer's purchasing and the suppliers' systems so that the entire purchasing process can be executed electronically.

In the context of competitive advantage and the influence of the Internet, Hackbarth and Kettinger's (2000) customer/supplier lifecycle is a useful framework for understanding an organization's business processes, as well as those of their customers, suppliers, and competitors. This framework provides a way of distinguishing between buying and selling activities to better understand the interrelationships between customers and suppliers' business processes, and what they term 'TouchPoints' in the company. This is shown in Figure 1. The buying-supplying process impacts three major areas, including the nature of the products being bought and sold; the type of value being exchanged between buyers, suppliers, and other members of the value chain; and the definition of a buyer or a supplier. Hackbarth and Kettinger (2000) argue that a successful electronic business strategy will alter the nature of the product or service being offered, its value in the marketplace, or the buyer-supplier relationship.

The Strategic Implications of B2B Commerce Streamlining the Order Management Process

A key requirement for the effective implementation of an effective delivery management system is a high frequency of information sharing between the supply chain partners (Yasin, Small, & Wafa, 1997). This is a crucial area in which Internet technologies are having a major impact. Timely and accurate information sharing is crucial in this process. The information sharing strategies of the trading partners is related to supplier performance (Walton & Marucheck, 1997). Effective use of electronic commerce has the potential to improve the materials management process of both the buyer and supplier in areas such as inventory reduction, delivery lot size reduction, and purchase order and invoice reduction. A key success factor in ensuring collaborative relations between trading partners is accurate customer demand forecasting. This is an area where electronic commerce technologies are having a major impact. One industry where supplier reliability and effective forecasting is crucial is the supermarket industry, due to the perishable nature of most of the items on sale. For example, over-supply means the supermarket is reducing cashflow, while under-supply means gaps on the shelves and poor customer service. Traditionally, the supermarkets operated EDI with their larger suppliers, while traditional paper-based approaches have been used to manage smaller suppliers. However, large supermarket chains are now linking with smaller suppliers via the Web, taking advantage of the open standards technology of the Internet (Hewson, 1999). For example, Tesco has enabled remote suppliers to access everything from manuals on how to deliver goods to particular stores to a directory of Tesco staff and locations, news, and service levels. Such 'links' allow suppliers to see how stocks stand within the different stores through exactly the same database as Tesco staff use. Such innovations impact the performance of both the customer and the supplier. For example, when Sainsbury set up an extranet link with Nestlé, availability on the shelves rose by 2% to 97%, while overstocking fell by a quarter (Hewson, 2000). Chrysler has also used information technology to improve relationships with its suppliers by using a computerized online system that transfers delivery and quality to suppliers in real time (Anonymous, 1995). The implications of this evidence is that electronic commerce not only benefits the customer, but there can be benefits to the supply chain as well. Such a situation creates a higher level of dependency in the relationship, with both partners being more willing to make shared investments in information technology in order to reduce costs.

The implementation of electronic commerce not only occurs at the buyer-supplier interface, but can also enable the trading partners to build a closer relationship with the end-consumer. For example, in the retail industry information technologies are enabling retailers to identify trends and target individual consumers. Using relational databases and data mining techniques, retailers are able to identify customer requirements and shopping habits (Taylor, 1997). One company that has successfully employed this technology is Wal-Mart. Wal-Mart stores data on point of sale, inventory, products in transit, market statistics, customer demographics finance, product returns, and supplier performance (Turban et al., 2000). The data is used for three broad areas of decision support: analyzing trends, managing inventory, and understanding customers. In particular, Wal-Mart has been able to build up 'personality traits' of each customer by analyzing relationships and patterns in customer purchases. Such innovations provide greater forward demand visibility throughout the supply chain by knowing which consumer buys which products where and at what time of the day. Milgrom and Roberts (1992) argue that information technology can enhance the customer's information management capabilities and transaction processing efficiency, which in turn can be used to foster closer relations with suppliers.

Building a More Intensive and Interactive Buyer-Supplier Relationship

Electronic linkages in the supply chain have been fundamentally changing the nature of inter-organizational relationships (Roberts & Mackay, 1998). Electronic commerce technologies have supported more collaborative relationships by changing the multi-functional interactions between customers and their suppliers. For example, Grover and Malhotra (1997) have argued that innovations in Internet technologies such as 'intranets' and 'extranets' are critical in integrating and coordinating cross-functional teams across organizational boundaries. The trend towards more collaborative relations has led organizations to reduce the number of suppliers, while at the same time fundamentally changing the way in which they do business with their remaining suppliers (McIvor, Humphreys, & McAleer, 1997). One of the most prominent indicators for a move towards partnerships is the rationalization and consolidation of the supplier base (Matthyssens & Van den Builte, 1994). Organizations cannot develop successful collaborative relationships with a large supply base. The underlying reason is that reducing the number of suppliers is a prerequisite for improved and deepened supplier relationships. Reducing the immediate supply chain has led to a changing of the structure of the chain and the number of tiers in it. In a manufacturing context, OEMs are buying assembled systems or complete sub-assemblies rather than individual components, thus introducing another level into the supply chain. Since the introduction of these policies, subcontractors are now commonly referred to as belonging to a particular level or tier of the supply chain. The first-tier supplier will supply the assembled system and is likely to be responsible for investment in product design and process development. The first-tier supplier will then be responsible for coordinating the required supply of inputs from the second-tier suppliers. First-tier suppliers take on the main burden of coordinating the activities of second-tier suppliers.

Information technology has played a key role in managing such an inter-organizational network of supply chain members. Electronic commerce can reduce the costs of closely integrating buyers and suppliers, and through electronic networks, firms can achieve greater integration at the buyer-supplier interface. The evolution of electronic commerce technologies is having a considerable impact on the communication patterns between the supply chain members. Traditional electronic commerce such as EDI transactions have been conducted over proprietary value-added networks (VANs) between the OEMs and tier one suppliers. However, Internet-based electronic communication is facilitating increased information sharing between members at lower levels in the inter-organizational network. For example, in an analysis of the buyer-supplier relations in the European automobile component industry, Hyun (1994) found increasing communication exchange between the various parties involved like the OEMs, the sub-assemblers, and the sub-suppliers. The information flows are multi-directional within this supplier network. The degree of communication linkage between the three parties could vary depending upon the nature of collaboration.

A crucial area of collaboration between the customer and supplier supported by Internet technologies is integrated product development. This involves using multi-functional teams from both the customer and supplier organizations. It is important to have all the customer representatives—such as research and development, engineering, purchasing, production, and logistics—involved in the process. Caterpillar has adopted such an approach with its key suppliers in the design process. Caterpillar has adopted an 'open' standards approach with its suppliers which enables partners to access spreadsheets, charts, documents, scheduling charts, databases, and computer-generated drawings electronically (Houlder, 1997). Such an approach is vital for Caterpillar, with large and small suppliers having instant access to mutually shared information. This reduces time-to-market and creates a lot of value that can be shared between the buyer and supplier.

Enhancing the Role of Intermediaries

Many of the intermediaries that have been established have attempted to create commodity-like markets for everything from chemicals to steel. A lot of these operations have been start-up companies that have been expected to replace traditional distributors by brokering transactions electronically between buyers and suppliers without being involved in fulfillment. These companies are established on IT platforms providing standard services, such as online auctions, typically earning a commission on the transaction volume generated. However, it must be stressed that most items within a company's purchasing portfolio cannot be purchased through auctions. Typically, 80% of a company's purchasing portfolio are traded through negotiated contracts that may last for more than a year. Therefore, these types of items are inappropriate to 'spot' sourcing. By focusing on these types of items, many of these intermediaries have not achieved the necessary liquidity to survive. In effect, these B2B operations have been attempting to replicate eBay's business-to-consumer business model in a business-to-business environment. Therefore, this model has struggled due to a proliferation of new entrants into the marketplace that has led to the squeezing of margins. For example, AMR Research in the U.S. found that not a single one of the 600 B2B intermediaries studies had reached even 1% of overall trading volume in the industry (Anonymous, 2000).

It is clear that these intermediaries will have to provide more sophisticated services to potential users rather than purely transaction and auction facilities. For example, Freemarkets has developed to provide far more than an auctioning service. It now assists customers in the collection and analysis of information required in purchasing more complex products and services online. It creates value for the customer through identifying and qualifying bidders, and creating detailed, standardized requests for proposals that enable the bidders to provide comparable quotes even on highly specialized products. Due to the ease with which start-up companies can replicate the auctioning process, it has now become a commodity service. Wise and Morrison (2000) argue that as Freemarkets handles more transactions, its product descriptions will become more refined and standardized, reducing the investment it has to make in subsequent auctions and expanding the range of auctionable items. In this way, these intermediaries will take on some of the roles traditionally undertaken by the purchasing function in the customer organization. For example, they will provide the online capability to identify product features that best meet a particular buyer's needs. Another feature emerging on these intermediaries is online communities that allow members to participate in discussions on common issues. Intermediaries are using communities to add value to the services on offer. For example, Medoxline was set up to allow buyers and suppliers to interact and carry out transactions in the healthcare sector. A key feature of this site is an online community that replicates the sharing of ideas and the discussion of problems normally carried out at conferences (Prigg, 2000).

The greater liquidity and transparency that flow from e-marketplaces have enabled more efficient pricing and more effective matching of customers and suppliers, and most important, value has shifted from the product itself to information about the product. Therefore, value resides in the information management rather than the processing of transactions. While the transfer of physical products will remain the end result of a business transaction, the information that shapes the transaction—price, availability, quality, quantity—can now be separated and exchanged electronically. This distinction between the Internet and the physical purchasing process is a significant factor. For example, a trading firm in Hong Kong, which deals directly with retailers in the U.S., has created an intermediary to link retailers with suppliers as a means of achieving competitive advantage (Humphreys, Lai, & Sculli, 2001). The intermediary, known as Factory Network, supplies retailers in the U.S. with simple commodity-type products, such as toys, clocks, and Chinese porcelain. A network of approximately 50 small to medium-sized companies in Southern China provide these products. The intermediary facilitates the creation, storage, transformation, and transmission of information across the organizational boundaries, between the parties involved in the relationship. It allows the retailers to shop for products and to place order requests, and at the same time to check on the status of orders. The system also provides information on product suggestions, delivery, and pricing options, and promotes special items. The intermediary transfers the order requests to the relevant enterprises based on an analysis of current production schedules and available capacity, in order to meet the customer lead-time requests. This intermediary enables retailers to gain access to detailed information on potential supply sources. Under the traditional purchasing process, this type of information would have been very difficult to obtain. In effect, access to this information can be as valuable to the retailers as the physical product.

Empowering the Participants at the Buyer-Supplier Interface

The application of electronic commerce technologies is blurring the traditional boundaries in the value chain between suppliers, manufacturers, retailers, and end-customers. A key capability of electronic commerce is the automation of routine and clerical tasks at both the buyer and supplier interfaces. Electronic commerce technologies are eliminating activities traditionally carried out by the relevant participants in both the customer and supplier. Electronic commerce technologies can provide facilities such as Web-based interfaces, integration with supplier catalogs and internal information systems, and built-in business transaction rules based on purchase limits or negotiated contracts. These facilities allow end-users to order products and services online without intervention by the purchasing department, including automatic fulfillment by the supplier and payment via electronic funds transfer or purchasing cards. Also, in relation to intermediaries the customer is outsourcing procurement activities traditionally carried out internally. These developments provide both a challenge and an opportunity to the relevant participants. With electronic commerce technologies automating the transaction type activities, the participants at both the buyer and supplier interface are now able to focus on 'value adding activities', as illustrated in the following areas:

- On the customer side, the role of the purchasing professional is moving from being involved in clerical type activities, such as invoice processing and expediting, to include activities such as integrating suppliers into their new product development processes and joint involvement in total cost analysis. For example, McIvor, Humphreys, and Huang (2000) have found that the successful implementation of IT at the buyer-supplier interface can reduce costs and allow purchasing personnel to have greater time and ability to engage in more sophisticated vendor evaluation programs and value analyses, build closer relationships with key suppliers, and rationalize their supply bases. In this way, it is possible for the purchasing function to make the transition from being a transaction-oriented operation to one that has a strategic focus.

- On the supply side, with the customer service function having limited involvement in handling routine order queries, they are able to focus more of their time on activities such as managing and building the relationship with their key customers. For example, the use of electronic commerce has enabled Nortel, a strategic supplier of BT, to devote more time to improvements in the product launch process, and in dealing with queries to enable faster provision and product installation. This provides Nortel with the opportunity to add value as part of collaboration by increasing end customer service and product utilization (Roberts & Mackay, 1998).

Such changes have considerable behavioral implications. For example, with the participants at both the buyer and supplier interface performing a more value-adding role, there are training and development implications. Related to this is the fact that the participants are being empowered to make more informed decisions through greater access to information.

Barriers to Achieving the Potential of B2B Commerce

However, there are considerable barriers to B2B commerce achieving its full strategic potential as outlined below.

Seamless Integration?

Much of the evidence presented has shown how companies can exploit the open standards technology of the Internet to link up with suppliers that they have traditionally traded with manually or to access new suppliers. The Internet has made a communication medium similar to EDI available universally, so that adding or deleting trading partners is a much more straightforward process (Tyler, 1999). With better linkages, transaction costs will be reduced, and the relationship between the buyer and supplier will be more efficient and effective. Tapscott, Ticoll, and Lowy (2000) argue that "pervasive, elegant, and cheap Internet technologies enable true end-to-end integration, fusing enterprises with one another and bringing the customer inside the value chain." However, there is still the significant problem of incompatibility of the systems of the trading partners. There is evidence to suggest that closed network problems can also affect the Internet with business-to-business electronic commerce running up against application interfaces that inhibit the operation of a fully transparent environment between trading partners. For example, with an e-procurement system, it is important to ensure consistency of purchase, and that the purchasing professional has control of the system with the necessary authorization procedures established. The system should have to be integrated with the internal systems of the customer organization. Also, externally, order information from this system should be easily transferable to the systems of suppliers. Therefore, standards would have to be agreed on so that the systems of the customer and suppliers would be directly interfacing with each other.

In the case of intermediaries, this problem is further exacerbated due to the number of buyers and suppliers that are brought together. Ideally, it should be possible for the participants involved to access the appropriate information to support the relationship. Information is sent and received for a number of purposes, including product and pricing information in an electronic catalog, placing orders, and managing inventory. To ensure integration it is necessary to get all the participants involved to agree to a common set of rules. However, it is very difficult to ensure integration from order placement to payment due to the range of systems involved that cut across both internal and external systems. For example, Wheatley (2000) has found that digital links to core financial functions, such as general ledger and payments systems, do not exist in many organizations. As a result, companies are buying and selling online, but are settling invoices with devices such as purchasing cards, and this is still standard practice with many intermediaries. Therefore, in many circumstances it may be of no advantage to become involved with an intermediary to source or sell items due to problems associated with systems integration. For example, a buyer may use an auction process to obtain lower prices for commodity-type items. However, the savings obtained as a result of the reduction in the price of the items may be offset against the costs associated with upgrading and adapting the systems to ensure efficient and effective integration in the order management process. The Chartered Institute of Purchasing and Supply (CIPS) has found that price is only about one-third of the cost of incorporating the goods and services into the final product

(Newing, 2000). Also, suppliers may be unwilling to become involved with intermediaries. Although suppliers may have more access to customers with a reduction in marketing costs, the consequent downward pressure on price will seriously undermine those potential benefits. Suppliers are likely to be unwilling to become anonymous participants in ruthless price bidding wars.

This evidence would appear to contradict the argument of Benjamin and Yates (1991) that "innovations in information technology will enable the unit costs of coordination transactions to approach zero, thus enabling the design of innovative coordination transactions to fit new business needs." Although commodity-type items are conducive to electronic trading through intermediaries, the difficulties associated with integrating systems across organizational boundaries pose enormous challenges. Also, this evidence shows that with the implementation of information technology at the buyer-supplier interface, it is very difficult to eliminate the human element. Also, recent evidence suggests that the barriers to the successful exploitation of Internet technologies at the buyer-supplier interface do not lie primarily with the technology, but with the business processes (Taylor, 1997). The perception is growing that the real benefits of electronic linkages will not come from 'streamlining' the supply chain management process electronically, but from re-defining it completely. Seamless integration of buyers' and suppliers' key systems across the total purchasing portfolio, rather than commodity-type items, should be the key objective, rather than attempting to reduce price or administration costs. Even in the most successful companies, there are few processes that are fully integrated horizontally. Effective implementation of electronic commerce to support supplier relationships and to optimize the supply chain requires that electronic commerce is fully integrated into both the business architecture and technology infrastructure of both the customer and the supplier. The redesign of processes must not only include internal organizational processes, but must include the wider business network. An organization is just one entity in a value system carrying out processes that extend beyond the boundaries of the organization into both its customers and suppliers. While companies may have focused on individual processes, systems, and departments, and optimized such activities, they have not considered the whole chain and identified activities and links that are adding most value. MIT's 'Management in the 1990s' research project has shown that a clear distinction exists between business process re-engineering (BPR) and what is usually referred to as business network redesign (BNR) (Venkatraman, 1994). BPR has clearly focused on the redesign of internal organizational processes. BNR is concerned with the wider business network. The underlying premise is that the firm is just one entity in an industry value system. Business network processes are those processes that extend beyond the boundaries of the organization into suppliers, customers, regulators, and alliance partners.

Collaborative Buyer-Supplier Relations?

In the case of established buyer-supplier relationships, it is important to consider the nature of the buyer-supplier relationship on the exploitation of Internet technologies. Successful implementation of electronic commerce at the buyer-supplier interface requires collaboration among customers and their suppliers (Roberts & Mackay, 1988). However, both customers and suppliers have had extreme difficulties with embracing this new ethos of openness, trust, and collaboration. Collaborative buyer-supplier relations are often perceived as the optimum approach to achieving supply chain improvement through the development of more effective customer-supplier relationships. Evidence has shown that this is an area where rhetoric seems to be moving well ahead of reality (McIvor et al., 1997; Burnes & New, 1996; Lamming, 1994). It is certainly true that partnership is described in simplistic terms, thus making the potential benefits appear easier to achieve than is the case. In addition, the distribution of the benefits that can be achieved through customer-supplier improvement activities is a more contentious issue than much of the literature acknowledges. New and Burnes (1997) conducted an empirical study of the benefits to be gained from collaborative buyer-supplier relationships. They found that the distribution of the costs of improvement activities was biased towards suppliers rather than customers. McIvor, Humphreys, and McAleer (1996) present evidence to suggest that procurement personnel have found it difficult to adapt to the new ethos of openness with suppliers. In addition, suppliers are expected to embrace a collaborative relationship, after many years of operating in a system in which trust was the last thing they expected. This evidence poses problems in the following areas:

- On the supplier side, there may be an unwillingness to share information on prices or costs, fearing that the customer might use such information to erode margins or disclose costs to competitors. For example, the sharing of cost information is an area which customers may use to obtain increased power over suppliers. In many cases, cost information is not used for mutual benefit, thus gaining a poor reputation because of its use as "just another weapon in the customer's arsenal" (Lamming, 1996).

- On the customer side, in a retail environment the retailer may not wish to disclose information to suppliers concerning sales promotions and product sales, fearing that the supplier might disclose such information to competitors. Clearly, if electronic commerce is to lead to the 'seamless integration' of supply chain partners, then a culture change is required to establish real partnerships in which information can be exchanged on a regular basis in an environment of trust.

Conclusion

This chapter has shown that the Internet represents a powerful technology for commerce and communication at the buyer-supplier interface. It has been shown how Internet technologies can have a considerable impact in a number of ways at the buyer-supplier interface. Effective use of electronic commerce has the potential to improve the materials management process of both the buyer and supplier in areas such as inventory reduction, delivery lot-size reduction, and purchase order and invoice reduction. Electronic commerce can reduce the costs of closely integrating buyers and suppliers, and through electronic networks firms can achieve greater integration at the buyer-supplier interface. For example, electronic commerce technologies can enhance the customer's information management and transaction processing efficiency that in turn improves customer demand forecasting and fosters closer relationships with suppliers. The evidence presented in this paper supports Porter's (2001) view that the Internet provides opportunities for organizations to establish distinctive strategic positionings than previous information technologies. It is essential for top management to understand that the Internet is more than a tool or technique, but rather something that is integral to the strategic development of the organization and the relationship with its environment. Adopting such an approach represents a drastic change from traditional management thinking and, more importantly, for management's behavior. The availability of information through the Internet allows organizations to overcome traditionally cost-prohibitive infrastructure barriers and establish a global presence.

It must be pointed out that the Internet is in its infancy, with the underlying infrastructure having some way to go before full development. For example, Internet search tools will become more sophisticated. Advances in the Extensible Markup Language (XML) will make it possible to identify products, features, and prices with far greater precision. Buyers will be able to set much more detailed search criteria, which gives them immediate access to even richer sources of information. In particular, innovations in technology will dictate the pace at which intermediaries will evolve to add more value and encapsulate items of greater complexity. Currently the core skills of intermediaries are information technology, commodity management, and an understanding of point-to-point buyer-supplier interactions. It is quite clear that intermediaries must redefine their roles and functions if they are take on a strategic role for buyers and suppliers. In the main, these intermediaries provide commodity-type items and act as a 'meeting' facility for buyers and suppliers. At the moment, the advantages are not clear for buyers and suppliers to embrace these intermediaries as a channel for commerce. In the case of intermediaries, it has been shown that it is necessary that the buyer and supplier adopt the same standards and invest in the infrastructure to enable seamless integration. However, adopting this approach is more akin to pursuing single sourcing rather than embracing the concept of an electronic marketplace. In order to develop further, these intermediaries will have to develop services such as greater intelligence in the product search process and richer information, and facilitate integration between buyers and suppliers.

While Internet technology offers ways for organizations to communicate and trade more effectively with their suppliers, and gives consumers higher levels of service and sophistication, it also poses major challenges to those within organizations who have to manage it. For example, the greater transparency that flows from an organization trading on the Internet will lead to a greater reluctance to pay full prices and further emphasis on cost reduction. In this way, the Internet may no longer be perceived as an opportunity, but a threat to organizations. A culture change must occur to establish relationships between buyers and suppliers in which information can be exchanged on a regular basis in an environment of trust. Such a change is essential to creating a 'seamless integration' of supply chain members. Considerable efforts must be made in ensuring the compatibility of systems between the trading partners. Closed network problems can also affect the Internet, with business-to-business electronic commerce running up against application interfaces that inhibit the operation of a fully transparent environment between trading partners. Important to further research and investigation are the change management implications of these new technologies. Processes that extend across organizational boundaries need to be jointly designed and managed. Electronic commerce facilitates information exchange and enhanced communications between organizations; it can reduce costs, risk, and uncertainty, while also increasing interdependency and joint investment. The level of adaptation and cooperation that is becoming necessary in the supply chain means that electronic commerce takes on an increasingly critical role. An understanding of how electronic commerce can be deployed by firms to exchange information and to maintain and build relationships is important, as it may impact on their ability to participate in a particular supply chain. Therefore, electronic commerce needs to be viewed in the context of its wider impact in enabling business process redesign, the opportunities it offers for exploiting information, the challenge of integration with internal systems, and its implementation through supporting technologies and applications.

References

Aberdeen. (1999). *Business resource management: A proactive approach to managing operations.* Boston, MA: Aberdeen Group.

Afuah, A., & Tucci, C.L. (2001). *Internet business models and strategies: Text and cases.* New York: McGraw-Hill.

Amit, R., & Zott, C. (2001). Value creation in e-business. *Strategic Management Journal, 22,* 493-520.

Anonymous. (1995). Chrysler pushes quality down the supply chain. *Purchasing,* (July 13), 125-128.

Anonymous. (2000). B2B exchanges—the container case. *The Economist,* (October 21), 76.

Archer, N., & Yuan, Y. (2000). Managing business-to-business relationships throughout the e-commerce procurement life cycle. *Internet Research, 10*(5), 385-395.

Barnatt, C. (2000). E-legacy: The IP systems challenge. *Journal of General Management, 25*(4), 1-16.

Benjamin, R., & Yates, J. (1991). The past and present as a window on the future. In M.S. Scott Morton (Ed.), *The corporation of the 1990s.* New York: Oxford University Press.

Benjamin, R.I., Malone, W.T., & Yates, J. (1986). *Electronic markets and electronic hierarchies.* CISR Working Paper No. 137, Center for Information Systems Research, Sloan School of Management, Massachusetts Institute of Technology.

Borman, M., & Williams, H. (1996). *Collaboration: More than the exchange of information technology.* Management Science Working Paper 96/4, Strathclyde Business School.

Bray, P (2000). Buy-side, sell-side meet at the hub. *Sunday Times Supplement: B2B Collaborating With Business Partners in the Digital Economy,* (December 3), 4.

Burnes, B., & New, S. (1996). *Strategic advantage and supply chain collaboration.* London: A.T. Kearney.

Croom, S.R. (2000). The impact of Web-based procurement on the management of operating resources supply. *The Journal of Supply Chain Management,* (Winter), 4-13.

Dutta, S., & Segev, A. (1999). Business transformation on the Internet. *European Management Journal, 17*(5), 466-476.

Evans, P.B., & Wurster, T.S. (1999). *Blown to bits: How the new economics of information transforms strategy.* Boston, MA: Harvard Business School Press.

Grover, V., & Malhotra, M. (1997). Business process reengineering: A tutorial on the concept, evolution, method, technology and application. *Journal of Operations Management, 15,* 192-213.

Hackbarth, G., & Kettinger, W.J. (2000). Building an e-business strategy. *Information Systems Management,* (Summer), 78-93.

Hewson, D. (1999). Teamwork with suppliers. *Sunday Times: E-Commerce Supplement,* (March 26), 8.

Hewson, D. (2000). Sharing can mean more for all. *Sunday Times: E-Business Supplement,* (November 26), 4.

Houlder, V. (1997). Design and production benefit from wired collaboration. *Financial Times: Information Technology: Make it on the Internet: Online Manufacturing,* (July 16), 34.

Humphreys, P.K., Lai, M.K., & Sculli, D. (2001) An inter-organizational information system for supply chain management. *International Journal of Production Economics, 70,* 245-255.

Hyun, J. (1994). Buyer-supplier relations in the European automobile component industry. *Long Range Planning, 27*(2), 66-75.

John, G. (2000). Wired science. *Supply Management,* (May 18), 30-31.

Kaplan, S., & Sawhney, M. (2000). E-hubs: The new B2B marketplaces. *Harvard Business Review, 78*(3), 97-103.

Lamming, R. (1994). *A review of the relationship between vehicle manufacturers and suppliers.* London: DTI/SMMT.

Lamming, R. (1996). Squaring lean supply with supply chain management. *International Journal of Operations and Production Management, 16*(2), 183-196.

Li, F., & Williams, H. (2000). Inter-organizational systems to support strategic collaboration between firms. *E-commerce and v-business: Business models for global success.* Oxford, UK: Butterworth-Heinemann.

Matthyssens, P., & Van den Builte, C. (1994). Getting closer and nicer: Partnerships in the supply chain. *Long Range Planning, 27*(1), 72-83.

McFarlan, E.W. (1984). Information technology changes the way you compete. *Harvard Business Review, 62*(3), 98-103.

McIvor, R., Humphreys, P., & McAleer, E. (1997). Implications of partnership sourcing on buyer-supplier relations. *Journal of General Management, 23*(1), 53-70.

McIvor, R.T., Humphreys, P.K., & Huang, G. (2000). Electronic commerce: Reengineering the buyer-supplier interface. *The Business Process Management Journal, 6*(2), 122-138.

McIvor, R.T., Humphreys, P.K., & McAleer, W.E. (1996). The evolution of the purchasing function. *The Journal of Strategic Change, 5*(6), 165-179.

Milgrom, P., & Roberts, J. (1992). *Economics, organization and management.* Englewood Cliffs, NJ: Prentice-Hall.

Nakamoto, M. (1997). NEC to use Internet to order supplies. *Financial Times,* (March 27), 8.

New, S., & Burnes, B. (1997). Developing effective customer-supplier relationships: More than one way to skin a cat. *International Journal of Quality and Reliability Management, 15*(4), 377-388.

Newing, R. (2000). Going, going, gone…to the best prepared. *FT.Com Financial Times,* (October 18).

Perry, D. (2000). *The blueprint for B2B success.* Available online at: www.ventro.com.

Porter, M.E. (2001). Strategy and the Internet. *Harvard Business Review, 79*(3), 63-78.

Porter, M.E., & Millar, V.E. (1985). How information gives you competitive advantage. *Harvard Business Review, 63*(4), 149-160.

Prigg, M. (2000). Healthy growth in the B2B field. *Sunday Times: E-Business Supplement,* (December 3), 8.

Rayport, J.F., & Sviokla, J.J. (1995). Exploring the virtual value chain. *Harvard Business Review, 73*(6), 75-85.

Roberts, B., & Mackay, M. (1998). IT supporting supplier relationships: The role of electronic commerce. *European Journal of Purchasing and Supply Management, 4*(2), 175-184.

Segev, A., Porra, J., & Roldan, M. (1997). Internet-based EDI strategy. *Decision Support Systems, 21,* 157-170.

Shapiro, C., & Varian, H.R. (1999). *Information rules: A strategic guide to the network economy.* Boston, MA: Harvard Business School Press.

Tapscott, D., Ticoll, D., & Lowy, A. (2000). *Digital capital: Harnessing the power of business webs.* Brealey Publishing.

Taylor, P. (1997). Electronic revolution in the retailing world. *Financial Times: Information Technology Survey,* (September 3), 3.

Turban, E., Lee, J., King, D., & Chung, H.M. (2000). *Electronic commerce: A managerial perspective (1st ed.).* Englewood Cliffs, NJ: Prentice-Hall.

Tyler, G. (1999). Identity crisis. *Supply Management,* (March 4), 42-43.

Venkatraman, N. (1994). IT-enabled business transformation: From automation to business scope redefinition. *Sloan Management Review, 35*(2), 73-87.

Walton, S.V., & Marucheck, A. (1997). The relationship between EDI and supplier reliability. *International Journal of Purchasing and Materials Management,* (Summer), 30-35.

Weiber, R., & Kollmann, T. (1998). Competitive advantages in virtual markets—perspectives of 'information-based marketing' in cyberspace. *European Journal of Marketing, 32*(7/8), 603-615.

Weill, P. (1992). The relationship between investment in information technology and firm performance: A study of the valve manufacturing sector. *Information Systems Research, 3,* 307-333.

Wheatley, M. (2000). Online auctions. *Supply Management,* (June 1), 25-27.

Yasin, M.M., Small, M., & Wafa, M.A. (1997). An empirical investigation of JIT effectiveness: An organizational perspective. *OMEGA, 25*(4), 461-471.

Zahra, S.A. (1999). The changing rules of global competitiveness in the 21st century. *The Academy of Management Executive, 13*(1) 36-43.

Chapter VI

Know Your Why's and How's –
Towards a Contingency Model for Industrial E-Procurement

Jakob Rehme
University of Linköping, Sweden

Daniel Kindström
University of Linköping, Sweden

Staffan Brege
University of Linköping, Sweden

Abstract

This chapter uses traditional marketing and purchasing strategy models to forward a model for e-procurement. It maintains that there are two major classes of e-procurement solutions used in industry, both deriving from traditional marketing models: e-procurement solutions that focus on enhancing relationships to enable integration between buyer and seller, and solutions that are transaction-oriented and have their primary function in strengthening market forces, thus making industrial markets more competitive. It is argued that the e-procurement solutions used should be related to the purchasing strategies employed and the different steps of the purchasing process. We propose a model based on purchasing strategies that identify appropriate e-procurement solutions to be considered for different types of purchased items. This model can be used to evaluate purchasing initiatives, both from an academic and a practical perspective.

Introduction

Procurement is becoming a strategic function (Kraljic, 1983; McGinnis & McCarty, 1998), contributing to the overall company success. Procurement is also one of the business processes where e-commerce solutions have the greatest potential for cost reductions and to increase efficiency. This is partly due to the fact that EDI has been used in procurement for a long time and therefore there is a high level of understanding of the benefits involved in doing business electronically.

Another interesting aspect is the importance of procurement as a driving force for e-commerce development. In B2B settings this mirrors the overall power balance in most value chains. Large customers' purchasing clout is a major rationale for cost reductions in corporations (and value chains). The large system integrators and/or end-user companies are increasingly exercising their buying power upstream in the value chain (cf. Brege & Brehmer, 2002). E-procurement is a powerful tool for industrial companies to reduce prices and costs for purchased goods.

As we can see, the focus of e-commerce solutions is more and more leaning towards procurement and not sales, and therefore needs to be adapted to the purchasing strategies and procurement processes employed. It can be argued that e-commerce plays different roles depending on the purchasing situation (Bhatt & Emdad, 2001; Rayport & Sviokla, 1995). Therefore there is a need for a differentiated approach to the inclusion of e-commerce into the procurement function. For selling companies it is also important to understand the driving forces and priorities that their customers have, in order to better adapt their e-commerce solution to their customer base.

The purpose of this chapter is to describe and analyze the relationship between purchasing strategies and e-commerce solutions handling different steps in the purchasing processes. Our analysis is empirically based on the experience gained by Swedish multinational companies between 1998 and 2003—where these examples are primarily used as illustrations.

Procurement and E-Commerce

In the wake of current SCM thinking, procurement is becoming an increasingly important function for overall operations (Spekman, Kamauff & Myhr, 1994). Purchasing managers have moved from being transaction accountants to information brokers, and from being the primary point of contact with suppliers to managers of external manufacturing (Spekman, Kamauff, & Myhr, 1994). More often than not, procurement involves other organizational units, such as production and engineering, making the function complex. Therefore, to improve buyer/seller interaction in complex procurement situations, issues regarding technical, commercial, logistical, and social/communication elements and activities need to be handled in a relational approach (cf. Håkansson, 1982; 1993; Rehme, 2001). At the same time, for less complex types of procurement (e.g., commodity type products), there may *not* be a need for establishing long-lasting relationships. Instead it may be desirable to keep suppliers at arm's length. Inevitably, there are large discrepancies between different strategic and processual considerations depending on the various types of purchased goods. Thus there is a need to direct appropriate purchasing measures and tools for different types of goods purchased and for different steps in the procurement process. Van Weele (1997), for instance, emphasizes the need for different purchasing strategies. He forwards a multitude of variables that affect the purchasing process, such as product characteristics, strategic importance of the purchase, financial impact of the purchase, market characteristics, relative risk, effects on existing routines and processes, and the role of the purchasing department. These variables can in many ways affect the different tools and solutions that are needed in procurement.

An e-commerce survey conducted in 1998 reported that purchasing managers expected that Web-based solutions would enable tighter and cheaper supplier relationships and thus reduce the length of the supply chain (Segev, Gebauer et al., 1998). Moreover (in the same report) purchasing managers stated that e-procurement would provide them with cost-reduction means through, e.g., bidding models via the Internet. These perceived benefits of e-commerce appear to be contradictory, since employing market forces (i.e., bidding models) in buyer/supplier relationships often means retorting to arm's length relationships not compatible with tighter supplier relationships. They also indicate the purchasing manager's goal: to attain the best of two worlds, i.e., to improve supplier relationships while still exercising market forces. In summary, the purchasing managers saw e-commerce as beneficial when it comes to reducing buying and transaction costs (Segev, Gebauer et al., 1998). In addition, according to a purchasing director at Volvo Cars (the car manufacturer), suppliers that do not utilize the opportunities for rationalizations that e-commerce can provide will face the risk of losing business (NyTeknik, 2001). Most of these benefits and value-adds can be attributed to the automation of various processes, enhancing speed and improving correctness of information.

E-Procurement: Strategy and Process Contingencies

Many of the e-procurement initiatives have been geared towards process automation. For instance, when Ericsson (the telecom company) and ABB (the power and automation company) introduced their more comprehensive e-commerce solutions, they focused on automating parts of the purchasing process for indirect material, with their solutions *Click-to-Buy* and *Easy-to-Buy*, in order to cut costs. Other companies, such as Dell or Cisco, attempted, through their use of e-commerce, to increase efficiency in logistics and marketing processes in order to achieve cost reductions and improve the competitive situation, e.g., in the form of decreased TTC (Time-To-Customer), TTM (Time-To-Market), and lower inventory levels. Another example of e-commerce for reducing costs is Pipe-Chain, an Internet-based solution for VMI (Vendor Managed Inventory), which is used by Ericsson and a number of their suppliers.

It is clear that strategic considerations in purchasing have great impact on the requirements of e-procurement solutions. The predominant purchasing efforts in e-commerce have been directed towards indirect material, where the items are often non-strategic and low in value. As mentioned above, the first and largest e-procurement investments in ABB and Ericsson, for instance, were for indirect material. These e-procurement solutions are often solely aimed at reducing costs of the procurement process rather than focusing on price negotiations and supplier relationship improvements.

In Figure 1 the importance of procurement denotes the overall impact of the cost of purchased goods on business performance (cost of material/total costs, etc.), and the complexity of the market marks the degree of logistics costs and complexity, monopoly or oligopoly conditions, technological development, etc. (Kraljic, 1983). This means that purchased items are classified based on their overall business impact, on the one hand, and how difficult they are to come by, on the other. Kraljic's matrix illustrates the difference between purchasing strategies when handling different sets of items (goods), i.e., non-critical, leverage, bottleneck, and strategic items. This classification of items purchased ranges from a market situation where suppliers are kept at arm's length, to a situation where it is necessary to adopt policies to support tight integration with

Figure 1. E-procurement solutions for different purchased items (Adapted from Kraljic, 1983, p. 111)

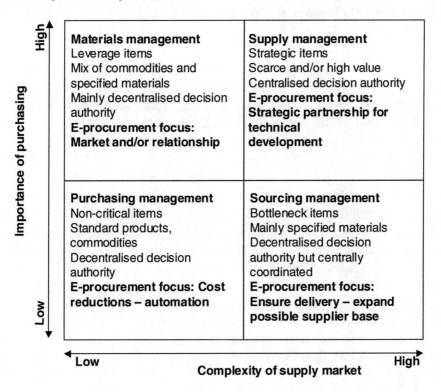

suppliers. Furthermore, the matrix denotes the way that purchasing decisions are authorized, i.e., the degree of centralized decision making in the purchasing process. The Kraljic classification scheme is quite often used in industry (for instance, in ABB and Ericsson). From a supply strategy perspective, it is important to understand the different strategies for which different e-commerce solutions are appropriate. In order to evaluate different solutions and make suggestions for appropriateness, as well as to investigate the usefulness of different e-procurement solutions, we use the matrix in Figure 1.

Non-Critical Items

For non-critical items, i.e., standard products and commodities with a large number of suppliers being able to supply the goods, e-procurement solutions ought to be aimed primarily at cost reductions. Products purchased do not significantly burden overall cost. Instead, the process cost is, in comparison to the purchased goods, high. Therefore, the automation of processes in order to cut costs is a desirable function for an e-procurement solution.

Many e-commerce solutions for purchasing have had their focus on this group of materials. ABB and Ericsson, among others, have come up with their most comprehensive solutions for this type of purchase, where contracts have been established at the corporate centers along with electronic catalogs. Ericsson's solution handles goods such as stationery, hand tools, and other items that are indirect by nature. The e-procurement solution is organized as an electronic catalog where the corporate purchasing department arranges the contractual agreements and the suppliers need to meet certain criteria in order to be included in the catalog. The solution is operated by a third party, who updates and maintains the catalog.

There are several reasons why non-critical items have been among the first to be handled by e-commerce solutions. First, as these materials are non-critical, purchasing managers take less risk in introducing this new purchasing measure, since a failure does not affect overall operations to any great extent. Therefore, managers can be proactive without risking any major operations. Second, for this type of material, the cost of the purchasing process itself is a substantial part of the overall cost, and since one of the more obvious upsides of e-procurement is process cost reduction, an investment in this group can provide a fairly easy return-on-investment. E-procurement leads to a centralization of contracting and the upholding of product databases whereas purchasing decisions remain decentralized. This way of doing business is also a way for the purchasing center to reduce maverick buying. In the long run, the e-catalog can be expanded with more suppliers to improve "online competition," thus reducing prices. However, this aim has so far been secondary (at best). Finally, it is interesting to note that catalog services are one of the few applications of e-marketplaces that suppliers have a positive attitude towards as compared to, e.g., Internet auctions where they are forced to underbid each other (NyTeknik, 2001).

Bottleneck Items

For bottleneck items, it is important to "control" the supplier in order to secure deliveries (cf. Kraljic, 1983). These products are not so important from an overall cost perspective, whereas to ensure deliveries is. Price should therefore be of secondary importance. Since the material in question is mainly specified, it is not easy to swap suppliers. Instead it will be important for the buyer to be able to efficiently provide technical data to the supplier, and in turn be provided with current production and inventory information from the supplier. Information exchange on product and production is therefore important, whereas the actual ordering is less so. Furthermore, in a long-term perspective, the possibility to search for future suppliers may be one of the largest benefits.

For instance, a company in the Swedish food industry incorporated new Internet-based search routines in order to find new or alternate suppliers for maintenance and repair type of products. Each buying situation is similar to a new-buy situation. Company or business search engines and directories, such as Business.com and Manufacturing.com, are designed to aid users in finding companies, products, services, and information with regards to wanted products. Still, the most common way to search for suppliers is through general search engines such as Google, Yahoo, or Alta Vista. To be able to search for new suppliers in order to ensure deliveries in a fairly cost-efficient way means that the buyer is able to reduce his dependency on suppliers with limited production capacity, thus reducing the complexity of the supply market and creating higher flexibility. Correctly designed e-procurement initiatives enable the buyer to better manage (or control) this supplier base.

Strategic Items

From an e-procurement perspective, strategic materials are highly interesting. They have a great impact on overall cost *and* functionality of the final products. Long-term relationships that are controlled from a corporate purchasing center are seen as the (viable) way to ensure the supply of goods, whereas bargaining is not an option (cf. Kraljic, 1983). Furthermore, these items often involve highly technical exchange of information, particularly in the product development stages, such as CAD-drawings and specification. The e-procurement system is thus able to cater for the exchange of technical information. In fact, it is important that the system aid the participants in all relationship-enhancing activities concerning issues such as commercial agreements, logistical arrangements, as well as any interpersonal relationships between the two parties. This is particularly crucial since it is not easy to find alternative suppliers, and more importantly, the products are often developed in cooperation between buyer and seller (Håkansson, 1982, 1993). Due to the importance of the products in this group, investments in solutions to improve the buyer/seller process ought to be fairly defendable. Although there are clearly benefits that could be drawn from employing e-procurement initiatives in this area, it is hard to come by successful cases (cf. Öhrwall-Rönnbäck, 2002).

SAAB Aerospace, a manufacturer of military airplanes, put a lot of effort in adopting Internet solutions with a number of key suppliers. This was done to make joint development projects more efficient and effective. However, caused, for instance, by the technical complexities of the products and high demands on security in the transfer of information, the Internet solutions were never used or developed to their full potential (Öhrwall-Rönnbäck, 2002).

Leverage Items

These items are very important for the overall business cost (see Kraljic, 1983). They consist of a mix of commodities and specified materials, and have probably the greatest potential for e-commerce solutions. For these products, two strategies related to e-procurement can be seen. The first strategy is to enhance the relationship in order to create a more efficient way for the operations. Comprehensive supply-chain management (SCM) solutions are viable, while the volume-value is large enough and the business is characterized by a high level of re-buy. The potential savings are often quite large and affect a range of operations in both the buying and selling firm (e.g., Ericsson & Pipe-Chain). Ericsson's Pipe-Chain solution involved first-tier suppliers that, with the help of Internet-based software, delivered products to the Ericsson assembly line. The software highlights product requirements and results in a transparent buyer/supplier interface, in so much as the suppliers can see Ericsson's stock status and deliver accordingly.

The second strategy is to exercise the purchasing clout that is available. This leads to a more market-oriented approach and is, consequently, quite different in its functionality from a relationship-enhancing one. The savings that may be generated from increased competition are also potentially large, but then predominantly based on the purchasing price (e.g., e-auctions). Both solutions, however, are quite comprehensive and affect activities in the purchasing department. E-procurement solutions of the SCM type are even more comprehensive and have major effects on other operational units as well.

Process and E-Procurement

Industrial procurement is a complex process, especially in a new-buy situation (see Figure 2) that involves several steps all the way from the search of suppliers to the resulting delivery and invoicing of goods (Van Weele, 1997). It can be very time consuming (up to several months) (see, e.g., Emiliani, 2000). For instance, for scarce or strategic items, there are normally a limited number of suppliers available, and the procurement process involves building up personal relationships between representatives not only in the procurement departments, but also with representatives from quality, product support, production, design, and corporate management. On the other hand for non-critical items, which are more transaction oriented, it might not be necessary to establish relationships at all, but rely on market forces. It is obvious that depending on the step of the process, different skills and support are necessary.

The process perspective states that there are discrepancies between the e-commerce solutions that are pertinent, useful, and value adding to an organization, where these discrepancies depend on what the procurement process looks like and on what steps process emphasis is placed. A procurement process differs with what kind of product is purchased, but is generally long and structured from tender to delivery, and involves many parties and requirements within the buying organization (see e.g., Van Weele, 1997; cf. Figure 2). E-procurement must cater for the length, the involvement of many parties on both the buying and selling sides, and the negotiation complexities that come with technical and commercial agendas. This means that the whole process may not be well suited to e-commerce initiatives. Rather, steps in the purchasing process will be performed with e-commerce *depending* on the situation. The extent to which the process can be computerized differs depending on the complexity of the product and the value, volume, and frequency with which it is purchased. New-buy and one-off complex purchases are less likely to be performed through e-commerce if compared to standard products purchased in large volumes.

We claim that the nature of the product flow, i.e., volume and value, and the business complexity of the individual process are related to the degree of automation in the e-procurement process. High degrees of automation are therefore expected to be associated with high volume/frequency, low variety of goods, and predictable environments. This is seen in the discussions regarding

Figure 2. The procurement process and some examples of associated functionality needed by an e-commerce solution (Adapted from Van Weele, 1997)

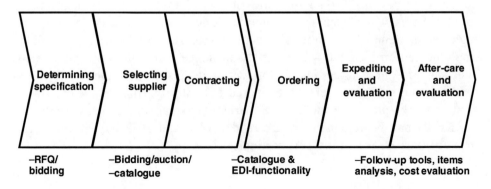

the e-ification of the procurement process which have been heavily geared towards cost reductions mostly associated with, e.g., economies-of-scale benefits and increased competition between suppliers.

By analyzing the procurement process, we can determine what functionality is in focus in what steps of the process (see Figure 2). Since different steps in the process demand different skills and different support, it is obvious that an e-procurement system ought to supply functionality depending on what is needed; e.g., the searching capabilities needed when selecting a supplier are not needed when performing evaluation and follow-up activities and vice versa. In addition, there is the dimension of what good is to be purchased (as seen earlier). There are also great differences in how the steps are executed depending on the product, e.g., buying commodities or engaging in a strategic partnership with co-development.

In the earliest step, i.e., *determining specifications*, when engaging in co-development and/or close relationships for complex products, e-commerce and IT solutions often include the exchange of sensitive information, such as CAD files and ERP data, as well as various platforms for real-time, multi-user environments. With standard products (commodities) in an arm's length relationship with a comparable short time-horizon, transaction efficiency and price agents become a priority. In this area there is great potential for integrative tools that enable companies to take advantage of the virtual dimension in the procurement process (cf. Bhatt & Emdad, 2001; Rayport & Sviokla, 1995).

The second and third steps of the general model of the purchasing process used, *selecting supplier* and *contracting,* in combination with the fourth, *ordering*, are what most commercial e-commerce solutions to date cater for, notably the e-marketplaces. The number of orders placed plays an important role in these process steps, since the more orders, the larger the cost reduction potential. These solutions are geared towards the purchasing of standard products and raw materials, such as the automotive industry portal Covisint. On Internet auctions with Covisint, some companies claim to have lowered the price by up to 20% percent, but at the same time many suppliers are hesitant about taking part in auctions (NyTeknik, 2001). Economies of scale and scope, and efficiency are of pivotal interest when discussing standard products (commodities). For strategic, high-value. items the solutions are more specific, and utilized as well as implemented on a case-by-case basis, and hence a complete different set of needs are present. Another interesting feature in these steps is the possibility to search for suppliers in order to, e.g., increase flexibility. An example of a stand-alone e-marketplace is Endorsia, a e-marketplace that was started with the aid of SKF, the ball-bearing manufacturer, and involves industrial buyers and sellers, primarily large international corporations.

After a supplier is selected and contracted, during the steps of *expediting and evaluation* and *after care and evaluation*, e-commerce solutions become more and more specialized, depending on the relationship needed and wanted between the supplier and the buyer. They can, e.g., include ERP systems and direct links into each other's functional IT systems and inventory systems. To a great extent it becomes a question of the degree of integration sought after (and the level of trust present between the involved parties). However, if the goods purchased are acquired on a spot-market (typically standardized products such as raw materials), with little or no contact between seller and buyer, these last phases become less important.

A Model for E-Procurement

Merging the procurement process model with the procurement strategies matrix (see Figure 3) makes it possible to identify—depending on the strategy employed—what phases of the process are most important, and subsequently what e-procurement solutions and models are pertinent. Table 1 summarizes the Kraljic matrix, process focus, and the e-procurement models. It also exemplifies some solutions in use.

In the category "Purchasing Management," e-procurement has been "used" to a fairly great extent. Since there are few risks involved, it is relatively easy to set up these kinds of solutions. At the same time however, the impact on total

Table 1. Summary of the discussion and identifying e-procurement models

Purchasing Type	Goods Supplied	Purchasing Importance	Supply Market Complexity	E-Purchasing Strategy	E-Model Solution	Process Focus	Solution Examples
Purchasing Management	Non-Critical, Standard, Commodities	Low	Low	Corporate Assortment of Goods	E-Catalog	Order Focus	Ericsson's Click-to-Buy
Sourcing Management	Mainly Specified Materials	Low	High	Relationship but Searching New Suppliers	Information Exchange and/or E-Agent	Information Exchange Search and Select Supplier	Manufac- turing.com, Google, Yahoo
Supply Management	Strategic Items	High	High	Tight Relationship	Resource Network. Stable Members	Strategic Information Exchange (Incl. Sensitive Information)	SAAB Aerospace
Materials Management	Leverage Items, Commodities and Specified	High	Low	Tight Relationship, or Marketplace	E-SCM, E-Marketplace	Comprehensiveness	Ericsson Pipe- Chain, GE TPN

business is limited, although there are cost savings to be generated by adopting lean processes. From a process perspective, e-procurement initiatives are predominantly appropriate for the ordering process, where the actual order, payment authorization, and invoicing are sub-processes that can be automated fairly easily (e.g., self-billing, etc.), and thus lower the transaction costs for this material. One example is Ericsson's Click-to Buy solution, which holds indirect material in a purchasing catalog, such as hand tools, etc. Their solution has resulted in fewer suppliers that subsequently become more important.

E-procurement initiatives in the category "Sourcing Management" are somewhat difficult to extract large-cost savings from. The investments should be directed towards information exchange in the areas of product and production, for the short term, and searching alternate suppliers for the long term. As with purchasing management, however, the impact on the overall operations remains low, and does not contribute significantly to total business. For this type of product, the e-procurement solution should aid in the procurement process rather than automate it, e.g., in terms of search engines and/or solutions that help transfer product and production information. On the one hand resource coordination for order fulfillment is vital, and on the other hand supporting the search for suppliers is important. One example of structured search engines to help find suppliers is Manufacturing.com, which lists suppliers in different industrial segments, and includes product descriptions and contact information.

The category "Supply Management" involves strategic considerations on a high level in the organization. E-procurement investments should be designed primarily to cater for the exchange of technical and commercial information. As with sourcing management, the e-procurement solution should support the ongoing process, rather than automate parts of it. Since the exchange involves sensitive information, the solution needs to be as secure as possible, and requires long-term relationships based on trust. Effects on the buyer's business may be substantial, particularly with regards to product development and innovation. As for the impact of e-procurement on the purchasing process, e-procurement does not need to be connected to the ordering per se. Instead it is important that the solutions contribute to tight integration and resource coordination between the parties, since close cooperation in, e.g., product development efforts are of interest. With SAAB Aerospace the solution exemplifies the difficulty in adopting Internet solutions for this group of materials.

The category "Materials Management" is the most interesting group of purchases in relation to e-procurement. This is due to the large effects on the overall business that can be a result of efficiencies and price pressures for this type of material. However, to be meaningful for e-procurement, this "strategic group" needs to be divided into two subgroups. One is for materials that ought to be handled in tight relationships, such as specified materials, or materials with high technical content or high volume-value that benefit from an SCM type of efficiency effort. This is exemplified by the Ericsson/Pipe-Chain solution that was particularly aimed at improving the logistics processes. The other is made up of the products that can be supplied adequately on a more open market, where purchasing clout can be exercised in order to benefit from price negotiations. One example is the early GE TPN that was aimed at cutting costs, but also at providing a better market for the supply of goods, for instance in auctions. Also, the early intentions of Covisint can be attributed to improving the market.

Clearly, the division between the two groups is a strategic decision in itself and results in two new distinct groups of materials. It is important to maintain that the division means that the segmentation needs to be done in order to define the different e-procurement functionalities required. However, the products in the two groups can vary over time, and it requires deliberate action in order to change a product from a relationship focus to a market focus. Despite their different forms, e-models for these product groups are quite comprehensive, regardless of focus, though they are fairly different from each other. One model needs to cater for SCM functionality or VMI approaches, which means that the focus is aimed at logistics issues. The other approach is directed towards commercial content with RFQ and bidding functionalities, which also includes contracting and ordering. Since the functionality for these two strategic decisions is comprehensive, the resulting investments are therefore large. In particular, for relationship/SCM focus, other departments and operations than purchasing are highly affected. Process-wise comprehensiveness is of importance. In both cases it is a matter of being able to work through the entire process and utilize e-procurement models in many steps.

A Contingency Model for E-Procurement

The e-procurement model in Figure 3 shows the various strategies and the corresponding importance in the purchasing process. It implies that different strategic considerations have a great impact on the corresponding e-procurement solution. The model also implies that there are large discrepancies between the required functionality for different types of goods purchased. For a company engaging in e-procurement solutions, it is therefore very important to determine the type of goods that should be handled electronically. We maintain that a fruitful way to define the purchased goods is to assess the importance of the purchasing to overall business performance, as well as by assessing the complexity in supply market—that is, to find out how difficult the goods are to come by (Kraljic, 1983). When the complexity of the supply market is high so that the logistics are complex and/or the goods hard to come by, e-procurement solutions appear to be less common. However, for e-sourcing, (bottleneck items, see Figure 3), solutions such as search engines may contribute to make the available market larger (larger number of suppliers and more international) and thus less complex. This implicates that the e-commerce solution as such may contribute to making the items easier to come by, thus in the long term enabling a re-classification of the items.

For purchased items with a low level of complexity in the supply market, the e-commerce solutions are both more integrated with the purchasing process and more comprehensive. Furthermore, for goods that have a low impact on overall business, i.e., e-purchasing in Figure 3, e-procurement initiatives are fairly risk-free to engage in, and the purchasing process cost savings are fairly large in comparison with the value of the purchased goods. Therefore the diffusion of these solutions is quite large. However, the business impact is low and does not

Figure 3. A synthesis of strategy and process in e-procurement

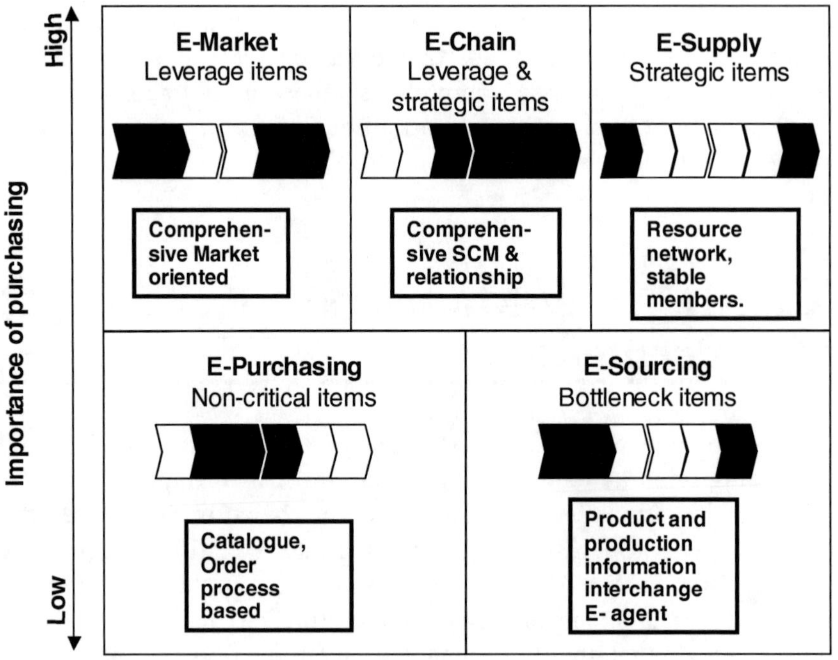

change any major operations. For the long term, initiatives in this group of materials appear to be reducing the number of suppliers, making the remaining suppliers more important, whereas the individual items do not necessarily become more critical.

For items with low to medium supply risk and high business impact, i.e., e-market and e-chain in Figure 3, we maintain that the cost-saving potential is much larger, that the process impact is bigger, and that the e-solution is required to be more comprehensive and thus more expensive. In addition we propose that these items are divided into two groups based on the strategic choice between tighter supplier relationships (SCM system, VMI solutions, etc.) or a more "open" market (bidding, auction, e-marketplace).

E-Supply, with high supply risk and high business impact, is probably the most difficult solution to maintain. We propose that the potential benefits are high, as is the business risk. There are high demands for information exchange of sensitive information for items belonging to this group. The predominant functionalities include solutions adapted to CAD drawings and technological databases, where the demand for security is high.

E-Procurement Dynamics and Development

Over time, e-commerce appears to have changed from focusing on business opportunities, to price and cost reductions (see, e.g., Kraljic, 1983). Since procurement costs can represent up to 75% of the total cost of goods sold, cost initiatives in business relationships are more often than not initiated and managed by the buyer (see, e.g., Emiliani, 2000). Electronic marketplaces (Brehmer & Johansson, 2001; Kaplan & Sawhney, 2000) increasingly focus on lowering prices and reducing costs in procurement. Also, within established supplier relationships, e-commerce development is very much focused on the cost aspects and on establishing transaction cost-effective extranet solutions (Brehmer, 2002). Consequently, many e-procurement solutions are thus aimed at rationalizing and strengthening established relationships rather than focusing on purchasing price alone (Clemons & Reddi, 1993; Stump & Sriram, 1997).

We argue that different purchasing situations call for different strategies when employing e-commerce solutions. Recent supply chain research states that a move to closer relationships is a necessity if competitiveness is to be preserved. However, much of the activity in the purchasing area gives evidence that this is not always the case; instead, many of the solutions and ideas are heavily geared towards arm's length relationships. We do not claim that this is the solution for all situations, but we do not agree with many SCM researchers that everything must go towards close integration between parties involved. Instead, e-commerce solutions for procurement enable different strategic choices depending on the market situation, the e-commerce solutions at hand, and the strategic focus of the firm. In light of this, it is argued that the degree of integration and the particularities of the used solutions depend on a variety of contingencies such as the purchasing strategy employed, items purchased, and the layout of the purchasing process.

Differences in a desired buyer/supplier relationship influence what e-commerce solutions are pertinent. In a situation with close relationships and tight integration, ERP integration and information exchange will be of the essence. When market characteristics are present, e-marketplaces and bidding models are interesting. Facing a situation with low supply complexity and high purchasing importance, it is more difficult to evaluate what e-commerce solution is pertinent, and a more careful analysis of the contingencies might be called for, i.e., whether tight relationships with suppliers are important or not. Due to this and the fact that here the impact of procurement on total operations is high, we argue that this is where companies have the most to gain if they analyze their purchasing situation carefully and adopting the correct e-commerce solutions. Our proposed model can help companies in this endeavor.

We believe that there are a number of interesting areas where the inclusion of e-solutions will alter the way in which procurement is carried out, which offer both academic challenges as well as practical opportunities. For example, e-supply type of goods (see Figure 3 above) can be transferred to e-chain type of goods when the situation so allows (such as when the products have been developed and the relationship moves into an operational phase). The dynamics of purchased items are therefore crucial to address in the evaluation of suitable e-procurement solutions. Another important aspect is that for certain type of goods, the e-procurement solution can change the buyer from buying items to buying from suppliers. For instance, for non-critical items in the e-purchasing category, the inclusion of electronic catalogs makes an addition of an item to the catalog easier to do if it comes from the same supplier. This also means that the employed e-procurement solution influences strategy, thus creating possibilities for engaging in new strategies for the purchase of goods. In order to better understand the appropriate e-procurement solution, we believe it is important to analyze the above-mentioned model with regards to the linkages between strategy, process, and e-procurement solutions.

References

Bhatt, G.D., &. Emdad, A.F (2001). An analysis of the virtual value chain in electronic commerce. *Logistics Information Management,* 1/2(14), 78-84.

Brege, S., & Brehmer, P.O. (2002). Turning technology into business: Organizing for e-business. *E-business value creation* (pp. 23-27). Stockholm, Sweden: The Foundation of Marketing Technology Center.

Brehmer, P.O. (2002). Market channels and e-business: Matching the demands of purchasing and sales. *E-business value creation* (pp. 7-15). Stockholm, Sweden: The Foundation of Marketing Technology Center.

Brehmer, P.O., & Johansson, A. (2001). B2B marketplaces—strategic value for whom? *Proceedings of the IMP Conference 2001,* Oslo, Norway.

Clemons, E., & Reddi, S. (1993). The impact of information technology on the organization of economic activity: The "move to the middle" hypothesis. *Journal of Management Information System, 10*(2).

Emiliani, M.L. (2000). Business-to-business online auctions: Key issues for purchasing process improvement. *Supply Chain Management: An International Journal, 4*(5), 176-186.

Håkansson, H. (1982). *International marketing and purchasing of industrial goods.* Chichester: John Wiley & Sons.

Håkansson, H. (1993). Networks as a mechanism to develop resources. In P. Beije, J. Groenewegen, & O. Nuys (Eds.), *Networking in Dutch industries* (pp. 207-223). Leuven/Apeldoorn, Garant.

Kaplan, S., & Sawhney, M. (2000). E-hubs: The new B2B marketplaces. *Harvard Business Review, 78*(May/June), 97-100.

Kraljic, P. (1983). Purchasing must become supply management. *Harvard Business Review, 61*(September/October), 109-117.

McGinnis, F., & McCarty, L. (1998). Strategic account management in the new procurement environment. *Supply Chain Management, 1*(3), 12-16.

NyTeknik. (2001). *Volvo demands e-commerce from the suppliers.* October 10.

Öhrwall-Rönnbäck, A. (2002). *Interorganizational IT support for collaborative product development.* Dissertation, Department of Management and Economics, Linköping University, Sweden.

Rayport, J.F., & Sviokla, J.J. (1995). Exploiting the virtual value chain. *Harvard Business Review, 73*(November-December), 75-85.

Rehme, J. (2001). *Sales coordination in multinational corporations: Development and management of key account programs.* Dissertation, Department of Management and Economics, Linköping University, Sweden.

Segev, A., & Gebauer, J. (1998). *Procurement in the Internet age—current practices and emerging trends (results from a field study).* CMIT Working Paper, WP-98-1033.

Spekman, R.E., Kamauff, J.W. Jr., & Myhr, N. (1994). An empirical investigation into supply chain management: A perspective on partnerships. *International Journal of Physical Distribution & Logistics Management, 28*(8), 630-650.

Stump, R.L, & Sriram, V. (1997). Employing information technology in purchasing: Buyer-supplier relationships and size of the supplier base. *Industrial Marketing Management, 26*(March), 27-136.

Van Weele, J.A. (1997). *Purchasing management: Analysis, planning, and practice.* London: International Thomson Business Press.

Chapter VII

A Framework for Addressing Minority Suppliers as an E-Business Strategy

Dale Young
Georgia College and State University, USA

Abstract

Financial returns from a corporate website are improved by broadening the site's audience to include minority (e.g., small and women-owned) suppliers. Firms believe that it is good for business if their supplier base has the same racial and gender composition as their customer base. This chapter directly addresses supply chain relationships, diverse suppliers, and investment returns by examining how large corporations use their public websites to communicate with small, minority-owned and women-owned trading partners. The chapter is based on findings from a large-scale study of corporate, public websites. The researcher visited all of the public websites of the Fortune 500 to understand Web-based supplier communications, and analyze how large firms use their public website to communicate with minority suppliers.

Introduction

Businesses are using the Web to communicate with a variety of audiences, including consumers and other businesses. One strategy for improving the return on investment from either a transactional or an informational website is to broaden the target audience for the site to include as many participants as possible. Corporations are now using outlets such as websites to communicate with and attract minority groups because of the growing importance of minority populations in the U.S. (Fields, 2001; Krause, Ragatz, & Hughley, 1999; Milken, 2000).

The number of minority-owned firms is growing at a faster rate than non-minority firms, and sales per employee grow more quickly at minority businesses than at Fortune 500 firms (Milken, 2000). These minority-owned firms are on the Web; nearly half of the largest minority-owned firms in the U.S. have a website (Hernandez, 2002). One way firms learn about these minority populations is by building relationships with minority suppliers. Firms are convinced that it is good for business—and thus a driver of investment return—for their supplier base to have the same racial and gender composition as their customer base (Carter, Auskalnis, & Ketchum, 1999; Morgan, 2002; Reese, 2001). Creating firms that are representative of all Americans, in turn, creates value for all Americans (Fraser, 2002). Women- and minority-owned enterprises make excellent trading partners because they offer competitive prices and high-quality products and services (Carter, Auskalnis, & Ketchum, 1999; Weaver, Stovell, & Romney, 2003). Thus, minority supplier programs are properly viewed in terms of business development rather than social advancement (Morgan, 2002).

This chapter directly addresses the issues of supply chain relationships, diverse audiences, and investment returns by examining how large corporations use their public websites to communicate with small, minority-owned and women-owned trading partners. The chapter is based on findings from a large-scale study of corporate, public websites. The researcher visited all of the public websites of the Fortune 500 to better understand Web-based supplier communications, and analyze how large firms use their public website to communicate with minority suppliers.

The objectives of this chapter are to review related studies, describe the Fortune 500 website study and explain its results, identify common practices for Web-based supplier diversity efforts, and propose a framework for using the Web to initiate minority supplier contacts. The research described here is distinctive because it focuses on the minority supplier content of corporate public websites. This chapter describes the supplier diversity items that appear on corporate public websites, and analyzes the role of these websites in identifying and attracting minority supplier prospects from whom these firms may purchase.

Background

The Web is an important channel for business-to-business (B2B) commerce. There are significant time and cost savings associated with online sourcing (Crockett, 2002). Most electronic commerce investments have been in customer-facing systems, with procurement and supplier relationships slow to develop (META Group, 2000). This chapter focuses on a single aspect of the emerging Web-based B2B marketplace—how large firms are using their public websites to communicate with and attract a more diverse set of suppliers. A diverse supplier base includes small or disadvantaged firms directed by minorities, and/or women, or disabled veterans. Using the Web to address minority- and women-owned firms is a productive strategy because the gender and racial composition of Web users approximates the race and gender composition of the overall U.S. population (Thompson, 2000a, 2000b). Corporations want to insure that their supplier base is as diverse as the many different types of customers they deal with; developing purchasing relationships with minority suppliers helps to achieve this goal and strengthen the minority business sector (Dollinger, Enz, & Daily, 1991).

Several studies have inventoried the content of corporate public websites. Young and Benamati (2000) found that Fortune 500 websites include four key content categories: product sales or financial transactions, customer service (e.g., check order status), communication (e.g., email), and information publishing (e.g., financials, product descriptions). In their study just over one-third of the sites had Web-based supplier content. Earlier, Liu, Arnett, Capella, and Beatty (1997) found that approximately one-quarter of the Fortune 500 conducted business through their website. A review of 250 of the Fortune 500 websites found that the sites were used for online sales and customer service (Palmer & Griffith, 1998). A survey among Fortune 500 Webmasters found key site content to be publicity, customer support, and revenue generation (Gardner, 1998). These studies find that corporate public websites include both customer-facing and supplier-facing content.

The trading partner content of corporate public websites includes Web-based B2B forms and processes for procurement, such as ordering, confirmation, invoicing, and payments (Baron, Shaw, & Bailey, 2000). These categories overlap Internet applications such as purchasing, order processing, and relations with vendors that are used for supply chain management (Lancioni, Smith, & Oliva, 2000). These studies categorize corporate website content related to the types of transactions carried out with both suppliers and customers. The most common usage of corporate websites for trading partner communication is publishing technical or operational information to majority/large suppliers (Young, 2001). Noticeably missing from most of these prior studies of corporate public websites is the supplier diversity or minority supplier content on the sites.

Prior literature reviews of minority supplier research find that few academic studies deal with the topic (Carter, Auskalnis, & Ketchum, 1999; Krause, Ragatz, & Hughley, 1999). However, some common themes do emerge from the minority supplier studies completed to date. Components of minority supplier programs that improve their chances of success include: assisting suppliers with bidding procedures, buying-firm participation in trade fairs, and the development of performance metrics and minority supplier spending targets (Dollinger, Enz, & Daily, 1991). Top management support and setting performance goals for minority supplier programs are critically important components of program success (Carter, Auskalnis, & Ketchum, 1999). Supplier development—efforts to improve the performance or capabilities of a supplier—is primarily performed by large firms and can include certification programs, supplier site visits, and awards programs (Krause, 1997). Minority suppliers must be able to compete against larger firms in the areas of quality, timely delivery, and competitive price (Krause, Ragatz, & Hughley, 1999) without the aid of set asides, price preferences, or acceptance of late delivery (Carter, Auskalnis, & Ketchum, 1999).

The number of women-owned firms is growing in every major ethnic group, and women in advanced-market economies own a quarter of all businesses (Fraser, 2002). Women-owned businesses are especially reliant on large corporations for much of their business (Weaver, Stovell, & Romney, 2003). Those women-owned businesses are challenged by current purchasing practices such as contract bundling and the reduction in the number of key suppliers that are maintained by the buying firms. Buying firms are reducing the size of their supplier base (Krause, 1997). Small minority firms are especially challenged by supply base reductions of buying firms (Krause, Ragatz, & Hughley, 1999). Bundling and preferred supplier programs increase the importance of second-tier supplier programs in which that second-tier supplier to the large buyer generates much of the minority- and women-owned business opportunity (Morgan, 2002; Munk, 2003; Weaver, Stovell, & Romney, 2003).

Few supply chain studies to date have tried to link supplier diversity issues and public websites. Interviews with Fortune 500 diversity managers found minority supplier usage to be one component of diversity evaluation, but the study did not cover the respondent's public websites (Wentling & Palma-Rivas, 2000). No single industry seems to be dominant in using the Web for supplier contacts (Young, 2001). Obstacles to supplier diversity include: a lack of management support, failure to educate internal customers, and implementation problems (Anonymous, 1998) —but there is no mention of Web access issues in this list of obstacles. The Krause (1997) study only makes one brief mention of minority suppliers, and those suppliers were not considered separately during the data analysis.

Using the Web to communicate with diverse suppliers can be viewed as an innovation. An innovation is an idea or practice that is new to an adoption organization or is the first/early usage of an idea by an organization (Nord & Tucker, 1987; Rogers, 1995). Innovation diffusion theory has been used to explain the adoption and implementation of information technology in a number of studies, including studies of EDI (Ramamurthy & Premkumar, 1995), inter-organizational systems (Grover, 1993), and telecommunications (Grover & Goslar, 1993). The rate of adoption focuses on the presence or absence of an innovation within an adopting unit—here the presence or absence of supplier diversity content on a corporate website—across a fixed set of potential adopters, 500 large corporations. This present study uses diffusion theory as the basis for evaluating the rate or percentage of occurrences of supplier diversity content on corporate public websites.

Examining Corporate Websites

The researcher visited each one of the public websites of all Fortune 500 firms to collect data for this study. The Fortune 500 were used because of their resources and the likelihood of having a public website, and the assumption that these firms would mention supplier diversity or minority supplier issues as part of majority or primary (i.e., large corporate trading partner) supplier programs. The site content relating to supplier diversity and majority suppliers was identified and cataloged. Both content areas were included because they were expected to appear together on these websites. The homepage, site index, and site search functions were used to identify references to diversity and to suppliers. When available, the site's search engine was used to search for terms related to this study: diversity, supplier, vendor, minority, women-owned, small business, and procurement.

All pages on these sites relating to suppliers were printed. Printing the pages created a fixed record of site content to control for page changes and updates during data collection. The printed pages were content analyzed by identifying and cataloging items regarding supplier diversity and majority suppliers. The cataloging allowed the researcher to identify common or recurring topics relating to supplier diversity as the topics appeared on these Web pages. The data analysis process follows the methodology of Strauss (1987) in which data are collected and systematically analyzed to develop categories by identifying similarities and differences (in this case across Web pages), the categories are named (the categories that emerged during this study are described in the framework at the end of this chapter), data are reexamined as new categories arise, and the results are integrated together. Findings are presented as percentages of the total number of sites visited during the study because the data are simply categorical.

The public website of a corporation is one component of electronic trading partner systems that may also include existing transactional private network links such as one-to-one or partner-to-partner electronic data interchange (EDI), one-to-many (i.e., one buyer to many sellers) value-added network connections, and Web-based extranets. This chapter focuses on supplier diversity content, specifically how a public website is used to identify and attract a diverse set of suppliers. Given that EDI and extranet systems presuppose an existing relationship between trading partners, focusing on public websites for identifying prospective suppliers is very reasonable. If a firm wants to attract a more diverse supplier base, its public website is an extremely logical place to accomplish that goal, along with other offline diversity efforts.

Web-Based Minority Supplier Communication

A critical finding from the study being reported in this chapter is that the number of corporations using a public website for communicating with potential or existing suppliers is low, considering the level of attention given to trading partner interactions in general, and more specifically to electronic supply chain interactions. Only 27.1% of Fortune 500 firms mention supplier diversity and/or majority/primary suppliers on their public website. The most common acronym for diverse suppliers is "MWBE"—*m*inority and *w*omen-owned *b*usiness *e*nterprises; disabled veterans and small or disadvantaged businesses are also MWBEs. Fortune 500 websites define MWBE as a minority- and/or women-owned business enterprise that is at least 51% owned, controlled, and operated by men and women who are African Americans, Hispanic Americans, Asian Americans, Native Americans, or non-minority women.

Of the Fortune 500 public websites with supplier content, a greater percentage discuss majority/primary suppliers without discussing supplier diversity (40.3%) than discuss supplier diversity exclusively (25.4%). Some sites discuss both (20.9%), and a few (13.4%) briefly mention one or the other topics, but provide no specific detail such as an MWBE contact name. For all of the Fortune 500 public websites, just 12.5% contain MWBE content and only 16.6% have majority/primary supplier content.

The low rate of MWBE content on Fortune 500 public websites is not completely surprising given the present level of corporate spending with minority firms. Minority businesses currently receive only 3.5% of total corporate purchasing expenditures (Hernandez, 2002). In addition, women business enterprises receive less than 3% of total purchasing by Fortune 500 firms (div2000.com; Munk,

Copyright © 2005, Idea Group Inc. Copying or distributing in print or electronic forms without written permission of Idea Group Inc. is prohibited.

2003). The rate of MWBE content on Fortune 500 public websites actually exceeds the level of purchasing those firms have with minority suppliers. The U.S. government record for minority spending is similar to corporate efforts. For example, the General Accounting Office found that the Department of Defense awarded less that 2.5% of its contracts to women-owned firms (Fields, 2001).

MWBE Content Placement

These firms place MWBE materials in several areas on their public websites. Supplier diversity materials may be in a firm's Web-based purchasing or procurement instructions to all suppliers. LTV, for example, views MWBE activities as part of purchasing: "The use of (MWBEs) is a function of our normal purchasing procedures, just as equal employment opportunity is an integral part of normal personnel policy." Other firms mention supplier diversity when discussing overall corporate diversity efforts. Pitney Bowes' strategic plan for diversity covers workplace diversity, business partner diversity, strengthening communities, and becoming a global firm. PPL says, "The value PP&L Inc. places on diversity in its employees, communities, and customers carries over to the people from which the company purchases goods and services." Some firms include diversity statements or pledges in the diversity segment of their website; these diversity statements always mention employees, but may or may not mention suppliers. A few organizations publish on their website a diversity report covering MWBE supplier issues. For example, Monsanto's Web-based corporate diversity report includes a supplier diversity segment.

Supplier Diversity Content Categories

There are three primary categories of supplier diversity content on corporate public websites—*requirements, reaching the firm,* and *rationale.* These categories emerged during the content analysis of the pages of each website that had supplier diversity content. Corporate websites are used to describe the requirements for creating a business relationship, to explain how to reach the firm, and to justify the firm's involvement in supplier diversity.

Requirements for establishing a business relationship cover various issues (Table 1). Over a third of the buying firms require prospect certification to prove MWBE status as a prerequisite to doing business. Some of the sites provide written definitions for each category of MWBE business—small, minority- or women-owned. A few sites provide links to the certifying agencies. These websites discuss MWBE certification. Firms don't allow self-certification; suppliers must prove certification by a certifying agency. The organizations most

Table 1. Requirements for minority supplier participation

Supplier Diversity Content Item (N = 134)	# (%) Sites
Require third-party certification	50 (37.3)
Financial statements	34 (25.4)
Define MWBE categories	33 (24.6)
Operational requirements	26 (19.4)
Links to MWBE certifying agencies	22 (16.4)

commonly mentioned for MWBE certification are the National Minority Supplier Development Council (NMSDC), the Women's Business Enterprise National Council (WBENC), and the Small Business Administration (SBA). Both the NMSDC and the WBENC have rigorous certification procedures, and both offer a national database of certified minority- or women-owned firms.

A number of the firms use the supplier diversity section to mention financial requirements such as a D&B number and past year's sales. Others mention operational requirements such as bar coding or EDI. Financial submissions that are required from prospective MWBEs include financial statements (e.g., income, balance sheet, cash flow, prior years' sales), D&B number, evidence of product liability insurance, and marketing budgets. Prospective suppliers must demonstrate their financial stability, and not simply prove they are a small, disadvantaged, or minority business.

Operational requirements for existing or prospective MWBEs cover mainframe access, EDI, UPC labeling and bar coding, product safety, labor law compliance, ISO certification, geographic coverage, and the importance of quality, price, service, on-time delivery, and cycle time improvement. Applicants must have a certain level of technical sophistication, and be price and quality competitive, before consideration.

Prospects can use a variety of methods for reaching the buying firm (Table 2). Application procedures include electronic application forms. Contact informa-

Table 2. Methods for minority suppliers to reach buying firm

Supplier Diversity Content Item (N = 134)	# (%) Sites
Electronic application form	40 (29.9)
Contact information: name, address, phone, email	35 (26.1)
Contact information *without* a contact name	25 (18.7)

Table 3. Rationale for minority supplier programs

Supplier Diversity Content Item (N = 134)	# (%) Sites
Explain MWBE involvement	39 (29.1)
MWBE program metrics (e.g., spending w/ MWBEs)	32 (23.9)
Diversity letter on website from corporate officer	21 (15.7)
MWBE awards or case studies documented	18 (13.4)
Second-tier program	16 (11.9)
MWBE mentoring	13 (9.7)

tion includes an internal contact name, and their email, phone number, and address. Some sites provide contact information by job title only, without giving a name.

Regarding rationale (Table 3), a few sites display a letter from an officer, such as the chairman or CEO, to publicize the importance of the firm's supplier diversity efforts. Some firms list MWBE awards received or case studies of successful MWBEs. They measure the success of MWBE programs. Second-tier supplier programs are mentioned infrequently. Formal mentoring programs assist MWBEs in developing their businesses.

Firms cite both business and humanitarian reasons for their involvement in supplier diversity. MWBEs are potential customers, and supplier diversity enables the firm to be a more compelling place to shop and invest. By attracting minority suppliers the firm can better understand and attract diverse customers. MWBE programs provide competitive advantage and make good business sense. The programs are required for government contractors. They support continuous improvement of products and processes, and give evidence of a high-performance, value-driven culture. The sites cite supplier diversity programs as a way to invest in and help grow the communities operated in; they are one way to insure community growth. The firms state that supplier diversity is a way to express concern for the public good, it's the right thing to do, and a healthy company and society depend on enabling all to share in the national economic growth.

Firms track MWBE progress through metrics such as the percentage increase in the total number of minority suppliers in a given time period, specific number of firms in the MWBE program database, dollar amount spent or the percentage of total procurement given to MWBEs each year, and stated corporate annual goal—as dollars or a percentage—for MWBE spending. Firms list the program start date and note MWBE contribution to cost reductions.

Closely related to MWBE program metrics are a variety of non-Web initiatives to support contacts with prospective MWBEs, or to recognize existing MWBEs. Buying firms participate in forums, trade fairs, procurement conferences, and they host small business open houses. Some firms give a "small business of the year" or a "best MWBE" award.

Letters from the CEO/Chairman introduce some of the MWBE sections on these websites. The letters discuss forming partnerships with suppliers, using the words "alliances" and "collaboration," equal or fair business opportunities, reasons for MWBE programs (e.g., reflect the communities served, strategic advantage, gain new customers), and how supplier diversity helps accomplish corporate objectives. Some mention metrics such as awards received, dollars spent with MWBEs, or the number of years the firm has had a formal program. Others stress ethical conduct for suppliers, and note the importance of price and quality for goods and services delivered. These letters express commitment from the top of the organization for MWBE programs and suggest issues that are important to the buying firm.

Some firms encourage majority/primary suppliers to include MWBEs as second-tier suppliers by asking those suppliers to include MWBEs in contracting and procurement. Quaker says: "All suppliers as a condition of seeking new or continued business…agree to…carry out Quaker's policy of supplier diversity through…awarding subcontracts wherever such subcontracting would be consistent with the efficient performance of the contract." Lucent asks its own MWBEs to "exercise internal MWBE initiatives and present a diverse workforce." When an MWBE is unable to do business with a Fortune 500 firm, the buyer may try to match it with one of its existing majority or primary suppliers. Firms have subcontracting programs to link second-tier MWBE suppliers with their primary suppliers, while others link prospective suppliers and current vendors if the MWBE cannot meet its purchasing criteria.

These firms ask majority/primary suppliers to report their second-tier MWBE efforts. They require contractors to show how they will subcontract work to MWBEs and monitor MWBE participation during supplier performance evaluations. Firms may give a target dollar value for reporting on contracts, or give targets for second-tier MWBE purchases. They ask for monitoring and reporting from primary suppliers. They ask a primary supplier liaison officer to report second-tier MWBE activity, or they give dollar value credits for spending with second-tier MWBEs toward the expected annual cost reductions from those majority suppliers.

These large firms mentor MWBEs. Quaker says: "Our (MWBE) success is based on…mentoring…that teaches participants how large corporations can work with small business and help strengthen business relationships. [MWBEs] develop skills necessary to service Quaker and other companies. Quaker builds...well-trained, service-oriented [MWBEs] prepared to adhere to the same rigid standards...of quality as majority suppliers." Frequently used terms include locating resources, guidance, and consultation. Others mention "technical assistance" or support without discussing a formal MWBE mentoring program. PepsiCo, for example, says its MWBE program is purchasing focused, and it does not emphasize start-up support or business development. Some provide technical assistance and professional coaching, so underrepresented businesses can become suppliers. These corporations emphasize the value of mentoring. Cardinal Health's program is "designed to help businesses align...resources to increase their overall equity, and to understand the requirements for establishing a business relationship." U.S. Department of Defense contractors participate in the DOD's mentor-protégé program. Raytheon uses the program to "strengthen small business participation." Ball Aerospace, Unisys' Federal Systems Division, and Science Applications International also participate. These firms have programs for small/disadvantaged businesses on federal contracts, and mentor small businesses regarding procurement procedures, quality requirements, and internal processes.

These Web-based items—requirements, reaching the firm, and rationale—are important supplier diversity issues that are supported by the content of off-line or non-Web programs. A recent supplier diversity survey by the WBENC also identified CEO involvement, formal measures for supplier diversity program success (e.g., the percentage of outside vendor/supplier spending to women enterprises), and certification requirements as key practices of successful diverse corporate purchasing efforts (div2000.com). The websites in this study very closely mirror that critical supplier diversity program content.

Becoming a Certified Minority Supplier

Fortune 500 firms have formal processes that begin after a prospective MWBE has submitted an application and provided evidence of certification from a third party, such as the NMSDC. The procurement office or supplier diversity program office evaluates the application, determines the need for the products or services of the prospective MWBE, and passes the information to a buyer. If a need exists, the MWBE may be invited to a face-to-face meeting with procurement personnel to learn the firm's expectations. Approved MWBEs are entered into the corporate purchasing database and given access to the supplier extranet—the private, Web-based system accessed by selected trading partners.

Most firms tell the prospect, "We'll call you if we are interested." Some, however, use their public website to inform prospective MWBEs of their responsibility in pursuing a business relationship. They encourage potential MWBEs to call back, be persistent, and look for ways to differentiate their firm from the many others that are trying to develop a trading relationship. The buying firms encourage follow-up visits with the director/manager of minority business to develop personal contacts and relationships by emphasizing the importance of follow-up with key contacts. They tell prospects to submit an application and then call. First-time bidders may meet with purchasing officers prior to bidding to learn procedures and specifications. Firms note that the competition is extreme and the process requires perseverance over a period of several years. MWBEs must check with procurement for potential business and follow-up to determine upcoming opportunities, especially if the prospect has new products to sell. MWBEs translate their capabilities into purchaser needs by converting those needs into problems that the products/services of the MWBE can solve, thus becoming "solution-oriented" and taking a "value-added approach." Procedures such as follow-up and persistence are common sales activities, but they tell MWBEs they are entering a lengthy and difficult process. They are not simply going through the formality of a questionnaire that guarantees business because of their certified status as an MWBE.

Strategic Aspects of Web-Based Minority Supplier Communication

The study discussed in this chapter has identified a number of strategic issues for generating additional returns on e-business investments. These issues relate specifically to the usage of a public website to initiate trading relationships with minority businesses. A few large firms are using the Web to attract minority suppliers. These firms rely on external agencies to certify prospective minority suppliers. The programs are important enough that the firms have developed specific metrics to track the success of reaching minority suppliers. The content of these Web-based programs parallel existing, off-line supplier diversity programs.

Web-based minority supplier communications are included with either procurement or with corporate diversity materials. The site placement of Web-based supplier diversity material suggests these programs are either part of a narrow purchasing effort or a broader corporate diversity program. Supplier diversity programs should look beyond procurement. The stated reasons for involvement in supplier diversity, such as community support and common good, suggest that some firms already hold this broader, more strategic view of supplier diversity.

The key strategic reason for outreach programs to minority suppliers is economic. The employees of these businesses represent potential or existing customers for the buying firm's products/services. Improving the economic well-being of minority firms helps build loyalty for what the buying firm has to sell. This economic benefit not only serves the buying firm, but the communities in which the minority firms are located through increased job opportunities. Second-tier program requirements "spread" the economic benefit beyond the primary buyer and minority seller to other firms in that same supply chain.

However, supplier communications from public websites are not widespread. Only one out of eight Fortune 500 public websites mention supplier diversity; they more frequently use these sites—one out of six firms—to publish majority supplier information. These low rates of adoption show that pubic websites are slowly emerging as an outlet for communicating with either diverse suppliers or with primary suppliers. Public websites are barely used for communicating with either existing or prospective diverse and majority suppliers. Diverse suppliers tend to be smaller than majority/primary suppliers, so the Web could significantly improve communications with existing MWBE suppliers because it avoids costly EDI or proprietary linkages, and should be an important way, along with trade fairs and procurement conferences, for reaching prospective minority suppliers.

Firms with off-line supplier diversity programs may be underutilizing the Web as a component of those programs. Web-based supplier diversity efforts seem to parallel the slow rate of adoption of the Web for supplier interactions. This low rate of usage is less a supplier diversity issue than it is an issue of choosing between customer-facing and back-facing systems. In addition, the relatively low rate of Web-based communications to diverse suppliers reflects the general level of business that is given to these types of suppliers across the entire economy.

Web-based supplier diversity does not imply special treatment for MWBEs. The number of firms that have operational requirements such as price, quality, and geographic coverage, and that request financials, shows there is no special treatment for minority suppliers. Although the percentages of firms that publicize specific requirements are low (e.g., only 25.4% ask for sales and financial data), other statements about expectations concerning price and quality on these sites show how prospective MWBEs must compete against majority suppliers that have previously established relationships with these large buying firms. These Web-based supplier diversity initiatives place the responsibility on the prospect for certification, for follow-up contacts with the buying firm, and for meeting the buyer's requirements for electronic linkages and financial stability.

The economic objectives for creating supplier diversity programs, such as gaining new customers and supporting continuous improvement, also argue against altruistic motives for these large, buying firms. The corporate diversity statements of these firms reveal that they view diversity more broadly than gender or race. Firms see sound business reasons for developing a diverse supplier base; reasons include gaining competitive advantage through lower operating costs and gaining a better understanding their customer's needs. Supplier diversity is one way firms understand and sell to a very diverse set of customers in an increasingly diverse marketplace. Unfortunately, the current low number of public, Web-based supplier diversity programs contrasts sharply with these stated goals for selling to diverse markets.

Web-based supplier diversity content enables information publishing and prospect screening. These supplier diversity segments are used to publish materials such as contact information and MWBE definitions. The segments are also useful for initial screening of applicants by providing electronic application forms and links to certifying agencies.

Electronic forms and certification are the most frequently appearing supplier diversity content. Given the generally low percentages for all supplier diversity content, most Fortune 500 firms with supplier diversity content on their public website are currently in the publishing stage—the site is simply used to publicize some of the firm's MWBE activities or interests. There is some consensus regarding supplier diversity content, but a low level of interest in using the transactional capabilities of these sites to support screening of prospective diverse suppliers.

Several content items relate to minority supplier certification. Firms with supplier diversity content tell applicants they must have external certification, the sites define the MWBE categories, and a few provide links out to the certifying agencies. This emphasis on certification suggests a concern for regulatory or federal compliance and equal treatment for all MWBE applicants. An MWBE cannot begin the process of developing a formal trading partner relationship with the buyer without certification. However, the majority of these websites don't tell prospects this, suggesting they either use other channels to inform prospects of the certification requirement or operate under the assumption that MWBEs are already aware of it.

Web-Based Supplier Diversity Practices

The corporate sites described here represent the earliest adopters of Web-based supplier diversity initiatives. The key component categories of these MWBE Web pages include: giving evidence of commitment, describing expectations, assisting with the certification process, measuring and publicly reporting program success, and creating a user-friendly environment to encourage applications from prospective minority suppliers.

Firms give evidence of commitment in the form of a letter from a top officer of the firm, participation in non-Web MWBE recruiting activities such as open houses and associations, second-tier requirements, and minority supplier development or small business mentoring programs. They use these websites to describe expectations regarding product or service prices, on-time delivery, quality, financial stability, and technological capabilities. They provide assistance with the certification and screening process by giving process help such as directions about certification, electronic forms, names and email contact information, product/service lists, and selling opportunities in specific areas (e.g., MRO, production, and support functions). These firms publish success measures, including case studies of existing MWBEs and formal metrics (e.g., annual purchases from MWBEs) for charting the growth in MWBE activity. A user-friendly site means the MWBE materials are easy to find on the public website, and the tone of the material encourages prospective MWBEs to apply. Tone can be set with statements such as, "We actively look for and help develop a diverse supplier base." Unfortunately, only a quarter of the sites list the contact officer names and phone numbers.

Although supplier diversity segments are not widely used on corporate public websites, several critical content items for these segments emerge from this study. Firms that are developing Web-based links to prospective MWBE trading partners should consider these key content areas—commitment, expectations, process, measures, and tone—as they modify their public websites. Placing these content categories on a firm's public website suggests they are already part of that firm's off-line MWBE efforts.

A Framework for Web-Based Minority Supplier Communication

This study finds that public websites are a component in the process of identifying and developing relationships with minority suppliers. The critical components of a process for working with diverse suppliers are identified in the MWBE Framework (Figure 1) that emerged during the analysis of these findings. The categories that emerge from the website content analysis in this study indicate that corporate, public websites are currently assisting in the execution of three distinct activities related to MWBE programs: identification of prospective suppliers, screening and certification of those prospects, and building trading relationships with those MWBEs.

The objectives for including minority suppliers have been well documented in prior studies. For example, the opening arguments in this chapter note that

Figure 1. Creating Web-based MWBE relationships

Identification of Minority Suppliers
Web application forms for prospective suppliers
Contact information listed on the website
  o   Phone, email, mailing address, title(s)
Web "Promotional" material on MWBE programs
  o   Chairman's letter
  o   MWBE awards and activities
  o   Website stories of successful MWBE firms

Screening and Certifying Prospective Diverse Suppliers
Links to certifying agencies from the buyer's site
List financial & operational requirements on MWBE
Web pages
Evaluation of application and determination of
product/service "fit"
  o   Described onsite but executed off-line

Development of MWBE Trading Relationships
Web posting of business opportunities
Web access to procurement extranet
Mentoring and second-tier programs
  o   Described onsite but executed off-line

MWBE: Minority & Women-Owned Business Enterprise

MWBE programs are instituted for business and competitive reasons, not simply for altruistic or social reasons. The framework presented here explains how the three MWBE aspects of a public website facilitate or carry forward an MWBE program. (Other studies have explained "why"; this is the first study to examine "how" regarding Web-based MWBE.) As such, adopting Web-based MWBE content is a vital component of building an e-commerce strategy.

A public website helps describe the buying firm to prospective MWBE suppliers by publishing diversity reports, contact information, success stories, and awards received. These sites augment related MWBE prospect identification activities such as open houses and trade fairs. After prospect identification, these sites assist with prospect screening through publication of electronic application forms, which supplement telephone and personal interviews. Following certification and other application procedures, the supplier begins to develop a relationship with the buying firm by accessing the buyer's website to check for business opportunities. Ongoing relationships with MWBEs can be enhanced through a variety of methods, including public and private (e.g., extranet) website access.

The websites described in this chapter have implemented these features for identifying and screening prospective MWBEs, and then developing and maintaining relationships with them. However, given the small number of corporate public websites that mention supplier diversity, and the small number with specific supplier diversity content, much remains to be done regarding public websites as a component of MWBE relationship development.

The Future of Web-Based Supplier Diversity Initiatives

Web-based MWBE programs reflect the current state of two significant influences: the general state of minority firm participation in the economy, and the current level of adoption of the Web for B2B communications and transactions. Corporate public websites have great potential as an outlet for linking with diverse suppliers, but the external influences just identified will act to retard the rapid adoption of Web-based supplier diversity initiatives. In short, the firms most likely to use the Web for attracting and connecting to diverse suppliers are the firms with active, off-line diversity efforts. The rapid adoption of the Web by small to mid-sized minority firms will provide them with an outlet for easily accessing the Web-based supplier diversity initiatives of the firms that have made the commitment to minority suppliers.

More generally, Web-based MWBE programs are a component of a firm's broader e-commerce strategy. That corporate-level e-commerce strategy—in order to be most successful—must be directly linked to corporate-wide strategic and marketing objectives. In other words, firms don't have separate corporate strategic plans and Web strategies; the Web is rapidly becoming a key component of competitive strategy as firms provide multiple channels for trading partners such as suppliers and customers to execute business processes. This chapter concludes that the Web can support multiple aspects of MWBE programs, which in turn are a part of broader e-commerce strategies.

MWBEs will be aided, in part, by government efforts to support minority-owned firms. For example, the U.S. Department of Commerce Minority Business Development Agency (www.mbda.gov) has a number of Web-based resources for small firms. The U.S. Chamber of Commerce offers links from its website (www.uschamber.com/access/resources/default) to minority business organizations, such as the National Minority Supplier Development Council (http://www.nmsdc.org), which provide certification services to minority-owned firms. MWBEs have access to a number of Web resources to search for U.S. federal and state government contracting opportunities (see for example, http://www.ethnicmajority.com/mbecontracts.htm). Other Web-based resources for MWBEs include the Women's Business Enterprise National Council (www.wbenc.org), the Small Business Administration (www.sba.gov), the DiversityBusiness site (div2000.com), and MWBE.com. These government and private initiatives aid in the growth of MWBEs so they are better prepared to compete for corporate procurement contracts.

Conclusion

Large-firm, public websites are largely underutilized for encouraging supplier diversity. Given the growing access to the Web, and its inherent value in terms of both costs and speed in linking to small and mid-sized trading partners, large organizations with established supplier diversity programs should strongly consider the Web as one more outlet for implementing these efforts. Web-based B2B commerce provides a number of strategic benefits to adopting organizations. This chapter shows how the Web can be successfully applied to attract and screen minority suppliers, and how this process provides economic benefit to the adopting organization. The chapter presents a framework for successfully managing the MWBE process. The framework is based on observations of programs currently in existence and operating among some of the largest corporations in the world.

References

Anonymous. (1998). Obstacles on the road to supplier diversity. *Purchasing, 125*(2), 14-19.

Baron, J., Shaw, M., & Bailey, A. (2000). Web-based e-catalog systems in B2B procurement. *Communications of the ACM, 43*(5), 93-100.

Carter, C., Auskalnis, R., & Ketchum, C. (1999). Purchasing from minority business enterprises: Key success factors. *Journal of Supply Chain Management, 35*(1), 28-32.

Crockett, R. (2002). Going to the source, on the Web. *Business Week Online,* (May 13).

div2000.com. (2001). New survey provides roadmap for success for U.S. corporations seeking supplier diversity. Available online at: http://www.div2000.com/news/December2001/WBENCSurvey.html.

Dollinger, M., Enz, C., & Daily, C. (1991). Purchasing from minority small businesses. *Journal of Purchasing and Materials Management, 27*(2), 9-14.

Fields, J. (2001). Uncle Sam gives women the cold shoulder. *Business Week,* (February 21).

Fraser, E. (2002). Women and minorities in business. *Vital Speeches of the Day, 68*(10), 312-316.

Gardner, E. (1998). More work—more money. *Internet World,* (October 5).

Grover, V. (1993). An empirically derived model for the adoption of customer-based interorganizational systems. *Decision Sciences, 24*(3), 603-640.

Grover, V., & Goslar, M. (1993). The initiation, adoption, and implementation of telecommunication technologies in U.S. organizations. *Journal of Management Information Systems, 10*(1).

Hernandez, R. (2002). The supplier diversity digital divide. *e-MBE.net.* Available online at: http://www.e-mbe.net/tutorials/supdivdigdivide.htm.

Krause, D. (1997). Supplier development: Current practices and outcomes. *International Journal of Purchasing and Materials Management, 33*(2), 12-20.

Krause, D., Ragatz, G., & Hughley, S. (1999). Supplier development from the minority supplier's perspective. *Journal of Supply Chain Management, 35*(4), 33-41.

Lancioni, R., Smith, M., & Oliva, T. (2000). The role of the Internet in supply chain management. *Industrial Marketing Management, 29,* 45-56.

Liu, C., Arnett, K., Capella, L., & Beatty, R. (1997). Websites of the Fortune 500 companies: Facing customers through homepages. *Information and Management, 31,* 335-345.

META Group. (2000). Study finds most major firms are missing the mark on e-business. Press Release, February 9.

Milken Institute. (2000). *The minority business challenge: Democratizing capital for emerging domestic markets.* September 25.

Morgan, J. (2002). How well are supplier diversity programs doing? *Purchasing, 131*(13).

Munk, C. (2003). Women enterprises struggle for big customers. *Wall Street Journal,* (February 4), B3.

Nord, W., & Tucker, S. (1987). *Implementing routine and radical innovations.* Lexington, JA: Lexington Books.

Palmer, J., & Griffith, D. (1998). An emerging model of website design for marketing. *Communications of the ACM, 41*(3), 44-51.

Ramamurthy, K., & Premkumar, G. (1995). Determinants and outcomes of electronic data interchange diffusion. *IEEE Transactions on Engineering Management, 42*(4), 332-351.

Reese, A. (2001). Supplier diversity and e-procurement: Why your initiatives are not at odds. *Isourceonline.com.*

Rogers, E. (1995). *Diffusion of innovations (4ᵗʰ ed.).* New York: The Free Press.

Strauss, A. (1987). *A qualitative analysis for social scientists.* Boston, MA: Cambridge University Press.

Thompson, C. (2000). Americans online, part 2: Race. *eMarketer.com,* (May 28).

Thompson, C. (2000). Americans online, part 3: Gender. *EMarketer.com,* June 7.

Weaver, J., Stovell, D., & Romney, L. (2003). Access to markets: Perspectives from large corporations and women's business enterprises. Center for Women's Business Research. Available online at: http://www.nfwbo.org/Research.

Wentling, R., & Palma-Rivas, N. (2000). Current status of diversity initiatives in selected multinational corporations. *Human Resource Development Quarterly, 11*(1), 35-60.

Young, D. (2001). Categorizing corporate Web-based supplier diversity initiatives. *Journal of Computer Information Systems, 42*(2), 57-64.

Young, D., & Benamati, J. (2000). Differences in public websites: The current state of large U.S. firms. *Journal of Electronic Commerce Research, 1*(3).

Chapter VIII

Alaska's Embrace of Digital Opportunities

Ping Lan
University of Alaska Fairbanks, USA

David C. Yen
Miami University, USA

Abstract

There have been a very limited number of systematic studies of how a region is turning digital opportunities into a development force. In theory, major advances in information and communication technology (ICT) have successfully transformed traditional businesses and markets, revolutionized learning and knowledge-sharing, generated global information flows, and empowered citizens and communities in new ways to redefine governance (Afuah, 2003; Mullaney et al., 2003). At a regional level, this "digital revolution" could offer enormous opportunities to support sustainable local prosperity, and thus help to achieve the broader development goals (DOT Force, 2001). Alaska is one state that can be positioned to take advantage of Internet and e-commerce technologies. Isolated from the U.S. main economic centers and heavily reliant on the export of commodities in its economy, e-commerce or business via the Internet is an ideal choice for Alaska. However, the available statistics do not support this claim. Most economic indicators show a downward trend in Alaska since 1995, in spite of the fact that the federal government expenditure has been increasing

(ASTF, 2002). This chapter is dedicated to measuring the usage of the Internet in Alaska. It hypothesizes that geographical limitations help a region like Alaska embrace ICT and its applications without much hesitation, but also hinders the region to fully exploit the potential of ICT due to the limitations of resources. A large-scale survey was conducted to reveal the characteristics of Internet usage among individuals, government agencies, local communities, and private firms in Alaska. This research is of interest in two aspects: It could offer help for policymakers and enterprises within Alaska to realize the potential development brought about by the current digital revolution, and it could help enterprises outside Alaska to target this market more effectively. Theoretically, it could shed light on issues related to technology adoption and local innovation. Besides that, the platform-dependent approach used in this research can be applied in a broader context.

Background: The Alaska Context and a Digital Platform

Turning digital opportunities into a development force in Alaska involves collective efforts made by Alaska governments, enterprises, and individuals. It is basically the results from the interaction of the current digital platform and resources which can be used by Alaskans. The former indicates that development is "platform-dependent." With a different platform, different activities can be performed or the same activities can be conducted in different ways (Rosenberg, 1976, 1982; Sawhney, 2001). The latter suggests that development is "resource-dependent." Any given development is affected directly by previous conditions or status.

This section will briefly describe the structure and characteristics of the current digital platform. Then it will analyze the economic development status in Alaska. Finally, it will present the Digital Task Force's recommendation for deploying the digital platform for followers or latecomers.

A Digital Platform

Much has been written on the characteristics of the current new digital platform by using different metaphors. For example, Turban et al (1999) suggest that the whole structure of e-business looks like a house. The roof is various applications.

The basement is e-business management. The pillars are people, public policy, technical standards, and organizations. The infrastructure consists of common business service infrastructure, messaging and information distribution infrastructure, multimedia content and network publishing infrastructure, network infrastructure, and interfacing infrastructure. Kalakota and Robinson (2001) suggest that e-business is analogizing to a terrace, which is made up of three interlocking layers. The top layer is E-Business Design, which plans business applications. The middle is E-Business Infrastructure, which includes various software tools for realizing the applications. The bottom layer is E-Business InfoStructure, which includes Web servers, databases, middleware, application servers, and application supply providers (ASPs). Fingar, Kumar, and Sharma (2000) present a Ball model. It shows how e-business is becoming an infrastructure for changing a company's inward-focused business processes.

Synthesizing the previous research, a three-dimensional framework of the current digital platform can be identified. It consists of: 1) technological foundation or special technology capacities, 2) major applications for directly exploiting the technological capacities, and 3) deploying characteristics, i.e., unique features associated with further developing, deploying, and disrupting the technology foundation. The interaction among the three dimensions of the digital platform displays the novelty, diversity, and dynamic nature of the new platform (Lan, 2002).

The current technological foundation consists of several sets of technologies such as digitizing technology, networking technology, and authoring technology. The development of digitizing technologies dramatically increases computing power and offers possibilities for shifting business operations from a materials-based paradigm to an information-based paradigm (Shapiro & Varian, 1999; Lan, 2000). The development of networking technologies enables information exchange to enjoy unimaginable freedom, judged by bandwidth, connectivity, accessibility, and diversity. The development of authoring technologies provides solutions for changing interactions between an organization and its stakeholders by adding a virtual dimension, so that mass creation and decoupling of the front end and back end of an operation can be realized. These technologies determine either the capacity of the platform or the way it is functioning.

The applications of the new technology capacities display a spectrum. Within this spectrum, three usages are pervasive: digital messaging, digital transactions, and digital integration. All three are information oriented and can be measured by indicators such as scalability, reliability, hosting, storage, and security. One direct role of digital messaging is to reduce the existing asymmetry of information between buyers and sellers (Zott et al., 2000; Huizingh, 2002). Another role is to improve efficiency of coordinating activities and reduce operation costs (Clark & Fujimoto, 1991). The third role of digital messaging is to change peoples' behaviors towards information (Sawhney, 2001a) and decouple many traditionally bounded activities (Sawhney, 2001b).

Digital transactions are characterized by electronic payments and related information flows. The simplicity of the application either diminishes the spatial and temporal gaps in conducting transactions, or intensifies the battle for securing the transaction channel. Digital integration is reflected in structuring and restructuring activities, functions, and organizations. The vertical integration shows the changes of linkages along a value chain (Afuah, 2003). The horizontal integration shows the convergence of traditionally separated activities such as cultural activities and commercial activities (Mitchell, Inouye, & Blumenthal, 2003).

The realization of technological capacities and pervasive employment of these capacities bring new realities to the world such as virtuality, intelligence, and globalization. Virtuality means that products, services, or the delivery of these objects are not confined to their physical dimensions or material existence. Virtuality results from the digitization of activities and processes, and it follows a different set of rules in creation, exchange, delivery, and consumption of products and services (Shapiro & Varian, 1999; Gulati & Garino, 2000). Intelligence means that the operations of many activities can be conducted in a distributed, synchronized, or flexible way through capturing, retrieving, conveying, creating, processing, and distributing information. Intelligence is created through various decoupling processes, such as the decoupling of product and product information, delivery and delivery information, and the front end and back end of operations. Intelligence becomes fluid and no longer stays necessarily in where it was generated. It is mobile, modular, and processable (Sawhney, 2001b).

Globalization is one of network externalities exhibited. It means that the operational reach of an interface in the digital platform is without boundaries in the world. Global connections and unified networking protocols or standards make information distribution spontaneous. Easy access and the virtuality of operations enable interactions between different players continuously and ubiquitously. These faceless, stateless, and round-the-clock interactions, on one hand, are forces for homogeneity or scale economy by linking scattered niches. On the other hand, they are catalysts for creating or increasing conflicts by releasing various intrusions.

The Alaska Context

Alaska's economy is comparatively simple and small, as shown in Table 1. Petroleum has boosted Alaska's economy since the 1970s, peaked in 1988, and

Table 1. Alaska's gross state product 1988 and 1998 (ASTF, 2002)

Year	Total GSP Million in 1998 $	Government %	Infrastructure/ Support %	Other Basic Industries %	Petroleum %
1988	23,000	23	35	7	35
1998	22,500	24	42	13	21

has since been in decline. Other basic industries—e.g., seafood, tourism, logging, mining, air cargo, and agriculture—have contributed less to gross state product (GSP) than petroleum, but have created more jobs. Infrastructure and support industries—e.g., utilities, communications, trade, and service industry—have grown rapidly as Alaska's population has grown and its economy has matured. Government remains a large contributor to GSP. During the last decade, Alaska's growth in GSP has been low due to declines in the petroleum, fishing, and forest products industries. Alaska's average annual growth in real gross state product from 1993-2000 was negative 0.8%. Alaska's decline in real terms is attributed to declining oil production, the oil price slump in the late 1990s, and a decline in paper products due to pulp mill closures. Alaska's economy relies heavily on oil, and therefore fluctuations of oil price impacts Alaska's GSP significantly (most data used in this section comes from ASTF 2002).

Alaska is the biggest state by area in the United States of America, yet it has almost the smallest population, ranked 48 out of 50 states in 2001. In spite of its low population density, in 2000 Alaska was 74% urban (places with more than 2,500 people). Alaska's relatively stable population is aging and has been impacted by military personnel losses and less migration of young people to Alaska. With the overall population increasing by 14% over the 10-year period, Alaska's 25- to 34-year-old population declined by over 24,000 or 21%. Downsizing and restructure within the military, oil, fishing, and logging industries have also contributed to net emigration.

In 2001, Alaska ranked first out of 50 states in per capita federal expenditures, receiving $6.4 billion in total. The growth in federal spending from about $4 billion in 1992 to $6.4 billion in 2001 has helped offset declining petroleum revenues. Alaska was ranked fourth in the nation in median household income in 2000. Within Alaska, the Bristol Bay Borough had the highest per capita personal income ($42,238) due to commercial fishing; villages in the Wade Hampton Census Area had the lowest ($13,974). The state average is $29,642.

In 2001, Alaska's international export commodities were dominated by seafood ($1,190 million), minerals ($329 million), oil and gas ($297 million), fertilizer ($190 million), wood ($155 million), and other ($257 million). Overall exports are on the decline from $2,800 million in 1996 to less than $2,500 million in 2001. The sharp drop in manufactured commodities was primarily forest products. In contrast to the 1960-1990 period, Alaska's wage and salary employment growth in 1990-2000 lagged behind the rest of the nation. In 1995-2000, annual growth was only 61% of the national average. Government is the leading employer in Alaska, with 16,800 federal employees including military, 22,900 state, and 38,800 local government jobs (accounts for 27% in 2001). Services rank second with 73,000 employees, and trade is third with 58,200. Over the 1996-2001 period, Alaska's employment increased overall by about 26,400 jobs. The lower-paid services and miscellaneous sector had the largest increase (38%). The only bright spot in employment is the growth rate of technology industry jobs (36%). From 1994 to 2001, Alaska's technology jobs and total jobs increased from 9,050 to 12,353 and from 256, 829 to 287,938 respectively.

Another feature of Alaska's economy is that it does not follow the trend of the national economy. During the 1996-2001 time period, Alaska had only one new company (Alaska Communications Systems Group), and it held an initial public offering that raised $140 million. Only one company, livepostcard.com of Anchorage, received $3.5 million venture capital investment in 2000. While the national economy suffers from the crash of technology stocks, Alaska's economy continues to grow steadily.

Action Agenda for Followers

The Digital Opportunities Task Force (DOT Force), an international organization for promoting digital evolution in underdeveloped countries and regions, offers specific guidelines for followers and latecomers (DOT Force, 2001). According to the guidelines, strategy formation, access improvement, local content generation, and knowledge sharing are key elements in an action agenda for taking advantages of digital revolution.

In terms of strategy formation, the ideal model suggested by the DOT Force shows the following features:

1)   It should be the result of a consultative process involving all relevant interested parties in the region, including the private sector and non-profit organizations.

2)   Digital strategy should be regularly reviewed and updated, and benchmarked internationally.

3)   It should be reinforced by regional and sub-regional coordination efforts, notably in the context of economic integration.

Digital strategy formation should commit to the establishment of an enabling and pro-competitive regulatory policy framework. In addition, digital strategies should distinguish and recognize the importance of eGovernment for internal efficiency and effectiveness within a government. At the same time, eGovernance for institutional capacity building, transparent organizational structure, operational accountability, and the capability to enhance the democratic governance should be encouraged.

In terms of access improvement, the following items are important:

1) Multiple technologies should be allowed to compete for communications networks and services and access terminals.

2) The establishment of public and community ICT access points should be supported as a key means to facilitate timely, broad, affordable, and sustainable access to ICT.

3) Approaches that promote universal access for rural and remote areas should be pursued.

4) R&D efforts for the development and adaptation of cost-effective technologies suitable to meet local challenges should be encouraged.

In terms of supporting the creation of local content and applications, the following measures are recommended by DOT Force (2001):

1) to encourage the software community to include the open source, and commercial software communities to develop applications relevant to local context and localize software applications;

2) to encourage the growth of eGovernment as a means of achieving a critical mass of online content, and encouraging governments to provide widely available free-of-charge access to state-owned information and local content;

3) to encourage local content development, to translate into and/or adapt to local context to fulfill the needs of various learners, scholars, professionals, and citizens for education, learning, training, and application development;

4) to support national and international programs for digitizing and putting public content online, focusing on multilingual applications and local heritage;

5) to encourage networking of bodies which acquire, adapt, and distribute content on a non-commercial basis;

6)   to encourage commercial publishers to explore possible business models to enhance greater accessibility for poor people to relevant content, support university-based "networked centers of excellence," which are focusing on research and learning at the intersection of ICT and development;

7)   to foster enterprise and entrepreneurship for sustainable economic development. including incubation activities; and

8)   to encourage private-public partnerships involving companies, local entrepreneurs, governments, non-profit organizations, and labor organizations.

Research Methodology

Combining the features of the digital platform, current status of Alaska's economy, and actions needed for reaping digital opportunities, this research aims to examine the characteristics of Alaska in turning digital opportunities into a development force by exploring the Internet usage among different stakeholders in Alaska.

The research hypothesis is set up to display the linkage between the digital platform and online operation in a given region. It states that geographical limitations help Alaska embrace ICT and its applications without much hesitation, while the exploitation of full benefits of ICT is limited by available resources in a region like Alaska.

To test the hypothesis, a survey framework is developed with five measurements: 1) the Internet usage of government agencies, 2) of local communities, 3) of technology providers, 4) of other private firms, and 5) of individuals in Alaska. The measurement of the online usage of government agencies and local communities aims to check eStrategy formation and implementation, since they play important roles in setting infrastructure, improving access, and initiating digital activities. The measurement of online usage of technology providers aims to check either local roots of ICT technology, or the technological capacity of local content creation. The measurement of the online usage of individuals and private firms aims to examine the scope and depth of digital penetration in Alaska. A generic picture of embracing a new digital platform in Alaska can be painted through these examinations.

The information collection was conducted in three ways. First was a literature review, which collected and reviewed all available reports and government documents. Another was an individual survey, which aimed to find out the characteristics of online usage among Alaskans (about 200), such as usage in daily life, as well as the changes and considerations for the usage. The third was a large-scale Website analysis where more than 1,600 Alaskan websites were checked based on their functionalities.

Alaska's Online Operations

Technology Providers' Online Operations

As mentioned in the last section, Alaska's growth in GSP has declined during the last decade. Among a few bright spots is the growth of the technology industry. However, this technology platform is very small. For example, total technology jobs in Alaska were only 12,353 in 2002. Upon examining the structure of the technology industry, an imbalance can be seen, i.e., most expertise in Alaska is confined to the area of networking. Only 9% of jobs are directly related to digitizing technology.

Starting from the fact that Alaska ICT technology dimension is short and imbalanced; a survey was conducted to check the online activeness of ICT technology providers. In order to understand who provides information technology, what information technology is provided, and how information technology is provided, eight sectors listed in *Alaska Science & Technology Innovation Index* were selected. These include wireless phones, text messaging, online transactions, and so forth. By using specific SIC codes to search the Alaskan corporation database, 121 Alaska-based companies among the eight sectors

Table 2. Online activeness of Alaskan ICT technology providers

Sector	No. of firms	No. of firms with a website	% of firms with a website in the sector
Cable & other pay television services	12	3	25
Computer & data processing	42	6	14
Computer data services	5	5	100
Miscellaneous communication services	11	3	27
Research & testing services	11	2	18
Telegraph & other message communications	11	0	0
Telephone communications	31	6	19
Utilities services	3	3	100
Total	**121**	**28**	**23**

Source: Alaskan corporation database and websites analysis

were identified. After the company names were found, a systematic online survey was conducted through search engines and site analysis. Table 2 shows the sector distribution of these companies, as well as the Website usage among these firms.

It is apparent that computer and data processing, and telephone communications sectors have the majority of firms. However, most of them did not even have a Website. Added up, less than a quarter of ICT providers in Alaska had a Website. Among the 28 companies with websites, 23 are located in Anchorage, the largest city in Alaska. The other five are located in five small cities. Most of those websites only have a digital messaging function, and do not show much digital transaction and digital integration functionalities.

This imbalance of the technology sector and the poor Website usage show negative impacts on Alaska in two aspects. One is that it makes Alaska rely on outsourcing from other states for a majority of its digitizing services, and it limits local content development.

Private Firms' Usage of the Internet

Two measurements were carried out in the survey to understand the current state of businesses use of the electronic medium. The first is to examine the depth of the Internet usage among the top 100 private firms in Alaska. The second is to examine the width of the Internet usage among various firms, particularly small firms.

In terms of the examination of the top 100 private firms, information on the number of Web pages for each Website that businesses used to convey information, the number of links that other companies had to these websites (Google and AltaVista were the tools used for carrying out the investigation), and the recording of these websites' usage of messaging, transaction, and integration were collected, as shown in Table 3.

Of the 100 companies studied, only 54 were based in Alaska and the rest were based elsewhere throughout the country. The average size of Alaska-based companies' websites is much smaller than firms based in other states, and the number of links to designated websites is also smaller. The average Web pages per site for companies based in Alaska are 258, while it is 2,640 for firms based outside Alaska. The average external links per site based in Alaska are 92, while it is 555 for firms based outside Alaska. The size of a Website reflects its richness in the content, and the number of external linkages is a good indicator for measuring the exposure of a site on the World Wide Web.

In examining the Website usage of the top 100 companies in Alaska, messaging, transaction, and integration functionalities were checked. Three types of indica-

Table 3. Usage of Websites among the top 100 private companies in Alaska

Industry	No. of firms	Online marketing Online interaction				Online sale	Community formation	Intranet & extranet usage			
		Customize	Search	Point	Other	Yes	Yes	Intra	Extra	None	Both
Health Care/ Social Service	17	0%	3%	13%	1%	1%	12%	2%	2%	12%	1%
Air Carrier/Bus/ Shipping Service	13	5%	1%	5%	2%	8%	6%	2%	5%	6%	0%
Hotel/Eating Service	13	5%	5%	3%	0%	10%	6%	1%	1%	8%	3%
Oil/Gas Extraction	13	0%	3%	10%	0%	0%	5%	2%	4%	7%	0%
Seafood Processing	9	0%	2%	7%	0%	0%	5%	1%	2%	6%	0%
Grocery/General Merchandise	8	3%	0%	3%	2%	5%	4%	0%	2%	6%	0%
Hospital/Medical Center	6	1%	0%	5%	0%	0%	4%	0%	0%	5%	1%
Communication/ Public Utility	5	1%	1%	1%	2%	5%	3%	0%	0%	4%	1%
Building/Facility Construction	4	0%	1%	2%	1%	1%	2%	0%	0%	4%	0%
Pine/Mining	4	0%	0%	4%	0%	0%	2%	1%	0%	3%	0%
Banking/Credit Union	3	0%	2%	0%	1%	3%	2%	0%	2%	1%	0%
Department Store	2	0%	2%	0%	0%	2%	0%	0%	0%	2%	0%
Others	3	1%	0%	2%	0%	1%	1%	0%	1%	2%	0%
Total	100	16%	20%	55%	9%	36%	52%	9%	19%	66%	6%

Source: Websites analysis.

tors were used in the analysis of online messaging or marketing. "Point and click" is designated for websites that just have links to sort their information. It reflects a low level of messaging capacity. "Search and query" is labeled for websites that allowed users to search for the information they want to know about. It shows a medium level of messaging capacity and allows users to quickly find information. "Product/service customization" describes companies like Dell, where you can take their product and change it to fit your needs right on the Website. It shows the highest level of messaging capacity, and provides a vast quantity of information in a format that is easy to understand and navigate.

Table 4. Usage of the Internet in Alaska's small firms

Program	No. of firms	Email usage	Website usage
MIA	709	77.6%	31.5%
ASTF	31	46.4%	44.0%

Source: Alaskan corporation database and websites analysis.

Community formation, extranet, and intranet usage were used to measure the integration tendency of a company to link with its customers, partners, and employees.

The survey finds that high-end activities were used much less than low-end activities among the 100 top private firms. For example, in terms of online marketing, the percentage of websites that possessed high, medium, and low messaging capacity were respectively 16%, 20%, and 55%.

In order to overcome the bias in analysis of the 100 top private firms, a much larger scale examination on the usage of the Internet was undertaken, which targeted two programs. One is "Made in Alaska" (MIA). The other is technology sectors of certain importance to Alaska, listed by the Alaska Science & Technology Foundation (ASTF).

As shown in Table 4, 709 firms **were** selected from the MIA grogram, which consisted of 17 industries according to MIA's statistics. In addition, 31 firms were randomly selected from the ASTF technology sector listing, except sectors which were regarded as ICT providers, because they were covered previously.

The data shows a big market gap in the usage of the Internet for small Alaska firms. For example, in the arts & crafts industry of MIA, which accounts for about 40% of all the samples of the survey, 89% have email access, 28% have websites, and 22% have email and a Website. Out of the 28% of the websites, 35% have some sort of online marketing, and 28% have online transactions. The clothing & apparel industry (which has 192 small firms and accounts for 25% of the total samples) is not much better: 25% have email access, 24% have a Website, 70% of the 24% have online marketing, and only 7% have online transactions. In the Alaskan novelty wood products industry (which ranks number three and accounts for 9.1% of the total MIA samples), 48% have email, 27% have websites, and 1% have both; and out of the 27% that have websites, only 28% have online transaction functionality.

Usage of Government Websites

The Alaskan government's Website includes about 150 state government Web links. After the exploration of all the websites, 81 were selected in this research. The reason for this minimization was due to the unnecessary detail in which some departments were sub-divided.

To formulate a consistent guideline for checking the contents of the government websites, a simple five-criterium method was adopted in the survey. The five criteria were: 1) valuable information, which determines if the information in the Website gives viewers a clear picture of that department's main function, and the availability of that department's resources; 2) the amount of "filler" information, which in this study was defined as information located on the site that was invaluable to the citizens in terms of the function of that department; 3) existence of a mission statement on the homepage, which shows viewers what they feel is valuable and what services are provided; 4) the department's contact information on the homepage; and 5) the information orientation, which aims to find out if a site is more community oriented or focused more along the lines of a form of intranet for the department. If all of the criteria points were met, the site received a score of 5, which is the highest amount possible. Table 5 displays the results of the ranking of Alaska government websites based on these criteria.

The office of the Lieutenant Governor Website, www.gov.state.ak.us/ltgov, was filled with relevant information about the main function of that department. There was no "filler" information, and could be understood by the common man or woman. Another site that received high rank was the Alaska Commission on Judicial Conduct at www.ajc.state.ak.us/CONDUCT.htm. Not only did this site meet all five criteria, it added some additional factors. The amount of resource information was vast, ranging from what services they offer to the types of cases they can handle. This site included contact information for every court judge, statutes and laws that are valuable to the community, and other good examples of uses of the Internet. For example, the DMV's Website offers vehicle registration online, as well as allowing users to purchase fishing licenses over the Internet. The Department of Law Website allows you to send them legal questions or concerns, and you will receive a response via email for free.

Table 5. User-friendly ranking of Alaska government's Websites

Total sites	Ranking: 1 lowest and 5 highest				
	1	2	3	4	5
81	3	15	27	19	17

Source: Alaska government websites analysis.

On this grading scale, 18 sites scored below the average of 3, and three of the 18 sites received a score of 1, including The Department of Revenue/Tax Division site at www.tax.state.ak.us/#top . Many people have questions about their taxes on a daily basis, yet the Website is not user-friendly. The source of information is rather obscure and not relevant to the department's main function, which is not stated on the homepage.

Out of the 81 selected, only eight had online transaction capability. Users are able to purchase a variety of things online, such as fishing licenses, hunting licenses, personalized driving plates, land leases, mining rentals, vessel licenses, and Alaska railroad gift items. Most of the departments' websites allowed users to retrieve copies of applications or forms from their websites, but the user had to mail in the form with a check or money order.

Community Usage of the Internet

In order to obtain a complete picture of Internet usage in Alaska, a survey on varied communities was conducted. Only 6% of communities have a population of over 5,000 people, and of the 94% of small communities, 68% have a population that is less than 500 people. Considering the number of communities in Alaska, 90 were selected, which included all the larger cities and randomly selected smaller communities. The samples covered all locations and 95% of the population in Alaska.

In addition to checking the usage of community websites in marketing, transaction, and community formation for private firms and the government, special

Table 6. Online popularity and community size

Community size Population	<100	100-499	500-999	1,000-4,999	>=5,000
Community numbers	12	27	18	24	11
Average online name search results	2,555	2,301	13,615	23,768	29,504
% of websites with good online marketing ranking*	8	7	11	46	100

* Good online marketing means that many services are available online such as reservations, email contact information, visitor guest books, etc. The ranking is divided into good, fair, and poor.

Source: Websites analysis.

Table 7. Online popularity and community main business activity

Main business activity	Community no.	Average community name search hits	% of websites with good online marketing ranking*
Commercial fishing	23	11,648	13
Comprehensive	3	112,974	100
Fishing	5	7,606	80
Government	8	10,492	75
Local services	8	6,300	25
Logging	3	3,860	67
Military	2	806	50
Oil/gas/mining	11	19,262	33
Subsistence	10	1,602	0
Tourism	14	31,313	29
Transportation	6	4,033	0

* Good online marketing means that many services are available online such as reservations, email contact information, visitor guest books, etc. The ranking is divided into good, fair, and poor.

Source: Websites analysis.

attention was paid to checking online popularity of different communities. It was conducted by checking online search engines such as Google for full community name search. The number of hits was used to indicate its online exposure. Tables 6 and 7 summarize the relationships between the community size, main business activities, and Website usage.

It is apparent that the large communities in the state have the best Internet access and online usage. For example, no community in the state with a population over 1,000 got lower than a good grade on their online marketing, and every city over 5,000 received a rating of excellent. Some smaller cities did very well, but most of them received poor ratings. Some remote communities had no ISPs and no known Internet usage. In order to have Internet access, some have to dial long distance and pay as much as $6.00 an hour. Other communities are able to obtain Internet access through satellite dishes.

A community's main business did influence their online activities. Communities that had the government as their major business usually had higher online marketing scores. Communities that listed subsistence as an economic resource typically received a poor rating. Communities with a service-based economy were shown to have better Internet usage than communities with a fishing-based economy. Aside from fishing communities, most communities fit nicely into the above patterns of Internet use in Alaska.

Individual Usage of the Internet

To find the characteristics of online usage among Alaskans, various methods including personal interviews and questionnaire surveys were used to collect information. Some survey findings are presented in Table 8, which show some interesting features.

First, about two-thirds of responses indicate an increase in online shopping in the last four years. Alaskans are supportive of both B2B and B2C e-business enterprises. Individuals from rural areas indicated a larger increase in shopping on the Internet than those in the cities. The main reason quoted for this increase is that they are purchasing items that they cannot get locally. Many people who recently moved to Alaska shared the idea that a person in the continental U.S. views the Internet as a convenience, but a person who lives in Alaska views the Internet as a necessity.

Secondly, the usage of the Internet among Alaskans is quite wide. The average Alaskan is familiar with Internet use, shopping and conducting financial operations via the Internet. Most people are using the Internet for things like email, checking the latest news and information, and online shopping. However, only a very small proportion of the interviewees used the Internet as a means of entertainment. Another prominent observation is that online job searching is not

Table 8: Web usage among Alaskans

No. of people	Age group (%)	Online usage hours per week (%)	Changes of online shopping (%)	Areas of Web usage (%)	Special concerns (%)
191	<18, (4)	<7 (35)	Increase online shopping last 4 years (65%)	Communications (95%) Shopping (64%) Banking (35%) Business 25%	No concerns (30%)
	18-29 (36)	7-14 (20)			Security (42%)
	30-39 (30)	15-21 (10)		Research and information (25%)	
	40-49 (19)	>21 (35)	Decrease or no change online shopping last 4 years (35%)	Advertising (15%)	Privacy and spam (63%)
	50-59 (8)			News (15%)	Delivery and product return (23%)
	>=60 (3)			Entertainment (10%)	

Source: Individual surveys.

popular. It is reported by some interviewees that it might not be feasible for them to research or apply for some jobs due to isolated location.

Thirdly, individual Web usage in Alaska shows an even distribution in terms of time spent on the Internet. One-third of users spend less than one hour per day. Another one-third spent one to three hours per day, and the final one-third surfs the Internet over three hours per day. Although the time spent is different, a high loyalty to certain websites, such as eBay, Google, Amazon, CNN, and Yahoo, remains constant across categories.

Fourthly, there is not much hesitation for Alaskan buying online, although Alaskans do consider privacy and security to be an issue. About one-third of the Alaskans surveyed had no complaints about using the Internet. However, most of those surveyed stated that they hate getting spam mail and most of all hate pop-up ads. Another special consideration for Alaskans was delivery and product return, which is most likely a result of the geographical isolation.

Case Studies: Alaska's Embrace of Digital Opportunities

To support the discussion above, the authors provide three interesting cases here to reinforce Alaska's embrace of digital opportunities. The three cases introduced below not only showed that Alaskan government and business took advantage of the digital opportunities and have realized some substantial benefits.

Case 1: Issue Licenses Electronically via US West/ NBTEL by Alaska's Department of Fish and Game
(www.state.ak.us/adfg/adfghome.htm, www.admin.adfg.state.ak.us/ license/, and www.sf.adfg.state.ak.us/statewide/html/sf_home.htm)

This case study places much of the emphasis on the new technology that Alaska's Department of Fish and Game has recently put in place. This new technology, a combination of "US West e-Network platform and NBTel's Global Multi-Channel Web Server," will give residents and non-residents the ability to apply, obtain, and pay for "fishing, hunting, trapping, or commercial crew licenses," either with the use of a touchtone phone or through access to the Internet. Some of the advantages for both the agency and citizens of the state include, "the ability to be more convenient and accessible to the public" and "the expedited processes for the department and enforcement."

Case 2: Alaska Airlines' Usage of Mainframe to Take Advantage of the Digital Opportunities

(http://search.epnet.com/direct.asp?an=2501504&db=buh, http://www.cisco.com, and http://www.neonsys.com)

The problem focused on in this case study was "enabling Alaska Airlines customers to access and manage mileage plan data residing in an IMS environment on the corporate mainframe." Alaska Airlines quickly jumped into frequent flier miles when they were first introduced, but found the relay of information to their customers difficult and were faced with extremely high volumes of calls. Several major benefits and important effects to take advantage of digital opportunities include items such as: the mileage plan page allows members to check accounts, request mileage credits, redeem or debit mileage for tickets, make reservations for Alaska Airlines and Horizon Air flights, upgrade flights to first class using mileage credits, and even donate mileage to the Red Cross. In addition, new members can enroll via the site as well and locate information, guidelines, and a Q&A about all aspects of the plan. By allowing customers to access this information online, Alaska Airlines has reduced costs for the company by reducing the number of calls on the frequent flier mile plans, reducing the paperwork needed and allowing customers to determine the benefits they receive.

Furthermore, Alaska Airlines has also embarked on new programs that improve service and its relationships with customers and employees, while boosting performance and cutting costs. It has made embracing the Internet and using it to maximum advantage a priority. Alaska Airlines began using the Internet in 1995, established an e-commerce division in 1999, and was the first U.S. carrier to offer ticket purchase online. A multidisciplinary team identifies and develops Internet business opportunities. This company introduces online services for customers and employees in phases, based on potential gains.

One of the biggest advantages is its ability to allow the reader to see an overall picture of the company. The reader has the unique opportunity to grasp where the airline started technologically eight years ago, where they were two years ago and the depth of the services they offered, and what they'd like to see happen in the future with regards to e-commerce

Case 3: State of Alaska's Usage of Internet Application Form

(http://www.businesswire.com)

Each year more than 500,000 residents in the state of Alaska fill out time-consuming paperwork in order to receive dividend checks, an opportunity for the state to share some of the wealth that is generated through oil revenues. However, beginning in 2000 the state had plans to place the application online using PureEdge InternetForms, allowing the state's citizens to file online. Where in the past, the process had required 35 full-time seasonal employees to accomplish all the required work in four months, the new system would greatly reduce the timeframe and labor force needed, creating in the end happier citizens.

Several major benefits highlighted include: half of all state dividend applications will be filed online in the future, associated labor costs will be reduced by 50%, incomplete applications will be eliminated, error-free submission process, prompt acknowledgement of receipt, faster processing time, and the elimination of duplicate submissions.

Discussion: Features of Alaska's Responses to Digital Opportunities

The above usages of the Internet and /or digital opportunities are a snapshot of the collective efforts committed by all stakeholders in Alaska to realize and appreciate the digital opportunities. The survey finds that Alaska is very committed to transforming digital opportunities into a development force. However, the digital transition in Alaska is at various stages throughout the state. It is an ongoing process; three features of the process can be drawn from the current use of the Internet in Alaska. First, it benefits consumers instead of suppliers. Second, it is driven by the government instead of the private sector. Third, it is strong at basic components or lower levels, instead of having a balanced structure.

The current digital transition benefiting consumers instead of technological suppliers is reflected in the combination of the following facts: 1) broad individual usage of the Internet among Alaskans, 2) good operation of government websites, and 3) low engagement of local technology providers in the digitizing process. The survey finds that households and individual consumers benefit greatly from digital messaging and digital transactions. By using the Internet, Alaskans not only increase their purchasing power and their choice for products and services, but also obtain much more convenience and customer satisfaction. The survey also finds that Alaskans can easily access various services offered by the state and local governments through their websites. All of them directly contribute to the improvement of the quality of life in Alaska.

In contrast to the bright picture, technology providers' engagement in the digital transition in Alaska is very low. The Website analysis and literature review reveals that the overall base of ICT technology foundation in Alaska is very small, and its industrial structure is incomplete. Besides that, less than one-quarter of ICT technology providers are active online. The results indicate that local technology providers do not benefit much from the digital transition due to their size and capacity, and resource limitations.

The current digital transition, driven by government instead of the private sector, can be observed from their performances. The survey finds that there is a huge gap in Website usage among private firms, particularly small firms. Internet business offers an ideal medium for export-oriented operations to reach a large market. However, only 31.5% of surveyed firms have their own websites. The cases in the top 100 private firms also show a large development gap in their online operations. As shown in Table 3, a very low adoption rate is shown across many popular e-business practices. This limits the technology transfer from private firms to other identities in the digital transition process.

The Alaskan government's role in promoting digital transition is very prominent. Its dedication and commitment go beyond the suggestion of DOT Force. As early as 1996, the Alaskan government made its *Telecommunications and Information Technology Plan* with a statewide consultation. In the plan, the following goals and implementation timeline were set up: 1) improve public access to government information; 2) maximize service to the public through voice, video, and data systems; 3) increase government efficiency; 4) explore innovative and cost-effective services that meet Alaska's challenges; and 5) stimulate the development of private and public services. Based on the achievements during the previous several years, a more technical implementation-oriented plan was formulated in 2002. This plan paid more attention to improving the overall infrastructure for maximizing digital opportunity, particularly for the government.

In addition to making a plan, Alaska has paid much more attention to building a digital government for internal efficiency and effectiveness, as well as for institutional capacity building, transparency, accountability, and its ability to provide democratic governance. The previous online usage of the government has proven that their efforts are productive. Alaska ranked third overall in the 2000 survey, up from ninth in 1998. In the 2001 survey, Alaska regained its number one position in digital democracy. One of Alaska's significant accomplishments was the passage of a digital signature law that updates state statutes and codes to make digital signatures legally binding. In March 2002, the Progressive Policy Institute ranked Alaska sixth in the nation in their study, "The Best States for E-Commerce," which examined how state governments make it easy or difficult for their citizens to fully take advantage of the Internet to buy things, engage in legally binding transactions, and interact with government.

An imbalanced structure in the current digital transition can be observed from the fact that Alaska enjoys a high level of online access, but shows a low level of local content generation. Due to the infrastructure construction, Alaska enjoys a higher level connection rate among all households, as shown in Table 9. Online access as a whole and online access for school students in Alaska are both better than the national average. The number of people online is probably the most fundamental indication of a state's progress toward the digital economy. In 2000 Alaska ranked second in the nation in terms of percentage of households with Internet access, and second in the nation in terms of percentage of households with computers. In addition to online access, basic online existence, particularly for local communities, is well planned and well executed. The analysis on various community websites shows wide usage of messaging functionality of the digital platform and increasing publicity of the communities.

In contrast to the high level of online access, Alaska's achievements in developing local contents and applications are very limited, which can be seen from two perspectives. One is the lack of established local websites. Most websites used are those of national or international companies. The other perspective is that most local websites do not show functionalities beyond basic marketing or "broucheware," for which several reasons may be attributed. One is Alaska's weakness in generating new knowledge as shown by patent generation, a good indication of how active the idea creation process is. The second is the lack of expertise in software development. Thirdly, the generation of local application, the sharing of knowledge, and the facilitation of innovation did not appear or did not get enough attention on the agendas of stakeholders.

Table 9. Online access rates in Alaska

Items	Households with home Internet access %		Households with Computers %	
	1998	2000	1998	2000
Alaska	44	56	62	65
U.S. average	26	42	42	51

Source: U.S. Department of Commerce.

Given the features of Alaska's current digital transition, several issues have to be dealt with carefully in order to effectively turn digital opportunities into a development force. Firstly, it is important to accelerate technology transfer from the public sector to the private sector in the area of digital operations. The survey displays that the Alaskan Government possesses the capacity and expertise in developing applications, while the private sector is quite weak in this area. Releasing the power of government agencies in ICT would bridge the gap in a cost-effective way. Secondly, it is important to run certain programs for promoting the applications of e-business in the Alaskan private sector. Given the fact that two-thirds of small firms do not exist online, a large-scale promotion should be formulated. Thirdly, innovation has to be put into the agenda of embracing digital opportunities with a higher priority. The sound infrastructure and high rate of Internet connection offer opportunities for Alaskans to broadly participate in national and international business. To adopt such a new platform, both technological and managerial innovations are needed.

Conclusions

Great expectations for implementing and/or adopting e-business have grown at an incredible pace in Alaska since the late 1990s. This rapid advancement has led to significant progress in the development of the digitizing processes. This chapter conducts a preliminary assessment of the impacts of this digital transition process in Alaska by systematically examining the usage of the Internet in Alaska from five different players: 1) local information and communication technology providers, 2) top 100 private firms and a large quantity of small-size firms with different scopes of operations, 3) the state government, 4) local communities, and 5) individuals. About 200 users and more than 1,000 websites were interviewed and analyzed in this study. The findings indicate that Alaska is very committed to taking advantage of digital opportunities. Currently, the digital transition and adoption in Alaska is at various implementation stages throughout the state. Three features of the process can be identified. First, it benefits consumers instead of suppliers. Second, it is driven by the government instead of the private sector. Third, it is strong at basic components or lower levels, instead of having a balanced structure. Based on the survey findings, this research suggests handling the following issues in this manner: accelerating technology transfer from government agencies to the private sector in the area of digital operations, promoting e-business usage in small business, and setting innovation as a key item in the development agenda.

The assessment of the collective efforts committed by major Alaskan stakeholders presented in this chapter is only a snapshot. When it displays the digital transition from one aspect—online usage—it fails to analyze the internal mechanisms driving this transition due to the limited nature of research. To further promote this transition, in-depth research on the linkage of different components in the process is needed, in which the synergy of different factors can be better understood.

References

Afuah, A. (2003). Redefining firm boundaries in the face of the Internet: Are firms really shrinking? *The Academy of Management Review*, *28*(1), 34-53.

ASTF. (2002). *2002 Alaska Science & Technology Innovation Index*. Report of the Foundation Alaska Science & Technology Foundation (ASTF). Available online at: http://www.astf.org.

DOT Force. (2001). *Digital opportunities for all: Meeting the challenge.* Report of the Digital Opportunity Task Force (DOT Force). Available online at: http://www.dotforce.org./reports/DOT_Force_Report_V_5.0 h.html#ac.

Dunt, E., & Harper, I. (2002). E-commerce and the Australian economy. *The Economic Record, 78*(242), 327-342.

Evans, R. (2002). E-commerce, competitiveness and local and regional governance in Greater Manchester and Merseyside: A preliminary assessment. *Urban Studies*, *39*(5-6), 947-975.

Fingar, P., Kumar, H., & Sharma, T. (2000). *Enterprise e-commerce*. Tampa, FL: Meghan-Kiffer Press.

Gulati, R., & Garino, J. (2000). Get the right mix of bricks & clicks. *Harvard Business Review, 78*(5), 107-114.

Kalakota, R., & Robinson, M. (2001). *E-business 2.0: Roadmap for success*. Boston, MA: Addison-Wesley.

Lan, P. (2000). Changing production paradigm and the transformation of knowledge existing form. *International Journal of Technology Management*, *20*(1/2), 44-57.

Lan, P. (2002). An interface between digital platform and innovation progress. *Journal of E-Business, 2*(2). Available online at: http://www.ecob.iup.edu/jeb/.

Mitchell, W.J., Inouye, A.S., & Blumenthal, M.S. (Eds.). (2003). *Beyond productivity: Information, technology, innovation, and creativity.*

Committee on Information Technology and Creativity, National Research Council.

Mullaney, T.J., Green, H., Arndt, M., Robert, D., Hof, R.D., & Himelstein, L. (2003).The e-biz surprise. *BusinessWeek*, (May 12).

Panko, R.R. (2001). *Business data communications and networking* (3rd edition). Upper Saddle River, NJ: Prentice-Hall.

Rayport, J., & Jaworski, B. (2001). *E-commerce.* Boston, MA: McGraw-Hill/ Irwin.

Rosenburg, N. (1976). *Perspectives on technology.* London: Cambridge University Press.

Rosenburg, N. (1982). *Inside the black box: Technology and economics.* London: Cambridge University Press.

Sawhney, M. (2001a). Where value lives in a networked world. *Harvard Business Review, 79*(1), 79-86.

Sawhney, M. (2001b). Synchronization. *Harvard Business Review, 79*(7), 100-108.

Sawhney, M., & Prandelli, E. (2000). Communities of creation: Managing distributed innovation in turbulent markets. *California Management Review, 42*(4), 24-54.

Shapiro, C., & Varian, H.R. (1999). *Information rules: A strategic guide to the network economy.* Boston, MA: Harvard Business School Press.

Turban, E. et al. (1999). *Information technology for management (2nd ed.).* New York: John Wiley & Sons.

Chapter IX

Strategic Success Factors for Selling Content Online:
Which Success Factors will make Internet Content a Sustainable and Profitable Business?

Stephan A. Butscher
Simon, Kucher & Partners, UK

Frank Luby
Simon, Kucher & Partners, USA

Markus B. Hofer
Simon, Kucher & Partners, Germany

Abstract

In this chapter the authors provide an overview of strategic success factors for sustainable and profitable business with online content. Based on the practical experience of the authors gained in numerous consulting projects in this field, the chapter reveals that business success will depend fundamentally on the providers' ability to develop compelling and convenient new content forms of high quality that are easy to find and to buy. Another key factor is a sound integration of the product "content" in the overall business model, including realistic expectations regarding revenue streams. Furthermore, the conquest of new target markets is essential. Finally, they need to develop a sophisticated pricing strategy. The practical implications of the identified strategic success factors are illustrated by means of the case study, Selling Music Online, *and are summarized in concrete action guidelines.*

Introduction

Media companies, publishing houses, and portals—currently struggling with the broad-based downturn in the market for advertising—would love nothing more than to find a way to sell their content profitably to the vast online audience. Music publishers, film producers, sports teams, game designers, and other entertainers face the same challenge, though their situation is less precarious. The task sounds so deceptively simple: Get the product right, and get people to pay the right amount for it. But so few have succeeded in doing both, in part because the answers to these questions are quite complex. A wide range of psychological, technical, legal, creative, and marketing barriers currently hamper attempts to make money from content on the Internet.

Curiously, Old Economy companies have become quite adept at overcoming the same kinds of barriers. Just as the New Economy did not change the laws of economics and the nature of financial markets, they have also not changed the fundamentals of product development and marketing. This offers a glimmer of hope, and a wealth of expertise to draw upon, for companies looking to sell content online.

Over the past few years, we conducted numerous consulting projects related to these issues in Europe and the United States. The project work provided us with many opportunities to meet competitors, customers, and observers who participate actively in a market where Internet communication, mobile communication, and "premium content" are starting to meld together. As a result we gained valuable insights and a thorough understanding of the difficulties in selling content online.

Based on this experience, in this chapter we show concrete steps that companies can take to overcome the numerous problems and difficulties. Special focus will be put on business strategy and marketing issues. The chapter starts with an overview of the status quo of the content selling business on the Internet. We then provide a general introduction to the strategic success factors for sustainable and profitable business when selling content online. This includes a discussion of product characteristics to be considered, effective business models, the approach of new target markets, and pricing issues. The findings result from detailed analyses of practical applications and numerous discussions led in meetings with managers and marketers in the respective field. The implications of the previously discussed factors are then illustrated in detail by means of the case study, *Selling Music Online*. The next section includes main guidelines to be considered when starting a content selling business in the Internet. Finally, the main results are summarized and concluding remarks are made.

Difficulties of Selling Content Online Today

The frustrating thing about "premium content" is its simplicity. Our lives revolve around the content we buy. The physical manifestations become keepsakes or even collectibles with considerable emotional and monetary value. There are three reasons why the Internet can't do that.

First, the Internet has become synonymous with communication, not content. Revenue generated by the activity of the Internet's largest global content provider, a species called *Homo Contentus*, dwarfs the revenues earned by selling pre-packaged "premium content." What used to be called "correspondence" and "conversation" in simpler times is now referred to as "user-generated content." The Internet and the mobile phone have turned Homo Contentus into a publishing powerhouse. He writes countless emails and sends over one billion SMSs every day. Like his very name, his writings show a high tolerance for grammatical mistakes and word invention. He maintains his own homepage, where he publishes his own photos, videos, jokes, art, and music for the whole world to see. He chats tirelessly and sends instant messages to people he'll never meet personally. He posts his personal opinions on message boards and sends his criticisms to the websites of booksellers and auction houses. He can't remember the last time he licked a stamp. Keeping Homo Contentus happy and empowered will always be a crucial revenue source for ISPs and mobile phone carriers. Their growth and in some cases their survival depends on him.

Second, this focus on communication has relegated content to little more than a loss leader, which has fed an "everything-for-free" mentality. The *Wall Street Journal*, *The Economist*, *Playboy*, and Disney are high-profile exceptions, because they have charged for proprietary content in various forms and with various degrees of success. Companies in highly specialized and sensitive areas, such as personal dieting, have also entered the market. For most other companies, content has become their giveaway, available to all comers. This has fostered an expectation and, even worse, an appetite for free content which will take considerable time and effort to change.

Third, the market for premium content on the Internet is a vast, unexplored territory. For those who dare to try, pricing in the market currently depends more on gut feeling and guesswork than hard data. Product development is also driven by trial-and-error. Both on the creative side and technical side, we experience every day that the commercial Internet is still in its childhood. Television and radio have had decades to develop, film and the phonograph a whole century, and modern print media even longer. While they are capable of delivering high art in their own way, the Internet is struggling with the media equivalent of cave paintings and crude carvings.

To get online users to buy content as well as to generate it, providers will need to understand and meet a number of success factors.

Strategic Success Factors for Profitable Business with Online Content

Sellability of Content

Compelling Forms

If we wanted to merge the sentiments from observers in Europe and the United States into one sentence, it would sound like this: "To charge a fee for content, you need new products with entirely new content that is truly compelling, and that means things people have never seen before, never expected, or never assumed would be free."

The word "compelling" came up much more frequently in our discussions than the word "exclusive," which people generally consider to be the most important success factor for premium content. To develop compelling content, providers need to look well beyond the current spectrum of free content, and discover the shades and wavelengths we have not yet seen: new formats, new programming ideas, similar to CNN and MTV in the early days of cable television.

Much of this content can be drawn from forms of content we are already accustomed to paying for, but which have not yet been adapted to the online world. These include music concerts, which obviously lose their "live" character when shown on the Internet. The challenge is to use the clear advantages of the Internet—networking, nearly instantaneous two-way communication, low distribution costs—to make the online concert a unique product, not just a lame one-to-one copy of the transmission we would have seen on TV or in the arena. This kind of content reflects one important aspect of compelling, namely, the "wow, you've got to see this" feeling.

This feeling is rare nowadays. Who gets goosebumps on the Internet? We currently have as much emotional attachment to the open Internet as we do to our encyclopedias or old school books. That will change when these new forms emerge. Extra bandwidth will help, but this will remove only technical barriers, not creative ones. Content providers need to take advantage of this extra power to develop new forms and surprise us with compelling content, not just send bigger files faster through bigger pipes.

Convenient Forms

Stephen King's failed attempt to sell a novel online as a text file demonstrates why form matters as much as the actual content itself. When you only get Mr. King's words—a simple typed manuscript converted into a PDF file—you lose the comfort and ease-of-use of a printed book, a communication form perfected over centuries. Without this form, the novel is for most people no longer worth reading, much less paying for. The lesson in Stephen King's book is not that people are unwilling to pay for premium content. Rather, the lesson is that form is essential and that compelling content forms on the Internet are rare things indeed.

Form must also have a practical side. Premium content on the Internet must be easy to find and easy to buy. Charging for content can still work even if the content is not exclusive and also available elsewhere on the Internet for free, as long as the content provider can place that content prominently before the right audience. Like people who drive 20 miles out of their way to buy gasoline because the price is a few cents cheaper, there will always be Internet users who bypass websites that charge them for content. Some enjoy the sport of surfing for that very reason, because the free stuff is only a click away. This pervasive "free-of-charge" culture will not disappear overnight. It will take time to teach people to make the tradeoff of convenience and quality in exchange for money, and perceive that surfing is more work than it's worth.

How we access and pay for this content matters as well. Even in the Google era, surfing for content is work, and paying for it is often even more difficult. Oliver Samwer, a successful German Internet entrepreneur who currently is in the managing board of the company Jamba, estimates that at every time potential customers need to click on another icon or fill out another form on the Internet, around 30% of them give up and go elsewhere. If you're billing process requires lots of clicking and typing, you can be glad that anyone has the patience to make it to the end. Easy payment goes hand in hand with making content on the Internet a positive experience, which is easy to enjoy and easy to appreciate.

Effective Business Models

The first step to a realistic approach to premium content is to determine its role in your company's business model. For most companies, this model invariably involves some combination of access charges, usage, commissions, licensing, advertising revenue, and content sales. The balance between these elements is always shifting. Some years ago AOL depended on access and usage for more than 90% of its revenues. That amount has been reduced significantly. Despite its unrivaled access to film, music, news, and other content forms, AOL actually still realizes much of its revenue by helping *Homo Contentus* let his creative juices flow, either through email or instant messaging. In contrast, Yahoo traditionally earns more than 90% of its revenues from advertising, and companies such as Earthlink or T-Online still depend on access and usage charges for the bulk of their revenues, as do most mobile phone companies.

How the focus shifts can depend on a conscious decision or on external forces. When the downturn in online advertising revenue intensified, portals and other suppliers of content on the Internet learned something that their colleagues in the ink-and-paper world have known for years: revenue from fees and subscriptions tend to be more stable than revenues from advertising. The never-ending boom in advertising that was promised by the forecast factories two or three years ago never materialized. Even America Online's cross-selling muscle through the other AOL Time Warner properties was not enough to prevent their revenue from advertising and e-commerce from falling. The pain was greater at Yahoo! and was fatal for The Industry Standard, Germany's Net Business, and other colorful commentators of the dot.com era who have closed their doors because the advertising money has dried up.

The upshot is that companies who want to survive need a broad revenue basis. A company's vulnerability is a direct function of its dependence or narrow focus on a small number of revenue sources.

New Target Markets

Before the companies can create a sound offer, they need to understand the target segments and customize the benefits of their specific online content. The opportunities rest not only in the ability to serve a large number of customers at low cost, but also in greater access to smaller segments, which can be better cultivated and more economically served than currently possible. The potential for customization opens up possibilities for a finer segmentation based on customers' needs. In this context, content providers should not forget new opportunities resulting from partnerships with other media (ISPs, mobile phones, etc.) which have started to melt together. Customers increasingly will buy content following cross-promotions that in times of wireless Internet access by laptop and mobile phones are only clicks away.

A few conclusions about the market for premium content seem well supported. Creating the market will not involve simply charging money for the exact same content that used to be free. Restaurants would face a backlash if suddenly charging a few cents apiece for napkins and straws. Mass circulation magazines have learned that their websites serve as an effective trial subscription, and they will likely continue offering high-quality content free of charge. This means that topics with a "mass" following—general news, sports, weather, finance—will be supported by a large amount of familiar and free content. Earning money in these areas with today's content will be particularly difficult. But earning money with content has never been easy, because interest in a particular theme or subject is hard to translate into cash. Although The Wall Street Journal or Major League Baseball claim to have millions of visitors or sold paper versions, only a small fraction serves as paying customers for online services.

Another important point to state is that content providers must tap into a basic customer motivation. The best way to get people to pay for content online is to give them a clear reason to do so. The main motivations of Internet users fall into two categories: money and fun. Money itself encompasses two areas: saving it and making it. While not directly offering content for money, AOL has already worked these aspects into its communication to customers. The pop-up window that described AOL's recent price increase for unlimited service in the United States stressed that AOL plans to offer more "valuable benefits which help members save time and money." Right behind money on the list come "fun" aspects such as playing, laughing, and curiosity. NTT DoCoMo's i-mode service demonstrates that content does not need to be sophisticated or broadband to compel people to open their wallets. Simple games, ring tones, wallpaper or logos, and silly jokes are all unsophisticated, cost little, but can generate significant revenues. They are the ornaments that *Homo Contentus* uses to spice up his own communications. Customers in i-mode generate higher revenues than conventional mobile phone users, which can amount to a rather large pile of money when you have 25 million customers under contract. Germany's D2/Vodafone has learned from this and has introduced a range of downloadable games for mobile phones. Their high-profile advertising campaign shows they mean business.

A third but more nebulous aspect is community. Before its commercialization the Internet was essentially a loose network of niche communities—largely academic ones—exchanging their own content. Today the Internet is ideal for satisfying our basic need for interaction with other people and helps us discover others who share our interests. These niches can embrace many millions—such as people who want to lose weight—or thrive well outside the mainstream—such as people who collect snakes. The challenge is to define when such groups are large enough to have commercial potential, and when managing the community and providing its content generation is best left to the passions of *Homo Contentus*, who does the job for free.

Sophisticated Pricing Strategy

Pricing Model

Is $9.95 for 2,430 radio broadcasts an optimal price? You can't park your car at a ball park for $9.95, never mind watch a game or have a meal there. Even one actual baseball itself costs more than $9.95.

The lesson is that compelling content in the right form requires more support before it makes the cash register ring. You still need to determine how—and how much—to charge people for that content. There is no clear-cut recipe in this area. The choice of revenue model is both a strategic question for the individual company, as well as a direct result of customer input and reaction. In principle

Chart 1. Criteria of the successful revenue model

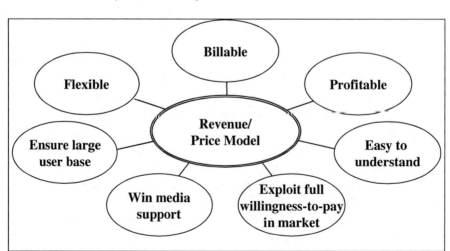

the revenue model must fulfill certain general criteria in order to be successful (see Chart 1).

As we have said over the last year in many different forums, pricing is a dangerous lever, and companies have little room for mistakes. This encompasses both the form and the price level. In terms of form, the dimensions are numerous. Should companies offer a subscription model, pay-per-use, or a combination? Should they offer a prepaid or postpaid model? Should they charge by time or volume? Should they subsidize hardware purchases? Because the market for premium content is so new, it lacks the anchor points and benchmarks that have accumulated over time in more mature markets. This does not mean, however, that content providers can feel free to ignore the knowledge from these mature markets.

One such insight concerns when to offer subscriptions and when to offer products on a per-use basis or with another kind of pricing model. While there is likewise no strict rule in this area, experience and common sense show that subscriptions are better suited for experienced users, not for those who are either beginning or who have had poor experiences in the past.

Price Structure

Let's say you want to watch a movie or play video games in a hotel room. Hotels will generally offer a teaser period of two to five minutes before asking you to commit to paying for a certain period of usage, usually 24 hours. Some charge for the period, others charge by the movie.

Now imagine that hotels abandoned their successful pay-per-use model and opted to follow the prevailing pricing wisdom for online premium content. Instead of a teaser and a one-time charge, we would be asked to commit to a whole year of hotel-movie-watching. Does that make sense? No, it doesn't. Nor would it make sense if sports teams offered only season tickets, but no tickets to individual games. But this is exactly what online content providers do when they confront their potential customers with subscription-only deals.

To optimize pricing means to optimize first the price structure and then the price levels. Let us focus first on the price structure, which offers many opportunities for differentiation. Several aspects need to be understood: What pricing elements matter most in the perception of the customer? Where will the customer's eye be drawn when he or she examines the offer? Would they pay more attention to one-off charges, a monthly fee, a price per download, a hardware subsidy, or some other element?

Those elements in the customers' focus require attractive prices to draw them in, while those outside the customers' main focus can be held at higher, less

attractive levels. The colorful mix of pricing elements in mobile telephony—
which range from one-off installation charges to monthly fees to per minute
charges (peak, off-peak, weekend) to billing intervals (full minutes, 10 seconds),
etc.—shows how many degrees of freedom such a complex pricing challenge
can present. In principle there are four alternative price structures, each with
certain advantages and disadvantages: a variable price per unit, a flat rate, a

Chart 2. Alternative price structures

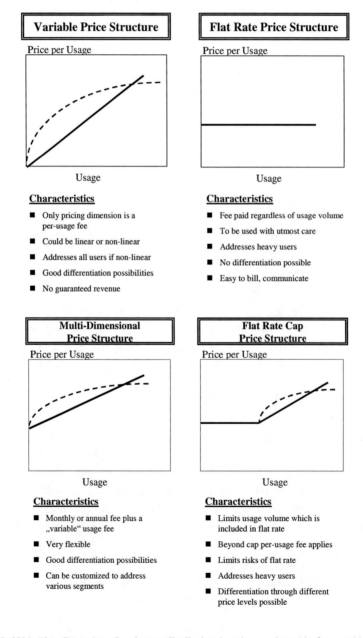

Variable Price Structure

Price per Usage

Usage

Characteristics

- Only pricing dimension is a per-usage fee
- Could be linear or non-linear
- Addresses all users if non-linear
- Good differentiation possibilities
- No guaranteed revenue

Flat Rate Price Structure

Price per Usage

Usage

Characteristics

- Fee paid regardless of usage volume
- To be used with utmost care
- Addresses heavy users
- No differentiation possible
- Easy to bill, communicate

Multi-Dimensional Price Structure

Price per Usage

Usage

Characteristics

- Monthly or annual fee plus a „variable" usage fee
- Very flexible
- Good differentiation possibilities
- Can be customized to address various segments

Flat Rate Cap Price Structure

Price per Usage

Usage

Characteristics

- Limits usage volume which is included in flat rate
- Beyond cap per-usage fee applies
- Limits risks of flat rate
- Addresses heavy users
- Differentiation through different price levels possible

combination of the two, or a flat rate with capped usage to keep costs under control (see Chart 2).

In many cases, neither per-download nor subscription—the two most obvious pricing structures—is ideal on its own. Depending on multiple membership tiers or service levels, a more intelligent pricing structure is required. Both components—subscription fee and pay-per-download—could be combined into multi-dimensional tariffs to avoid uneconomical usage while strengthening the relationship with the customer. Other pricing alternatives include bundling, price customization, and different types of volume discounts, all of which are designed to both manage and guide demand while optimizing profit.

Price Level

None of the pricing issues can be resolved without customer input. No matter how glorified content may become as a potential or revolutionary revenue source, it is still nothing more than a product. These products need prices that reflect their full value in the customer's eyes. Right now, pricing for online content is extraordinarily difficult because it is unexplored territory. There are few benchmarks, even fewer success stories, and hardly any empirical information to build on. It does seem clear that consumers are reluctant to commit to a subscription for online content before they have a positive experience with the content on a pay-per-use basis. All other information must be acquired on a product-by-product basis. In this constellation, input from customers—especially their views on value and price—give companies a firm basis for pricing decisions. Leave that part out, and the only other available method is trial-and-error.

Setting the right price level involves understanding how the customers perceive the features you are offering, and how much they are willing to pay for them. The benefits from many content forms we know disappear when they go online, as the example of Mr. King's novel showed. The words are still there, but the convenience and portability are gone. All of these features and benefits can be described in money terms.

The important thing to consider is: There is no difference when car companies determine whether and how much consumers will pay for more horsepower, more comfortable seats, telematic services, or certain styling features; then compare that information with the cost of developing them, and then the challenge that companies like Major League Baseball, AOL Time Warner, or Vivendi Universal face if they want to charge money for online content.

Case Study: Selling Music Online

When Napster made the headlines some years ago, it turned online music distribution into one of the most hotly debated issues in the news. Primarily the legal issues surrounding Napster and MP3.com have been focused on by the five major record labels at the beginning. Although these have not been finally settled yet, they worked on and tried to develop a workable online music distribution venture at the same time. Apple's iTunes Music Store and German Phonoline are first solutions for downloading music or MP3 files.

According to a study by Minneapolis-based Ipsos-Reid (see press release dated June 12, 2002), about one-fifth of the American population (aged 12 years and above) have used peer-to-peer file sharing service (Morpheus, Napster, AudioGalaxy, etc.) to download music or MP3 files. About four million users per day exchange 800 to 900 million pieces online—and that only using Kazaa (see FACTS, May 28, 2003).

But the market for online music distribution nonetheless remains in its infancy. The player who develops the keenest business model will have the best chance of taking this baby out of intensive care, providing it a nice home, and giving it the future it deserves.

Differentiation as Basis for Competitive Advantages

Three dimensions will determine the ultimate business models of these ventures: technology, legal issues, and marketing. The former two have held the spotlight over the last few months, as the Napsterites crusade on Capitol Hill showed. But marketing is the only area in which the players have a real opportunity for significant differentiation and for the creation of competitive advantages.

Technology will be standardized: Differentiation is nearly impossible, as all important technical solutions are currently available to all players. MusicNet— the platform created by RealNetworks, BMG, EMI, and Warner Music—can be licensed by any online outlet. The main format available for music files is .MP3. The (albeit slow) evolution of broadband will improve the possibilities of all players equally.

Legal issues will converge to universal licensing: Only a few ventures, namely MP3.com and MTV, have reached agreements with all five major labels. Duet (Sony and Universal's service) accounts for only about 37% of the world music market, MusicNet for about 39%. But let's be serious. No venture will be successful if it does not offer consumers access to the full range of music—and the labels and listeners know that. Key players in this market will need to offer very similar music catalogs to their customers, who often do not know or care about which labels publish their favorite artists.

Marketing is still virgin territory: Ironically, marketing is the only point where differentiation can succeed. With technology and legal issues progressing on a favorable path, at least for now, the record companies—and any other contenders for a piece of this market—must now invest the same level of energy and intensity into segmenting the market, developing the right products, and constructing the right revenue models. Two fundamental questions need to be answered: How do I bring value to the market, and how do I extract that value back through intelligent pricing?

Delivering Value to the Market

The question "Where's the value?" is closely linked to the question "What's the product?" Is the product really music? Is Tina Turner the real "product," or is it her studio recordings? What about the lyrics, the cover art, the song version, the file size, the sound quality, etc.? Answering these questions means understanding that any product is really a bundle of features, with in this case the music as one central element. The broad market of music listeners must be segmented in order to ensure that the right product bundles—those which maximize the perceived value for each segment—are created and offered.

A hardcore Lenny Kravitz fan will take advantage of the opportunity to download not only the latest Lenny Kravitz song, but also seek to download all upcoming new versions (unplugged, live) of the same song. Previously unreleased content or newly released versions of songs from the artist's earliest days—which may have too small an audience to warrant pressing a CD in commercial quantities—can be made available to all comers at minimal marginal cost. If you know that artists such as John Mellencamp record up to 25 new songs for an album, but only 10 make it in the end, you can imagine the largely untapped monetary opportunities these unreleased songs have within the Mellencamp fan community.

This desire among fans is nothing new, but it has remained largely outside the record companies' domains. Loyal fan communities of artists as diverse Bruce Springsteen and the Grateful Dead have been swapping bootleg concert tapes on the black market for nearly three decades, and fans of house music artists for nearly two decades. But these fans would now have the opportunity to gain access to more and better quality versions—all of it legal!

The same applies to niche markets such as blues. While most blues artists remain outside the mainstream, they all have hardcore followings who feel poorly served by mainstream record stores and would be willing to take their money online. Casual fans, in contrast, would appreciate a helping hand that guides them to certain songs and to other bands of the same genre. This segment may also include those who want to find an out-of-print nugget, but lack the time to search used record stores, cut-out bins, or flea markets.

The net benefit in all of these cases is nearly identical—someone gets a desired song—but the differences in perceived value are enormous. This leads to nearly endless opportunities for marketers to design relevant and exciting products.

Services Make the Real Difference

First things first: The online product has to provide high-quality downloads to distinguish itself from many of today's peer-to-peer exchanges. They may offer a wide range of files, but the sound quality and the completeness of the songs is highly unpredictable. Users only know the true quality of the desired track after they have downloaded and tested it. This is entirely unacceptable for a premium commercial offer from a reputable record company.

Furthermore, the network must have enough capacity so that customers will be able to log in at any time, and be robust enough so that customers can download files without disruptions or lost connections. Broadband connections will alleviate this problem to some degree, but the responsibility is primarily with the online venture.

But the real question concerns the "product" itself. Will all songs be available separately, or will some be available only on complete albums? Does this make the whole concept of the traditional pop album—which is really just a few singles and lots of filler—obsolete? In the Internet world, the only meaningful constraints are the capacity of the users' hard drives, the quality of their connections, and their ability to produce their own tapes or CDs. Finally freed from the constraints of vinyl and its successors, record companies can bundle music as they see fit in order to exploit customers' desires. Redefining these bundles attractively will be at the heart of any successful strategy for the online sale of music, because the possibilities—in terms of unit size, artists, genres, etc.—are nearly limitless.

In one sense, the vast file-sharing community has willingly taken on the production and distribution of music for the record companies, whether they like it or not. They hijacked Humpty Dumpty on his way to the record store, dragged him from the wall, and have swapped the fragments of egg shells ever since. They have unbundled and re-bundled them to fit their own needs. Allowed to thrive further, this trend will cement a major shift in power from suppliers to consumers.

Why? Without the bundles, we have the extreme situation in which every song is available as a separate unit. This creates a higher benefit for customers, for it allows them to fully customize their purchases. But it also effectively turns every song into a "single" which needs to survive on its own. What happens if just a tiny fraction of the songs account for the bulk of sales? Will this be the end of the 'fillers', which are, however, very popular with the true fan of an artist? Will the overall output of an artist be dramatically reduced? In this case, the Internet would prove a disaster for many. The record companies and artists have to weigh the outcomes here: higher costs for new releases on one hand, and higher benefits for customers on the other.

Online music ventures also have a wide range of possibilities to create additional revenue streams through totally new products for their customers:

- *Artist subscriptions:* A true Don Henley fan could subscribe to a special product that automatically sends new Don Henley songs or song versions to him via email. That way no time is spent on fruitless searches and the fan never misses anything. Of course the labels and artists would have to guarantee a regular flow of content, but especially for bands that have been around for several years, the files are full of material. Similar subscriptions could be offered for certain types of music (i.e., Latin American) or based on other value dimensions (i.e., #1 songs in Top 10 markets worldwide are automatically emailed). This also raises an intriguing question: If I want to subscribe to Don Henley, what role does the record company play? Do they become Don Henley's MSP (music service provider)? Or do they offer Mr. Henley's fans an array of value-added services which he cannot provide himself?

- *Taste matching:* Several companies have started to develop and fine-tune technology that helps to identify music tastes based on collaborative filtering, pattern analysis, music evaluation, and other techniques, in order to find out what other music could match a consumer's taste. While these technologies are not yet perfect, the idea of incorporating them into an online music distribution website in order to increase the site's cross-selling potential is very intriguing.

- *Mixing digital and physical:* Although the future will see wireless music-on-demand, current technologies such as the CD still have a role to play. Why not offer the customers a service in which they buy—or perhaps sample—individual tracks, decide how to compile them onto an album, and then have the CD produced and sent by the music company? Firs record stores already started to compile and burn CDs individually. The value-added is clear, in terms of time savings, quality control, and convenience.

- *Exclusivity:* A company could, for example, offer a special version of Beethoven's Ninth Symphony, played at the Vienna Festival, exclusively online to further differentiate between the channels. Companies could also make special bonus tracks available only to online subscribers.

The possibility for other services and product enhancements is nearly unlimited compared to CDs or old vinyl records. These range from cover art files, interviews (recorded and print), featured lyrics, previews of new songs, up-to-date notifications of tour dates, excerpts from tour magazines, the possibility to buy concert tickets and merchandise (posters, t-shirts, etc.), to interactive opportunities such as artist chats and review posting.

The ability to use other media as the basis of a product offer is an unexplored but potentially profitable territory for the record companies. From a technological standpoint, we are not all that far away from having listeners be able to hear a song on the radio, call their online music sales company on their Internet-compatible mobile phones, and order the song from wherever they are. This can happen spontaneously, or be promoted through sponsorship or cross-promotion. When next-generation mobile phone systems are launched, the carriers will be scrambling for high-traffic content. Working with them to promote online music sales could help both sides build their businesses.

Pricing Music Online

Forget Obvious Solutions Like Simple Subscriptions

Pricing will play a make-or-break role. If the record industry seizes the initiative and anchors the prices for online music sales at acceptable, sustainable, and profitable levels, it will strike a knock-out blow against the renegade systems and drive them to the margins. After all, studies by the record companies themselves and by independent sources such as Webnoize revealed that as many as three out of four Napster-type users would be willing to pay for a download offer in exchange for the assurance that they were not violating any laws. However, the danger is that the future major online distribution players like AOL Music, Duet, etc. will try to fight it out on the price dimension rather than the product and service dimension. Such a price war could ruin the profits of the entire music industry. Pricing is a dangerous lever, and the industry has little room for mistakes.

The two most discussed pricing elements for the record companies are a straightforward pay-per-download system and a flat subscription fee. A pay-per-download may hinder the companies in their efforts to gain a loyal user community and collect some valid data about it. Buyers who make separate purchases leave only a limited data trail. This makes Dell Computer an apt analogy for the record companies. One of the competitive advantages in Dell's business model is its unrivalled customer database gained through years of direct selling both on- and off-line.

A flat subscription fee might be more suitable, because it guarantees the record companies a stream of customer information. But watch out: Experience with pricing for Internet access shows that flat rates tend to attract heavy users who make up a small percentage of all customers, but block a large part of the available capacity. In the U.S., some 4% of AT&T's flat-rate users block 50% of the network resources, according to a company source.

In order to avoid such uneconomical usage and strengthen the customer relationship, a combination of subscription fee and pay-per-download, i.e., a multi-dimensional tariff, could be applied. Other pricing alternatives with the same objective include:

- *Bundling*, which fosters sales of products that might not seem too attractive when sold separately. Example: You can download Metallica's "S&M" at $14, or you can download "S&M" and another, older album together for $19.95. Or you buy the latest U2 single and receive future versions—live, unplugged, or maxi—automatically via email free of charge.

- *Multi-step discounts*, which encourage higher usage. Example: You can purchase your first 10 rap singles at $0.99 apiece, the next 10 singles at $0.79, and so on.

- *Price customization*, which is a useful tool to approach different segments in different ways. Example: To attract new users, a tariff with a low subscription and high per-download component makes sense, while heavy users are better served by a high subscription fee and low per-download fees. Once their usage surpasses a certain point, they are better off. The fencing between the segments, however, has to be supported by the product structure.

- *Stretch discounts*, which are designed to encourage a user to buy a marginal number of additional units in order to receive a certain bonus or discount. For example, if usage patterns reveal that someone buys three to four albums per month on a regular basis, they could be enticed to "stretch" to five albums, by being offered album six for free.

- *Bulk bundles*, which means that the basic monthly subscription fee includes the right to receive a certain number of songs or units automatically. The user then pays only for the songs or albums purchased beyond that basic amount. This model is common in mobile telephony in Europe, where a subscriber receives a fixed block of minutes per month for a regular fee, then pays only for minutes used beyond the fixed block.

How to Find the Magic Numbers

No matter how the record companies plan to get their money from customers, the big question still remains: How much will they be able to get? Good question. The main battleground for determining this answer is not the board room or the gut feeling of an experienced marketing executive, but in the field with the customers themselves. The revenue and profit at stake is not trivial, and to miss the optimal price levels by even just a few dimes means that tens of millions of dollars in profit are lost forever.

We would like to emphasize a point we made previously: If the music industry fails to act or sets the price anchors too low, prices will degenerate and gut the industry's profitability and stability. Pricing is a dangerous lever, and the industry has little room for mistakes.

One of the most important current trends working for the music industry is that there is a strong shift in nearly all online sectors away from giving content and products away for free or at heavily subsidized prices. These first attempts at business models have proven unsuccessful, and the remaining players are fighting hard to change the consumers' expectations and increase their willingness-to-pay.

The willingness-to-pay is of course closely linked to the benefits generated by the product. Herein lies the challenge for an offer for downloading music. The 'legal' ventures must differentiate themselves on the value-side vs. the Gnutella's of this world which are hard to beat in the courtroom. State-of-the-art research tools like conjoint measurement can measure those benefits and transform them into the underlying willingness-to-pay. It can isolate what various parts of the bundle are worth to the listeners.

The online music ventures should also not lose sight of the total cost from the consumer side. While customers may not always consider the travel, time, and research costs when they drive to the mall and spend $14.99 on a CD, they may be more sensitive to the additional—and transparent—costs incurred for downloading music. These include Internet access fees, hardware storage costs, online time, and so on, and not just the average cost per download.

Guidelines to Launch a Content-Based Online Business

Online ventures face huge marketing challenges. They must act quickly to optimize both the product and services they will offer, as well as the revenue model. To succeed, they need to:

1. *Segment their markets.* Not all customers can be treated the same. Identifying the most important segments is a must. Valid data will be crucial. Sophisticated research with state-of-the-art multivariate methods will provide indispensable insights that can be turned into a long-lasting strategic advantage.

2. *Start with the most promising segments.* Not every customer segment has to be served from the start. In order to get on the fast track to profitability, companies need to focus on those segments that hold a large enough potential to reach the critical mass that justifies large investments.

3. *Focus on premium quality offers.* Value for money. It's as simple as that. Premium products are an absolute must for the new services, because reliable, first-class quality is the one thing file-sharing pirates will never be able to deliver consistently.

4. *Develop sexy products.* The sale of content online is nearly constraint-free. It forces industries to think beyond its established borders and look for new products and services (bundles, additional services), as well as new partners (ISPs, mobile phone companies).

5. *Optimize the revenue models.* We are talking about multi-billion dollar markets at stake. This calls for a little more sophistication than mere subscription fees. A huge part of the potential profits will be generated by utilizing advanced pricing tools like stretch discounts. Neglecting those tools means sacrificing those profits. Not doing the necessary research most certainly means missing the optimal prices and giving away millions in profits.

Conclusion

Would-be content sellers will need to shift their thinking if they want online users to start shelling out money. *Homo Contentus*, who is already active online and who enjoys having high-quality information at his fingertips for free, earns his name not only because he creates his own content, but because he is also quite happy with the current arrangement. To get online users to spend money for purchasing content as well as to generate it, providers will need to understand various success factors. They will need to know how to get the product "content" right, then understand what role they want content to play in the business model. They need to describe and quantify their target market, and find the right pricing models and price levels to serve it profitably. If that sounds very Old Economy, it is. But that should be seen neither as a setback nor as a surrender. Realizing whatever potential the Internet has to sell content will require not just vision and creativity, but also discipline and rigor.

Considering the discussed strategic factors will help content providers to tackle successfully the challenges that they face when building their online businesses. The first point made was that business success will depend fundamentally on the providers' ability to develop compelling content forms which are of high quality and easy to handle, to find, and to buy. In contrast it is not necessary by all means to keep premium content exclusive. Second, it is important to integrate content into the overall business model. In doing so, expectations regarding revenues should be kept realistic. A third essential factor is the conquest of new target markets. Thereby it is important not to confuse interest with willingness-to-pay. In order to achieve the latter, content providers have to develop customer motivation by giving customers a clear reason to buy. What counts is to reach quickly a sustainable market size: The providers should start with the most promising customer segments that have a potential large enough to reach a critical mass which justifies large investments. Finally, selling content online requires a sophisticated pricing strategy. Pricing is a dangerous lever and there is little room for error. The definition of the optimal pricing model, with adequate price structure and level, should not result from guesswork but be based on customers' product preferences and willingness-to-pay. Furthermore, it has been proven to be effective in this context to apply advanced pricing tools like product bundles and different types of volume discounts.

We are now at a critical turning point in understanding what features need to be built into online content to make it valuable to customers and encourage them to buy it. The downturn in the New Economy has made the need for Internet companies to adopt old economy discipline and rigor all the more urgent. At the same time, content is poised to penetrate our lives to a greater degree than ever before—in our palms, in our cars, in our houses—as soon as somebody finds a way to make it compelling, make it useful, and make paying for it a no-brainer. The entire technical revolution of the last 20 years has been driven not by customers who bought things because they were possible, but because they were practical.

References

Albers, S. et al. (Eds.). (2000). *E-commerce. Einstieg, Strategie und Umsetzung im Unternehmen (2ⁿᵈ ed.)*. Frankfurt: FAZ-Institut.

Bilstein, F., & Luby, F. (2002). Casing America Online's faltering flat-price model. *The Wall Street Journal*, (December 10).

Butscher, S., & Luby, F. (2000). How to make the deal work. *The Wall Street Journal Europe*, (December 20).

Butscher, S., & Luby, F. (2001). Content, content everywhere.... *Business Online*, (July), 30-31.

Butscher, S., Luby, F., & Weber, A. (2001). *Selling music online.* Version 2. White paper. Bonn: Simon-Kucher & Partners.

Daum, J.H. (Ed.). (2002). *Intangible Assets oder die Kunst, Mehrwert zu schaffen. Mit Beiträgen von David P. Norton, Leif Edvinsson und Baruch Lev.* Bonn: Galileo-Press.

Eggers, B., & Hoppen, G. (2001). *Strategisches e-Commerce-Management. Erfolgsfaktoren für die Real Economy.* Wiesbaden: Gabler.

Hagel, J., & Singer, M. (1999). *Net worth.* Boston, MA: Harvard Business School Press.

Kelly, K. (1998). *New rules for the new economy: 10 radical strategies for a connected world.* New York: Viking.

Kröger, F. et al. (2001). *Ne(x)t Economy. Mit digitalen Geschäftsmodellen zum Erfolg.* Wiesbaden: Gabler.

Luby, F., & Tacke, G. (2002). Don't be afraid to make Internet content pay. *Financial Times*, (March 20).

Rother, S., Günter, L., & Butscher, S. (2001). Marketing und Management von content. *Information Management & Consulting, 16*(December 3), 55.

Schneider, D., & Schnetkamp, G. (2000). *E-markets. B2B-Strategien im Electronic Commerce.* Wiesbaden: Gabler.

Schreiber, G.A. (1998). *Electronic Commerce—Business in digitalen Medien. Geschäftsmodelle, Strategien, Umsetzung.* Neuwied: Luchterhand.

Shapiro, C., & Varian, H.R. (1998). *Information rules: A strategic guide to the network economy.* Boston, MA: Harvard Business School Press.

Silberer, G., Wohlfahrt, J., & Wilhelm, T. (Eds.). (2002). *Mobile Commerce. Grundlagen, Geschäftsmodelle, Erfolgsfaktoren.* Wiesbaden: Gabler.

Stolpmann, M. (2001). *Service und Support im Internet—intelligente Dienstleistungen—effizient zum Erfolg.* Bonn: Galileo Press.

Stone, M., & Butscher, S. (2002). Pricing the customer. *Database Marketing*, (December), 2-4.

Tacke, G., & Luby, F. (2000). *Selling content online.* White paper. Bonn: Simon-Kucher & Partners.

Whinston, A.B., Stahl, D.O., & Choi, S.-Y. (1997). *The economics of electronic commerce. The essential economics of doing business in the electronic marketplace.* Indianapolis, IN: Macmillan Technical Publ.

Wieder, G., & Hammer, C. (2003), *Internet-Geschäftsmodelle mit Rendite.* Bonn: Galileo Press.

Wirtz, B.W. (2001). *Electronic business (2nd ed.).* Wiesbaden: Gabler.

Zerdick, A. et al. (Eds.). (2001). *Die Internet-Ökonomie. Strategien für die digitale Wirtschaft (European Communication Council Report)* (3rd ed.). Berlin: Springer.

Zerdick, A. et al. (Eds.). (2003). *E- merging media.* Berlin: Springer.

Chapter X

Past Purchasing Behavior in E-Commerce:
The Impact on Intentions to Shop Online

TerryAnn Glandon
University of Texas at El Paso, USA

Christine M. Haynes
University of Texas at El Paso, USA

Abstract

As e-commerce becomes more competitive, it is increasingly important for Web vendors to understand why people choose to—or choose not to—buy online. Ajzen (1985, 1991) developed the Theory of Planned Behavior to predict and explain human behavior. The current study tests a modified form of the theory in an online shopping context. It is hypothesized that past online purchasing behavior will contribute toward explaining intentions to purchase online in the future, independent of the theory's original antecedents—attitude, subjective norm, and perceived behavioral control. Two-hundred-forty students from two universities completed a Web survey developed from an open-ended elicitation questionnaire. Results indicate that in addition to attitude, subjective norm, and perceived behavioral control, past purchasing behavior is directly related to intentions to shop online in the future. Adding past purchasing behavior also significantly improves the explanatory effect of the model. Unexpectedly, past behavior was independent of attitude and subjective norm, but interacted with perceived behavioral control. These results suggest that the challenge to Web vendors is to entice potential customers to try online shopping, as experienced shoppers quickly gain control and confidence in the online shopping process.

Introduction

Online shopping is attracting more consumers—Internet sales increased 46% during the year 2000. Nevertheless, during the same time period, more than 200 Internet firms ceased operations (Scott, 2001). As competition edges out inefficient firms, it becomes increasingly important for Web vendors to understand why people choose to—or choose not to—buy over the Internet.

For years, psychologists have recognized that understanding behavior is the first step toward influencing it (Fishbein & Ajzen, 1975). The Theory of Planned Behavior was designed to predict and explain human behavior in specific applied contexts (Ajzen, 1985, 1991). Recent research has indicated that the theory may provide a foundation for predicting future Web purchasing behavior (Pavlou & Chai, 2002; Limayem, Khalifa, & Frini, 2000). However, it remains unclear whether the theory's antecedents—attitude, subjective norm, and perceived behavioral control—are sufficient to fully understand behavior in an online purchasing context. As shoppers gain experience, the time, effort, and uncertainty associated with online shopping is reduced; thus, it is hypothesized that prior online purchasing behavior will directly influence intentions to shop online in the future, independent of attitude, subjective norm, and perceived behavioral control.

Marketing research has already established a link between past and future shopping behavior in traditional retail settings (Bellman, Lohse, & Johnson, 1999; Lilien, 1974) and industrial markets (Soderlund, Vilgon, & Gunnarsson, 2001). However, the effect of past behavior on consumers' intentions to purchase online has not been examined. In the current study, past online purchasing behavior was added as a fourth antecedent variable to the Theory of Planned Behavior to examine its impact on future online purchasing intentions. The addition of past purchasing behavior significantly improves the explanatory effect of the model. Furthermore, past purchasing behavior is directly related to intentions to shop online, independent of attitude and subjective norm. However, past purchasing behavior was found to moderate perceived behavioral control. This suggests that as consumers become familiar with online shopping, they perceive the process as easy, controllable, and simple to accomplish—it becomes a positive experience that is more likely to be repeated. Consequently, a major challenge for e-commerce vendors is to entice consumers to *try* online shopping so that they become comfortable with this new shopping experience.[1]

The remainder of this chapter is organized as follows. The second section reviews extant online shopping research. The third section develops the study's primary hypothesis. The fourth section describes the methodology used in the study. The fifth section relates results of the current study, while the final section discusses implications of these results, acknowledges limitations of the study, and offers suggestions for future research.

Literature Review

Although somewhat limited and fragmented, research addressing consumers' online purchasing behavior has begun to emerge. One area of research has examined obstacles to online shopping. Results indicate that consumers have several concerns about shopping online, including poor customer service, lack of Internet security, fear of having a credit card number stolen, and network reliability (Gefen, Karahanna, & Straub, 2003; Gefen & Straub, 2003; Gefen, 2000; Limayem et al., 2000; Cockburn & Wilson, 1999; Forrester Research, 1999; Salkin, 1999; Jarvenpaa & Todd, 1997).

In a separate line of research, factors affecting the length of website visits and features of vendor websites were studied. Raman and Leckenby (1998) found that consumers who attach utilitarian value to Web advertisements tend to spend longer periods of time at websites than do those who view advertisements as entertaining or intriguing. In addition, they concluded that Web browsing enjoyment is negatively related to time spent at any one site. They reasoned that consumers who frequently use the Web develop efficient navigation strategies and therefore do not need as much time at a particular site to obtain information. Another study examined certain elements of vendor websites. Srinivasan, Anderson, and Ponnavolu (2002) found that eight attributes of websites— customization, contact interactivity, cultivation, care, community, choice, conve- nience, and character—were all positively related to customer loyalty. Further- more, "e-loyalty" was positively related to word-of-mouth as well as a willing- ness to pay more for the product.

Finally, at least three studies have examined factors influencing the decision to buy online. In an exploratory study, Kovar, Burke, and Kovar (2000) asked open-ended questions to identify antecedents to online purchasing. Results indicated that several factors, including general attitudes toward online transactions, desire for personal contact, perceived convenience, perceived credibility of the site, and concerns about low information security, all affected consumers' decisions to purchase online.

Limayem et al. (2000) used a more theoretical approach to examine the factors that influence online shopping. Starting with the Theory of Planned Behavior (Ajzen, 1985, 1991), the authors developed a model to explain online purchasing intentions and behavior. The model included the three factors included in the original Theory of Planned Behavior—attitude, subjective norm, and perceived behavioral control—and two additional factors, personal innovativeness and perceived consequences. Results indicated that all five factors are strong indicators of behavioral intentions and that intentions significantly influence actual online shopping behavior.

Pavlou and Chai (2002) also relied on the Theory of Planned Behavior to examine cultural characteristics of Chinese and U.S. online shoppers. The authors found that culture moderates attitude, societal norm, and perceived behavioral control.[2]

Results from prior research suggest that although the Theory of Planned Behavior can be applied to an online shopping context, its antecedents may not be *sufficient* to fully explain Web purchasing behavior. The current study also begins with the Theory of Planned Behavior and examines whether another antecedent, past online purchasing behavior, adds to the theory's predictive value.

Theory and Hypothesis Development

The Theory of Planned Behavior

The Theory of Planned Behavior is a framework designed to predict and explain human behavior in specific contexts (Ajzen, 1985).[3] The theory maintains that a person's behavior will follow from his/her motivation (intention), if the behavior is under the person's volitional control (Ajzen, 1991). Intention, in turn, is a function of three factors: (1) the person's positive or negative evaluation toward performing the behavior (attitude), (2) the person's perceived pressure to perform or not perform the behavior (subjective norm), and (3) the person's perceptions that (s)he has the ability and resources to perform the behavior (perceived behavioral control). Figure 1 illustrates the relationship among behavior, intention, attitude, subjective norm, and perceived behavioral control. Mathematically, the Theory of Planned Behavior can be stated as follows:[4]

Behavior = Intention = w_1 (Attitude$_B$) + w_2 (Subjective Norm$_B$) +

   w_3 (Perceived Behavioral Control$_B$)   (1)

where,

w_i indicates weights that vary across people and contexts

$_B$ indicates the behavior

Each element of the model also has a specific meaning and mathematical definition.

Figure 1. Theory of planned behavior model

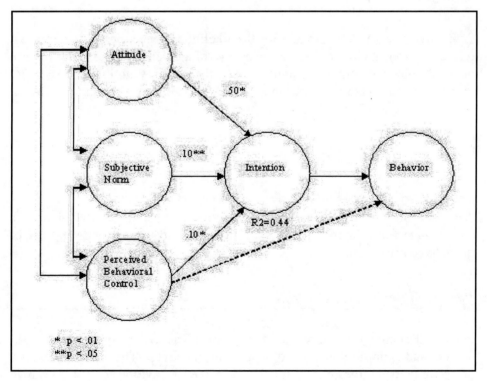

Based on Ajzen (1991, p. 182)

Attitude

Attitude is generally estimated by eliciting salient beliefs about the behavior and assessing the subjective probability associated with those beliefs. Thus, a person's attitude toward a given behavior is the sum of the products of the strength of the person's salient beliefs toward the behavior (b) and the person's subjective evaluation (e) of each belief. In other words:

$$\text{Attitude} = \sum_{i=1}^{n} b_i e_i \tag{2}$$

In general, if a person expects mostly favorable outcomes from a given behavior, (s)he will have a favorable attitude toward that behavior. If, on the other hand, a person expects mostly unfavorable outcomes, (s)he will hold a negative attitude (Harrison, Mykytyn, & Riemenschneider, 1997).

Subjective Norm

Subjective norm is concerned with the likelihood that a person's important reference groups will approve or disapprove of a given behavior. The strength of each subjective norm (n) is multiplied by the person's motivation to comply with the opinion of the reference group (m). The products are then summed. That is:

$$\text{Subjective Norm} = \sum_{i=1}^{n} n_i m_i \tag{3}$$

A measure of subjective norm is generally obtained by asking respondents to rate the extent to which important reference groups would approve or disapprove of the behavior in question.

Perceived Behavioral Control

Perceived behavioral control deals with the presence or absence of the resources and opportunities needed to perform a behavior. The fewer obstacles a person anticipates, the greater his or her perceived behavioral control. As shown in Equation (4), perceived behavioral control is measured by summing the product of each control belief (c) and the perceived power (p) of the control belief to facilitate or inhibit performance. In other words:

$$\text{Perceived Behavioral Control} = \sum_{i=1}^{n} c_i p_i \qquad (4)$$

Ideally, *actual* behavioral control would be measured instead of *perceived* behavioral control; however, actual behavioral control is difficult to operationalize. Accordingly, perceived behavioral control generally is used as a proxy (Ajzen, 1991).

The Role of Past Behavior

The Theory of Planned Behavior has been successful in predicting intentions and behavior in several contexts, including weight loss (Schifter & Ajzen, 1985), class attendance (Ajzen & Madden, 1986), and computer usage (Taylor & Todd, 1995). Nonetheless, some researchers have argued that *past behavior* should be included as an additional predictor of future behavior (Gefen, 2003; Ouellette & Wood, 1998; Fredericks & Dossett, 1983; Bentler & Speckart, 1979). These researchers maintain that past behavior is a surrogate for "habit"—a behavior that occurs automatically and without conscious thought.[5] They believe that past behavior (habit) has a significant effect on future behavior, *independent* of attitude, subjective norm, and perceived behavioral control (see Figure 2). In support of this argument, Ouellette and Wood (1998) conducted a meta-analytic synthesis of prior research and found that the effect of past behavior on later behavior was comparable with that of the other predictors of the Theory of Planned Behavior.

The underlying concept of habit formation is useful for understanding why past online purchasing behavior may affect intentions to purchase online in the future. According to Heckhausen and Beckmann (1990), performing a previously unlearned behavior requires consideration of how to initiate, implement, and terminate the action. This involves time and effort. Once the behavior becomes well-practiced, the time and effort needed to perform the action is minimized. Over time, the behavior becomes routine and unconscious, and a habit is formed. Thus, even though online shopping is not habitual for most shoppers, becoming experienced with the act (e.g., navigating the website, dealing with shopping carts, understanding site security, etc.) likely reduces the time, effort, and uncertainty associated with online shopping. As a result, past purchasing behavior is expected to be directly related to intentions to shop online in the future. This leads to the following hypothesis (stated in the alternate form):

Figure 2. Modified form of the theory of planned behavior model

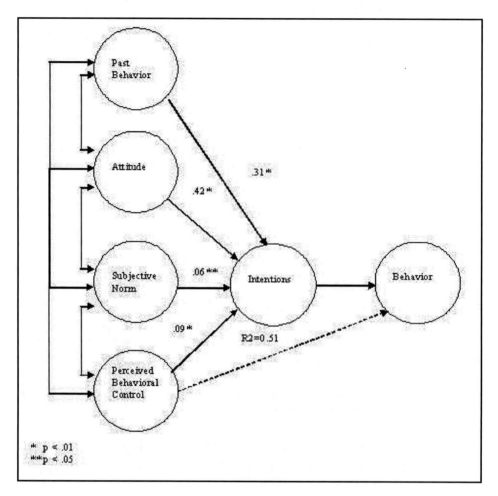

H$_a$:   Past purchasing behavior is directly related to intentions to shop online in the future, independent of attitude, subjective norm, and perceived behavioral control.

Methodology

The Sample

Two hundred forty college students from two universities participated in the study. Table 1 presents demographics of the participants. In total, participants

Table 1. Participant demographics

	Shoppers	Total
N	157	240
Male	50%	54%
Female	50%	46%
Minimum Age	18	18
Maximum Age	55	55
Average Age	26	25
Number of Times Shopped—Range	1-100	
Number of Times Shopped—Avg.	8	
Largest Online Purchase—Range	$10-$1000	
Largest Online Purchase—Avg.	$200	

ranged from 18 to 55 years of age, with an average age of 25 years. Fifty-four percent of the participants were male, while 46% were female. Of the 240 participants, 157 (65%) reported that they had shopped online in the past. To determine whether this sample of online shoppers is representative of the true population of online shoppers, separate demographics were calculated for participants who reported having shopped online in the past. Fifty percent of the "shopper" participants were male and 50% were female. This breakdown is similar to Princeton Survey Research Associates' 2002 report, which indicates 51% of online shoppers are male and 49% are female. Table 1 also reveals that "shopper" participants reported having shopped online an average of eight times in the past, with an average largest purchase of $200. This suggests that "shopper" participants are more than just casual website browsers. Furthermore, recent studies by Akhter (2003), Gibbs, Kraemer, and Dedrick (2003), and Joines, Scherer, and Scheufele (2003) all reported that most online shoppers are younger, with at least some college education. Gibbs et al. (2003) and Joines et al. (2003) also found that online shoppers are equally likely to be male or female. Accordingly, the "shopper" participants in the current study appear to provide an adequate proxy for the online shopping population.

The Instrument

To collect and measure the variables of interest, Ajzen and Fishbein (1980) suggest developing an elicitation survey to capture salient beliefs of the target sample. From those responses, a final survey is created and administered to a larger (and different) sample. This process has been organized succinctly by Mykytyn and Harrison (1993, p. 21) into six steps:[6]

1. Define the behavior of interest in terms of its action, target, context, and time elements.

2. Elicit perceived consequences of the behavior and social referents associated with it.

3. Choose the most often cited consequences and referents from the elicitation.

4. Create measures of behavioral beliefs, evaluations, normative beliefs, and motivations to comply, and control beliefs and perceived power.

5. Create measures of intention, attitude, subjective norm, and perceived behavioral control, all based on the earlier definition of the behavior of interest.

6. Integrate measures of all of these constructs into a single questionnaire and administer it to the sample in question.

The behavior of interest in the current research is the intention of individuals to shop online in the near future (within six months). There was no concern for a particular website, product, or service.

Elicitation Survey

For the initial survey, an open-ended questionnaire was developed to elicit salient consequences, referents, and resources or obstacles. After obtaining approval from the university's Institutional Review Board for Projects Involving Human Subjects (IRB), the initial survey was administered to 61 accounting majors enrolled in two upper-division accounting classes at a large university. The student population at the university consists of more mature, non-traditional students as well as traditional students. Almost all business students at the university work part time, and many are employed on a full-time basis. Responses listed most frequently were considered to be the most salient for the behavior in question and were retained for the final questionnaire. The responses were content analyzed by two raters who worked independently. Lacity and Janson (1994, p. 142) suggest that content analysis is a positivist approach to analyzing qualitative data. The positivist approach holds that understanding arises through the identification of non-random variation. This implies that frequency is an indicant of importance—the more a phenomenon occurs, the more likely it is non-random and thus important. Although causality cannot be inferred through this type of analysis, Weber (1990) asserts that it can be used to code the open-ended questions in an instrument such as an elicitation survey.

Final Survey

The final instrument was developed from the initial survey and posted on the university's website. It was approved by the university's IRB and pilot-tested by individuals who had not participated in the elicitation survey; no changes to the questionnaire were necessary. The target sample for the final questionnaire was composed of business students. Participants were enrolled at two universities; none were enrolled at the university where the elicitation survey was conducted. The demographics are similar at all three institutions. By completing the survey, student-participants earned extra credit points for an accounting course. To receive the points, they were instructed to print a certificate of completion after finishing the survey. JavaScript code was used to create and print a unique number on each certificate. Instructions on the certificate directed the student to fill in his or her name and submit to the class instructor for credit.

The survey measured: (1) intention to shop online; (2) a general measure of the Theory of Planned Behavior's primary constructs: attitude, subjective norm, and perceived behavioral control; (3) the underlying components of the three constructs; and (4) prior online purchasing behavior. A copy of the survey, describing each item and construct measure, is provided in the Appendix. The Web survey available to the participants did not include the description of the measurements.

Results

Preliminary Analyses

Internal consistency of the questionnaire items for each construct was tested using Cronbach's alpha. This technique focuses on the degree to which the same characteristic is being measured. For the current study, the reliability estimates (alpha) for each of the measures are as follows: behavioral intention ($r=0.92$), attitude ($r=0.92$), subjective norm ($r=0.87$), and perceived behavioral control ($r=0.80$). All of these values are above the recommended 0.70 levels.

The content validity of the survey instrument also was evaluated. Responses from a small group of potential shoppers were used to determine relevant obstacles, advantages, disadvantages, and social referents. Questionnaire items were developed from those responses to measure the underlying components of attitude, subjective norm, and perceived behavioral control in the final instrument. Harrison et al. (1997) advocate this process to ensure the content validity of the final survey instrument.

Table 2. Correlation matrix of average variance extracted (AVE) of principal components and descriptive statistics

Variable	BI	ATT	SN	PBC	PAST BEHAV
Panel A: Correlation Matrix					
Behavioral Intention (BI)	0.93[b]	0.63[a]	0.43[a]	0.45[a]	0.55[a]
Attitude (ATT)		0.92[b]	0.54[a]	0.46[a]	0.42[a]
Subjective Norm (SJ)			0.94[b]	0.37[a]	0.34[a]
Perceived Behavioral Control (PBC)				0.84[b]	0.44[a]
					1.00[b]
Panel B: Descriptive Statistics					
Mean (Scale: -3/+3)	-0.50	0.69	0.25	1.57	
Std. Deviation	1.88	1.18	1.62	1.30	

n=240
[a] Correlations between variables; all correlations are significant at p < 0.0001.
[b] Square root of each construct's AVE. Discriminant validity is indicated when the AVE of a construct is greater than its correlation with other constructs.

Discriminant and convergent validity of the questionnaire items were examined using exploratory factor analysis with an orthogonal (Varimax) rotation. All items load significantly on the three primary constructs; furthermore, all cross-loadings are far below the 0.40 benchmark. The three factors explain 82% of total variability.

Discriminant validity of the principal constructs was conducted using Partial Least Squares (PLS). Using the PLS method, discriminant validity is verified if the square root of each construct's Average Variance Extract (AVE) is larger than its correlations with other constructs (Chin, 1998). As shown in Table 2, Panel A, the square root of each variable's AVE is larger than all other cross-correlations. Table 2, Panel A also presents the correlation matrix of the principal constructs. According to the Theory of Planned Behavior, moderate to strong correlations are to be expected between behavioral intention and each of the independent variables (Fishbein & Azjen, 1975). As reported in Table 2, Panel A, correlations between behavioral intention and the primary constructs are moderate, except for a strong correlation between intention and attitude (r = 0.63). All correlations are significant at p<0.0001.

Analysis of the Hypothesis

PLS (PLS-Graph Version 3.0)[7] and multiple regression were both used to test the hypothesis. Some researchers argue that structural equation modeling is appropriate for analyzing the Theory of Planned Behavior (cf., Pavlou & Chai, 2002; Taylor & Todd, 1995), while others prefer multiple regression (Harrison et al., 1997; Ajzen, 1991; Mathieson, 1991). Both methods have advantages. Structural equation modeling uses the underlying questionnaire items in specifying the relationships among the primary constructs. As a result, the method simultaneously evaluates the acceptability of the hypothesized relationships as well as the relationship between the questionnaire items and the primary constructs. The primary advantage of multiple regression is that it allows for the evaluation of interactive effects among the independent variables.

Figure 1 (p.213) presents the PLS results for the original Theory of Planned Behavior. The PLS coefficients for all three constructs are statistically significant, thereby supporting the Theory of Planned Behavior in general (attitude b=0.50, p< 0.01; subjective norm b=0.10, p< 0.05; perceived behavioral control b=0.10, p< 0.01). However, according to Chin (1998), standardized path coefficients must be above 0.20 in order to be meaningful predictors of behavior. Attitude is the only construct in Figure 1 that exceeds this minimum standard.

Figure 2 (p.216) adds past purchasing behavior as an additional antecedent to the original model. As indicated by the figure, past purchasing behavior exceeds the 0.20 predictive meaningfulness criteria and also is significantly related to intentions to purchase in the future (b=0.31, p<0.01). In addition, as reported in Table 3, the model's adjusted R^2 increases from 0.44 to 0.51 when prior purchasing behavior is added. This change in R^2 is highly significant (F=33.57; p<0.001).

Taken together, these results indicate that knowing past purchasing behavior improves the predictive ability of the model. However, the hypothesis states that prior shopping behavior not only has a direct relationship with future intentions to shop, but also is independent of the theory's primary constructs. As an alternative hypothesis, past purchasing behavior might simply represent an additional antecedent to attitude.[8] Although the correlation between attitude and past purchasing behavior is not strong (0.42), a third PLS model was constructed in which past purchasing behavior was added as a precursor to attitude. The resulting R^2 drops from 0.51 down to its original level of 0.44. In addition, results of the multiple regression do not indicate a significant interactive effect between

Table 3. Analysis of predictors of behavioral intentions

Variable	Mean	b	t	p	Change in R-sq [a]	Adj. R^2	Adj. R^2
Attitude (ATT)	0.69	0.63	6.65	0.001	0.395		
Subjective Norm (SN)	0.25	0.09	2.80	0.084	0.014	.44	
Perceived Control (PBC)	1.57	0.10	0.33	0.741			
Past Behavior	0.67	2.03	4.91	0.000	0.061		.51*
Past Behavior * PBC		0.31	2.16	0.015	0.008		

n=240; [a] at successive stages of the modeling process.
* There was no measurable change in R^2 upon addition of the moderator term.

attitude and past purchasing behavior. Accordingly, past purchasing behavior does not moderate attitude. Finally, variance inflation factors did not reveal any problems with multicollinearity. The largest variance inflation factor was 1.6, far below a value of 10, which is the standard benchmark for the presence of multicollinearity (Neter, Kutner, Nachtsheim, & Wasserman, 1996). The sum of this evidence indicates that past purchasing behavior does not represent an additional antecedent to attitude, but is instead a fourth indicator of intentions to purchase online.

Although Table 3 does not indicate an interactive effect between attitude and past purchasing behavior, it does reveal that perceived behavioral control is moderated by past purchasing behavior (t=2.16, p<0.015). A graphical representation of the interaction (Figure 3) reveals that stronger perceived behavioral control is accompanied by stronger intentions to shop online. The effect is much more pronounced for shoppers than for non-shoppers, suggesting that prior shopping experience rapidly increases a person's belief that online shopping is easy, controllable, and simple to accomplish. In sum, the evidence from the current study supports the hypothesis that past purchasing behavior directly influences behavioral intentions, independent of attitude and subjective norm; however, it interacts with perceived behavioral control.

Figure 3. Interaction between perceived behavioral control and past purchasing behavior

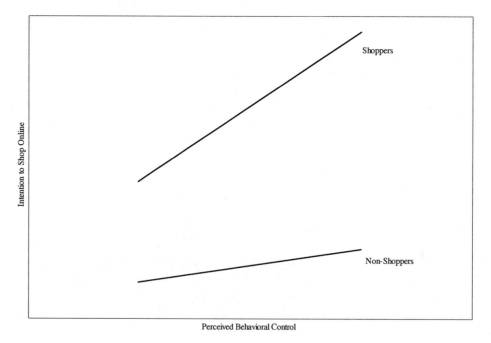

Conclusions

Implications

The purpose of this study was to examine the impact of past online purchasing behavior on intentions to purchase online in the future. The data support the Theory of Planned Behavior (Ajzen, 1985, 1991), with attitude explaining most of the variance in the model. Although subjective norm and perceived behavioral control are statistically significant factors in the PLS and regression models, their coefficients are small, suggesting they may not be good predictors of future online shopping intentions. The Theory of Planned Behavior postulates that all variables, other than attitude, subjective norm, and perceived behavioral control, are 'external' and are mediated by these three constructs. However, results of the current study indicate that past purchasing behavior also directly affects intentions to shop online and contributes to the explanatory power of the model. Furthermore, results indicate that past purchasing behavior moderates perceived behavioral control, suggesting that individuals who have shopped online in the past are more likely to respond that they have adequate control over the experience. As consumers become familiar with online shopping, they are likely to find it a positive experience to be repeated in the future. Thus, Web vendors may find it profitable to entice potential customers to *try* online shopping.

Limitations and Future Research

This study is subject to several limitations. First, the data were collected from self-reports. This data collection method increases the potential for inflated correlations between the dependent and independent variables due to common method variance, a limitation of the Theory of Planned Behavior (Ajzen, 1991). Second, the data in this study were correlational. The patterns observed are not sufficient to infer that the antecedents have causal influence on the decision to shop online. However, Ajzen (1988) reports many lab and field experiments of the theory that support the causal impact of these components on decisions.

Third, the study measured intentions, not actual behavior. Ajzen (1991) argues that a wealth of research has shown intentions to be highly correlated with actual behavior and, therefore, measuring actual behavior is not necessary. Furthermore, the online purchasing study by Limayen et al. (2000) found a strong correlation between intentions to purchase online and actual online purchasing behavior. For the current study, the initial plan included sending a follow-up survey to participants who provided their email addresses to ascertain whether their intentions had resulted in action. Unfortunately, only a few participants were willing to provide their email address and, accordingly, this part of the study could not be completed. In subsequent studies, researchers may want to consider some type of enticement to encourage participants to volunteer for follow-up interviews.

The study was restricted to university students in a single geographical region. Although 65% of the participants in this study actually had online shopping experience, non-students and/or persons outside the southwestern area of the United States may have responded to the survey differently. Thus, the generalizability of the final results remains unknown. Future studies may want to examine shopping habits of consumers not currently enrolled in college. Although the sample for the current study represents online shoppers in general, it is likely that non-student consumers have more disposable income and more leisure time. Without tuition payments or homework assignments, individuals may spend more time (and money) for both traditional and online shopping. Finally, national or international surveys may reveal other important characteristics in online shopping experiences that were not apparent in this study.

Endnotes

[1]   Amazon.com recently used this approach in its "Hard-Won Customer" promotion. The promotion consisted of mailing thousands of full-color brochures to individuals who had not yet purchased from the Internet bookstore; included was a $10 gift certificate to try their website.

[2]   Pavlou and Chai (2002) split subjective norm into societal norm and social influence to capture cultural differences between the two countries.

[3]   The Theory of Planned Behavior is an extension of the Theory of Reasoned Action, developed earlier by Fishbein and Ajzen (1975) and Ajzen and Fishbein (1980).

[4]   This discussion modeling the Theory of Planned Behavior is based on Ajzen (1991).

[5]   As an example of a habit, Ouellette and Wood (1998) refer to the act of automatically answering the telephone with a certain hand.

[6]   Mykytyn and Harrison (1993) created these steps for the Theory of Reasoned Action, a precursor to the Theory of Planned Behavior. The only difference between the Theory of Reasoned Action and the Theory of

Planned Behavior is that the latter model includes perceived behavioral control as an additional construct.

[7]   PLS was used as the structural equation modeling method because the small sample size precluded the use of LISREL (Pavlou & Chai, 2002). Similar results were found when AMOS was used.

[8]   We wish to thank an anonymous reviewer for this observation.

Acknowledgments

We would like to thank Lance Brouthers, Mo Adam Mahmood, and Rick Posthuma for their helpful comments and suggestions.

References

_____. (1988). *Attitudes, personality and behavior.* Chicago: Dorsey Press.

_____. (1991). The Theory of Planned Behavior. *Organizational Behavior and Human Decision Processes, 50,* 179-211.

_____ & Fishbein, M. (1980). *Understanding attitudes and predicting social behavior.* Englewood Cliffs, NJ: Prentice-Hall.

_____ & Madden, T.J. (1986). Prediction of goal-directed behavior: Attitudes, intentions, and perceived behavioral control. *Journal of Experimental Social Psychology, 22,* 453-474.

Ajzen, I. (1985). From intentions to actions: A theory of planned behavior. In J. Kuhl & J. Beckmann (Eds.), *Action control* (pp. 11-39). Berlin: Springer-Verlag.

Akhter, S.H. (2003). Digital divide and purchase intention: Why demographic psychology matters. *Journal of Economic Psychology, 24,* 321-327.

Bellman, S., Lohse, G.L., & Johnson, E.J. (1999). Predictors of online buying behavior. *Communications of the ACM, 42,* 32-38.

Bentler, P.M., & Speckart, G. (1979). Models of attitude-behavior relations. *Psychological Review, 86,* 452-464.

Chin, W. (1998). Issues and opinion on structural equation modeling. *MIS Quarterly, 22,* 7-16.

Cockburn, C., & Wilson, T. (1999). *Business use of the World Wide Web*. UK: Department Information Studies, University of Sheffield.

Fishbein, M., & Ajzen, I. (1975). *Belief, attitude, intention and behavior: An introduction to theory and research*. Reading, MA: Addison-Wesley.

Forrester Research. (1999, October 4). *Forrester Research.*

Fredricks, A.J., & Dossett, D.L. (1983). Attitude-behavior relations: A comparison of the Fishbein-Ajzen and the Bentler-Speckart Models. *Journal of Personality and Social Psychology, 45,* 501-512.

Gefen, D. (2000). E-commerce: The role of familiarity and trust. *Omega: The International Journal of Management Science, 28,* 725-737.

Gefen, D. (2003). TAM or just plain habit: A look at experienced online shoppers. *Journal of End User Computing, 15,* 1-13.

Gefen, D., & Straub, D. (2003). Managing user trust in B2C e-services. *e-Service Journal, 2,* 7-24.

Gefen, D., Karahanna, E., & Straub, D.W. (2003). Trust and TAM in online shopping: An integrated model. *MIS Quarterly, 27,* 51-90.

Gibbs, J., Kraemer, K.L., & Dedrick, J. (2003). Environment and policy factors shaping global e-commerce diffusion: A cross-country comparison. *The Information Society, 19,* 5-18.

Harrison, D.A., Mykytyn, Jr., P.P., & Riemenschneider, C.K. (1997). Executive decisions about adoption of information technology in small business: Theory and empirical tests. *Information Systems Research, 8,* 171-195.

Heckhausen, H., & Beckmann, J. (1990). Intentional action and action slips. *Psychological Review, 97,* 36-48.

Jarvenpaa, S.L., & Todd, P.A. (1997). Consumer reactions to electronic shopping on the World Wide Web. *International Journal of Electronic Commerce, 1,* 59-88.

Joines, J.L., Scherer, C.W., & Scheufele, D.A. (2003). Exploring motivations for consumer Web use and their implications for e-commerce. *Journal of Consumer Marketing, 20,* 90-108.

Kovar, S.E., Burke, K.G., & Kovar, B.R. (2000). Selling Webtrust: An exploratory examination of factors influencing consumers' decisions to use online distribution channels. *The Review of Accounting Information Systems, 4,* 39-52.

Lacity, M., & Janson, M. (1994). Understanding qualitative data: A framework of text analysis methods. *Journal of Management Information Systems, 11,* 137–155.

Lilien, G.L. (1974). A modified linear learning model of buyer behavior. *Management Science, 20,* 1027-1036.

Limayem, M., Khalifa, M., & Frini, A. (2000). What makes consumers buy from Internet? A longitudinal study of online shopping. *IEEE Transactions on Systems, Man, and Cybernetics—Part A: Systems and Humans, 30,* 421-432.

Mathieson, K. (1991). Predicting users intentions: Applying the Theory of Planned Behavior. *Information Systems Research, 2,* 173–191.

Mykytyn Jr., P.P., & Harrison, D.A. (1993). The application of the Theory of Reasoned Action to senior management and strategic information systems. *Information Resources Management Journal, 6,* 15-26.

Neter, J., Kutner, M.H., Nachtsheim, C.J., & Wasserman, W. (1996). *Applied linear statistical models* (4th edition) (pp. 386-387). Chicago: Irwin.

Ouellette, J.A., & Wood, W. (1998). Habit and intention in everyday life: The multiple processes by which past behavior predicts future behavior. *Psychological Bulletin, 124,* 54-74.

Pavlou, P.A., & Chai, L. (2002). What drives electronic commerce across cultures? A cross-cultural empirical investigation of the Theory of Planned Behavior. *Journal of Electronic Commerce, 3,* 240-253.

Princeton Survey Research Associates. (2002). A matter of trust: What users want from websites. *Consumer Webwatch News.* Retrieved July 26, 2003, from: http://www. consumerwebwatch.org/news/1_abstract.htm.

Raman, N.V., & Leckenby, J.D. (1998). Factors affecting consumers' "Webad" visits. *European Journal of Marketing, 32,* 737-748.

Salkin, S. (1999). Fear of buying. *Logistics Management and Distribution Report, 8,* 101-104.

Schifter, D.B., & Ajzen, I. (1985). Intention, perceived control, and weight loss: An application of the Theory of Planned Behavior. *Journal of Personality and Social Psychology, 49,* 843-851.

Scott, A. (2001). Online shopping on the rise. *Internal Auditing, 58,* 15-16.

Soderlund, M., Vilgon, M., & Gunnarsson, J. (2001). Predicting purchasing behavior on business-to-business markets. *European Journal of Marketing, 35,* 168-181.

Srinivasan, S., Anderson, R., & Ponnavolu, K. (2002). Customer loyalty in e-commerce: An exploration of its antecedents and consequences. *Journal of Retailing, 78,* 41-50.

Taylor, S., & Todd, P. (1995). Understanding information technology usage: A test of competing models. *Information Systems Research*, *6*, 144-176.

Weber, R. (1990). *Basic content analysis*. Newbury Park, CA: Sage Publications.

Appendix

Your response to the survey indicates you understand that records of your participation will be held strictly confidential and that your identity as a subject will not be disclosed to anyone beyond the investigators. Research at the University of XXXXXX that involves human subjects is carried out under the oversight of the Institutional Review Board. Phone: (###) ###-####.

Instructions: This survey consists of three sections—it should take you 10-15 minutes to complete. Please answer each question by selecting the best answer in the drop down box. Click the button at the bottom of the page to submit your answers. You will be given the opportunity to print out a "Certificate of Completion" at the end of the survey. *Thank you for your help!*

Behavioral Intention:

How **likely** is it that you will *purchase an item over the Internet* within the next six months?

- (Choices: Extremely unlikely/Quite unlikely/Slightly unlikely/Neither/Slightly likely/Quite likely/Extremely likely)

How **certain** are your plans to purchase an item over the Internet within the next six months?

- (Choices: Extremely certain I don't have plans/Quite certain I don't have plans/Slightly certain I don't have plans /Neither/Slightly certain I do have plans/Quite certain I do have plans/Extremely certain I do have plans)

My **commitment** to purchasing an item over the Internet in the next six months is...

- (Choices: Extremely weak/Quite weak/Slightly weak/Neither/Slightly strong/ Quite Strong/Extremely Strong)

General Measurement of Subjective Norm:

How likely is it that **most people who are important to you** would **strongly approve** of you purchasing an item over the Internet in the next six months?

- (Choices: Extremely unlikely/Quite unlikely/Slightly unlikely/Neither/Slightly likely/Quite likely/Extremely likely)

Most people who are important to you would:

- (Choices: Strongly disapprove/Somewhat disapprove/Slightly disapprove/ Neither/Slightly approve/Somewhat approve/Strongly approve)

General Measurement of Perceived Behavioral Control:

To purchase an item over the Internet in the next six months would be...

- (Choices: Extremely Difficult/Quite Difficult/Slightly Difficult/Neither/ Slightly Easy/Quite Easy/Extremely Easy)
- (Choices: Extremely difficult to control/Somewhat difficult to control/ Slightly difficult to control/Neither/Slightly under your control/Somewhat under your control/Definitely under your control)
- (Choices: Extremely complicated to accomplish/Quite complicated to accomplish/Slightly complicated to accomplish/Neither/Slightly simple to accomplish/Quite simple to accomplish/Extremely simple to accomplish)

General Measurement of Attitude:

Purchasing an item over the Internet would be...

- (Choices: Extremely bad/Quite bad/Slightly bad/Neither/Slightly good/ Quite good/Extremely good)
- (Choices: Extremely negative/Quite negative/Slightly negative/Neither/ Slightly positive/Quite positive/Extremely positive)
- (Choices: Extremely foolish/Quite foolish/Slightly foolish/Neither/Slightly wise/Quite wise/Extremely wise)

Underlying Beliefs of Subjective Norm:

Normative Beliefs:

How much would each of the following people approve or disapprove of you purchasing an item over the Internet in the next six months?

My family (example: parents, spouse or significant other, siblings) would

* (Choices: Strongly disapprove/Somewhat disapprove/Slightly disapprove/ Neither/Slightly approve/Somewhat approve/Strongly approve)

My friends would

* (Choices: Strongly disapprove/Somewhat disapprove/Slightly disapprove/ Neither/Slightly approve/Somewhat approve/Strongly approve)

Motivation to Comply:

IN GENERAL, how much do you usually do what your **family** thinks you should do?

* (Choices: Not at all/Somewhat/Very much)

IN GENERAL, how much do you usually do what your **friends** think you should do?

* (Choices: Not at all/Somewhat/Very much)

Underlying Beliefs of Perceived Behavioral Control:

Control Beliefs:

How LIKELY is it that you will have each of the following that would enable you to purchase an item over the Internet?

access to a computer

* (Choices: Extremely unlikely/Quite unlikely/Slightly unlikely/Neither/Slightly likely/Quite likely/Extremely likely)

access to the Internet

- (Choices: Extremely unlikely/Quite unlikely/Slightly unlikely/Neither/Slightly likely/Quite likely/Extremely likely)

credit card

- (Choices: Extremely unlikely/Quite unlikely/Slightly unlikely/Neither/Slightly likely/Quite likely/Extremely likely)

Perceived Power:

How IMPORTANT are each of the following with respect to making a purchase over the Internet?

access to a computer

- (Choices: Extremely unimportant/Quite unimportant/Slightly unimportant/ Neither/Slightly important/Quite important /Extremely important)

access to the Internet

- (Choices: Extremely unimportant/Quite unimportant/Slightly unimportant/ Neither/Slightly important/Quite important/Extremely important)

credit card

- (Choices: Extremely unimportant/Quite unimportant/Slightly unimportant/ Neither/Slightly important/Quite important/Extremely important)

Underlying Beliefs of Attitude:

Evaluative Beliefs:

Select the phrase that best expresses, IN GENERAL, how you feel about each item below.

Ability to shop from the comfort of home

- (Choices: Extremely bad/Quite bad/Slightly bad/Neither/Slightly good/ Quite good/Extremely good)

Saving time by shopping over Internet
- (Choices: Extremely bad/Quite bad/Slightly bad/Neither/Slightly good/ Quite good/Extremely good)

Ability to search for more choices
- (Choices: Extremely bad/Quite bad/Slightly bad/Neither/Slightly good/ Quite good/Extremely good)

Opportunity to get a better deal or cheaper price
- (Choices: Extremely bad/Quite bad/Slightly bad/Neither/Slightly good/ Quite good/Extremely good)

Behavioral beliefs:

The items in the list below all have to do with possible consequences or things you might associate with purchasing an item over the Internet. For each item, select the phrase that completes the statement in a way that best expresses **YOUR OPINION**.

If I purchase an item over the Internet in the next six months, it is...

...that shopping from home will be a comfortable experience
- (Choices: Extremely unlikely/Quite unlikely/Slightly unlikely/Neither/Slightly likely/Quite likely/Extremely likely)

...that I will save time shopping
- (Choices: Extremely unlikely/Quite unlikely/Slightly unlikely/Neither/Slightly likely/Quite likely/Extremely likely)

...that I will have the ability to search for more choices
- (Choices: Extremely unlikely/Quite unlikely/Slightly unlikely/Neither/Slightly likely/Quite likely/Extremely likely)

...that I will find a better deal/cheaper price

- (Choices: Extremely unlikely/Quite unlikely/Slightly unlikely/Neither/Slightly likely/Quite likely/Extremely likely)

Prior Online Purchasing Behavior:

Have you ever purchased anything over the Internet?

- (Choices: Yes/No)

If you answered YES to the previous question, approximately how many times have you purchased items over the Internet?_____

What was the largest dollar amount (approximate)? _____

Demographics:

A little information about you—please complete the following section for STATISTICAL PURPOSES ONLY.

Male ___ Female ___

Age ___

Would you be willing to answer 1 or 2 follow-up questions? If so, please enter your e-mail address here:_____

Thank you for completing this survey on Internet shopping! Please press the SUBMIT button to send your information and print your certificate of completion.

Chapter XI

Identifying Purchase Perceptions that Affect Consumers' Internet Buying

Thomas W. Dillon
James Madison University, USA

Harry L. Reif
James Madison University, USA

Abstract

This chapter examines how purchase perceptions influence consumers' Internet buying practices. Using traditional, pre-Internet era buying motivators as a starting point, a survey is developed specifically for Internet consumers. With the goal of developing a better understanding of Internet buyers, 16 influencers falling within four general categories— product perception, shopping experience, customer service, and consumer risk—are examined. Results are reported for each category and related to demographic variables. The survey instrument described in this chapter, along with the results of the survey, are important tools for furthering the understanding of the growth in electronic retailing. Successful electronic retailers, merchants, and e-commerce systems developers must understand

and acknowledge the effects that consumers' perceptions about the marketplace in general and about each vendor's website in particular play in consumer's decisions to buy or not to buy.

Introduction

Consumer buying practices traditionally are of interest to marketing professionals (Cox & Rich, 1964). With the advent of the Internet, traditional "brick-and-mortar" and catalog sales venues are being complemented by a global electronic selling arena. How well do the factors explaining consumers' buying in traditional venues explain consumers' behaviors in the Internet's e-commerce setting? Exploring what makes Internet customers satisfied is perhaps one of the most important challenges facing customer relationship managers in this decade. It is important because prior studies suggest that happy customers make repeat purchases and develop brand loyalty (Lee, Pi, Kwok, & Huynh, 2003). Shopping enjoyment, convenience in purchasing, and the product value (i.e., product quality and price) contribute significantly to the attainment of customer satisfaction (Lee et al., 2003; Liu, Arnett, Capella, & Taylor, 2001; Eastin, 2002).

The Internet environment differs significantly from traditional selling environments in that distance and time barriers are minimized or eliminated, supplemental and comparative product information is more easily obtained, and variables, such as pricing, can be changed dynamically. Accompanying these positive differences are potential problems created, in part, by the low cost-of-entry to the e-commerce marketplace and by the Internet technologies that enable e-commerce. Common problems include increased propensity for credit card fraud, product misrepresentation, unscrupulous sellers, and loss of buyers' privacy.

This chapter recaps 'brick-and-mortar' buying motivator explanatory analysis and uses it as the starting point for gaining an understanding of the role that Internet buyers' purchase perceptions have upon buying. This starting point is also the foundation for a questionnaire administered to e-commerce buyers to test whether traditional buying motivators also affect e-commerce buying. Not surprisingly, new buyer concerns are identified that have evolved simultaneously with the technology-enhanced e-commerce marketplace. These new concerns are classified into one of the existing four general purchase perception categories, and the accompanying statistical analysis justifying the validity of the results are presented. Additional analysis for the various demographics of the survey participants is presented as well.

The chapter concludes with an explanation of how these new findings can be applied to assist electronic retailers in understanding how to better package their offerings to positively influence prospective buyers to make purchases from their website.

Literature Review

Buyer behavior research has a long history, beginning with research about 'brick-and-mortar' types of purchases. Research into other non-store shopping methods (e.g., catalog and telemarketing) and, more recently, Internet purchases has extended the research base. There is continuity within the research, as evidenced by the continued presence of some of the same purchase perception factors over time as new methods have evolved. Nonetheless, O'Cass and Fenech (2003) caution that characteristics of shopping behaviors across non-store shopping methods are not necessarily consistent. They suggest that the perceptions underlying buyer behavior be reexamined independently for each shopping method.

This literature review considers purchase perceptions that affect all shopping methods, but emphasizes those that are most closely described as influencing Internet purchases.

Purchase-Perceptions

Perceptions believed to influence consumers' purchase decisions are extensively researched and documented in the context of traditional consumer behavior literature. Jarvenpaa and Todd (1996-97) cluster e-commerce purchase perceptions into four general categories: 1) Product Perception, 2) Shopping Experience, 3) Customer Service, and 4) Consumer Risk. Each of these four general factors contain multiple items which, taken together, form the basis for exploring how each of the four purchase perceptions apply to e-commerce purchases.

Product Perception

The three product perception items of price, product quality, and product variety are the most influential purchase perception issues cited in the literature (Arnold,

Handelman, & Tiger, 1996; Baker, Levy & Grewal, 1992; Cronin, 1996; Liao & Cheung, 2001).

Price is defined as the total monetary cost to the consumer for the purchase or the bargaining power available to the consumer (Bock & Uncles, 2002). New pricing strategies are being applied to goods and services sold over the Internet. Dynamic pricing, defined as a pricing strategy where prices change over time, based on buyer demographics, or across product bundles can be easily implemented and executed on the Internet (Kannan & Kopalle, 2001). This contrasts with conventional retail channels (Kannan & Kopalle, 2001) where pricing changes are traditionally performed only by specific product and maybe implemented over the course of days or weeks.

Product quality is defined as those distinguishing characteristics or traits inherent in the product or service that differentiate it from competitive product or service offerings (Cronin, 1996). For the purpose of clarifying this definition, *service* refers to the service that is being purchased and should not be confused with *customer service,* which is treated as a separate factor and is defined later in this chapter.

Product variety is the assortment of alternative and complementary goods available from the retailer. Product variety is important to shoppers because it provides them with the opportunity to compare, contrast, and select from among multiple potential solutions that meet their needs.

In a recent study, Lu and Lin (2002) developed a model to test the relationship between product equity and customer behavior. Product equity, used synonymously with value by other authors, is defined as a combination of quality and price that exists in the mind of the buyer. Their results indicate that customer behavior is influenced by belief about the product value.

Shopping Experience

The shopping experience is a mixture of effort (Baty & Lee, 1995), lifestyle compatibility or perceived convenience (Ratchford, Talukdar & Lee, 2001; Eastin, 2002), fun (Goldsmith, 2000), and playfulness (Liu et al., 2001; Hoffman & Novak, 1996, 1997). Web shopping compatibility, impulsiveness, satisfaction with websites, and shopping orientation are identified as positive influencers for the adoption of Internet technology for retail shopping (O'Cass & Fenech, 2003).

When engaged in e-commerce purchases over the Internet, effort is primarily a mental activity; shoppers work at their keyboard instead of having to plan for and travel to multiple shopping sites. For e-commerce shopping, the dominant components of effort are ease of use, coupled with the ease of placing and canceling orders (Eastin, 2002). These components may be described in terms of the time required to find and purchase products, the convenience of using the shopping engine or "shopping cart" as part of the purchasing process, and the availability of the desired products (Berkowitz, Walker & Walton, 1979; Bhatnagar, Misra & Rao, 2000; Swaminathan, Lepkowska-White, & Rao, 1999).

Lifestyle compatibility encompasses the buyer's lifestyle and shopping habits (Vellido, Lisboa & Meehan, 2000). The shopping tools must be easy to use and must provide the buyer with all of the information required to make a purchase decision. If ancillary support is required, such as telephone interaction to answer personal questions, the website must facilitate this linkage, and staff must be available to provide support. Extensive telephone wait times and lack of available staff negatively impact the buyer's perception of compatibility lifestyle. Research has found that those who have *not* made an e-commerce purchase categorize those who have made an e-commerce purchase as "nerds," suggesting that lifestyle compatibility is also affected by potential buyer's opinion of e-commerce buyers (Goldsmith & Bridges, 2000).

Playfulness and the perception of "fun" take into account the shopper's overall satisfaction with the shopping experience (Hoffman & Novak, 1996, 1997; Goldsmith, Bridges & Freiden, 2001; Lee et al., 2003). Playfulness is negatively affected by shopping sites that are cumbersome to navigate, insult the shopper's intelligence, or do anything to diminish the shopping experience. Unnecessary shopping time and the inability to locate in-stock products of the desired color and size are examples of occurrences that diminish the shopping experience (Bhatnagar, Misra & Rao, 2000).

Customer Service

Customer service affects purchase decisions through evidence of vendor knowledge, responsiveness, and reliability (Baker et al., 1992; Gefen, 2002). Liu and Arnett (2000) performed a factor analysis of six design quality features in order to determine factors associated with website success. Their findings show that two key customer service factors (service quality and reliability) influence Internet purchase behavior.

Vendor knowledge and responsiveness are embodied in the way that the service provider anticipates and responds promptly and effectively to customers' needs and requests, providing customers with the knowledge needed to make purchases (Jarvenpaa & Todd, 1996-97). An example of anticipating customers' needs occurs when a merchant clearly states which forms of payment are acceptable, and goes on to explain differences in expected delivery times and charges for different delivery options available to the customer.

Reliability occurs when the customer perceives that there is a high probability that the service provider will deliver all of what is promised in the agreed-upon time and at the agreed-upon price. Internet purchases present new challenges in this regard when compared with traditional 'brick-and-mortar' retail store purchases, because consumers do not have the opportunity to physically inspect goods on the Internet prior to purchasing them (Jarvenpaa & Todd, 1996-97). Instead, Internet purchasers must rely on mediated representations of the goods being purchased, are normally dependent on third parties for delivery of the purchased good, and may question the viability and convenience of a product return.

Consumer Risk

Consumer adoption of new retail innovations are influenced by perceived risks. Consumers must be able to trust (Huang, Keser, Leland, & Shachat, 2003) the Internet transaction and must perceive that trust in all risk dimensions—economic, privacy, personal (Simpson & Lakner, 1993), and performance (Jarvenpaa & Todd, 1996-97). Economic or financial risk encompasses monetary losses associated with poor purchase decisions, the inability to return a product, and the non-receipt of a product ordered (Perterson, Albaum & Ridgway, 1989; Bhatnagar, Misra & Rao, 2000).

Personal risk refers to the possibility that the consumer will be harmed or injured by either the product or the shopping process. Koyuncu and Lien (2003) found that shoppers that successfully seek out a secure shopping environment (i.e., their home) are disposed to order more from the Internet. Credit card security is cited as the predominant example of a personal risk inherent in e-commerce purchase transactions (Jarvenpaa & Todd, 1996-97; Goldsmith & Bridges, 2000; Liao & Cheung, 2001), with buyers exhibiting fears that their credit card information may be misappropriated or misused.

Privacy risk reflects the degree to which buyers may sacrifice their privacy when they are required to provide confidential information in the course of making retail e-commerce transactions (Bhatnagar, Misra, & Rao, 2000; Jarvenpaa & Todd, 1996-97; Vijayasarathy, 2002). Passwords, buying history, product preferences, home addresses, email addresses, and telephone numbers are all examples of private data often collected from the Internet.

Performance risk embodies the consumer's perception that a product or service may fail to meet expectations, the "fear of not getting what they want" (Cox & Rich, 1964).

Demographic Characteristics

Research into e-commerce purchases examines numerous demographic characteristics. Bhatnagar et al. (2000) include age, gender, marital status, and years on the Internet in a recent study on risk, convenience, and Internet shopping behavior. Their conclusions show that there are no effects on purchase behavior based upon marital status and find mixed results based upon gender (except for specific gender-related products), years on the Internet, and age. Other studies report that e-commerce purchasers are younger, more educated, and have higher incomes (Ratchford et al., 2001). A recent study finds that as many as 75% of those that shop via the Internet have not actually made an e-commerce purchase (Udo & Marquis, 2001-2002).

Method

Survey Instrument and Data Collection

A survey of e-commerce purchase perceptions is developed using the purchase perception literature previously presented. The survey originally consisted of 15 word/phrases related to general purchase perceptions representing the four determinants of the buying experience. To improve the survey's content validity, the 15 items were reviewed by a focus group of 14 e-commerce professionals. Some of the original phrases were revised, and three additional phrases were added. The final version of the survey contains 18 randomly listed items. Respondents were instructed to circle a number on a seven-point semantic distance scale to show how well they felt each word or phrase described an Internet purchase that they had made. The extremes are labeled "not at all" and "very influential."

In addition to purchase perceptions, the questionnaire includes demographic questions that identified respondent's age, gender, type of employment, occupation, estimated household income, level of education, and the number of children and adults in each household. There are also questions regarding computer ownership and the experience each respondent has using a computer and the Internet.

Data were collected from 190 adults living in Virginia, Maryland, Pennsylvania, and New Jersey. Data were collected by 19 college students who delivered and retrieved the self-administered questionnaires from field-worker-selected locations (shopping malls, neighborhoods, etc.). The self-administered questionnaire was completed without compensation and anonymously, with the exception of the voluntary collection of contact telephone numbers that were used solely for verification of the data collection process. Each student field-worker was assigned a flexible quota of 10 respondents to avoid survey bias, but since the field workers were located in a "college town," we expected a larger number of students for those respondents in their twenties, and we expected a larger number of respondents to be employed in education. Nineteen questionnaires were considered unusable do to erroneous or incomplete data.

Validity and Reliability

As previously noted, the original questionnaire items were drawn from the general purchase perceptions literature, in an effort to provide more reliable content validity for the selected variables. The 15 questionnaire items were reviewed by a focus group of e-commerce professionals for corrections, additions, and deletions. Eighteen scaled items reflecting product perception, shopping experience, customer service, and consumer risk were ultimately included on the survey.

The initial investigational factor validity was assessed by performing a factor analysis on the 18 product perception, shopping experience, customer service, and consumer risk scale items using principal component extraction and varimax rotation (Straub, 1989). The rotation converged in nine iterations identifying the four principle components with an Eigen value of at least 1. The four factors corresponded with the four purchase perceptions variables outlined in the literature (product perception, shopping experience, customer service, and consumer risk). Two scale items (*delivery time* and *acceptable payment method*) did not appear to be related to any one of the four purchase perception factors. One scale item (*amount of time spent shopping*) was evident in two factors.

The scale items that did not load on any of the four purchase perception factors were removed from further assessment, and a second factor analysis was performed. The scale item that loaded on two factors (*amount of time spent shopping*) remained. For the second factor analysis, limits were set to a maximum of four factors in order to force each word phase into each of the given multi-item factors. As predicted by the literature (Goldsmith, 2000), *amount of time spent shopping* loaded into the shopping experience factor.

As can be seen in Table 1, the 16 remaining scale items all loaded comfortably into the four purchase perception factors (i.e., customer service, shopping experience, consumer risk, and product perception). The customer service purchase perception factor contains the five scale items of vendor warranty/

Table 1. Construct validity (Factor analysis)

Scale Items	Customer Service	Shopping Experience	Consumer Risk	Product Perception
Vendor warranty/guarantee	.718		*	
Return policy	* .691			
Return convenience	* .686			
Product variety	.665			*
Product quantity	* .647			
Lifestyle compatibility		* .792		
Physical effort to shop		* .737		
Ease of shopping		* .662		
Enjoyable activity		* .700		
Shopping time		* .562		
Customer service/response	*		.805	
Vendor reliability	*		.794	
Confidentiality of data			* .710	
Credit card security			* .524	
Price				* .872
Quality				* .815

Notes: Asterisks indicate expected consumer purchase influencers. Factors evident below the .5 cutoff are not included in Table 1.

guarantee, return policy, return convenience, product variety, and product quantity. The shopping experience purchase perception factor contains the five scale items of lifestyle compatibility, physical effort to shop, ease of Internet shopping, enjoyable activity, and amount of time spent shopping. The four scale items contained in the consumer risk purchase perception are customer service/ responsiveness, vendor reliability, confidentiality of personal data, and credit card security. And finally, the product perception factor contains product price and product quality (an * appears where the consumer purchasing literature suggests each perception would be present).

Cronbach's alpha was used to assess inter-item reliability for each of the multi-item variables (Straub, 1989). As reported in Table 2, Cronbach's alphas were .8557 for product perception, .8486 for shopping experience, .8762 for customer

244 Dillon & Reif

Table 2. Inter-item reliability (Cronbach's alpha)

Variable	Alpha
Product perception	.8557
Shopping experience	.8486
Customer service	.8762
Consumer risk	.8610

service, and .8610 for consumer risk. These alpha scores exceed the .80 recommended in the literature for acceptable inter-item reliability, indicating that the factors within each multi-item variable are, in fact, inter-related (Straub, 1989).

Results

Analysis of Demographic Characteristics

The demographic distributions of the responding sample are presented in Table 3. As a consequence of the flexible quota, younger consumers, those employed in education, and those of higher educational and socio-economic status are somewhat more strongly represented in comparison to the public at large. The distribution also indicates a higher than expected response rate for home computer ownership that is attributed to the nature of the sample's demographics. The sample is evenly distributed between genders.

As with the demographics, the flexible quota allows the sample to include an increased number of long-term computer and Internet users. The mode response for the question determining the years of experience each respondent has using a computer is between six and 10 years, and the mode response for the years of experience each respondent has using the Internet is between four and six years.

For the two open-ended questions concerning years of computer experience and years of Internet experience, respondents simply record the number of years for each. For presentation in Table 4, responses are clustered into five-year intervals for years of computer experience and three-year intervals for years of Internet experience. Surprisingly, five respondents self-reported years of computer experience exceeding 25 years, and 19 respondents self-report 10 or more years

Copyright © 2005, Idea Group Inc. Copying or distributing in print or electronic forms without written permission of Idea Group Inc. is prohibited.

Table 3. Demographic distributions of responding sample

Characteristic	Num (%)	Characteristic	Num (%)
Age		**No. of children**	
Twenties	32(18.7)	**in the Household**	
Thirties	39(22.2)	Zero	104(60.8)
Forties	35(20.5)	One	42(24.6)
Fifties	37(21.6)	Two	20(11.7)
Sixty and over	28(16.4)	Three or more	5(2.9)
Gender		**Own a Computer**	
Male	84(49.1)	Yes	147(86.0)
Female	87(50.9)	No	24(14.0)
Type of		**Occupation**	
Employment		Professional	56(32.7)
Seeking	2(1.2)	Executive/manage	15(8.8)
Company	39(22.8)	Engineer/technical	10(5.8)
Education	41(24.0)	Clerical	15(8.8)
Government	17(9.9)	Sales/marketing	6(3.5)
Self-employed	15(8.8)	Skilled craft/trade	7(4.1)
Student	31(18.1)	Semi-skilled	3(1.8)
Homemaker	8(4.7)	Military	4(2.3)
Retired	18(10.5)	Homemaker	5(2.9)
		Retired	14(8.2)
		Student	29(17.0)
		Other	7(4.1)
Household		**Level of**	
Income	16(9.4)	**Education**	
Under $20,000	20(11.7)	Some high school	1(.6)
$20,000 to 39,000	29(17.0)	H.S. graduate	22(12.9)
$40,000 to 59,000	29(17.0)	Some college	48(28.1)
$60,000 to 79,000	20(11.7)	College graduate	51(29.8)
$80,000 to 99,000	28(16.4)	Post graduate	49(28.7)
$100,000 and	28(16.4)		
over			
refused			
No. of Adults in			
the Household			
One	23(13.3)		
Two	90(52.5)		
Three	31(18.0)		
Four or more	28(16.2)		

of Internet experience. Nine respondents report never having used a computer at home or at work, and 15 respondents report never having used the Internet.

In an attempt to isolate the overall demographic characteristics most likely to influence purchases over the Internet, we ran two regressions, one for the categorical variables (age, gender, type of employment, occupation, estimated household income, level of education, number of adults in the household, number of children in the household, and home computer ownership) and a second for the continuous variables (number of years of computer ownership and number of years of Internet use). Table 5 presents the result of both regression analyses. Three demographic characteristics reported in Table 5 presented as significant influencers of e-commerce purchases (i.e., age, level of education, and number

Table 4. Years of computer and Internet use

Years of Computer Use	Number(%)	Years of Internet Use	Number(%)
Never used	9(5.3)	Never used	15(8.8)
1 to 5	38(22.2)	1 to 3	31(18.1)
6 to 10	53(31.0)	4 to 6	90(52.7)
11 to 15	39(22.8)	7 to 9	16(9.4)
16 to 20	20(11.8)	10 to 12	17(9.9)
21 to 25	7(4.2)	13 to 15	2(1.2)
26 to 30	3(1.8)		
31 to 40	2(1.2)		

Table 5. Categorical demographic influencers of Internet purchases

Demographic Characteristic	B	Std. Error	Beta	t	Sig.
Age	-.253	.066	-.322	-3.844	*.000
Type of Employment	-.069	.053	-.131	-1.303	.194
Level of Education	.174	.087	.168	2.014	*.046
Gender	-.054	.154	-.025	-.349	.728
Occupation	-.007	.029	-.028	-.244	.808
Est. Income Range	.010	.041	.018	.245	.807
No. Adults/Household	.023	.078	.024	.297	.767
No. Child/Household	.152	.088	.128	1.736	.085
Computer Ownership	.050	.174	.021	.285	.776
Yrs. of Computer Use	.002	.013	.013	.144	.886
Yrs. of Internet Use	.096	.032	.271	3.040	*.003

* *Significant influencer of Internet purchases.*

of years of Internet use). The negative relationship for age suggests that younger, as opposed to older, consumers are more likely to make an Internet purchase. The positive relationship for level of education shows that consumers with higher levels of education are more likely to make Internet purchases. In addition, the longer a consumer has been using the Internet, the more likely he or she is to buy an item via the Internet.

Interestingly, the number of children in the household appears to be close to significant as an influencer of Internet buying. In casual conversations with colleagues that have multiple young children, many remark that the Internet is the shopping channel of choice for most items except groceries. Searching the Internet in the evening after the children are asleep is a favored shopping activity.

Analysis of Purchase Perceptions

The means of the influence scale for the 16 items that successfully loaded into the four purchase perception factors (customer service, shopping experience, consumer risk, and product perception) were clustered into each prospective factor as an index. The customer service index contains the mean of the influence scale scores for vendor warranty/guarantee, return policy, return convenience, product variety, and product quantity. The shopping experience index contains the mean of the influence scale scores for lifestyle compatibility, physical effort to shop, ease of Internet shopping, enjoyable activity, and amount of time spent shopping. The index score for consumer risk contains the mean of influences scores for customer service/responsiveness, vendor reliability, confidentiality of personal data, and credit card security. And finally, the product perception index contains the mean of product price and product quality influence scores.

Regression analysis was used to predict which overall purchase perception factors are most likely to influence a buyer to consummate a purchase via the Internet. Table 6 presents the results of the regression analysis. Two purchase

Table 6. Product perception influencers of Internet purchases

Demographic Characteristic	B	Std. Error	Beta	t	Sig.
Customer Service	-.048	.081	-.065	-.589	.557
Shopping Experience	.236	.068	.319	3.445	*.001
Consumer Risk	-.034	.071	-.048	-.480	.632
Product Perception	.135	.053	.226	2.521	*.013

Significant influencer of Internet purchases.

perception factors are found to be the primary influencers of Internet buying—the shopping experience and the perception of the product. Clearly, Internet buyers seek enjoyable shopping experiences that are easy to consummate and are compatible with their lifestyle. Not surprisingly, product quality and preferred pricing were also found to significantly influence Internet buying.

Discussion and Conclusions

This chapter examined how purchase perceptions influence consumers' Internet buying practices by building upon existing knowledge of pre-Internet buying motivators. Eighteen scaled items were used by survey teams to gather data from 190 adults in a four-state area which was subsequently analyzed. The discussion and conclusions are based upon the data and analysis that follow.

The four general categories of buyer motivator variables identified previously in the marketing literature were found to also be valid for Internet buyers. This finding should not be surprising, given that Internet shopping can be considered an evolutionary step in buying processes. Consider that, in its earliest stages, buying began as a negotiated exchange of goods or other consideration among two producers of goods, and evolved into marketplaces where sellers sold goods obtained from multiple sources and where buyers could easily compare and purchase goods. Niches evolved for manufacturers and sellers.

Catalog shopping was an important step in the evolutionary process. It set the stage for Internet shopping, where buyers purchased goods conveniently from their home, relying on pictorial and textual descriptions of the goods that they purchased. A new niche evolved for organizations that specialized in moving goods from sellers' warehouses to buyers' homes.

The Internet added automation to the shopping experience by making catalogs available online. Concomitantly, Internet technologies enabled sellers to add facets other than color and text to influence potential buyers. These new facets shifted buyers' behavior toward other influencers. Jarvenpaa and Todd (1996-97) grouped the items affecting buyer purchase perceptions into four purchase perception categories (product perception, shopping experience, customer service, and consumer risk), which were tested to ascertain the influence that each item has upon buying via the Internet.

The shopping experience and product perception variables emerged in this study as the most influential behavioral factors that encourage a consumer to buy via the Internet. The composition of the shopping experience factor contains five survey items: lifestyle compatibility, physical effort, ease of Internet shopping, enjoyable activity, and amount of time shopping. The product perception factor consists of the two questionnaire items, price and product quality, which together are often described as the *value* of the product. These findings are consistent with those reported by Lee et al. (2003), Liu et al. (2001), and Eastin (2002). These researchers reported that shopping enjoyment, convenience in purchasing, and product value (i.e., product quality and price) contribute significantly to the attainment of customer satisfaction.

Three demographic characteristics—age, level of education, and years of Internet experience—were found to be major Internet buying influencers. The study found that Internet purchasers are younger (lowest reported age was 20), have higher education levels (more than 75% had some college), and have significant Internet experience (most commonly four to six years). These findings differ from Bhatnagar et al.'s (2000) mixed results for Internet experience level and age demographic variables, but are similar to Ratchford et al.'s (2001) findings regarding buyers' education levels.

What implications do these findings have for electronic retailers, merchants, and e-commerce developers? How can the findings be incorporated to garner a competitive advantage in positively influencing Internet consumers to buy and to attract new consumers to the Internet? Parties interested in the answers to these questions should begin by recognizing that Internet consumers do not perceive that product variety affects their overall product perception. This implies that Internet retailers can offer a smaller variety of quality products for competitive prices. The caveat is that, since consumers relate product variety to customer service, e-commerce systems should offer potential consumer links to other websites when they cannot offer specific varieties of the product themselves. Doing this will reinforce consumers' positive perceptions of the referring vendor's customer service. Properly done, such referrals will generate revenue for the referring vendor. An example of this strategy can be viewed at Amazon.com's website, where customers desiring an unavailable product are offered fulfillment from Target or Toys-R-Us.

Successful e-commerce retailers must maintain a positive shopping experience to facilitate positive buyer behavior. This can be done by maintaining the positive features of their websites. Goldsmith (2000) recommends refreshing the website periodically to increase the fun of buying as a means to motivate positive buyer behavior.

Our second recommendation is that Internet shopping environments provide plenty of choices and sources of information for the buyer. An Internet shopper that enjoys the shopping experience may want to invest additional time to find a better product by searching more thoroughly. Lee et al. (2003) agree with this recommendation, noting that Internet buyers enjoy the activity of prioritizing their buying options and consolidating their purchase preferences, while taking pleasure in the Web surfing and shopping experience, finding it playful and fun.

Our final recommendation to the e-commerce retailer is to participate in product "bundling." Since Internet buyers enjoy the shopping experience and the time online, they may be influenced to buy an assortment of Internet products. For example, Eastin (2002) recommends that electronic retailers provide a bundle of Internet purchasable products and services, such as online shopping, online banking, online investing, and electronic payment methods.

Taken together, these recommendations all serve to maximize the buyer's shopping experience. A positive shopping experience has been demonstrated to provide the highest propensity of encouraging consumers to engage in Internet buying.

As future research occurs in the area of Internet purchasing, we encourage researchers to build upon our findings by concentrating on developing a better understanding of items demonstrated as affecting each of the four purchase perceptions.

References

Arnold, S.J., Handelman, J., & Tiger, D.J. (1996). Organizational legitimacy and retail store patronage. *Journal of Business Research, 35,* 229-239.

Baker, J. Levy, M., & Grewal, D. (1992). An experimental approach to making retail store environment decisions. *Journal of Retailing, 64*(4), 445-460.

Baty, J.B., & Lee, R.M. (1995). InterShop: Enhancing the vendor/customer dialectic in electronic shopping. *Journal of Management Information Systems, 11*(4), 9-31.

Berkowitz, E.M., Walker, O.C., & Walton, J.R. (1979). In-home shoppers: The market for innovative distribution systems. *Journal of Retailing, 55,* 15-33.

Bhatnagar, A., Misra, S., & Rao, H.R. (2000). On risk, convenience, and Internet shopping behavior. *Communications of the ACM, 43*(11), 98-105.

Bock, T., & Uncles, M. (2002). A taxonomy of differences between consumers for market segmentation. *International Journal of Research in Marketing, 19,* 215-224.

Bredin, R., Granitz, N., & Koernig, S. (2001). Toward an understanding of gender differences in the use of e-commerce: An expansion of the technology acceptance model. *Quarterly Journal of Electronic Commerce, 2*(3), 261-278.

Cox, D.F., & Rich, S.U. (1964). Perceived risk and consumer decision making the case of telephone shopping. *Journal of Marketing Research, 1,* 32-39.

Cronin, M.J. (1996). *Global advantage on the World Wide Web.* New York: Van Nostrand Reinhold.

Eastin, M.S. (2002). Diffusion of e-commerce: An analysis of the adoption of four e-commerce activities. *Telematics and Informatics, 19,* 251-267.

EMarketer. (2002). *North America online: Access, demographics, and usage.* New York.

Gefen, D. (2002). Customer loyalty in e-commerce. *Journal of Association for Information Systems, 3,* 27-50.

Goldsmith, R.E. (2000). How innovativeness differentiates online buyers. *Quarterly Journal of Electronic Commerce, 1*(4), 223-333.

Goldsmith, R.E., & Bridges, E. (2000). E-tailing vs. retailing: Using attitudes to predict online buying behavior. *Quarterly Journal of Electronic Commerce, 1*(3), 245-253.

Goldsmith, R.E., Bridges, E., & Freiden, J. (2001). Characterizing online buyers: Who goes with the flow? *Quarterly Journal of Electronic Commerce, 2*(3), 189-197.

Hoffman, D.L., & Novak, T.P. (1996). Marketing in the hypermedia computer-mediated environments: Conceptual foundations. *Journal of Marketing, 60,* 50-68.

Hoffman, D.L., & Novak, T.P. (1997). A new market for paradigm for electronic commerce. *Information Society, 13,* 43-54.

Huang, H., Keser, C., Leland, J., & Shachat, J. (2003). Trust, the Internet, and the digital divide. *IBM Systems Journal, 42*(3), 507-518.

Jarvenpaa, S.L., & Todd, P.A. (1996-97). Consumer reactions to electronic shopping on the World Wide Web. *International Journal of Electronic Commerce, 1*(2), 59-88.

Kannan, P.K., & Kopalle, P.K. (2001). Dynamic pricing on the Internet: Importance and implications for consumer behavior. *International Journal of Electronic Commerce, 5*(3), 63-83.

Koyuncu, C., & Lien, D. (2003). E-commerce and consumer's purchasing behavior. *Applied Economics, 35*(6), 721-729.

Lee, J.N., Pi, S.M., Kwok, R.C., & Huynh, M.Q. (2003). The contribution of commitment value in Internet commerce: An empirical investigation. *Journal of the Association for Information Systems, 4,* 39-64.

Liao, Z., & Cheung, M.T. (2001). Internet-based e-shopping and consumer attitudes: An empirical study. *Information and Management, 38,* 299-306.

Liu, C., & Arnett, K.P. (2000). Exploring the factors associated with website success in the context of electronic commerce. *Information and Management, 38,* 23-33.

Liu, C., Armett, K.P., Capella, L.M., & Taylor, R.D. (2001). Key dimensions of Web design quality as related to consumer response. Journal *of Computer Information Systems, 42*(1), 70-82.

Lu, H., & Lin, J.C.C. (2002). Predicting customer behavior in the market-space: A study of Rayport and Sviokla's framework. *Information and Management, 40,* 1-10.

O'Cass, A., & Fenech, T. (2003). Web retailing adoption: Exploring the nature of Internet users Web retailing behavior. *Journal of Retailing and Consumer Services, 10,* 81-94.

Park, C. (2001). Discriminating factors of cyber shoppers in Korea. *Quarterly Journal of Electronic Commerce, 2*(2), 147-155.

Perterson, R.A., Albaum, G., & Ridgway, N.M. (1989). Consumers who buy from direct sales companies. *Journal of Retailing, 65*(2), 273-286.

Ratchford, B.T., Talukdar, D., & Lee, M.S. (2001). A model of consumer choice of the Internet as an information source. *International Journal of Electronic Commerce, 5*(3), 7-22.

Settle, R.B., Dillon, T.W., & Alreck, P.L. (1999). Acceptance of the phone-based interface for automated call direction. *Behaviour & Information Technology, 18*(2), 97-107.

Simpson, L., & Lakner, H.B. (1993). Perceived risk and mail order shopping for apparel. *Journal of Consumer Studies and Home Economics, 17,* 377-398.

Straub, D.W. (1989). Validating instruments in MIS research. *MIS Quarterly, 13*(2), 147-166.

Swaminathan, V., Lepkowska-White, E., & Rao, B.P. (1999). Browsers or buyers in cyberspace? An investigation of factors influencing electronic exchange. *Journal of Computer-Mediated Communication, 5*(2), 1-24.

Udo, G.J., & Marquis, G.P. (2001-2002). Factors affecting e-commerce website effectiveness. *Journal of Computer Information Systems, 42*(2), 10-16.

Vellido, A., Lisboa, P.J.G., & Meehan, K. (2000). Quantitative characterization and prediction of online purchasing behavior: A latent variable approach. *International Journal of Electronic Commerce, 4*(4), 83-104.

Vijayasarathy, L.R. (2001). The impact of shopping orientations, product types, and shopping aids on attitude and intention to use online shopping. *Quarterly Journal of Electronic Commerce, 2*(2), 99-113.

Vijayasarathy, L.R. (2002). Internet taxation, privacy and security: Opinions of the taxed and legislated. *Quarterly Journal of Electronic Commerce, 3*(1), 53-71.

Chapter XII

Strategic E-Commerce Aspects of the E-Banking/ E-Lending Industry

William T. Rupp
University of Montevallo, USA

Alan D. Smith
Robert Morris University, USA

Abstract

Major advances in technology, especially those that leverage the growth of the Internet, are playing a key role in the development and evolution of the banking and lending industry. In order to succeed, banks must create and implement a more aggressive strategy and move away from the primarily defensive strategy if they are to return to acceptable levels of ROI. E-banking/e-lending can significantly reduce the amount of time it takes to process loans and related services by allowing the potential borrower to do much of the work themselves. The cost savings for presumably many thousands of applications per year will be substantial. However, the start-up costs for e-banking/e-lending can be significant. Lenders must be confident of sustainable volume projections. E-banking/e-lending also allows lenders to reach borrowers outside of their traditional market areas.

Several strategic factors and various models are discussed to identify the emerging tendencies and to explore the opportunities and threats within a strategic framework.

Introduction to the Emergent Nature of E-Commerce

Internet as a Change Agent

This chapter deals with the emergent nature of the e-lending/e-banking industry as it relates to the dynamic nature of the e-commerce environment. The main objectives of this chapter are to define those aspects of the e-commerce environment that have a direct bearing on the complexities of the e-lending/e-banking industry, and dissect those strategic elements that management should understand in order to leverage the power of the Internet and turn theses aspects into elements of sustainable competitive advantage. The next major objective is to model the major forces in the industry to present in such a way that management and interested persons can make intelligent decisions about the future of the banking industry within an e-commerce framework. The last objective is to use the concepts of Diffusion Theory to understand the practitioner's viewpoint of the many changes within the e-lending/e-banking industry.

The Internet is changing the global marketplace, including the banking industry. The use of the Internet is lowering entry costs and removing barriers to entry for many businesses. The lowering of barriers has led to a flood of banks entering the industry, ultimately increasing competition and providing increased value to potential customers. However, most of the traditional banking industry has been slow to join the Internet bandwagon. At the end of 2000, only 19% of the countries' FDIC (Federal Deposit Insurance Corporation) insured commercial banks and saving institutions offered e-banking, which allows the customer to perform all of their normal bank transactions via the Internet instead of at the traditional branch (Orr, 2001, p. 40). The percentage of companies offering these online services continues to rise, but as of December 2001, almost half of all financial institutions had no plans to offer e-banking in the future (Orr, 2001a, p. 42). In contrast, approximately 66% of the U.S. population is accessing the Internet and "that figure continues to grow exponentially" (Nigro, 2002, p. 39). As a result, consumers today are more knowledgeable than ever and are consequently demanding more from their bank in both services and products. However, the one major issue that is keeping the consumer from utilizing more

Figure 1. Some of the major factors influencing the development of e-banking strategies

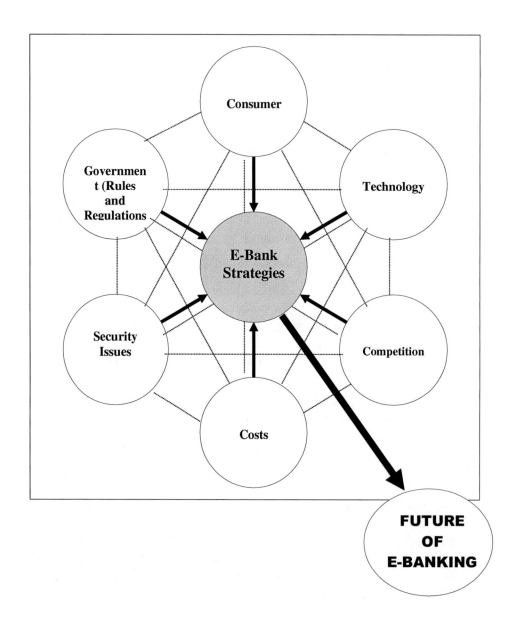

of the Internet's capabilities is the concern of inadequate privacy protection and limited regulations. Therefore, the future success of financial institutions will depend on how well they understand the market drivers and the threats to position themselves best to adapt to the new Internet Age. In this new Digital Age, "the Principal of Information Darwinism will determine who thrives and who becomes extinct in the years to come" (Marks, 2001, p. 1).

Electronic commerce continues to gain significant increases in consumer usage, confidence, and spending, and although the banking industry has been relatively slow to adapt, its time is fast approaching. A recent Fannie Mae study revealed that, although only 2% of recent homebuyers used the Internet for the entire mortgage process in 2000, half of all Americans anticipate that most home mortgage loans will be handled over the Internet within five years. The portion of respondents that would "definitely" or "probably" use the Internet to apply for a mortgage loan was 30%, up from 20% in 1996 (*The New York Times,* 2000). The market for Internet mortgage applications could grow 150% over the next four years, to $150-$200 billion (Bergsman, 2000). However, even taking these trends into consideration, the state of electronic banking at present is not healthy as compared to comparable mature industries. According to Orr (2001c), approximately 10% of all banks offer e-banking in any form, and 90% of banking households are still choosing not to take advantage of handling their financial affairs over the Internet. In 2001, there are about 50 Internet-only e-banks— most of them unprofitable and many compromising their reason for being by opening physical branches. Orr (2001a, 2001b, 2001c, 2001d, 2001e) suggested that the slow growth of e-banking is mainly due to the fact that banks are slow to offer it, and when they do offer it, they usually do not promote it aggressively. Still, e-banking should be the wave of the future, since demographics are pointing to the next generation that has grown up with the Net. In fact, "All banks, especially large ones, will rapidly shift the bull's eye of their e-banking target to the top 10-20% of their customers who deliver 70% or so of the banks' profits. The buzzword here is 'wealth management'" (Orr, 2001c, p. 53).

Mortgage lending has so far been the focal point in the e-lending industry, but other areas of consumer credit are emerging. Details from Forrester Research predict that one of every six credit cards will be issued online by 2003, and that home equity loans, auto loans, and student loans will follow mortgages into hyper growth (Orr, 2000). In fact, online student loans are expected to increase from 12,000 to 3.3 million, or 25% of all such loans in the U.S. The graph in Figure 2 shows Forrester Research's projected market for online credit over the next few years.

Another small, but emerging market for online lending is small business loans. Small businesses are connecting to the Web at an even faster rate than private households (50% are connected, 75% are expected to be by 2002), and about

75% of small businesses need to utilize outside funding to meet working capital and asset acquisition needs (Orr, 2000). Credit scoring models, relying heavily on the owners' personal financial information, are being used for fast loan approval or rejection. Many small businesses need the convenience of that quick response time. Some lenders approve or reject within minutes for loans of $50,000 or less (Garcia, 2000). Obviously, in order to compete in the Internet market, e-lenders need to consider the benefits to lender and customer, the credit risks, the problems, and the alternatives that are quickly developing in the Web-based environment. Some popular e-lenders cope with this environment by being multiple site lenders. "Multi-lender websites are portals-gateways to affiliated institutions that actually originate loans. Prospective borrowers submit profiles

Figure 2. Mortgage lending has so far been the focal point in the e-banking/e-lending industry, but other areas of consumer credit are emerging (Details from Forrester Research cited in Orr, 2000)

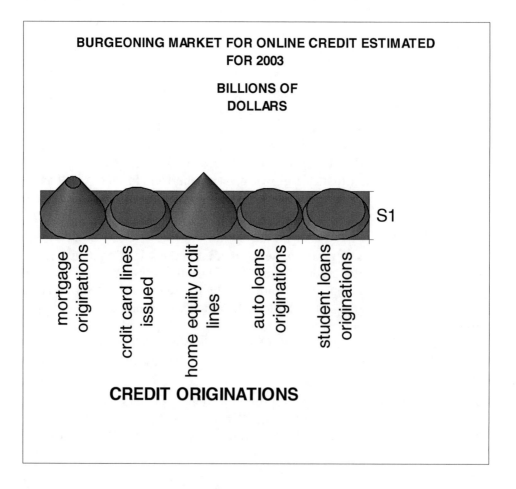

of their intended home purchase and their own financial resources" (Orr, 2000, p. 45). Thus the website serves as a shopping place for borrowers and a source of prospects for lenders, "which seems like a win-win situation" (Orr, 2000, p. 45). Also, another tactic is to target small business for e-banking/e-lending services and products.

Although until recently, lending to small businesses has not been a high priority for most lending institutions, especially large banks—primarily due to the labor intensiveness of the underwriting process, the high risks, and the relatively small income per loan—this market is especially favorable to e-banking/e-lending since it minimizes the previously mentioned disadvantages that larger, more financially comprehensive banks find in dealing with these relatively small businesses.

What is at Stake for a Financial Web-Enabled Strategy?

Model Element: Internet-Empowered Consumers

Referring to the basic outline of interrelationships portrayed in Figure 1, and with approximately two-thirds of the U.S. population using the Internet and taking advantage of all of the information is has to offer, customers are becoming more

Figure 3. Impact of the change in demographics on e-banking usage (Next generation will bring an increase in online acceptance)

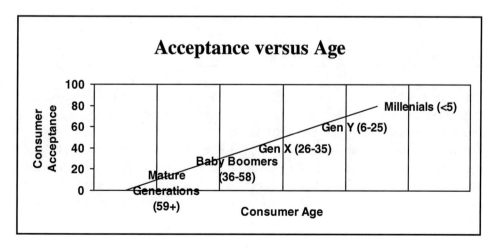

knowledgeable and sophisticated and, thus, "demanding higher expectations" (Fuhrman, 2002, p. 2). To compound this, the American demographics are changing, and according to the U.S. Census Bureau, 50.5% of the population is less than 35 years of age. Roughly 30% of the population has grown up on the Internet, and "that number continues to rise each year" (Wellner, 2000, p. 57). Consequently, as demonstrated in Figure 3, there is a natural inverse relationship developing: as the age of the consumer declines, the demand for Internet services, including e-banking, will rise.

In just the past three years, the number of visitors to the websites of financial institutions has increased by 150% (*Bank News,* 2001, p. 31), and in 2001 alone the number of e-banking customers increased by 100% from 11 million to 22 million (Draenos, 2001). Consumers are taking advantage of the benefits that e-banking has to offer, primarily due to:

1. Convenience—access from anywhere, 24 hours a day, seven days a week.
2. Flexibility—access from any handheld personal computing device from anywhere.
3. Time Savings—reduced travel time to branches and avoid slow moving lines.
4. Immediate Feedback—real-time transactions.

However, even though total use is rising and more people are visiting bank websites, as of January 2001, only about 10% of households had chosen to handle their financial transactions over the Internet (Orr, 2001a, 2001d, 2001e). The main concern expressed by the average consumer is the security of the system. Therefore, "increasing the confidence level of the consumer and selling the services they expect will play key roles in the acceptance and growth of e-banking" (Lamberg, 2001, p. 6).

Model Element: Technology

The changes taking place in the banking industry, in particular in reference to customer demand as a result of the Internet, demonstrate the power of technology and the "importance of taking advantage of these new ways of delivering a long established product" (McRae, 1999, p. 22). The survival of banks will depend on how well they incorporate new technology and applications to deliver a more sophisticated product that will satisfy customer expectations. However, one of the problems for banks is that many of them have inherited old, outdated operating systems and technology as a result of all of the recent mergers and acquisitions that took place in the 1990s. Therefore, it can be extremely costly trying to choose which of the largely unproven technologies they should purchase (Orr, 2001d). Banks should incorporate technology that is open, flexible, and easily integrated in order to accommodate shifts and changes in the market. With the correct technology, banks can improve efficiency in core markets and penetrate new markets. Banks should depend on a clear definition of the business, its market objectives and strategies, and the return on investment (ROI) in choosing technology. The key for banks is to focus on selecting technology that matches their organization's objectives. Banks should not dwell on all of the features the other technology can offer or on what all of the competition is doing (Fuhrman, 2002).

Model Element: Competition

As a result of the changes in technology and customer expectations, the banking industry is becoming an increasingly competitive market. With the revolution in information processing, entry costs have been significantly lowered, thereby increasing competition among banks and other non-bank institutions offering similar services and products. Banks are discovering that in this crowded marketplace, in order to stay alive and prosper, they must re-evaluate their strategy and start focusing on gaining customer loyalty (Schwlizer Bank, 2001). With the increase in competition, it is generally assumed that gaining customer loyalty is more difficult. However, due to the nature of the industry, banks have at least two important advantages working in their favor. First, it takes a significant amount of effort to break a pre-existing relationship. Second, banks possess an extensive amount of personal information about their customers. These two advantages make it easier for banks to maintain and strengthen customer loyalty (Nigro, 2002).

Banks will need to develop a more competitive strategy that will add value to the customer and differentiate them to outmaneuver the growing competition (Nigro, 2002). The banks that are able to best incorporate and surpass customers' expectations in building their digital business design will be the most effective (*Bank News,* 2001). The technology is available and the range of services that it can provide is endless. However, there are certain threats that will impact the success of e-banking. The banks that are aware of and understand these challenges the best will survive.

Model Element: Costs

As banks are starting to integrate the Internet into their business strategies, they are also "starting to alter their spending patterns and begin budgeting for e-banking expenses" (Marlin, 2001, p. 10). However, there are a few things banks must be aware of before they make that final technology purchase. Banks need to learn from the mistakes committed by many of the Internet-only banks that have failed in the past three years. These unsuccessful companies suffered from high costs due to new technology, heavy marketing expenses, and higher salaries that were needed to attract the people capable of managing the new system. The companies were not able to cover the high capital costs because of insufficient demand (Orr, 2001d, 2001e). Banks in the planning stage will need to better align their costs with their objectives, strategies, and expected demand.

In order to succeed, e-banks will need to stay away from mass marketing and focus on gaining a larger share of their targeted niche market (Orr, 2001d, 2001e). As depicted in Figure 4, banks need to budget the funds necessary to satisfy the expectations of the customers in a specific market. Banks should make a strategic investment in organization, process, and technology that will retain current customers and improve relationships. The banks that are able to achieve this challenge will find that acquiring new customers and controlling a

Figure 4. Costs vs. customer expectations (As banks continue to try and cut costs, customer expectations continue to grow)

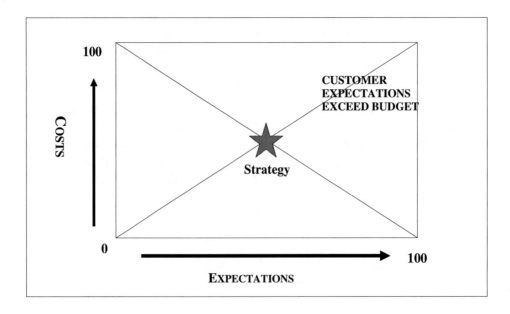

niche market will become easier. To minimize costs, banks will need to keep their technology planning in line with the overall business plan (Fuhrman, 2002). While banks are trying to control costs, there is one technology requirement that all banks must not neglect and that is an effective security system.

Model Element: Security Issues

Alarmingly, recent surveys of Fortune 500 companies have confirmed that the consumer's biggest fear is that many companies are not prepared to handle the e-commerce risks (see Figure 5). These risks include hackers, cyber-thieves, viruses, internal saboteurs, and terrorists (Smith & Rupp, 2002a, 2002b; *Security Sense,* 2000). Even the FBI has warned banks to be more vigilant in protecting their online products to reduce the number of hackers illegally stealing personal information. As more banks introduce e-banking services, they will need to provide a cost-effective secure solution.

Customer concern with the security of the systems and the integrity of the transaction data is the major factor affecting the acceptance of online banking. As demonstrated in Figure 6, consumer confidence in the product will increase as the number of security violations decrease.

Figure 5. A selection of e-commerce security risks that must be factored in at the strategic level

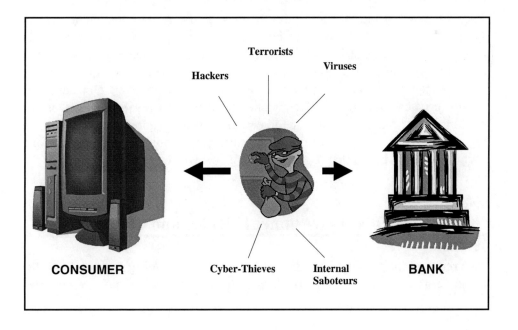

Figure 6. Confidence level of consumer versus security of e-banking/e-lending

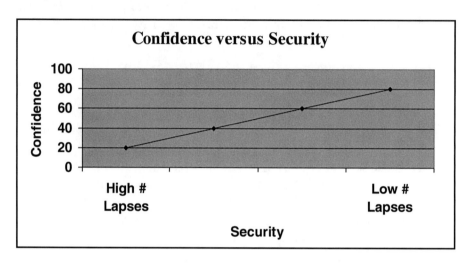

Despite all of the technical weaknesses with Internet technology, human interaction within the system's components still present a potential great to the security of e-banking. Ultimately, the greatest threat to the success of e-banking is carelessness on the part of customers or bank insiders. In recent bank fraud cases, the violators were unhappy or former employees or external service providers (Smith & Rupp, 2002b; *Security Sense,* 2001).

Today, the only solution to minimize the privacy risk is to implement a security system that finds the best balance between cost, complexity, and convenience (RMA Conference, 2001). In addition, banks need to educate their customers about the types of security that they have put into place (Lamberg, 2001). Banks also need to train their employees and educate them on the severe consequences of any privacy violations. As consumers' confidence levels towards online banking rises, more and more people will sign up. Therefore, even though regulatory action has been limited in ensuring that banks implement a strong security system, banks that take that extra effort will win the confidence of the consumer.

Model Elements: Government (Rules and Regulations)

As a result of the Internet's borderless nature, it is becoming more difficult for the government to regulate the banking industry. The lack of enforcement and limited regulations could negatively affect the banking industry's stability. Several government agencies are trying to impose and enforce stricter regulations. In 1999, the Gramm-Leach-Bliley Act was implemented, which calls for reasonable levels of security and requires financial institutions to notify their customers of their information sharing practices and their privacy policies (Whiting, 2002). In addition, the Office of the Comptroller of the Currency (OCC) reserves "the right to review all new proposed electronic activities to ensure that they are in accordance with the law" (Moeller, 2002, p. 10A). However, until government regulations are tough enough, banks need to develop their own privacy policies.

There are a few important things that banks need to consider when developing their privacy policy. Banks need to inform and communicate their policy to their customers. Customers need to know what information is being gathered and whom they can contact if they have an issue. Banks also need to explain the consequences that will occur if anyone breaches their privacy policy. Banks need to make sure their customers are confident that their personal information is secure. The aggressive companies are realizing the benefits of a security system, which includes not only meeting government regulations, but also avoiding bad publicity and improving customer loyalty (Aaron, 1999). The banks that are taking that extra effort and providing privacy protection are definitely gaining a strategic advantage.

Reasons Why Lenders Should Consider E-Banking/E-Lending Services

A primary reason that lenders may consider e-banking/e-lending is the potential in cost savings. Processing loan applications takes time, personnel, and, therefore, money. E-banking/e-lending can significantly reduce the amount of time it takes to process loans by allowing the potential borrower to do much of the work, including data entry. The cost savings for thousands of applications per year will be substantial (Warson, 2000). Keep in mind, however, that the start-up costs for e-banking/e-lending can be significantly cost prohibitive in nature (Britt, 2000). Lenders must be confident of volume projections. E-banking/e-lending provides another opportunity to gain the much-valued and lucrative "wallet share." Offering e-banking/e-lending services to your already savvy Internet customers allows banks to increase the amount of business with that customer. Lenders can use the increased flow of information and real-time interaction to offer a variety of products and services that are relevant to a particular customer (Kassarjian, 2000). E-banking/e-lending also allows lenders to reach borrowers outside of their traditional market areas.

Finally, the growth in e-banking/e-lending, as discussed previously, will tend to force lenders to keep up with lending technology or risk being left behind by the competition (Cofran, 2000). Grant Thornton's annual survey of community bank executives revealed that 28% of respondents were concerned about competition from Internet portals and Internet banks. Only 11% of those surveyed offered online lending services, but 75% stated that they would establish an Internet lending program within the next three years (Lamb, 2000). In 2001, there are about 50 Internet-only e-banks—most of which are unprofitable (Orr, 2001c).

Why Consumers Consider E-Borrowing

The major impact of the Internet has been the shift of power from businesses to consumers, who now have unprecedented amounts of information available and have come to expect unprecedented levels of service. Lending is becoming a self-service industry (Lamb, 2000). Customers are looking to the Internet for many different reasons, and e-commerce companies, including lenders, need to have the capabilities to quickly address all of them. Customers are looking for choice, convenience, security, the ability to quickly compare prices, education about products and services, and speed of service (Waller, 2000). E-borrowers in particular like applying for loans in anonymity. The process frees the borrower from the pressures of dealing with a real person. They do not have to be embarrassed to tell their computer how much debt they have, how much money they make, or how many payments they may have missed. And should the loan be rejected for any reason, customers avoid the shame of being told by a person. This avoidance of embarrassment and shame may mean that riskier customers are using the Internet, so lenders have to be wary (RMA Conference, 2000).

So far, customers' interests in Internet borrowing have been largely educational in nature (Hewitt, 2000). Hence, as these interested parities gain more confidence in matters of information expertise and security, the acceptance rate of this form of financial transaction could grow exponentially in nature. These interested parties may gather information about loans, rates, repayment options, and competitors, and then go into their bank or credit union fully armed with information. Lenders, therefore, need to make sure that information and education is available and easy to find on websites. Banks and all other e-companies need to understand the customer. Customer acquisition and retention is the key to e-business, and retention is less costly than acquisition. The groups of customers that use the Internet for banking services has some common characteristics that, if understood, can help banks maximize the appeal of their websites (Rosen, 2000):

1. Internet banking customers tend to be either under 40, or over 55 (retired or semi-retired).

2. Generally, Internet banking customers want, and even demand, the right to use the Internet, even if it is not their primary delivery channel.

3. Internet banking customers generally want to be left alone to do their business, but, when they need help, they expect it immediately. 24/7 live help has become a right rather than a privilege.

4. Most Internet users are not afraid to use the "chat" mode for help.

5. Internet banking customers are not particularly concerned with the bank's heritage and reputation, but rather, about the security, functionality, and convenience of the delivery channel.

Typically, one out of two customers abandon Internet banking channels in frustration, citing two basic reasons: It is too complicated, and there is a lack of customer service (Rosen, 2000). According to Rory Rowland, President of Rowland Consulting Services, Internet shoppers tend to move through four basic stages (Waller, 2000):

1. Looking for information
2. Exchanging information about themselves
3. Buying something small
4. Buying something large

A consideration of these stages led to the development of the Continuum Model of Internet Shopping, which is presented in Figure 7. The model shows how consumers move from looking for information to exchanging personal information as they gain confidence in the system, the process, and the provider. Continued confidence and motivation to try a transaction leads to the purchase of something small. Continued confidence, continued motivation, and familiarity lead to the purchase of something larger. The customer then can extend the process into other areas of e-commerce (investing, banking, borrowing, or purchasing elsewhere online).

A key aspect in this continuum model is that once confidence is broken or motivation or familiarity is stifled, the arrows are broken and the cycle ends. One of the main thrusts of this model is to explain the relative lack of customer service (confidence) or a complex process (motivation) can result in the abandonment of Internet channels. The model builds on the work of Porter (1996, 1999a, 1999b), who states that, although operational effectiveness (OE)—performing

Figure 7. The proposed continuum model of Internet shopping

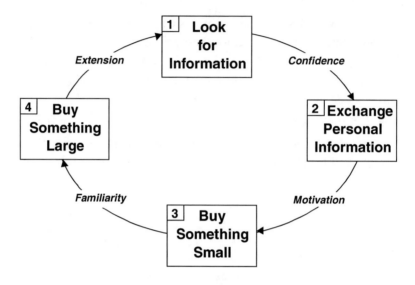

similar activities better than rivals perform them—is necessary for superior performance, there is a difference between operational effectiveness and strategy.

The Need for Strategic Foresight and Porter's Operational Effectiveness: Adding Value Through Competitive Performance

Strategy should involve performing activities differently than rivals do in order to maintain competitive advantage. As stated by Porter: "A company can outperform rivals only if it can establish a difference that it can preserve, and it must deliver greater value to customers or create comparable value at a lower cost, or do both" (1996, p. 62). Basically, Porter suggested that there is a "productivity frontier" "that constitutes the sum of all existing best practices at any given time" (1996, p. 62). This frontier could apply to individual activities, groups of linked activities, and to an entire company's activities, or in this case the concept of e-banking/e-lending. Improving OE moves a company toward the frontier, but this frontier "is constantly shifting outward as new technologies and management approaches are developed and as new inputs become available" (1996, p. 62). In order for e-banking/e-lending companies to become e-leading companies, there is a need to keep up with this frontier—managers have been too preoccupied with improving only OE. One tool of OE, benchmarking, ultimately causes companies to begin to look alike—therefore it is important for e-leaders to think outside the box defined by other financial leaders. Thus, according to Porter, "competitive strategy is about being different" (p. 64) by "deliberately choosing a different set of activities to deliver a unique mix of value" (1996, p. 64). This concept certainly applies to customer acquisition and retention as the key to e-business in general and e-banking/e-leading more specifically; retention is also less costly than acquisition. To support this idea, the classical Southwest Airlines' profitable policy of serving price-sensitive and convenience-sensitive travelers, and also Ikea who targets young furniture buyers who want style at low cost, are role models that e-leaning firms could imitate.

For e-lending institutions to grow in this dynamically changing business and economic environment, a certain degree of strategic foresight is necessary. According to Prahalad and Hamel (1994a, 1994b, 1994c), to develop a prescient and distinctive point of view about the future, senior management must be willing to spend 20 to 50% of their time on this subject over a period of months, not days. Senior management "must then be willing to continually revise that point of view, elaborating and adjusting it as the future unfolds" (Prahalad & Hamel, 1994b, p. 65). The first step in this process is the "quest for industry foresight—a deep understanding of the trends and discontinuities (technological, demographic, regulatory, or lifestyle)—that can be used to transform "industry boundaries and create new competitive space." Of course, the trick is to foresee the future before your competition.

From this foresight comes a sustainable vision for the firm. "While understanding the implications of such trends requires creativity and imagination, any "vision" that is not based on a solid factual foundation is likely to be fantastical" (Prahalad & Hamel, 1994b, p. 66). Thus, building industry foresight demands that e-banking/e-lending management accept the challenges to move beyond the issues on which they claim expert status. The future of e-banking/e-lending can be found in the intersection of changes in technology, lifestyles, regulation, demographics, and geopolitics. By insight into new product possibilities and going beyond traditional modes of marketing research, a firm can develop industry foresight to prosper in the future in a highly competitive environment. Therefore, strategy "is the creation of a unique and valuable position, involving a different set of activities" (Porter, 1996, p. 68). These concepts are partially integrated in the proposed model (Figure 2), so that e-leading "strategy is about combining activities" that "fit and reinforce one another," and that "fit is a far more central component of competitive advantage than most realize" (1996, p. 70).

The Internet and Its Special Set of Financial Risks

An audio-conference conducted by the Risk Management Association (RMA) (formerly Robert Morris Associates) stressed that while the Internet offers new types of financial rewards for the financial services industry, e-commerce practices also have their own special set of risks (RMA Conference, 2000). Those risks include lower approval rates (every denied application costs money), higher-risk customers, unknown borrowers, and an increased occurrence of fraud. Panelists agreed that, in the "virtual environment," approval rates fall because there is a greater number of higher-risk applicants. One cause is heavy marketing that leads to heavy volume. Another is anonymity. Higher risk applicants are more likely to apply online since they do not want be told no face to face (Orr, 2000; Smith & Rupp, 2002b). The panelists also agreed that fraud on the application is the most common source of risk. Chris Conrad, Vice President for Fraud Management at First USA Bank One (Wilmington, Delaware) suggested of fraud that his bank sees little of any other type of risk (RMA Conference, 2000).

The key to combating fraud and higher risk applicants is to remember that banks (and other lenders) determine who will become a customer. Lenders must establish and enforce credit standards with which they feel comfortable (RMA Conference, 2000). Credit bureau information should be used to help identify fraud attempts. Banks need tools that can immediately verify such simple data as name, social security number, address, and phone number, and credit bureaus are a good source of such information. Any information that does not match should raise a red flag. Banks also need to implement training programs in fraud identification. Banks should use technology to create a database of fraud experience. Many in management are extremely surprised when they monitored the volume of repeat offenders coming in and how significant of a burden it places on the operational effectiveness of the firm. In addition, any detailed discussion of lending risk should be coupled with an equally detailed discussion of interest rates.

In determining interest rates, banks traditionally consider three primary costs: the risk factors inherent in the loan, the administrative costs, and the cost of funds (McDonald & McKinley, 1981). E-commerce companies historically tend to try to compete on the basis of price. In lending, however, price of capital (interest rate) should have a direct relationship with risk. As risk increases, so should the interest rate charged to compensate the lender for taking that risk. To charge a lower rate of interest on e-loans despite a higher level of risk as discussed above violates that basic law of lending.

Special Online Leading Problems

Of course, there are problems other than credit risk. From a customer's point of view, security is probably the most important issue. Stoneman (2000, p. 56) cited a statement from Richard Biell of TowerGroup: "It's one thing to submit a credit card number online to buy a product. It's quite another thing to put your entire personal dossier online and hope that no one intercepts it, particularly if you're not familiar with the lender." These confidence and familiarity issues tie into the presented model. A borrower will not proceed to exchanging personal information without a sufficient level of confidence, and will not pursue other products and services without being familiar with the vendor and the process. For lenders, online loan origination volume has so far been under-whelming (Hewitt, 2000; Stoneman, 2000, 2001). Volume projections have been under some criticism largely because there is not a standard definition of what an Internet origination is. Hewitt (2000) quoted Fannie Mae's Michael Williams as saying that if you're looking for an online origination volume quote, "you probably can get a quote to match any number you want" (p. 4).

Another interesting problem that has been making news lately is that of the ownership of information. For example, in February of 2000, an online lender, e-Loan, allowed its customers to check their credit scores online. A credit score, a three-digit number derived by a computer algorithm from a customer's credit history, can determine approval or rejection, interest rates, and loan terms. These scores are one of the bases of fast credit decisions. Fair-Isaac, the credit reporting company, demanded that the scores are proprietary, and forced e-Loan to stop offering them to customers. E-Loan officials, the Federal Trade Commission, and consumer advocate groups have been pushing for legislation to make Fair-Isaac and other credit reporting companies divulge credit scores (Bicknell, 2000). Obviously, this chapter is not the place for a debate on credit scores, but the issue clearly demonstrates that, in this information-based society, the question of ownership of key information is an important issue, and one that is not going to go away. If customers feel that they have a right to certain information, keeping it away from them is another way of breaking the arrow in the suggested Model of Internet Shopping (Figure 2). Customers become frustrated and suspicious. They lose the confidence and, perhaps more so, the motivation that it takes to pursue Internet transactions.

E-Banking/E-Lending as an Acceptable Alternative in a Competitive Environment

Although for most dot.com startups, the last 25 months have been a nightmare, two Internet-only banks have managed the takeoff phase and climbed to substantial size and even profitability (Orr, 2001a, 2001b). According to Orr (2001a), NetBank, started in 1996, has more than $1 billion in deposits, and its operations have been profitable for the past 13 quarters, and E*Trade Bank, formed from the acquisition of TeLebank by E*Trade, the online brokerage firm, has almost $7 billion in deposits. However, as suggested by Orr (2001a), profitability is rare among the rapidly dwindling number of Internet-only banks. "Virginia Philipp, an analyst at TowerGroup, identified 40 Internet-only banks at the beginning of this year. Her 'hunch' is that the number is now in the 25-30 range, on its way down to 5-10 within five years" (Orr, 2001a, p. 62). It may be that the best alternative for larger banks is to establish an e-banking/e-lending presence on their own websites—accessible sites that offer other banking products and services. Many believe that the ultimate winners in the online lending market will be those with both an online and offline presence (Julavits, 2000). In addition, larger banks tend to instill more confidence in consumers, leading, according to the model displayed in Figure 2, to more online activity by those consumers. Banks should strive to be vertical portals, as described below. If banks plan to survive in the Internet market, they must become more user friendly and provide live customer service. According to the website at Forbes.com (2000), there are a number of suggestions, including three fairly sensible ways of introducing customers to the convenience, security, and speed of online banking:

1. Place PCs in lobbies so that customers can try the service with real help nearby.
2. Copy the Amazon.com model of using customer information already collected so that customers do not have to keep entering the same information for credit card or loan applications.
3. Install an online help button that immediately connects to a live customer service representative.

Consider the effect that these actions will have on confidence, motivation, and familiarity, the key components for movement through the Continuum Model of Internet Shopping (Figure 2).

Lamb (2000) offered three models for Internet delivery: aggregators, portals, and specialty providers. Specifically, aggregators are those sites that offer information and products from hundreds of different lenders, some of which may not be depository institutions. These sites can be in the form of malls or auctions. In malls, the customer can do research on products, rates, terms, etc., and then choose a lender. In auctions, the process is that of the reverse auction, where lenders bid for the customer's business based on the information that the customer provides. QuickenLoans, OnMoney.com, and GetSmart.com are examples of the banking mall, while LendingTree.com, Priceline.com, and LoanWeb.com are reverse auctions (Lamb, 2000).

There is, however, a gap between the promise of aggregators and the reality. Aggregators are not "scouring the planet for great rates": they are using a finite list of lenders that are paying referral fees (Stoneman, 2000). In addition, lenders using aggregators for loan volume are contributing to the reality that financing is becoming a commodity. Some industry analysts consider aggregators a short-term solution to e-banking/e-lending, to be used until banks develop sufficient brand recognition to draw customers away (Lamb, 2000). According to Dan Gilbert, CEO of QuickenLoans, who was recently quoted by Orr (2000), "Multi-lender sites are not profitable. They don't work. They never will" (Orr, p. 61). QuickenLoans recently purchased Rock Financial Corporation, a leading mortgage originator, and abandoned its QuickenMortgage.com aggregator site. Portals are large sites that have a section that offers financial products. AOL and MSN both offer such services. Portals offer access to not only online loans, but also to bill payment services, insurance, and investments. There are some portals that are specifically financial, such as Quicken.com, American Express, and Charles Schwab, along with some strictly Internet banks like CompuBank.com and WingspanBank.com. The range of products available to the consumer is what distinguishes portals from regular banking sites (Lamb, 2000).

Morgan Stanley believes that portals are going to become financial supermarkets. Successful ones will offer Web, telephone, and brick-and-mortar distribution channels. Charles Schwab is a successful example of this strategy, offering a network of brick-and-mortar branches and a strong Internet presence (Lamb, 2000; Stoneman, 2001). Specialty providers are those lenders that can distinguish themselves in the Internet market by carving out a certain niche. Hence, the 2000 class of online banks is no longer trying to attract a mass clientele with a universal model. In fact, they are adopting niche-focused models or are teaming up with affinity groups to generate specialized products (Ptacek, 2000). Specialty providers can market not only through their own websites, but also through aggregators and non-financial sites. PeopleFirst.com has been very successful in the online vehicle financing market. PeopleFirst.com, which can approve an online car loan application in 15 minutes, formed alliances with online auto dealers (examples include but are not limited to AutoByTel.com and Autoweb.com), information providers (like Kelley Blue Book), and aggregators (like LendingTree.com). In small business lending, Crestmark Bank (Troy,

Michigan), a "cashless bank" dealing with commercial transactions, uses a combination of the Internet and personal contact to solicit and sell factoring services and loans (Lamb, 2000).

E-Bank Strategies (Strategy Development and Implementation)

Defensive Strategies

Strategy is difficult to define, and Porter (1996, 1999a, 1999b) addresses several issues that bring strategy to life. There were five direct issues addressed that help define strategy. These issues will help organizations define what they are and what they want to accomplish. These five ideas expressed by Porter are: (1) operational effectiveness is not strategy, (2) strategy rests on unique activities, (3) a sustainable strategic position requires trade-offs, (4) fit drives both competitive advantage and sustainability, and (5) rediscovering strategy is an important issue for every industry. The banking industries for the most part are continuing to use a defensive Internet strategy and are choosing to watch from the sidelines. The banks' main motive to implement Internet banking is to prevent defection of their customers to other Internet banks or financial service providers. Banks are seeing the Internet as something that they cannot ignore, but "from which it will be difficult to actually make money" (Pyun, 2002, p. 73). Obviously, Internet banking is still in a stage of growth through experiment. Banks are still challenged with trying to automate their labor-intensive back-office operations. As a result, banks are finding it difficult to keep up with the Internet technology while competing with other banks and non-bank financial institutions for new products and new delivery systems. Technological innovations will continue in the financial industry, and they will constantly challenge the ability of banks to manage their competition with other financial service providers in a complex and dynamic e-commerce environment (Pyun, 2002).

Aggressive Internet Strategy

Banks will need to focus on the key elements of an aggressive Internet strategy. Banks need to offer incentives that will push the customer to switch to the online services and at the same time will satisfy the customer's expectations and strengthen customer loyalty. Banks need to provide a higher quality of service and not to compete entirely based on price and costs. Banks need to determine their niche market, but they should pursue corporate as well as retail banking initiatives. As suggested by Prahalad and Hamel (1994a, 1994b, 1994c), having strategic foresight is important for a more aggressive strategy by establishing what they are doing compared to what they could be doing to become leaders in their industries. Companies are taking a reactive approach versus a proactive approach to industry leadership. The banking industry must be willing to ask the right questions to see where they stand in their specific industries in order to take a proactive approach. For example, Hamel and Prahalad posed a question to some top officials of a U.S. company to find a trend in their industry that could change the industry as a whole. Once the company found the trend, they were asked if they could sustain a debate for a full day, among themselves, about the implications of this trend to your company and the industry. The company officials, unfortunately, were unable to perform this task. They were, however, able to perform the task on a much simpler question, such as: Could you sustain a debate for eight hours on the issue of how you allocate corporate overheads, set sales targets, and manage transfer prices? For example, Bayer Corporation, headquartered in Pittsburgh, Pennsylvania, is a type of company that does look into the future proactively. The company looks at what it can do for the industry. This has been proven through products the company has developed as well as receiving patents. This shows the community as a whole that Bayer is looking into the welfare of its future. This strategic foresight is not a procedure that can be done in a few hours of brainstorming. It is a procedure that takes time and effort to evaluate and research as much of the industry as possible. The banking industry needs to build a portfolio of information and use this as a continual learning tool. Most companies perform this continual learning, but only on certain issues. They may not realize the extent and importance of this, which will need to be performed in all functions of their business decisions. The banks that will be most effective are the ones with the strategic foresight which become aware and incorporate consumer wants into their digital business designs. Finally, banks need to implement technology that integrates front- and back-end systems. It is becoming evident that "more banks are starting to demonstrate the desire, capability, and strategic drive that will be required to win the e-banking race" (Hoppe, 2000, p. 128).

However, developing an aggressive strategy is only the first part; banks must then ensure an effective implementation and execution of that strategy. Banks must next "focus on the organizational structure, systems, shared values (culture), skills, style, and staff" (Pearce & Robinson, 2002, p. 340). Banks must match their organizational structure to the strategy to ensure that the critical tasks and activities are organized most effectively (Pearce & Robinson, 2002). When implementing a new strategy, companies must also make sure that they have the right managers in the correct positions to best handle the change. Banks will need to make sure both management and staff have the skills necessary, and that there is proper leadership within the organization. All systems need to be in line with the strategy from policies and controls to the company reward and recognition programs. How well banks address each of these components will play a critical role in the shaping of the organization's culture (shared values) and ultimately will lead to a well-executed strategy (Pearce & Robinson, 2002, Porter, 1996, 1999a, 1999b).

Bottom-Line Benefits to the E-Banking/E-Lending Industry

Up to this point, we have basically focused on what the customer wants and how banks can best develop strategies to position themselves to best satisfy those needs. But how exactly will banks themselves benefit on the bottom line from e-banking? Although the initial investment and start-up fees will be costly, costs will drastically decline for two main reasons. First, traditionally manually intensive work will now be automated. Second, the Internet is cheaper per transaction in comparison to the costs of the traditional ATM and telephone transactions (Orr, 2001a, 2001b, 2001c, 2001d, 2001e). In addition, while the banks' costs will decline, their revenues will rise. E-banking will improve customer relationships and therefore banks will experience greater retention. As a result of a more satisfied customer base and the added ability to reach customers in new geographic markets, banks will win new customers. Finally, banks will see an increase in the cross-selling of their products (Draenos, 2001). All of these opportunities will result in more assets and higher balances per customer. As revenues grow and costs decline, banks will definitely see the benefits in the bottom line.

Diffusion of Innovations Theory

At this point we have looked at the market drivers and threats that will shape the development of e-banking strategies and thus ultimately impact the future of e-banking. We have also looked at what banks need to do internally, within their organization, in order to effectively implement that strategy. But how can banks be sure that their innovation will be adopted and accepted by society, especially by their niche market? Rogers (1986, 1995) may provide an insight to this process through an application of the Diffusion of Innovations Theory. Diffusion of Innovation gives a theoretical basis on how innovations become widely accepted within society by explaining the patterns of adoption and thus determining whether a new innovation will become successful or not. When discussing

Diffusion Theory, it is important to remember that it is not one well-defined, comprehensive theory, but rather a combination of a number of theories from several disciplines (Surry, 1997).

We will now apply the Theory of Diffusion to the innovation of e-banking. The four main elements in the diffusion process include (Gregor, 1999, p. 71):

1.   The innovation
2.   Communication and promotion of the innovation
3.   Time/rate of adoption
4.   The members of a social system/niche market

There are five characteristics on how innovations are perceived: complexity, compatibility, trial ability, observability, and relative advantage. With more people using and becoming more comfortable on the Internet, e-banking will become less confusing and more people will perceive it as easy to understand. As banks continue to develop better privacy protection policies, e-banking will be less risky to the consumer and thus become more compatible with existing values (Williams, 2001). Banks that offer incentives such as free online banking will entice the consumer to try the product faster. The benefits of e-banking must be obvious to the consumer, and they must be better than the idea it is trying to supersede. Research shows that innovations like e-banking, which are easy to understand, offer several benefits, are available to use on a trial basis, and are compatible with current operations, will be adopted much faster and will experience an increased rate of diffusion (Rogers, 1986, 1995; Williams, 2001).

Innovations must be communicated through certain channels, over time. The innovation will actually pass through five stages that include: knowledge, persuasion, decision, implementation, and confirmation. Banks should use mass media and creative marketing at the knowledge stage to promote, attract, and tempt users to try e-banking/e-lending. However, in order to actually sell the product and gain consumer acceptance, banks will need to persuade the customer through interpersonal channels of communication versus mass media. Once the consumer has developed a favorable attitude towards e-banking/e-lending and decides to use it, adoption has occurred. However, the process does not end there; banks will need to ensure that the implementation goes well and that there is adequate confirmation and reinforcement based on positive out-comes (Clarke, 1999). Banks must keep in mind that the adoption of e-banking will go through a period of slow, gradual growth, then it will hit a period of rapid growth, eventually it will stabilize, and then decline. Therefore, the rate of adoption theory is very similar to the normal product lifecycle, and the banks that understand that will be able to better position themselves for each stage.

In every society and market, there are different types of people, each with there own predisposition as to how quickly they will adopt to new innovations. On one extreme are the Innovators who are risk takers, quick to adopt to new innovations; on the other end you have the laggards who resist to adopting a new innovation until rather late in the diffusion process, if ever (Surry, 1997). All members of a given society fall somewhere on this spectrum. The e-banking/e-lending industry in general needs to identify their niche market of potential adopters, research and measure their expectations and perceptions, design and develop a product that fits their needs, inform the potential adopters of the product, and provide support to the adopters (Surry, 1997, p. 10). Once the niche market has adopted e-banking, acceptance will continue to grow and diffuse to other markets and parts of society. The key to banks then is to look to the potential adopters to learn what they want and then gradually introduce the innovations into their market/societies (Rogers, 1986, 1995; Surry, 1997).

Rogers' Diffusion Theory emphasizes the importance of creating innovations that will improve society, but more importantly focusing on what society wants. Research shows that even if an innovation provides more benefits than the idea before it, if it is not integrated and adopted by society, it will fail. The firms within the e-banking/e-lending industries that address the market drivers and the threats in developing their e-banking strategies will see their innovations being adopted and diffused throughout society.

Future Aspects of E-Banking/E-Lending

Imagine a day when a customer, while driving in his car in China on a business trip, can pick up his mobile phone or plug in his handheld personal computing device and complete all of his banking transactions in just a few minutes. He/she can move money from one account to another, review the status of all of his/her accounts, or open up a new account or even a new insurance policy. The range of services that can be offered is not only diverse and secure, but also more personal. The future technology roadmap for the banking industry includes acceptance, enhancement, and expansion in the field of e-commerce. Internet speed and information will undoubtedly fuel the continued growth of Internet-friendly households in the U.S. In addition, continued widespread wireless access and stronger privacy protection will turn current customers into more regular users, and will also increase the number of new online banking customers. These advances in technology, coupled with the explosive growth of the Internet, will create a more demanding customer. Banks that embrace the challenge and keep their focus on business development and growth as the primary goal, with new technology as the means, will no doubt survive in the future. It seems that digital-age Darwinism is here with a vengeance, and financial institutions that wait too long to integrate these communication channels into their e-commerce strategies are going to find themselves wondering what happened to their customers and will ultimately miss the wave of the future.

General Conclusions and E-Commerce Implications to E-Banking/E-Lending

This chapter on the e-commerce implications to the e-banking industry is deeply embedded in the proposition that as a mature industry, it finds itself as an emerging entity as the technology associated with e-commerce diffuses through the banking industry. A general summary of the main findings of the present, contributions, and implications to e-commerce are contained in this section. The advances in technology, especially the Internet, are constantly playing a key role in the development and evolution of the banking industry. As banks develop more aggressive strategies, there are several market drivers and threats that they cannot overlook. Customers, technology, competition, costs, security issues, and regulations will definitely impact banks' strategies and ultimately the future of e-banking/e-lending.

For financial institutions, the Internet redefines the "rules of engagement" for customer interaction, acquisition, and relationship management. The opportunity for forward-looking organizations lies in redefining the role of credit by exploiting the improved information flow and real-time interaction that the Internet offers. By providing additional services and access to physical-world infrastructure, established players can move competition on the Web away from being merely a pricing issue (Kassarjian, 2000).

A successful Internet strategy requires both strategic thinking—strategic fore-sight—as well as strategic operational planning—Porter's operational effectiveness. Despite a slow start compared to other Internet ventures, it is the authors' opinion that Internet banking will continue to grow. Those firms that do not address this particular need in the financial area of competition are likely to be left behind in a very short timeframe. Hence, there are four primary areas of intensive competitive leverage that lenders need to address in the near future:

1. Integration of Internet, telephone, and branch operations
2. Security and privacy
3. Education
4. Technology alternatives

Figure 8. A relational strategic fit model between company focus and proposed model of Internet shopping component (see Figure 7)

FOCUS	Confidence	Motivation	Familiarity	Extension
Integration	☐	☐		☐
Security and Privacy	☐	☐	☐	
Education	☐	☐	☐	☐
Technology	☐	☐		

By addressing these four areas, lenders can affect the way that consumers are likely to act according to the Continuum Model of Internet Shopping (Figure 2), as displayed in the relationship among company focus and model of Internet shopping component, as graphically represented in Figure 8.

Hence, a bank entering the Internet arena needs to understand its requirements and expectations, and the delivery costs involved. Most importantly, banks need to integrate Internet operations with all other delivery channels. To the customer, the transition from Internet to call center to branch should appear seamless. Hence, according to Raab (2000):

> "Despite all the advances in delivering financial services online, there's one tried-and-true delivery system that customers won't give up: branches. Banks continue to make investments and upgrades in their brick-and-mortar structures as customers integrate branch use into a multi-channel approach based on what's most convenient at any given moment." (p. 12)

Banks must also spend the time and money to invest in security and privacy, primarily because it's the right thing to do, but also because it is one of the OCC's top priorities (Moeller, 2002; *The New York Times,* 2000). This means using the latest encryption technologies, tracking technology developments closely, and constantly monitoring and updating processes to ensure compliance with the highest standards. As previously discussed, most Internet borrowers are using currently using the Web for education, to secure information on rates, companies, services, products, and options. Even as more and more originations and closings are done online, education will remain an important part of e-banking/e-lending. Thus, positive strategies include keeping the customer informed through Web presences and shared databases, and making sure that price is a major issue, but not the only issue. Service also comes with a price, and most customers understand that. In mortgage originations, there are four parts to price that customers need to know: the origination fee, the discount fee, the actual rate, and the closing costs.

According to Ernest Knudsen, President of Lowrates USA, a mortgage bank:

> *"Currently, [consumers] think that there's only one rate, and don't understand that I can actually make more money on a 7.5% loan than an 8% loan, depending on my fees. The industry needs to explain that."* (Quinn, 2000, p. 1)

The overall goal is to provide an Internet portal, but all banks cannot start from this position, and in-house technology may not be enough (Habal, 2000). More banks are partnering with new entrants rather than trying to develop technology and online capabilities in house, due to the enormous capital outlays and the speed to market as compared to in-house. Habal (2000) basically suggested that people in and out of the banking industry would eventually find core competencies of their organization and try to sell it to others who do not have the same competencies, especially in dealing with IT infrastructures. Hence, IT technologies and its competent management are the keys—if you do not have it, join with someone who does, or simply outsource. In general, Rosen (2000) suggested some advantages to outsourcing:

1.   Staying competitive with bank and non-bank competitors
2.   Avoiding cost and obsolescence
3.   Keeping the cost variable
4.   Conserving management skill and attention

Further, Rosen (2000) states that outsourcing is an increasingly viable option for small to mid-sized institutions and should be considered as a strategic option. This allows banks' top talent to focus on core issues of competing in an increasingly crowded and complex brave new world. Of technology, Orr (2000, 2001a, 2001b,

2001c, 2001d, 2001e) reported the e-banking/e-lending processes must be designed to eliminate human intervention, or they will not able to handle the problems associated with the transition of hyper growth online. Obviously, e-lenders must start now with strategic foresight, since once hyper growth becomes the norm in the financial world, unprepared bankers will be inundated with applications and fighting for resources to keep pace as a laggard in an e-commerce environment.

REFERENCES

Aaron, E.A. (1999). Consumer privacy. *Independent Banker,* 18-19.

Bank News. (2001). Consumers still wary of Internet financial services. 101, 31.

Bergsman, S. (2000). Bricks and clicks. *Mortgage Banking, 60*(11), 36-41.

Bicknell, C. (2000). Who's credit is it anyway? *Wired News,* (September 22).

Britt, P. (2000). Exploring new lending niches. *Community Banker, 9*(8), 30-34.

Clarke, R. (1999). *A primer in Diffusion of Innovations Theory* (pp. 1-3). Xamax Consultancy Pty Ltd.

Cofran, J. (2000). Online credit networks offer bank cost-effective 'e-Lending' solution. *Bank Systems & Technology, 37*(7), S2, S12.

Draenos, S. (2001). Round one knockout: Electronic banks vs. bricks & mortar banks. Upside, 13(7), 54-59.

Forbes.com. (2000, February 14). Consumer penetration of online banking still low. Available online at: www.Forbes.com.

Fuhrman, A. (2002). Your e-banking future. *Strategic Finance,* 1-8.

Garcia, E. (2000). Techs tumble, Fannie Mae soars. *Money, 29*(12), 46.

Gregor, S., & Jones, K. (1999). Beef producers online: Diffusion Theory applied. *Information Technology and People,* 71-83.

Habal, H. (2000). Banks get over their online lending jitters. *American Banker Special Report: Retail Delivery*, (October 12).

Hewitt, J.R. (2000). An engineering feat. *Mortgage Banking, 60*(5), 4.

Hoppe, D., & Smith, J. (2000). Weapons are they ready? *The Banker, 150*(893), 128-129.

Johnson, T.P. (2000a). Team effort. *Banking Strategies, 76*(1), 4.

Johnson, T.P. (2000b). Bridging the divide. *Banking Strategies, 76*(2), 4.

Johnson, T.P. (2000c). Front line solution. *Banking Strategies, 76*(3), 4.

Julavits, R. (2000). AppOnline goes its own way in Web divorce plan. *American Bankers Association's Banking Journal, 92*(3).

Kassarjian, R. (2000). Internet redefines 'rules of engagement' for customer interaction in lending. *Bank Systems and Technology, 37*(7), S4, S14.

Lamb, E.C. (2000). Internet lending: Happily ever after? How the Internet affects consumers, banks, and business. *Community Banker, 9*(10), 28-33.

Lamberg, E. (2001). Online banking gaining acceptance. *Mercer Business, 77*(4), 6.

Marks, E.A. (2001). Information Darwinism: The impact of the Internet on global manufacturing. *Information Strategy, 17*(2), 40-48.

Marlin, S. (2000). Study: 3000 U.S. banks will offer e-banking services by 2005. *Bank Systems and Technology, 10* (September).

McDonald, J.M., & McKinley, J.E. (1981) *Corporate banking, a practical approach to lending.* Washington, DC: American Bankers Association.

McRae, H. (1999). Paying bills will never be the same as banking takes off in cyberspace. *The Independent, 22* (October 8).

Moeller, R.H. (2002). E-banking ground rules just got clearer. *American Banker, 167*(159), 10A.

The New York Times. (2000). Online mortgages may grow fast. (October 6).

Nigro, F. (2002). From the outside: Mastering e-customer loyalty. *Bank Technology, 15*(1), 39.

Orr, B. (2000). Easy money. *American Bankers Association's Banking Journal, 92*(3), 41-47.

Orr, B. (2001a). Dot.com bank prospers in tough times. *American Bankers Association's Banking Journal, 93*(10), 61-62.

Orr, B. (2001b). Should eBanking programs speak OFX and IFX—or both? *American Bankers Association's Banking Journal, 93*(3), 56-60.

Orr, B. (2001c). E-banking 2001: Where are we headed? *American Bankers Association's Banking Journal, 93*(1), 52-53.

Orr, B. (2001d). E-banking what next? *American Bankers Association's Banking Journal, 93*(12), 40-46.

Orr, B. (2001e). Is Internet banking profitable yet? *American Bankers Association's Banking Journal, 93*(7), 57-58.

Pearce, J.A., & Robinson, R.B. (2002). *Strategic management: Formulation, implementation, and control* (8th edition). Chicago: Irwin Publishing.

Porter, M.E. (1996). What is strategy? *Harvard Business Review, 74*(6), 58-77.

Porter, M.E. (1999). Michael Porter on competition. *Antitrust Bulletin, 44*(4), 841-880.

Prahalad, C.K., & Hamel, G. (1994a). Strategy as a field of study: Why search for a new paradigm? *Strategic Management Journal, 1*(5), 5-16.

Prahalad, C.K., & Hamel, G. (1994b). Seeing the future first. *Fortune, 130*(5), 64-70.

Prahalad, C.K., & Hamel, G. (1994c). Competing for the future. *Harvard Business Review, 72*(4), 122-129.

Ptacek, M. (2000). Online banks develop niche strategies. *American Banker's Special Report: Retail Delivery,* (October 12).

Pyun, C.S., Scruggs, L., & Nam, K. (2002). Internet banking in the U.S., Japan, and Europe. *Multinational Business Review, 2*(2), 73-81.

Quinn, L.R. (2000). Some consumers exploit Internet; others burned. *American Banker's Special Report: Mortgages 2.0,* (August 14).

Raab, M. (2000). Changing times, changing strategies. *American Banker's Special Report: Retail Delivery,* (October 12).

RMA Conference. (2000). *E-banking offers new types of financial risk along with its rewards, experts advise.* Available online at: http://www/rmah1.org/News_PR/July 28-00.html.

Rogers, E.M. (1986). *Communication: The new media in society.* New York: The Free Press.

Rogers, E.M. (1995). *Diffusion of innovations (4th ed.).* New York: The Free Press.

Rosen, C. (2000). Online marketplaces arrive with customers in tow. *Informationweek, 787,* 32.

Rosen, T.A. (2000). Don't let your Internet customer become a statistic. *The RMA Journal,* (November).

Schwlizer Bank. (2001). *E-banking with Hewlett-Packard: Secure, comprehensive, tried and tested.* Public Forum, 1-2.

Security Sense. (2000). Survey: Companies not prepared for e-commerce risks. *3*(11), 1.

Security Sense (2001). Study finds companies underestimate internal threat. *4*(7), 1.

Smith, A.D., & Rupp, W.T. (2002a). Application Service Providers (ASPs): Moving downstream to enhance competitive advantage. *Information Management and Computer Security, 10*(2), 64-72.

Smith, A.D., & Rupp, W.T. (2002b). Issues in cybersecurity: Understanding the potential risks associated with hackers/crackers. *Information Management and Computer Security, 10*(4), 178-183.

South China Morning Post. (2002). Diversity of options helps push e-banking expansion. 11.

Stoneman, B. (2000). Fitting it all together. *Banking Strategies, 76*(2), 50-58.

Stoneman, B. (2001). Passing the buck. *Banking Strategies, 77*(4), 35-40.

Surry, D.W. (1997). *Diffusion Theory and instructional technology.* University of Southern Mississippi.

Waller, E. (2000). Online lending is becoming a lender expectation. *Credit Union Magazine, 66*(6), 60-62.

Warson, A. (2000). Lenders of the world unite! (In Cyberspace). *Mortgage Banking, 60*(11), 44-51.

Wellner, A.S. (2000). Generation divide. *American Demographics, 22*(10), 52-58.

Whiting, R. (2002). Making privacy work. *InformationWeek*, (August 19). 30-36.

Williams, W.L. (2001). Embracing innovation: Aerial applicators scrutinize proposed technology. *Resource, 8*(12), 13-14.

Chapter XIII

An E-Business System Development and Modernization Model to Improve the Profitability of Investment Decisions

Bahador Ghahramani
University of Nebraska at Omaha, USA

Abstract

An Internet-based Systems Development and Modernization Model (SDMM) is an information technology (IT) method that system designers and developers (SD&Ds) can use to develop new systems, to modernize legacy systems, and to increase the net present worth of the systems. The SDMM is, therefore, implemented for three primary purposes: to design and develop leading-edge technology systems, to modernize legacy systems, and to increase profitability of the systems. The model satisfies SD&Ds' specifications as well as user requirements from the concept phase to the operational phase of the development process. It is a structured approach through which users and SD&Ds interact before the system is designed; thus, the users can affect system development when it is most cost-effective to do so. The model uses online modules to develop products that are fully capable of bridging the design to the system development lifecycle phases. The SDMM implements IT principles to standardize system development throughout its lifecycle phases.

Introduction

The Systems Development and Modernization Model (SDMM) adheres to information technology (IT) concepts through which system designers and developers (SD&Ds) begin to understand the user's business requirements for developing a system. The model enables the users and SD&Ds to communicate with a common language about the system before it is designed. The users can influence the development of a system when it is most cost effective. A variety of products are created during system design and development, depending on the type of project and on the SD&Ds' preference. The model also develops a system following the most updated industry and government standards and practices. Figure 1 shows the SDMM architecture and information flow process.

Figure 1. SDMM architecture and information flow process

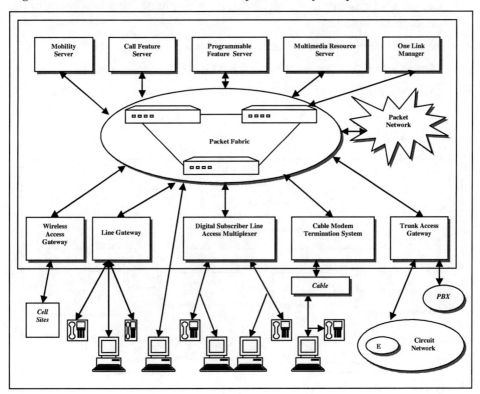

SDMM employs CASE tools to support the SD&Ds' efforts after the system design methodology is in place and before it is deployed. The SDMM also uses its System Modernization Module (SMM) to modernize hardware, software, and interfaces (HSIs) of legacy systems. The SMM consists of a set of algorithms that are used throughout the lifecycle phases of the development process. The SDMM therefore develops a blueprint for the new system showing how SD&Ds' specification documents and methodologies are customized. This methodology is then implemented to fashion a requirement specification list for CASE tools (Meyer, 1993).

SDMM addresses various system products in terms of their "lifecycle" development phases. In order to acknowledge the bridge to design, products developed in the design are included. The SDMM development phases include six online files: (1) Requirements Analysis, (2) Data Analysis, (3) Function Decompositions, (4) Logic Specifications, (5) Design Specifications, and (6) Cost Ledgers. Figure 2 illustrates the interdependent and online SDMM files.

The objectives of the SDMM are to:

1.   Standardize the development phases.

2.   Use a common language to describe the development phases.

3.   Create a framework in which CASE tools might be used in support of the development phases.

4.   Apply modern modules to develop a system.

5.   Move system development away from an art form toward an IT discipline.

6.   Integrate the function of human factors in application development.

Figure 2. SDMM online development files

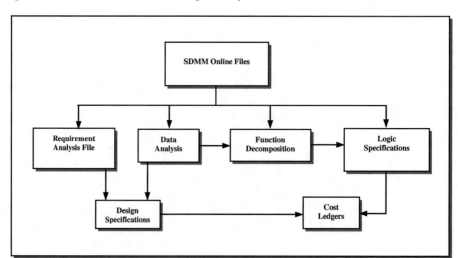

In order to satisfy the above objectives, the SD&Ds have to evaluate the system's programming environment and its applications. Products produced in one system may differ from those developed in another, depending on user requirements and the SD&Ds' expertise. To standardize the system development phases, this model provides checklists for various lifecycle phases of the system development process. The SDMM modules continuously monitor and support the lifecycle development process. As Figure 3 indicates, the SDMM has a set of six primary interdependent modules: (1) System Specification Modules,

Figure 3. SDMM primary modules

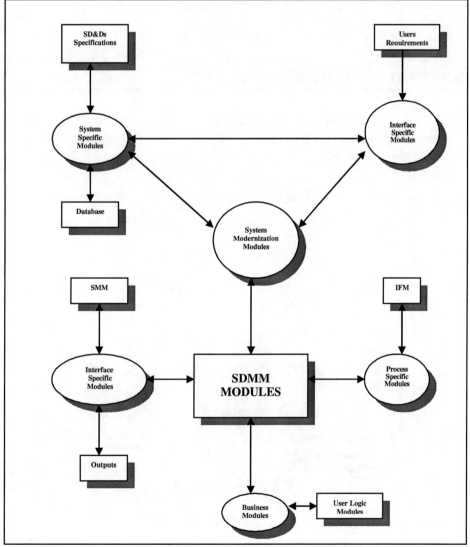

(2) Interface Specific Modules, (3) Process Specific Modules, (4) Business Modules, (5) User Logic Modules, and (6) System Modernization Modules that will be discussed later. In addition to their definitions and to standardize the development process, the SDMM modules have the following characteristics:

1. *Rationale*: Whether the module is required or recommended during the development effort.
2. *Client:* The development team members who make use of the modules.
3. *Developer:* The primary creator of a module.
4. *Precedence:* The Systems Development modules that are completed before work on the product can be initiated.

System Specific Modules

The SDMM uses various specific modules to develop a system. The lifecycle development process is the backbone of the SDMM architecture, which is shown in Figure 4. The SDMM System Specific Modules consist of Requirement

Figure 4. SDMM lifecycle development process

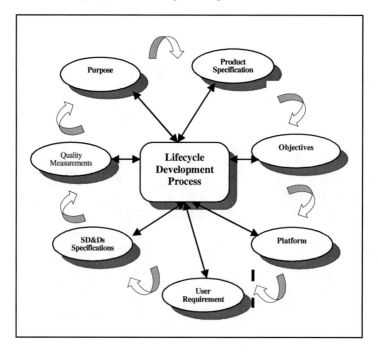

Analysis, Provisioning, Assumption List, User Profile Modules, and Internet-Based Forecasting Module.

Requirement Analysis Module

This is an online module that states a business problem or opportunity. The module supplies a sufficient level of information about the users' needs and their current mode of operation to provide an understanding of their business requirements. It documents and communicates the information with the SD&Ds. It also provides a starting point, direction, and information-gathering capabilities. Users' requirements are an online list of their needs and constraints to be imposed in the development phase of the system. A solution to the users' problems is not likely to be satisfactory if it does not meet these needs within their constraints. User requirements change during the lifecycle development phases of the system. User requirements are a collaborative effort of SD&Ds and users; users alone rarely produce requirements. User requirements are not a solution or an implementation. Therefore, requirements should not imply a computer system solution to a problem. User requirements must be clearly articulated to focus the system development effort. As Figure 5 shows, the SDMM lifecycle effort is an evolutionary process that demands continuous evaluation.

Figure 5. SDMM lifecycle development evaluation

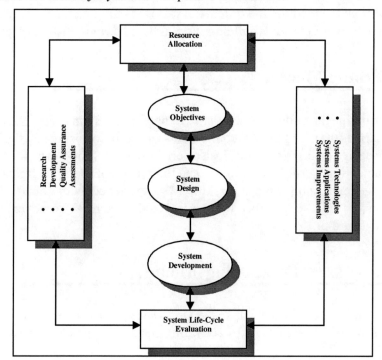

User requirements may contain such needs as: (1) features/functionality, (2) new user work function, and (3) interface to another system. The user requirements must also work within such constraints as cost, delivery date, data volumes, input domain (the limits of valid inputs), transaction frequency response time, allowable error rate and down time, number of users, user location and training, existing system interfaces, HSI, disaster recovery, safety, legal, and usability.

Provisioning Module

This is an online module that supplies the SD&Ds with direction and activity numbers for online HSI provisioning. Because of this module, some of the system's HSI is installed before they are activated into operation.

Assumption List Module

This is an online module that monitors user requirements and profiles, cost effectiveness, usability, or design of a system. This module is activated during the development phase of the lifecycle process. It is a tool to verify and update assumptions in a timely manner. Once an assumption is verified, it should be added to the appropriate SD&Ds' specification and development document and removed from the module. It explicitly clarifies assumptions that are related to a certain risk level and avoids building systems based on unrealistic expectations.

User Profile Module

This is an online list of the characteristics of potential system users. The module clearly defines the user group's requirements and helps to ensure that the human interface design meets user needs. It also defines the user group(s) by identifying and documenting: (1) unique strengths and limitations of users, (2) frequency of use, (3) general knowledge and skill, (4) experience with job (task) and computers, (5) job responsibility, (6) physical environment, (7) turnover rate, and (8) average age of the users.

Internet-Based Forecasting Module

This is an online module that helps SD&Ds and users perform trendline analysis and other statistical evaluations by activating one or a sequence of five methods:

(1) Least Square, (2) Logarithmic Regression, (3) Polynomial Regression, (4) Power Regression, and (5) Exponential Regression. It also computes the R-squared or error value of a set of data points. This module is also linked to the other modules to gather information, measure lifecycle development process, and support the SD&Ds' activities.

Interface Specific Modules

Online Interface Specific Modules bridge system development scope to its organizational environment, interface environment, and functional responsibility. These modules are intelligent and are designed to help users make correct decisions and add value to their work. They help users maintain direct interaction with the system's development process. They ensure a common set of user interface standards that covers all aspects of the system inputs to its physical design. The contents of these modules include:

1. Established human factor guidelines to be followed.
2. A description of the interface procedures (i.e., dialogue style such as menu driven, command driven, etc.).
3. Any standards specific to the system.
4. General screen formats.
5. Any specific HSI requirements.
6. Conventions to be followed for terminology and abbreviations.

An online list of the system interfaces is developed in the beginning phase of the development process. These online modules bridge the system with its identified customers and suppliers.

Interface Documentation Module

This is a combination of event and interface lists. Each interface is listed with all its associated characteristics and events. An event is an occurrence that affects a business process (input event) or is caused by a business process (output event). Input events come from an interface, while output events affect an interface. Each event has a name, direction (input or output), and frequency. It is the first step in identifying system functions. A comprehensive event list helps ensure the completeness of the function list.

Process Documentation Module

This is an ongoing range of activities, with no single start or end. Depending on the size of a system, its scope may contain only one process or multiple processes. This module is a stepping-stone to the functional design of the system and helps to initiate the development phase of a system.

Process Specific Modules

Process Specific Modules are online simulations of the system's lifecycle development phases and processes. They show the system's development process using its data flow activities throughout its lifecycle phases.

Dataflow Simulation Module

This is a presentation of the system's dataflow input and output functions. The functions are represented as rounded boxes and may be "exploded" for decomposition into other simulation models. Interfaces appear as square boxes and data stores as rectangles with an open side at the right. During decomposition, care must be taken to preserve precedence among functions, inputs, and outputs. This is referred to as a "level balance." This module is used to decompose processes and functional hierarchies. Evaluation of the legacy systems suggests that the module is appropriate for analysis only when defining precedence among the elementary functions subordinate to primitive functions. Recent advances in IT suggest that the primitive functions should not be decomposed at all during analysis. That would make the module optional at analysis time, depending on the preference of the SD&Ds for the module over function hierarchies. Modeling the proposed physical functionality of a new system and flow of information between those functions are design activities, but can be accomplished through a physical presentation of the module.

Entity Relationship Simulation Module

This is an online presentation of normalized entity types (business objects) and the relationship between them. It includes certain properties of the relationship, especially the entity and relationship names, and the number of occurrences of one entity associated with an occurrence of another entity (e.g., one to one, one to many). It also includes an entity-element list that helps the SD&Ds understand data relationships and where to store them. User inspection of the module verifies that the SD&Ds have captured the business environment of the system throughout its lifecycle development phases.

Logical Data Dictionary Module

This is an online simulation of the basic information structure that supports the system's scope being analyzed. It identifies and defines the entities and associated data elements needed to operate the system. It also contains definitions and descriptions of the elements and entities, the associations between the elements and entities, sourcing information, valid value sets, and the number of occurrences that could be expected. Primary identifiers must be identified. The module is not complete until the data is normalized. It is also used by the SD&Ds to develop the physical structure of the data.

Functional Logic Module

This is a simulation of the sequential steps that must be performed by a function in order for it to accomplish its purpose. The logic is generally developed for elementary functions, and documents the function to its lowest level of decomposition that allows the SD&Ds (as well as the customers of the product) to gain a full understanding of the function down to its lowest level of detail. The module is: (1) independent of any particular physical implementation; (2) specific and identifies inputs and outputs; (3) unambiguous; and (4) expressed using the systems approach, decision tables, or decision trees.

Business Modules

The SDMM Business Modules represent a system's customary or desired environment, occurrence, and practice in an operation. Each of these modules has a unique set of identifiers that describes the basis for various functional logic documents. These modules include Logical Access Path, System Model, and Prototypes.

Logical Access Path Module

This is a representation of the data accessed or created by a function. It may be graphical or tabular, but shows the entities (including entry and selection criteria) and relationships that are involved in the logic of the function, actions that the function performs on the entities, and access volumes. The logical access path also details navigation through the data, giving both sequence and direction. The database used by the SD&Ds provides pertinent information to complete the lifecycle development phases and to design an efficient schema for the physical database. The SD&Ds verify that the data model and functions support each other, and that the logical access paths to create the physical access exist.

System Model Module

This is a printed report that contains a high-level description of the system to be built. The module is written in terms of business functions, interfaces, general system inputs and outputs, operational recommendations, and selected alternatives (such as the physical hardware, operating environment, and communications needs). It includes the underlying assumptions and constraints, a profile of the target user population, and flow diagrams (e.g., system, data, and process flows). The module facilitates discussions between the users and the project team regarding the system's scope and functionality. These participants in the development of the system should sign-off on the module when it is considered final, although further changes may be negotiated if requirements change.

Prototype Modules

This falls into two basic categories, working and non-working prototypes. Working prototypes may be discarded or may serve as a basis to build upon. Non-working prototypes (interface prototypes) may be either simple or sophisticated. All prototypes serve as a vehicle for communication with the user. The basic idea behind prototypes is to show the users what the SD&Ds have in mind before the system is built. Working prototypes show feasibility as well as answering "what if" questions.

User Logic Modules

User Logic Modules identify and document the SD&Ds' specifications that are required to develop the system. Although these modules have the same standard-ized formats as function logic, they include validations that are required by a particular physical implementation. They bridge the overall SD&Ds' specifica-tions into the user requirements and to design specifications. They also develop a set of system-reusable codes, clarify design logic, reference logical or physical data, and develop input and output logics.

User Specification Module

This is an online document that lists specific information for every action and data entry field, and for every screen or window to be developed. It provides specific information pertaining to fields on the screen layout. It also provides the following information for every action (e.g., add, change, delete) of each screen/window: (1) field name, format, size (in bytes); (2) edit number (if the field is edited); (3) message number (if the field edit is linked to a message); and (4) data element name.

Message List Module

This is a separate list that is compiled and maintained on an ongoing basis and supplements the design specifications. It provides a single source of system messages. For every edit, status, diagnostic, and warning message, the list contains a unique identifier of the message, and a literal text of the message.

System Modernization Module

The primary objective of the System Modernization Module (SMM) is to help the SD&Ds modernize legacy systems. The SMM assists the SD&Ds in assessing the modernization of HSI. The SMM technology is based on mathematical and optimization algorithms, as well as implementing financial and economics prin-ciples. The SMM is an automated and online module addressing present and future HSI modernization requirements. It is an interdependent module generat-ing one of the two conclusive results: to either modernize or not to modernize a system. The SMM uses a perceptive approach that is dependent upon preventive and corrective variables (Baker, 1997). The SMM's development and evaluation process is presented in Figure 5. This figure also explains the application of mathematical algorithms and optimization techniques in conjunction with economic and finance principles.

The SD&Ds frequently decide whether a system should continue operating without any major modernization plans, or whether it should be modernized to meet current and future technology requirements. HSI modernization decisions are being considered with increasing frequency, as SD&Ds have to operate in today's competitive and cost-effective IT market. For SD&Ds, unfortunately, financial constraints and technology limitations always accompany HSI modernization requirements.

This module enables SD&Ds to determine intuitively, quantitatively, and objectively the need to replace HSI by one or a combination of the following four alternatives (Cebesoy, 1997):

1.   **Purchase:** From outside sources
2.   **Reuse:** An old HSI or part
3.   **Update:** Rebuild using internal resources
4.   **Replace:** New HSI or part that was stored

SMM provides SD&Ds with a clear method of determining HSI modernization needs by referring to a part's original design intent, latest part specifications, barcode, and performance record. This, in turn, permits SD&Ds to select the proper method of modernizing the part at an appropriate time and with exact specifications (Garg, Puliafito, Telek, &Trivedi, 1998). It is imperative to note that SMM becomes the driving force in HSI modernization efforts. For SD&Ds, SMM is a multi-dimensional, multi-functional, fully automated, and user-friendly online system that significantly and positively affects the HSI modernization process (Avizienis, 1997).

SMM Added Value

The fully automated, user-friendly, and online SMM is a benefit to SD&Ds because most HSIs are continuously used for an extended time. As a result of extended use and technology evolution, over time a system's HSI becomes outdated and a decision regarding the need for modernization becomes necessary, which is due to two criteria:

1.   **Loss of efficiency and effectiveness:** This leads to an economic decline. In this case, there is no clearly defined point indicating an obvious need for modernization. SMM determines optimum modernization schedules by weighing the increased maintenance and operation costs of used HSIs, along with the costs related to technological and economic obsolescence, against the costs associated with modernization. In this way, SMM allows SD&Ds to make economically appropriate decisions regarding the modernization of outdated HSIs (Laprie, 1992).

2.   **Failure or impending failure:** This leads to work stoppage. Since the failure of some pieces of HSI can have wide-ranging implications throughout an organization in terms of downtime and emergency modernization costs, there are times when it is advantageous to replace HSI before failures. SMM determines the probability of a failure and recommends that key pieces of HSI be replaced prior to the failure (Laprie, 1992).

SMM Decision-Making Process

SMM considers the fact that since the life span of HSI in most legacy systems is about one to five years, the modernization decision is primarily based on the following five criteria (Liu, Lin, Shih, Chung, & Zhao, 1991):

- Modernization due to loss of efficiency
  - Increased maintenance costs
  - Technological and economic obsolescence
  - Extended service life
  - Obsolescence due to age
- Modernization due to failure
  - Availability of new equipment or parts
  - Replacement before failure
  - Probability of failure
  - Physical impairment
  - Inadequacy of current equipment
- Modernization or rebuilding of existing HSI or parts
  - Appropriateness for alternative use
  - Need for rehabilitation or retooling

- Determination of acquisition strategy
  - Purchase
  - Reuse
  - Update
  - Replace
- Computation of the Net Present Worth and other related information
  - Forecasting analysis
  - Trendline analysis
  - Analysis of Variance
  - Other statistical analysis

SMM Analysis

The proposed SMM better satisfies the goal of modernizing a legacy system with lower cost, and higher reliability and performance than the existing fault-tolerance methods. The existing methods rely on HSI availability after their failures instead of the preventive process that is inherent in SMM. The module provides a preventive approach that enhances the SD&Ds' efforts to modernize HSI before their mean time before failure (MTBF). The SMM is based on a structured preventive and effective maintenance and long-term monitoring of primary HSI.

The SMM is defined as the type that does not require actual modernization of HSI since the module replaces parts before the MTBF (Dargan & Hermes, 1997). SMM takes advantage of modern tools and technologies, fault-tolerance analysis, and software engineering to compare modernization alternatives.

SMM is able to provide appropriate modernization periods and strategies by recommending what must be replaced before or when a failure occurs. In this case, a cost trade-off exists between the lengthened service life and the accompanying lower average investment cost in comparison to the cost of emergency or unscheduled modernization due to failure during operation (Meywe, 1980). In many situations, shutdown costs caused by an unscheduled failure are extremely high because of downtime expenses and the cost of expedited modernization, replacement, or repair. In these cases, SMM recommends modernization or repair of the HSI just before their failures because it is economically more desirable. If the cost of modernization after failure is not high enough to justify modernization and replacement until failure occurs, SMM recommends the optimum economic course of action to follow. If the impending failure of HSI is probabilistic, SMM incorporates stochastic values to the events to estimate the expected value of each failure at a given period. Should the failure time be known with certainty, SMM recommends scheduling HSI modernization or part replacements just before failure. However, SMM takes advantage of the fact that failures in most HSI tends to be a random process and thus must be treated as a probabilistic event, or the event could be a premature failure (Alkalai & Underwood, 1995).

Probability of Failure

The module identifies HSI stochastic failures and their distributions by using their historical or experimental data. The module uses past data to predict the probability of future HSI failures.

Premature Failure

The module decides whether this failure is due to infant mortality or other factors. The module discards the infant mortality failure since it happens during the breaking-in periods; SMM assumes that the part has already been subjected to any necessary run-in time. If the premature failure is due to other factors, the module performs root-cause-analysis of the failure and provides appropriate reasons and best courses of action. The module also determines the economic life of depreciable HSI and compares it with similar ones for future selection purposes.

SMM Operation

The operational process of SMM is based on a primary and centralized database management system (DBMS) located in a Central Office that contains historical data of the HSI currently in use. The SMM modernization strategy depends on three interdependent requirements: (1) perceptive modernization, (2) preventive modernization, and (3) corrective modernization. The SMM modernization strategy is shown in Figure 6.

As a part is purchased, reused, updated, or replaced, the SD&Ds regularly update the DBMS. The system subsequently updates all related information and provides accurate online results automatically. The historical data consist of the following criteria (Martin, 1996):

Figure 6. SMM selection strategy

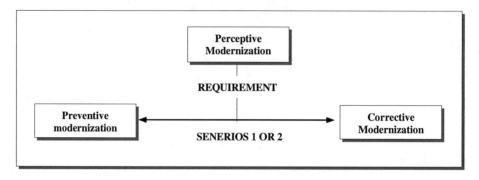

- Purchase date and cost
- Reuse date and cost
- Update date and cost
- Replacement date and cost
- Average time before failure
- Average repair time and cost
- Part availability and location

To efficiently and effectively process information, the DBMS data can further be divided into and accessed from the following two categories (Lykins, 1997):

1. **Technical information:** This includes type of HSI, production rate (units per hour), annual or cycle working hour, MTBF, useful life, and remaining life.
2. **Economic information:** This includes purchase cost, operating costs, salvage value, depreciation, taxes (federal, state), and discount rate.

The SMM operation is shown in Figure 7. As this figure illustrates, the SMM operations cover eight activities: (1) application of modules, algorithms, and CASE tools; (2) application of finance and economic tools; (3) performance enhancement of existing modernization process; (4) fault tolerance enhancement of the existing process; (5) designing and coding of the fault removal process; (6) imprecise computation or forward recovery; (7) resourceful systems or forward recovery; and (8) roll back and update.

Figure 7. SMM operations interdependent activities

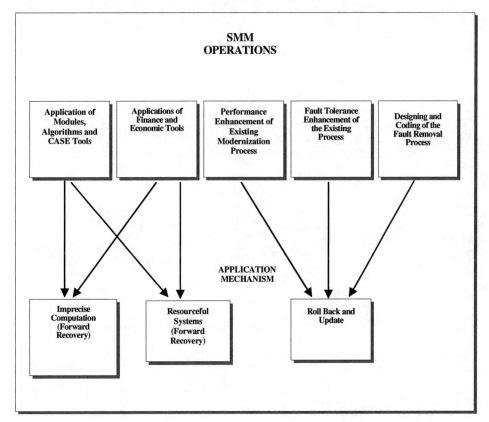

SMM Algorithms

The SMM employs the following modern optimization algorithms to evaluate a system's modernization process. The SMM assumes that operation and maintenance costs of HSI are considered as production costs (Cebesoy, 1997).

Operation Cost + Maintenance Cost = Production Cost   (1)

$$O_i + M_i = P_i \equiv \text{Production Cost} \qquad\qquad i = 1,2,\dots n \qquad\qquad (2)$$

If the time value of money and its effects are considered, the mean investment of an existing or replacement cost is the difference between the initial investment cost and the trade-in or salvage value of the HSI (capital expense) at the end of the nth period, divided by the n number of periods.

Capital Expense = Initial Investment Cost −

   Trade-in or salvage value at period n   (3)

$$\text{Average investment cost} = \frac{I - T_n}{n} \qquad (4)$$

$$\text{Average investment cost} = \frac{\sum_{i=1}^{n} O_i + M_i}{n} \qquad (5)$$

where, $\sum_{i=1}^{n}(O_i + M_i)$ is a summation of the operating and maintenance costs for the nth period of an existing HSI.

When to Modernize?

Let us assume that the average or mean cost for period n is MTC_n. Therefore, in all cases, an HSI satisfies $MTC_{n-1} > MTC_n > MTC_{n+1}$. We can therefore conclude that for costs $c_0, c_1, ..., c_n$ at the end of modernization periods $0, 1, ..., n$ the mean cost is:

$$MTC_{n-1} - MTC_n > 0, \text{ and similarly } MTC_{n+1} - MTC_n > 0 \qquad (6)$$

$$MTC_n = \frac{1}{n}\left[I - T_n + \sum_{i=1}^{n}(P_i)\right] \qquad (7)$$

For the $n+1$ period

$$MTC_{n+1} = \frac{1}{n+1}\left[I - T_{n+1} + \sum_{i=1}^{n+1}(P_i)\right]$$

(8)

$$MTC_{n+1} = \frac{1}{n+1}\left[I - T_n + T_n + T_{n+1} + \sum_{i=1}^{n+1}(P_i) + P_{n+1}\right]$$

(9)

$$MTC_{n+1} - MTC_n = MTC_n \frac{-1}{n+1} + \frac{1}{n+1}\left(\left[T_n - T_{n+1} + P_{n+1}\right]\right)$$

(10)

Since $MTC_{n+1} - MTC_n > 0$, and multiplying both sides by $n+1$:

$$MTC_n < T_n - T_{n-1} + P_{n+1}$$

(11)

Scenario 1: It is feasible to modernize only if the summation of the salvage value of an HSI for the $n+1$ period $(T_n - T_{n+1})$ and the production cost P_{n+1} is greater than the MTC_n.

When Not to Modernize?

From the previous discussions, we know that:

$$MTC_{n-1} = \frac{1}{n-1}\left[I - T_{n-1} + \sum_{i=1}^{n-1}(P_i)\right]$$

(12)

Equation 12 can further be simplified by expressing $MTC_n - MTC_{n-1}$:

$$MTC_n - MTC_{n-1} = \frac{-MTC_{n-1} + T_{n-1} - T_n + P_n}{n}$$

(13)

Since $MTC_n - MTC_{n-1} < 0$, thus:

$$MTC_{n-1} > T_{n-1} - T_n + P_n \qquad (14)$$

Therefore, initiate the modernization process.

Scenario 2: It is not feasible to modernize only if the summation of the production and trade-in costs is less than the present MTC_n.

Furthermore, it is expected that as the result of modernization, the new system becomes more efficient and profitable. To identify the most optimum modernization alternative, the SMM computes net present worth (NPW) of each alternative by comparing the present worth of profits, or CR (cash receipts) and present worth of costs, or C.

For a constant cost of capital, $K \geq 0$, the modernization efforts generate regular profits or cash returns of $r_0, r_1, ..., r_n$ at the end of periods $0, 1, ..., n$ respectively. The SMM uses the following formula to compute R.

$$CR = \sum_{i=0}^{n} \frac{r_i}{(1+k)^i} \qquad (15)$$

Similarly, the SMM computes the present value of the modernization costs for $c_0, c_1, ..., c_n$ at the end of periods $0, 1, 2, ..., n$.

$$C = \sum_{i=0}^{n} \frac{c_i}{(1+k)^i} \qquad (16)$$

The net present worth (NPW) of the efforts which is the difference between CR and C is computed using the following formula:

$$NPW = CR\text{-}C = \sum_{i=0}^{n} \frac{r_i - c_i}{(1+k)^i} \qquad (17)$$

When the *NPW>0*, the modernization alternative is accepted and when $NPW \leq 0$ the alternative is rejected. If there is more than one alternative with positive NPW, the SMM ranks the NPW values starting with the most positive value to help the SD&Ds decide which one of the alternatives best satisfies their specifications and user requirements. In most cases, the optimum alternative is the one with the highest positive NPW (Tai, Meyer, & Avizienis, 1996).

Applications

This section discusses two unique applications of the Internet-based Forecasting Module (IFM). The IFM bridges to all other SDMM modules and is used by SD&Ds to perform forecasting, trendline analysis, Analysis of Variance, and a host of other statistical evaluations.

The IFM is one of the primary modules of the SDMM that was created in Microsoft Excel for Windows to perform trend analysis of the MTC_n, *CR, C,* and *NPW* using Equations 11, 15, 16, and 17; it also measures R-squared or error value of a set of information. Microsoft Excel was selected because it can be easily bridged with other SDMM modules and software, and is readily available to all users. The IFM is a Multiple Regression technique capable of helping SD&Ds and users predict and analyze future values gathered through other SDMM modules. The forecasting and trendline applications of the IFM provide statistical information by adding and inserting a trendline to a set of data series. The module can also be used to forecast forward and backward analysis simultaneously. However, most users do not use the backward application because they have the actual backward data points and the future values that are points of interests in most cases. In this chapter the online forecasting and trendline analysis applications of the IFM are discussed; other applications are available by request.

The IFM forecasting and trendline applications display the specific regression equation that corresponds to the given data points that are drawn on a graph. By using future x and y coordinate values in the regression equation, specific future values are predicted. The IFM uses the following five methods to develop the trendlines:

1. **Least Square or Linear Regression:** It minimizes the sum of the squared deviation around the data points given and creates the trendline using the linear equation $y = mx + b$ where *m* is the slope and *b* is the y intercept.

2.   **Logarithmic Regression:** It creates the trendline using the logarithm equation $y = lnx + b$ where b and c are constants and ln is the natural logarithm.

3.   **Polynomial Regression:** It uses the equation $y = b + c_1x + c_2x^2 + ... + c_6x^6$ where b and c are constants.

4.   **Power Regression:** It uses the power equation $y = cx^b$ where c and b are constants. This method cannot be used if data contains negative values.

5.   **Exponential Regression:** It creates a trendline using the exponential equation $y = ce^{bx}$ where c and b are constants and e is the base of the normal logarithm. Similar to the Power Regression, negative values can be used in this method.

The IFM also displays the R-squared or error value on the graph to test accuracy and reliability of the trendline using the following model:

$$R = 1 - \left[\frac{\sum_{i=1}^{n}(y_i - \hat{y})^2}{(\sum_{i=1}^{n} y_i^2) - \frac{(\sum_{i=1}^{n} y_i)^2}{n}} \right] \qquad i = 0, 1, 2, ..., n \qquad (18)$$

Steps to Run the IFM

Users are given a complete package of SDMM software and two manuals: a users' manual and a specification manual. The software package includes the IFM software and the following instructions:

1.   Put the forecast disk in one of your drives or install it on your hard drive.

2.   Activate the **EXCEL** software by double clicking on the Excel icon.

3. To open the file go to the file menu at the top of your screen, and pull down to **OPEN**. The following box will appear on the screen. The drive box must be changed to the selected drive, and then the files from the disk will appear in the File Name Box. Double click on the FILE **camcopy.xls** or highlight the file and click **OK**.

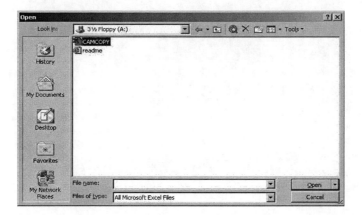

4. What appears to be a blank spreadsheet will appear on your screen. Hit **Crtl-F** to activate the forecast model.

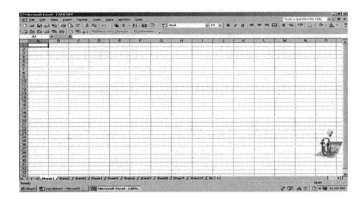

5.   The forecast model will rename the first five worksheets and start drawing an INPUT BOX and blank graphs. Nothing should be done until the module prompts you.

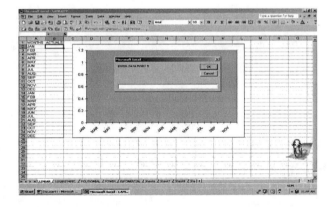

6.   The module will prompt the user TO **INPUT DATA POINTS 1 THROUGH 12**. After each data point is entered, you must tap the entry key or click the OK button.

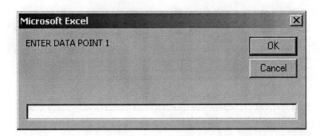

7. After the 12th data point has been **ENTERED, THE MODEL WILL CONTINUE** by putting the data points into the INPUT BOX, plotting the points, and drawing the trendlines associated with the points. The model will also input Equation 18 for the trendline and the error (R-Squared value).

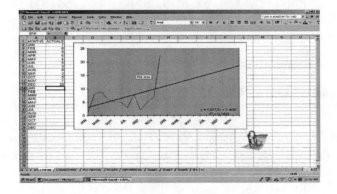

8. Now the user can **CLICK ON THE INDIVIDUAL TABS** for each worksheet and browse each trendline method.

9. The method with the **LOWEST R-SQUARED VALUE** is the trend method with the closest fit to the original points.

10. If the **INPUT DATA POINTS NEED TO BE CHANGED** or altered, this has to be done on the linear worksheet (all other data is fed from this worksheet).

11. Do a **FILE SAVE AS** and rename the file so that the original blank sheet will always stay in track to be used again.

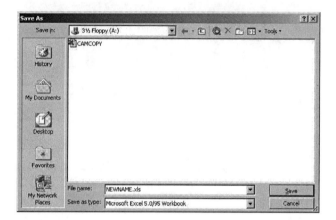

12. Have fun trying your forecast module and if you have **QUESTIONS OR PROBLEMS** running the module, please contact the author.

Applicability of the Model

The proposed model better satisfies the goal of helping SD&Ds to develop high-technology systems or to modernize legacy systems. The SDMM's applicability in e-business environment stems from its ability to guide the SD&Ds to communicate with a common language using various online and Internet-based modules. The SDMM helps systems development by increasing the ease and speed of the lifecycle development process, and provides the SD&D the ability to monitor the development process by employing the SMM algorithms. The SDMM applications help SD&Ds to standardize the development phases, use a common language to discuss the development phases, use CASE tolls to support the lifecycle development phases, apply modern modules in the development process, use IT principles to develop a system, and integrate the human factors principles to create an efficient and user-friendly system.

The Requirement Analysis Module provides SD&Ds with a sufficient amount of information to help them identify users' business problems or opportunities. The Provisioning Module provides the SD&Ds a list of online HIS provisioning needs. The Assumption List Module monitors user requirements and profiles, as well as cost effectiveness, usability, and design of the system, and maps them with the SD&Ds' specifications to identify changes throughout the lifecycle phases. The User Profile Module lists users' characteristics, defines users' requirements, and ensures user satisfaction. The Internet-based Forecasting Module provides SD&Ds with online trend analysis and other statistical evaluation that helps them to assess the lifecycle development process. The Interface Specific Modules help users to make correct decisions and add value to their work by linking the life cycle development phases to organizational environment, interface environment, and functional responsibility. The Process Specific Modules simulate the system's lifecycle phases, showing the SD&Ds the development process using data flow activities. The Business Modules provide the SD&D with a blueprint of the system's desired environment, occurrence, and practice in an operation that describes the basis for various lifecycle functional logic requirements. The User Logic Modules identify and document SD&Ds' specifications that are needed for the lifecycle phases.

To modernize the legacy systems' HSI, the SD&Ds implement the online System Modernization Module, or SMM. The SMM is based on mathematical, financial, and economic algorithms that provide the SD&Ds with a means to develop the most cost-effective modernization requirements. The SMM significantly benefits the SD&Ds modernization efforts by reducing the loss of efficiency and effectiveness, and failure or impending failures throughout the lifecycle phases. The SMM provides the SD&Ds with a technology, based on the historical data and vendor specifications, to modernize a legacy system based on five criteria: modernization due to loss of efficiency, failure, rebuilding of existing HIS or parts, acquisition strategy, and NPV of the HSI. In comparison to the fault-tolerance methods, the SMM satisfies a system's modernization process more efficiently and cost effectively. The SMM is a preventive method that is more cost effective than the fault-tolerance techniques that rely on HSI availability after their failures. The SMM measures the expected value of HIS failures as well as their premature breakdowns to help the SD&Ds decide when to replace a part before its mean time failure or actual failure. The SMM modernization algorithms provide the SD&Ds a decisive method to decide when to modernize, when not to modernize, and how to compute the NPW of various modernization alternatives (e.g., purchase, reuse, update, replace, etc.).

The Internet-based IFM modules provide a means to bridge with the system's databases to help the SD&Ds perform forecasting, trendline analysis, Analysis of Variance, and related financial and statistical analysis. The IFM is user friendly and is created in Microsoft Excel for Windows to compute MTC_n, CR, C, and NPW using the SMM algorithms. IFM uses the Multiple Regression technique to bridge various modules together to function as a cohesive unit and to measure R-squared or fault analysis of the information stream through the system. The IFM also provides the SD&Ds needed information to perform forward and backward analysis simultaneously during the modernization period.

Conclusions

The Systems Development and Modernization Model (SDMM) uses the most modern decision-making process to satisfy two primary objectives of System Designers and Developers (SD&Ds). The SDMM design and development decision-making process is illustrated in Figure 8.

The first SDMM objective is to design and develop a new state-of-the-art system, and the second objective is to modernize existing legacy systems. The model employs various modules to meet both objectives. To reach the first objective, the model uses System Specification Modules, Interface Specific

Figure 8. Systems design and development decision making process

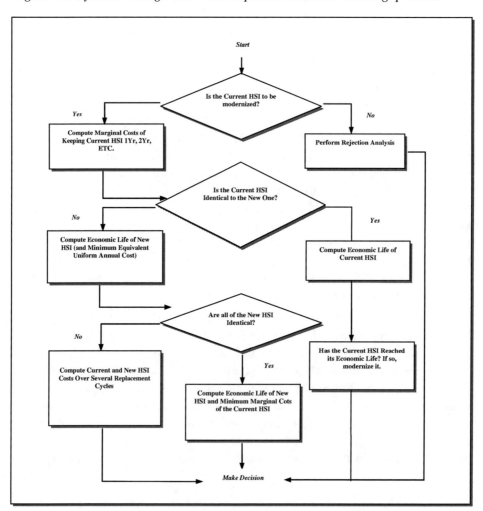

Modules, Process Specific Modules, Business Modules, and User Logic Modules. The System Specific Modules consist of various online modules that are system development specific and guide the SD&Ds' efforts throughout the lifecycle phases of the system development process. Interface Specific Modules are intelligent and online modules that bridge the system development process with the user's environment. Process Specific Modules are online modules that simulate the development process throughout its lifecycle phases and dataflow processes. The Business Modules are also online modules that project users' desired environments, are based on user requirements, and are dependent on a set of identifiers (Chevalier & Marshall, 1997).

For the second objective, the SDMM uses the System Modernization Module (SMM). The SMM mathematical algorithms and optimization techniques are employed in conjunction with finance and economics principles to help SD&Ds decide whether to replace or not replace HSI at any given time. The SMM algorithms help the SD&Ds decide how to modernize a legacy system and chose the optimum strategy. The SMM is a decision-making blueprint that helps the SD&Ds to perform sensitivity analysis of pertinent modernization decisions, to answer "What if?" questions, and to address "When to modernize?" and "When not to modernize?" questions. The model takes into account the operation and maintenance costs of HSI and other related factors influencing the SD&Ds' decisions. SMM offers four basic HIS alternatives—(1) purchase, (2) reuse, (3) update, or (4) replace—to determine whether to replace or not (two scenarios). The model determines profitability of the modernization by comparing the lifecycle development and modernization costs with its benefits. Through implementation of the IFM, the SD&Ds and users are able to determine the NPW of the modernization process, to perform trendline analysis, to compute forecasting and expected values, to provide Analysis of Variance tables, and to conduct other statistical evaluations.

Acknowledgments

The author greatly appreciates his colleagues at the University of Nebraska at Omaha for their encouragement and support. This book chapter and project would not have been possible without generous grants from the NJK Holding Corporation and its subsidiaries. He is extremely grateful to his colleagues Dr. Mark Pauley, Dr. Rosalie Saltzman, and Professor Mary Levesque, for their reviews and editing. He also thanks graduate students Linfeng Cao and Louis Weitkam of the University of Nebraska at Omaha for their efforts and input. In addition, his sincere gratitude is given to systems engineers at Bell Laboratories and IBM Watson Research Center for their reviews and recommendations.

References

Alkalai, L., & Underwood, M. (1995). *Micro-electronics systems IPDT technology roadmap.* Technical Report D-13276, Jet Propulsion Laboratory, California Institute of Technology, Pasadena, California.

Avizienis, A. (1997). Towards systematic design of fault-tolerant systems. *IEEE Computer, 30,* 51-58.

Baker, L. (1997). Lessons learned applying model-driven system design. *Proceedings of the 7th Annual INCOSE Symposium* (pp. 751-756).

Cebesoy, T. (1997). Surface mining equipment cost analysis with a developed linear break-even model. *International Journal of Surface Mining, Reclamation and Environment, 11,* 53-58.

Chevalier, J., & Marshall, R.M. (1997). How to properly specify and control essential project data. *Proceedings of the 7th Annual INCOSE Symposium* (pp. 729-736).

Dargan, P.A., & Hermes, M.A. (1997). Challenges in designing open systems. *Proceedings of the 7th Annual INCOSE Symposium* (pp. 799-806).

Garg, S., Puliafito, A., Telek, M., & Trivedi, K.S. (1998). Analysis of preventive maintenance in transaction-based software systems. *IEEE Transaction Computers, 47,* 96-107.

Laprie, J.C. (1992). *Dependability: Basic concepts and terminology. Dependable computing and fault-tolerant systems* (Volume 5). Wien, New York: Springer-Verlag.

Liu, J.W., Lin, K.J., Shih, W.K., Yu, A.C., Chung, J.Y., & Zhao, W. (1991). Algorithms for scheduling imprecise computation. *IEEE Computers, 24,* 58-68.

Lykins, H. (1997). A framework for research into model-driven system design. *Proceedings of the 7th Annual INCOSE Symposium* (pp. 765-772).

Martin, J.M. (1996). On the nature of integration: An essential task in the engineering of systems. *Proceedings of the 6th Annual INCOSE Symposium* (pp. 637-642).

Meyer, B.C. (1993). Market obsolescence and strategic replacement models. *The Engineering Economist, 38*(3), 209-221.

Meyer, J. F. (1980). On evaluating the performability of degradable computing systems. *IEEE Transaction Computers, C29, C29,* 720-731.

Tai, A.T., Meyer, J.F., & Avizienis, A. (1996). *Software performability: From concepts to applications.* City: Kluwer Academic Publishers.

Chapter XIV

A Complementary Tele-Working Platform for Data and Voice Networks

Philip Sotiriades
University of Patras, Greece

G.-P. K. Economou
University of Patras, Greece

Abstract

*Post, telephone, and telegraph (PTT) enterprises, due to the incessant advances of telecommunications, have to provide for novel value-added services and to be able to supply their customers with the means to reap the full advantages of new technology so both commercially survive (Kurland, 1988). On the other hand, the market trends that favored the birth of many dot.com companies asked for service providers (SPs) that lead PTTs to gradually extend their services towards e-business and become x-service providers (x-SPs); x-SPs mainly stand for **Application** (ASPs), **Interactive Voice Response Systems** (IVRSPs), **email/Messaging** (eMSPs), **Network** (NSPs), **Management** (MSPs), **Storage** (SSPs), **Data Center** (DCSPs), **Hosting** (HSPs), and **e-Commerce** (eCSPs) ones. This chapter introduces the premises, the implementation, and the evaluation performance of a tele-*

working platform that was put into operation in order to equip the Public Bureaus of Thessaly's rural county (Hellas) with the resources to build and provide their citizens those services. This novel platform complies with x-SP specifications and is built on a distributed computing basis.

Introduction

Market trends influencing telecommunication service providers (SPs) led the Hellenic PTT [OTE] and the University of Patras three years ago to the initiation of a collaborative large-scale project aiming to make OTE able to supply novel value-added services. This corporate project outcome had to be a novel integrated tele-working platform (TWP) supporting e-business facilities, and a ready-to-be-applied x-SP system to satisfy the increasing new technology demands of OTE clients. To this end a market investigation was performed and its results thoroughly analyzed so as to establish this project's main features; technical know-how for those services was not made public then (Economou, Karavatselou, Chassomeris, & Lymberopoulos, 2001).

Generally, x-SPs, in order to satisfy these demands, utilize a number of already mature fields, such as personal computers computing power, telecommunication networking facets, and experience in the field of building software applications and remote collaboration between distant parties, a must-supply issue for modern PTTs (Jereb, 1999; Shin, 1999). The proposed tele-working platform also satisfies the need to exchange data without human intervention and access remote resources, in order to both de-centralize their operations and take advantage of the benefits of e-business, while reducing the huge amounts of paperwork that they handle. It can be equally attractive to large/smaller enterprises. The platform meets the following demands:

- Fast exchanging data procedures
- Remote update/service features in order to be always ahead of the market
- Decreased costs of ownership and accountability
- Reduced manual data processing, resulting in reduced relative costs
- Chance offered to small/medium-sized enterprises to attract new customers
- Simplified Web forms for e-business

- Very small elapsing time between business-to-business, business to its partners, and between a business and its customers online and offline transactions

- Compatibility for interacting with the Internet, supporting a variety of file transfer protocols (SMTP, FTP, HTTP) and new standards (e.g., XML) (CCITT Recommendations, 1988)

Complementarity between Internet-based and traditional activities led to the integration of an Interactive Voice Response System (IVRS), designed to meet the ever-expanding requirements for business information transport over telephone lines; it can also support voice processing application solutions through a Web application. By bringing together existing telephone network equipment, business logic servers, and data communications networks, voice processing provides customers with new services such as phone banking or stock market exchange via both telephone and Web networks.

The TWP was strategically built as a distributed computing system (OMG, 1994), thus enacting the benefit to exploit resources within the service such as printers, file servers, and other resources. Data present within the distributed service may be shared across all similar Platforms (nodes). This aspect of jointly operating gives to the TWP flexibility, robustness, and potentially limitless scalability (Sotiriades, Economou, & Lymberopoulos, 2002).

The tele-working platform has been developed with built-in fault tolerance attributes, seeking to enable the users' non-stop availability. By making use of idle processing power within the distributed service, the overall efficiency can be increased by 'load balancing' all the nodes. Also, control data synchronization across this system presents a management challenge that requires specialized technologies to meet; security enforcement can also be less than trivial to achieve.

OTE, in order to demonstrate the resources of the TWP and be able to sell the x-SP, decided to the implement it and focus on a closed user group. The Public Administrational Bureaus of Thessaly, a rural Hellenic county, was chosen as such, considering its geographic particularity, its sparsely populated region, and the need to offer quality of e-business service to the citizens at any time.

The next section describes the architecture of the application-consolidated tele-working platform. We then refer to its operational modes, and the pilot implementation of the platform and the x-SP performance evaluation are discussed. The chapter concludes with an overall discussion about present tele-working platforms and their future potential.

Architecture

General Characteristics

The goal of the project was to create a TWP that would be supported by a distributed computing system, including several joined x-SPs and networks to which OTE would offer 24-hour operational support through its established network. The undergone quest was to achieve the implementation of the x-SP domain's infrastructure and software-dependent basis that would be hosted at OTE (hence referred to as the x-SPD) capable to fulfill the e-business demands and future trends.

This infrastructure should allow for adaptability to the customer's intranet, extranet, or other network protocol requirements such as ISDN, DSL, and/or ATM. The x-SPD support team experience ensured that TWPs would be operated at a high quality of service, while significantly reducing operation costs. Access via private networks to the x-SPD are configured on a client-per-client basis. A simplified view of this interaction of the x-SPD to the clients' TWPs is shown in Figure 1.

The distributed computing system consists of a software layer between the communications facilities provided on each host and the application (Crowcroft, 1996). The software layer (Figure 2) acts like an in-between service between

Figure 1. x-SPD interaction with a client's tele-working platform

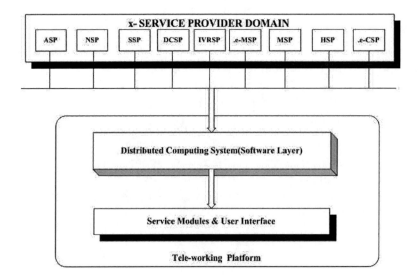

application programs and networks, managing the interactions between disparate applications across heterogeneous computing platforms.

This layer ensures a high degree of independence between the underlying host and the set of distributed applications. It is used to transfer information from one application to one or more others, shielding its user from dependencies inherent in communications protocols, operating systems, and hardware platforms. Generally, this layer provides a set of services specifically geared towards supporting distributed computing. These services ensure that the tele-working platform is scalable, reliable, secure, and available for use, accomplishing high performance.

The integration of the interactive voice response system within the overall tele-working platform aims to utilize new, additional value-added services such as:

- Information and transaction services (e.g., phone banking, stock market)
- Sales force automation
- Location-based services for residential users and businesses (e.g., city guides)

Figure 2. Software layer

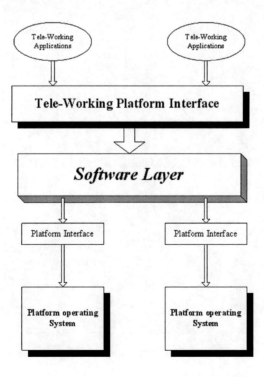

- Voice access to vending machines and convenience services
- Mobile productivity (e.g., voice access to email, conferences, and database services)
- Mass-calling (tele-voting)

Figure 3. Physical view of the x-SP distributed architecture

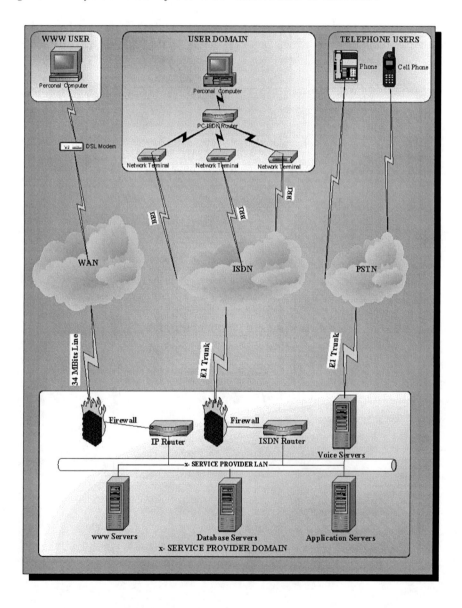

The key points of the distributed architecture are as follows (also shown in Figure 3):

- Internet access is protected by firewalls. The x-SPD consists of a local area network (LAN) that contains all services to Web users, including commerce applications, Web servers, etc.

  The LAN substructure includes two routers: the first one is connected to a wide area network (WAN) through a 34Mbps line; the second one, is connected to a PRI (30B channels) and is used to establish ISDN dial-up connections between the clients and the VS/MCU (§2.2), accessing as many channels as the local network and the database-server ports allow.

- The IVRS is a voice/speech processing platform, integrated into the voice servers, offering:
  - Speech recognition resources
  - Text-to-speech resources
  - Voice/XML browser
  - Resource management
  - E1 trunk connectivity
  - FAX support
  - CTI integration
  - Call control

- The Hosting Service Provider (HSP): Hosting special-purpose applications, network support (unvarying bandwidth), and surveillance checking are supplied by the x-SPD.

- The Management Service Provider (§2.2) satisfies standard ITU protocols.

- The Application Service Provider (§2.2) bridges the interoperability among the voice and Web applications, and the multiple database servers that are integrated in the TWPs network, as well as the calls, and the router connections according to free server ports in the network layer.

- Local and remote databases are in use, incorporating service, querying, and maintenance tools, as well as the user interface, to handle the data traffic.

- The Network Terminals connect the x-SPD to the ISDN lines.

- The DSL cable modem connects the client's hosts to the WAN.

- The PC-ISDN router that handles up to three ISDN BRIs.

A user's interaction with the novel service is facilitated by both applying multimedia information technology and visual programming, which provide for an interactive user-interface. For example, Figure 4 represents the main real-time conference (§3.2.2) instantiation screen with its buttons, multimedia icons, camera output, etc. Each of those objects reveals a help tip each time the pointing device (mouse) is placed on its top. Software tools also exchange audio/voice/data information.

This distributed architecture was thus structured and its main features selected in order to both reduce cost and accomplish a number of important specifications such as:

- *Software utility components re-use.* Updating of existing software-components need not be re-integrated and re-leveraged, thus resulting in reduced development and deployment time.

- *Location independence.* The aforementioned software layer (SL) hides completely the location of a component, whether it is in the same process as the client or on any other node of the service. The way the client connects to a component of the platform is identical.

- *Connection management set-up.* In the case of a network/hardware failure, the components in tele-working applications need to be notified if a client is not active anymore. The SL manages connections to components shared by multiple clients or dedicated to a single one, cheaply.

- *Scalability.* The proposed platform's applications have the ability to grow with the number of users, the amount of data, and the required functionality by remote administration.

Figure 4. Interactive user interface

- *Performance.* In the SL, the applications never see the server object itself; yet, the application is never separated from the server due to the fact that it communicates with the component through method calls. By using these methods' software addresses (utilizing a simple address table), the performance of the TWP augmented to a factor of up to 90%.

- *Bandwidth and latency.* The SL minimizes network round trips wherever possible to avoid the impact of network latency; also, it utilizes the connectionless transport protocol UDP, which is subset of the TCP/IP protocol suite (Howes & Smith, 1997). Its connectionless nature allows the SL to perform several optimizations by merging many low-level acknowledging packages with actual data and pinging messages (OMG, 1994).

- *Security.* The SL programming model hides a component's location and also the security requirements of a component. This security inaudibility is achieved remotely.

- *Load balancing.* A referral component is used by the SL that utilizes the information about the server's load, the network topology between a client and available servers, and statistics about past demands of a given client. Every time a client connects to a component, the referral component can be assigned to the most appropriate server available at that moment.

Communication software modules have been designed to deal with the administrative and the application needs of the TWP, and the interoperability between a client's host and a network terminal. Also included are procedures implementing operational scenarios depending on particular needs. The aforementioned modules are responsible for the online and offline use of the tele-working service, supporting transfer rates up to 384Kbps. Their implementation follows the H.320 and T.120 ITU-T recommendations (online use), and the LDAP (X.500) and DAP standard protocols (Howes & Smith, 1997). TCP/IP handles offline secure file transfer.

The Domain Structure of an x-Service Provider

The idea behind the platform's application was the creation of an x-SPD that would be able to provide various services (through the Public Administrational Bureaus and State Banks nodes) to the citizens. Services such as phone banking, city navigation by the IVRS provider, certificates from the municipal roll records by the application service provider, and citizens websites hosting allow for e-business (through the e-commerce service provider) to professionals at their request.

These services have to adhere to operational standards and a good quality of service. In order to fulfill both requirements and keep clients' private information inaccessible to the provider of the service, a number of modules were designed. All handle data that the x-SPDs administrate (Figure 5):

- The Management Service Provider (MSP) is responsible for the platform's administration, the control data that remain unaffected to the features of the application (Blue Book, 1988).

- The Network Service Provider (NSP) handles the control data that include the additional requested information (safety of transfer between collaborating users) (Blue Book, 1988; Kraemer, 1988; European Telecommunication Standard Institute, 1996; International Telecommunication Union, 1997).

- The IVRS provider (IVRSP) has integrated voice servers that are used to enable callers to access e-business applications using their voice or the

Figure 5. The architecture of the x-SPD

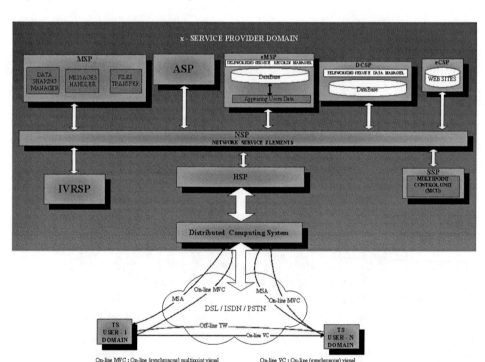

buttons on their telephone. The users' experience is enhanced by a number of features, such as:

- A speech-recognition engine that matches spoken words to a list of possible words in a lexicon. The speech-recognition engine recognizes caller utterances by means of one or more application specific grammars and converts spoken audio into text.

- A text-to-speech engine that produces a speech audio stream from text provided by the speech application or stored in databases for playback over a telephone. The voice server provides unlimited vocabularies using human voices.

- Support of a variety of telephony platforms for inbound and outbound voice calls. The telephony platform connector is the run-time platform for speech applications that connects the voice audio streams from the public telephone network or Voice over Internet Protocol (VoIP) to recognition and text-to-speech engines.

- Voice application development tools are used to develop and test speech applications using speech recognition and/or text-to-speech. These tools include support for applications written in Voice XML (Wyke, 2002).

- A system management component, handling the browsers' initialization/termination.

- Support for automatic/dialed number identification service, and call transfers.

- Barge-in detection.

- Support to enable the voice server to reside behind a firewall.

- Support for secure sockets layer.

The connection environment by which the IVRS provider performs is shown in Figure 6.

- The Application Service Provider (ASP) provides for the correct timing of the combined procedures. A tele-working service has to anticipate the following timing levels: the various events time-schedule of the main application, asynchronously fired operations while in an active application (multi-point calls (Fruscio, 1998), participants' identification, definition of certain types of messaging, i.e., from the conference chair), the definition of the priorities per client, municipal roll record certificate execution, and

Figure 6. The connection environment of the IVRS provider

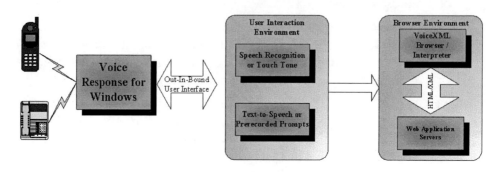

various synchronization levels that are irrelative to the application or the hardware capabilities (Blue Book, 1988).

The voice server of the IVRS provider, supplies the structure for voice-enabled applications that are handled by the ASP, using dialog management which enables the caller to use a natural interface just by speaking. The IVRS provider consists of:

- The Storage Service Provider (SSP), which incorporates a non-natural user (server). In the case of multi-user tele-working applications, it manages the exchange of a large amount of data amid the participants while the establishments of many connections with every other part result. Often, multi-user applications influence the quality of the service (i.e., the audio/video/data flow) that has to be compensated by a high functional cost. So ITU suggests the insertion of a virtual server (VS), to temporally store or collect the user concerning information. The characteristics of a VS (Blue Book, 1988) are:

  - Information control (International Telecommunication Union, 1997; Fruscio, 1998)

  - Data transferring error correction

  - Creation of storage temporary spaces

  - Messages synchronization (eMSP) for chat-like conferences (European Telecommunication Standard Institute, 1996)

  - Virtual port resources

- Surveillance tools for the service, implementing the access controls, right alteration, and information updating for active conferences

A Multi-point Control Unit (MCU) often implements a VS, having many more capabilities; its specifications are also set by the ITU (International Telecommunication Union, 1997).

- The e-Commerce Service Provider's (eCSP's) domain, where the clients' catalog is hosted. It contains the identification information for each client and also additional information related to their activities, their current state, and their business profile, providing a form of data warehousing. Additional information is derived from the clients' personal databases, and some user-selected data of those can be arranged to appear in websites through the central databases. These websites may also contain active server pages in order to serve the e-commerce activities such as transactions, orders, etc. The eCSP interacts with the IVRS provider in order to reach a much larger audience, anyone with a telephone.

Implemented Protocols

As aforementioned, a number of international standards were implemented in both the x-SPD and the TWP in order to grant the project quality of service and reduced cost performance. The tele-working service's architecture was built on the ITU standards such as SMTP, POP3, IMAP4, LDAP version 3, and NNTP for handling data exchange. The videoconferencing structure is based on H.323 and T.120 protocols (Blue Book, 1988; European Telecommunication Standard Institute, 1996; International Telecommunication Union, 1997). The H.323 ITU standard also specifies how clients' hosts (PCs), equipment, and applications are to link, share data, and synchronize their packets' traffic.

H.323 terminals and equipment can handle real-time video, voice, and data, or any combination of those. H.323 also defines how calls are set up, the capability negotiation framework (the process of getting user terminals to communicate), the way data is transmitted, and audio and video codecs (encoders/decoders of input/output audio and video sources that can be user refined). H.323 specifies the utilization of the T.120 standard for data conferencing.

The T.120 standard provides for collaboration conferences using data conferencing features such as application sharing, conferencing white board, and file transfer. Finally, the implemented Lightweight Directory Access Protocol (LDAP) is a method for clients to query and access information stored on directory servers over TCP/IP connections (Blue Book, 1988).

Tele-Working Platform Services Operational Modes

The platform provides the clients with on- and offline communication, advertising of their offered e-business, interactive participation in chat-like conferences, set-up of real-time collaborative conferences, file transfer utilization, access agenda/client catalog facilities, and exploitation of central databases facilities. All data exchange takes place in a secure environment.

Offline Communication

Offline communication refers to services such as electronic mail messages/ attachments, agenda data, publicity, and application forms that do not involve real-time multimedia conferences. It mainly relates the data exchange between the central databases. The following x-SPs are offered:

- *Messaging services.* Tools are included to compose, access, and read messages/attachments. Supported are also the clients' address book services, monitoring of sent messages/attachments, voice access to email, notification service, etc.

- *E-business and phone banking services.* Clients can set-up any e-commerce service and access bank accounts, make transactions, etc., through voice-enabled applications. Building, hosting, and updating Web pages that support all commercial activities by active server pages built into the application and voice servers, can be organized according to the enterprise variety.

- *Agenda/client catalog.* The agenda facility stores proposed, accepted, and/or modified data regarding clients' e-meetings. The catalog stores clients' personal/professional data.

- *Central databases.* They are responsible for the message handling and the data exchanging between the clients. They administer (add/delete/modify) the clients' and their pre-arranged advertising-submission data, send the meeting notification (acceptance, modification, postponing) to the proper clients, and monitor conference scheduling.

Online Communication

Online communication refers to conference services (i.e., chat-like and real-time collaborative conferences) where audio/video/data collaboration takes place among the clients.

- *Chat-like conferences.* The database-server can create upon demand virtual 'rooms' in which the clients 'chat' by writing messages in real time, handling the floor control operations and rights. Several 'rooms' can be made and accessed by the same clients simultaneously.

- *Real-time collaborative conferences.* The x-SPD provides the clients with the appropriate tools for the establishment, management, and application of collaborative, real-time conferences. Proper signaling and a set of controls support the synchronization of commands and resulting events, as well as application sharing, real-time data exchanging, floor control managing, whiteboard facilities, etc. Password-locked procedures are implemented, to allow the clients to safely join multi-collaborative sessions (by utilizing an MCU) (Blue Book, 1988; Kraemer, 1988). Figure 7 shows this operation by a relative diagram.

Figure 7. Schematic representation of real-time collaborative conferences

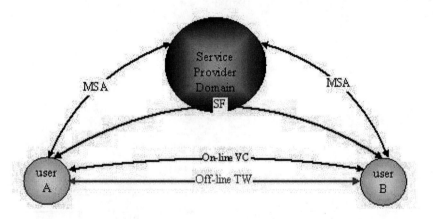

On-line VC : On-line (synchronous) visual collaboration

Off-line TW : Off-line (asynchronous) teleworking

MSA : Maintenance, Surveillance and administration process

SF : Store and forward of users data

Pilot Implementation

As soon as OTE implemented the x-SPD, the installment of a number of TWPs took place at the rural area of Thessaly, an agricultural Hellenic county. Its geographic particularity chose the region, where the city is in the lowland and most of the people are in the highland. Personal presence was required for a citizen to carry on bureaucratic tasks along to frequently bad weather conditions.

A network of 10 nodes was set with the purpose of linking the local administration bureaus and simplify/accelerate the work of the employees, hence serving the public in a better way. Alternatively, it provided the citizens with new services such as advertising their region for tourist exploitation, digital maps use, citizens' websites hosting, processing of bureaucratic procedures, etc.

The x-SP responded successfully over the duration of the pilot project (nine months), while the pilot project itself is considered a success. For this period of time, well over 250 cases were serviced (75/190 online/offline collaboration ratio). A total of 112,459,591MBs were exchanged (to and from) amid nodes. Usage time during collaborative sessions was 90 minutes, in average. The topics covered were 72% service in nature, 9% administrative, 10% financial, and 9% social talk.

Table 1 shows how public servants (employees-PS) judged the service's performance. The great majority of the answers ('good' + 'very good') were positive; the best ratio was achieved for the one regarding execution time. Service reliability rated second, whereas recovering capability regarding the services and PSs' errors were satisfactory. System resources management was also well accepted.

Table 1. Service's performance rates

	Rates (%)		
	(VB)&(B)	NG	(G)+(VG)
Response/task execution time	0	4	96
System reliability	8	12	80
Recover capability/terminal errors	12.5	12.5	75
Recover capability/PS errors	4.2	16.7	79.2
System resources management	4.3	17.4	78.3

VB: Very Bad, B: Bad, NG: Not Good, G: Good, VG: Very Good.

Table 2. PS routine without the X-SP operation

	Rates (%)		
	(VS)&(S)	N	(L)+(VL)
Response/task execution time	0	0	100[*]
System reliability	23	18	59
Recover capability/in-bureau errors	0	100	0
Recover capability/off-bureau errors	21.6	15.2	63.2
Bureau resources management	48	32	20

VL: Very Larger, L: Larger, N: Neutral, S: Smaller, VS: Very Smaller.
[*]*Opinion taken after the training period.*

Table 2, on the other hand, shows that PSs believe the overall performance of their bureaus before and after the x-SP operation significantly defers only in the time saved by operating the x-SP. Their belief, however, in the 'bureaucratic operation mode' (before the x-SP operation) as a more error-free procedure can be explained by the 'new technology phobia' they use to demonstrate. This 'phobia' was greatly eased during their training period (two weeks), but mostly by operating the TWPs.

Table 3 shows the results of collaborative sessions. PSs found the connection process and its needed time to be good (i.e., 'good' + 'very good'). On data operations—both file transfer and application sharing—they were satisfied. Utilization of real-time communication and sharing tasks was also positive, as their answers showed (i.e., 'good' + 'very good' again).

Table 3. Connection's process performance rates

	Rates (%)		
	(VB)&(B)	NG	(G)+(VG)
Connection process	0	12	88
Connection time	0	8.3	91.7
Real-time communication	0	0	100
File transfer	8	8	84
Sharing tasks	0	0	100

VB: Very Bad, B: Bad, NG: Not Good, G: Good, VG: Very Good.

Discussion

In the previous section's tables, PSs of the pilot nodes embraced the new service in general. Notwithstanding their disquietude towards computers, networking equipment, and the other necessary apparatus, they exhibited a genuine enthusiasm about the perspectives the service brought to them.

They strongly believe their needs—to constantly get informed about developmental programs, tele-conferencingly consult major experts in a field, virtually attend seminars, and create and learn from special set-up distance learning educational projects—can be met by the presented tele-working x-service. On the other hand, the overall cost for installing, upgrading, and maintaining such a service (and a tele-working network) is much less than the cost of the DSL/ISDN/PSTN calls transacted.

On the other hand, to enable the future adaptability of the service, embedment of Component Object Model (COM) protocol within the aforementioned software layer (§2.1) is the agent that has been lately integrated in the tele-working platform. COM defines how components and their clients interact. This interaction is defined such that the client and the component can connect without the need of any intermediary system component. Microsoft's Distributed COM (DCOM, 1996; Lockhart, 1994; Rosenberry, 1993) extends the protocol to support communication among objects on different computers on a LAN, a WAN, or even the Internet. DCOM advantages are:

- Location independence
- Connection management
- Scalability
- Performance
- Bandwidth and latency
- Security
- Load balancing
- Fault tolerance
- Ease of deployment
- Protocol neutrality
- Platform neutrality
- Integration with other Internet protocols

Also, the reader has to keep in mind that very little is made public about tele-working services of such a magnitude. Most recently, however, a publication about an Internet-based system facilitating commerce of medical devices (Palamas, 2002) appeared. This special-purpose platform aims to help possible customers of medical devices select the appropriate equipment by building a powerful Internet portal. The developers' main objective was to maintain control over the detailed information of products, and be able to drag data from linked websites and online catalogs.

Although the level of the portal's potential is not similar to the proposed platform, the interest for building commercial applications that would link 'clients' is a given fact. In addition, since another facet of the Internet-based application, a fragment of our proposed platform, is the adoption of Java and XML technologies, this application also sustains the key decisions of our own platform.

Alternatively, from the part of the Hellenic PTT (OTE), the backer of the whole project, the team of developing engineers can only mention this set of specifications:

- Acquire the capability to enter the tele-working market by means of a reliable x-SP and TWP that would be based on standard protocols, software, and hardware components.

- The cost of the non-communication equipment was to be kept low.

- The obtained x-SPD and TWP, as well as the connectivity equipment and tools, and the team of technicians that would back-up the new x-SP, would have to rely on its organization facets and utilize the already present telephone, mobile, and ISDN networks.

- Service backing-up (i.e., the training of the clients, the structuring of 'help desks', the forwarding of the new x-SP), updating, and monitoring of the pilot project was to weigh on it the minimum possible. Later on, the team of developing engineers would train its technicians.

- The service had to be ready to migrate to DSL/ADSL and ATM networks with minimum effort, low cost, and without having to re-train clients/technician on its use/maintain.

Pondering the above specifications, the architecture, operational modes, and the pilot implementation characteristics of both the x-SPD and the TWP implementations are better explained. Nevertheless, all OTE specifications were satisfied; actually, the Hellenic PTT extended its collaboration with the University of Patras for a period of three more years.

Moreover, we learned that the OTE initial investment funds turned to profit. More specifically, after the collaboration and buying out of a number of Eastern Europe's National PTTs (i.e., Romania, Georgia, Armenia), the Hellenic one enters their market by forwarding e-business solutions by means of its acquired know-how from the novel x-SP. The not-so-sophisticated, but otherwise very reliable network capabilities on which the design was based are very appropriate to ensure a steady market share gaining.

Finally, there a number of lessons that the developing engineers learned:

- People are eager to know about new technologies, even to get to utilize them, but they expect great funding to come from state programs, from various organizations' backing-up, or from decisions (i.e., laws) that would be applied to their work.

- 'New technology phobia', especially personal computer utilization, is still an everyday problem. People with no proper education tend to deny the benefits they offer, especially those running small/medium enterprises (of at most 50 employees) that developed by themselves.

- To build the necessary software to implement all communication protocols, the user interface, the control modules, etc., of the novel service, a lot of compromises had to be reached between the actual operation and the firm budget. The code's modularity was so adopted.

- Updating the software modules can be done remotely, a major cost-reducing facet.

- The x-SPD and TWP documentation proceeded simultaneously to their building.

Conclusions

The developed tele-working platform aims to be the base to establish the tele-working service in a flexible, user-friendly, foolproof, fruitful, and most convenient manner. It seeks to convey unexploited human and material resources, and to combine them with high-end technological solutions to facilitate labor and thus improve productivity. Attributes of the platform, such as classification of professional future clients' data and their promotion, easy and quick retrieval of significant data from the Web by means of secure connections, online and offline communication, real-time collaborative conferencing, and a friendly-man-to-computer interface, are met. On the other hand, the investment of the Hellenic

PTT (OTE) was returned since the technologies used are far from expensive. Naturally, when new features such as DSL/ADSL and ATM networks will be employed, the cost will have to increase, but the overall quality of service and connection rates will also manifold increase.

References

Blue Book (1988). *CCITT Recommendations: F710 to F730.*

Crowcroft, J. (1996). Open distributed systems. UCL.

DCOM (1996). Latest information available online at: http://www.microsoft.com.

Economou, G.-P.K., Karavatselou, E., Chassomeris, C., & Lymberopoulos, D. (2001). A novel tele-medicine system. *Online Symposium for Electronic Engineers,* March. Available online at: http://www.osee.net/pro_bio_systems.html.

European Telecommunication Standard Institute. (1996). *ETS 300 483— Terminal Equipment (TE); Integrated Services Digital Network (ISDN); Multi-point communications for audiovisual services; main function- ality and basic requirements for Multi-point Control Units (MCUs).*

Fruscio, G., Ishaq, A., & Petrone, V. (1998). *A signaling server prototype for the support of multipoint to multipoint multimedia services.* CoRiTel, Ericsson Telecomunicazioni S.p.A., Via di Tor Vergata, January.

Howes, T.A., & Smith, M.C. (1997). *LDAP programming directory-enabled application with lightweight directory access protocol.* Technology Series. MacMillan.

International Telecommunication Union. (1997). *ITU-T Recommendation H.320—Narrow-band visual telephone systems and terminal equip- ment.* July.

Jereb, E., & Gradisar, M. (1999). Research on tele-work in Slovenia. *Inf. (Ljubljana), 23*(1), 137–142.

Kraemer, K.L., & King, J.L. (1988). Computer-based systems for cooperative work and group comp. *Surveys, 20*(2), 115-146.

Kurland, N.B., & Bailey, D.E. (2000). Telework: The advantages and chal- lenges of working here, there, anywhere, and anytime. *IEEE Engineering Management Review, 28*(2), 49–60.

Lockhart, H.W. (1994). *OSF DCE, guide to developing distributed applica- tions.* McGraw-Hill.

OMG. (1994). *The common object request broker: Architecture and speci-fication. Revision 2.0.* Object Management Group.

Palamas, S., Kalivas, D., & Panou-Diamandi, O. (2002). An Internet-based system for the commerce of medical devices. *IEEE Engineering in Medicine and Biology,* 21(2), 26–32.

Rosenberry, W., & Teague, J. (1993). Distributing applications across DCE and MS-WindowsNT. O'Reilly.

Shin, B., Higa, K., Liu Sheng, O.R., & Ide, T., (1999). Analyzing the media usage behavior of tele-work groups: A contingency approach. *IEEE Transactions on Systems Management and Cyb.—Part C, 29*(1), 127-139.

Sotiriades P., Economou, G.- P.K., & Lymberopoulos, D. (2002). Enhanced applications of an ISDN-based tele-working platform. *IASTED International Conference Communication Systems and Networks (CSN 2002),* Malaga, Spain, September 9-12.

Wyke, R.A., Rehman, S., & Leupen, B. (2002). XML programming (core reference). Microsoft Press.

About the Editor

Namchul Shin is Associate Professor of Information Systems at Pace University (USA). He received his PhD in MIS from the University of California at Irvine, an MBA from the University of Toledo, and a BA from Seoul National University. His current research interests focus on the areas of IT business value, organizational and strategic impacts of IT, electronic commerce/electronic business, and business process management. His work has been published in journals such as *European Journal of Information Systems, Journal of Logistics Information Management, Journal of Electronic Commerce Research, International Journal of Services Technology and Management, International Journal of Electronic Business,* and *Business Process Management Journal.* He is currently a member of the Editorial Boards of *Journal of Electronic Commerce Research* and *Business Process Management Journal.*

About the Authors

Staffan Brege is Professor of Industrial Marketing. He has an MSc in Business Administration and a PhD in Industrial Marketing both from the Institute of Technology at Linköping University, Sweden. His research covers several different areas, including marketing strategy, value chains, outsourcing, and e-commerce. Dr. Brege also has extensive experience as a strategy consultant.

Stephan A. Butscher is a Partner with Simon, Kucher & Partners Strategy & Marketing Consultants (UK) and is Managing Director of SKP's London office. He has been with the firm since 1994 and has spent three-and-a-half years building up the US office in Boston. He is the author of the books, *Customer Clubs—A Modern Marketing Instrument* (German only) and *Customer Loyalty Programs and Clubs—A Practical Guide* (Gower Publishing, London, 2nd ed., 2002). He has published more than 80 articles on international marketing and strategy, retention marketing, pricing and so forth in various journals in Europe and the US.

Thomas W. Dillon is an Associate Professor of Computer Information Systems at James Madison University in Harrisonburg, Virginia (USA). He holds a PhD in Information Systems from the University of Maryland Baltimore County. He currently teaches courses in Electronic Commerce and Systems Analysis and Design. Dr. Dillon researches and publishes regularly on electronic commerce and healthcare informatics issues.

G.-P. K. Economou was born in Cagliari, Italy, in 1966. He received the Diploma in Electrical and Computer Engineering (five-year degree) and a specialization in Systems for Automatic Control from the University of Patras, Hellas (1990). He completed his PhD in 1995 and covered the design, development, and learning facets of decision support systems. He is at present a Senior Staff member of the Network Operation Centre with the University of Patras, Hellas, Greece. Dr. Economou most recently completed a major strategic national project aiming to plan, develop, and support tele-working networks. He has also played a chief part in the fruitful outcome of a number of EU projects, sponsored either by European projects or Hellenic SMEs. His research interests include tele-working and tele-medicine development platforms, decision support systems structuring, neural networks processing, VLSI architectures for the integration of tele-working platforms, and computer networking. He has published more than 40 articles, and is a member of the IEE, the Technical Chamber of Hellas, and the Hellenic Society of Electrical and Mechanical Engineers.

Cain Evans has worked on assignments in industry, in particular with eCRM, systems integration, and business transformation. His assignments have been both in the UK and overseas. Professor Evans spent a number of years with EDS during which he worked on several local and national blue-chip projects relating to integration of systems. His current responsibilities include teaching E-Commerce and Information Security (MSc, MBA, and BSc) with research in recent years in the field of e-Business/e-commerce systems and integration, which he has continued to the PhD level. He has a first degree and second degree in IT and Computer Science, and is a member of BCS, IIE (E-Business), and MIEEE.

Bahador Ghahramani is an Associate Professor in the Department of Information Systems and Quantitative Analysis at the University of Nebraska at Omaha (UNO) (USA). Prior to joining academia, he was a Distinguished Member of the Technical Staff (DMTS) at AT&T-Bell Laboratories. His work experience includes positions in academia, industry, and consulting. He has presented and published numerous papers, and has been an active participant and officer in several national and international organizations and honor societies. He holds seven patents and has copyrights on five AT&T global system designs. Dr. Ghahramani received his PhD in Industrial Engineering from Louisiana Technological University with a minor in Information Systems; an MBA in Information Systems from Louisiana State University; an MS in Industrial Engineering from Texas Technological University; an MS in Applied Mathematics and Computer Science from Southern University; and a BS in Industrial Engineering and Management from Oklahoma State University. He is the recipient of three outstanding teaching awards from major higher education entities.

TerryAnn Glandon is an Assistant Professor of Accounting at the University of Texas at El Paso (USA), where she teaches undergraduate and graduate courses in Accounting Information Systems and Computer Applications. In 2003, she was a recipient of the Outstanding Accounting Educator of the Year award by the Texas Society of CPAs. She has published articles in the *Journal of Accountancy, Advances in Management Accounting, Internal Auditing,* and *Journal of Applied Business Research.* She can be reached at tglandon@utep.edu.

Călin Gurău is a Lecturer of Marketing in the School of Management, Heriot-Watt University, Edinburgh (UK). He is a Junior Fellow of the World Academy of Art and Science, Minneapolis (USA). He worked as a Marketing Manager in two Romanian companies, and he has received degrees and distinctions for studies and research from the University of Triest, Italy, the University of Vienna, Austria, Duke University, USA, the University of Angers, France, and Oxford University, UK. His present research interest focuses on the marketing strategy of the biotechnology firms and the marketing strategies on the Internet.

Christine M. Haynes is an Associate Professor of Accounting and Associate Dean of the College of Business Administration at the University of Texas at El Paso (USA). She graduated *magna cum laude* with a BS in Accounting from the University of Utah (1986) and earned her PhD in Accounting from the University of Texas at Austin (1993). Her primary research interests are in the areas of auditor/client interactions and auditor judgment. Results of her research have appeared in such journals as *Auditing: A Journal of Practice and Theory* and the *Journal of Accounting Literature.* She can be reached at chaynes@utep.edu.

Markus B. Hofer, PhD, is a Director at Simon, Kucher & Partners Strategy & Marketing Consultants GmbH in Bonn. He studied Industrial Engineering and Business Administration at the University of Karlsruhe, Germany, where he received his master's degree. During his studies in the US, he attended Louisiana State University in Baton Rouge as a Fulbright scholar. In 2002 he completed a PhD at the University of Dortmund, Germany. He is a regular speaker at conferences, author of many articles, and editor of books, such as *Automotive Management* and *Investor Marketing.*

Paul Humphreys is currently a Reader in the Faculty of Business and Management at the University of Ulster, N. Ireland. He previously held positions at the University of Hong Kong and The Queen's University of Belfast. His current research and teaching interests are in supply chain management and electronic commerce.

Il Im is an Assistant Professor in Information Systems Department at the New Jersey Institute of Technology (USA. He received his BBA and MBA from Seoul National University and PhD from Marshall School of Business, University of Southern California. His research interests include supply chain management, personalization information systems, and individual behaviors in online environments.

Myung Soo Kang is a full-time Lecturer of Global Marketing at Hansung University, Korea. He received his BBA, MBA, and PhD degrees from Seoul National University, Korea. His research interests are in global marketing strategy and relationship marketing in online environments.

Ki-Chan Kim is a Professor of Business Administration at The Catholic University of Korea. He received a PhD from Seoul National University, Korea, and had researched at the University of Tokyo, Japan, and MIT as visiting scholar. His research interests are modularization with IT, inter-firm relationship at the automotive industry, and supply chain management.

Daniel Kindström is a doctoral student at the Institute of Technology at Linköping University (Sweden) and recently published his licentiate thesis, "Rearranging a Business Model Towards Market Orientation—Strategic and Operational Dimensions and the Impact of E-Commerce." His research interests revolve around business models and the impact of e-commerce on business development and change.

Ping Lan received his PhD from the University of Strathclyde, UK (1995), and is currently an Associate Professor of Business Management at the University of Alaska Fairbanks (UAF) (USA). Prior to joining UAF, Dr. Lan worked in Canada, Australia, Thailand, Britain, and China as an academic, a journalist, and an entrepreneur. He has been published widely, with articles in the *International Journal of Technology Management, Technovation, International Journal of E-Business, Asia Pacific Business Review, Regional Studies, Transnational Corporations, Journal of Euromarketing,* among others. His current teaching and research interests include e-commerce, innovation management, technology transfer, and international business.

Frank Luby is a Partner with Simon, Kucher & Partners Strategy & Marketing Consultants GmbH in Boston, MA. In his 15-year professional career, he has worked as a consultant, writer, and editor. He worked for A.T. Kearney, Lexecon, Inc. (Chicago, Illinois), Analysis Group (Cambridge, Massachusetts), and an affiliate of Dow Jones & Company outside of Frankfurt, Germany. He studied physics at the University of Chicago, which awarded him a bachelor's degree in 1985. He also worked for three years there as a Teaching Assistant in the Mathematics Department.

Nils Madeja is a Research Associate and doctoral candidate at the Otto-Beisheim Graduate School of Management (WHU) (Germany). His research and teaching activities include success factors in electronic and mobile business. His research has been featured in journals like the *JECR* and presented at international conferences such as the HICSS and ICEB. Prior to joining the chair, he spent two years in Japan, where he worked in the semiconductor industry and for an e-commerce system vendor. He also gained professional experience in the semiconductor and telecommunications industry in Germany. Mr. Madeja holds an advanced degree in electrical engineering (Dipl-Ing) from the University of Kiel, Germany.

Ronan McIvor is a Senior Lecturer within the Faculty of Business and Management at the University of Ulster (N. Ireland). He has carried out extensive research in the areas of supply chain management and information systems. His doctorate is in the area of supply chain management. He is currently carrying out research in the areas of outsourcing and the application of electronic commerce at the buyer-supplier interface.

Jakob Rehme is an Assistant Professor of Industrial Marketing, with an MSc in Industrial Engineering and Management, a Licentiate of Technology in Industrial Marketing, and a PhD in Industrial Marketing, all from the Institute of Technology at Linköping University (Sweden). His research interests include: marketing and distribution channels, sales and purchasing management, and electronic commerce. Dr. Rehme has extensive experience in industry as a consultant in fields such as industrial marketing, distribution/logistics, and electronic commerce. Prior to his dissertation he spent three years at various positions at ABB working with distribution strategies, sales/marketing, and project management.

Harry L. Reif is an Assistant Professor of Computer Information Systems at James Madison University (USA). He earned his doctorate at Virginia Commonwealth University and his MBA at Michigan State University. His primary teaching duties include telecommunications, networking, systems analysis and design, and project management courses at the undergraduate level. Dr. Reif also teaches master's level students in JMU's Information Security MBA program. His research interests include systems implementation, e-commerce, intelligent systems, project management, and information systems/telecommunications curriculum development.

William T. Rupp is currently an Associate Professor of Management at Robert Morris University, Pittsburgh, Pennsylvania (USA). He is serving as the Acting Associate Dean of the School of Business and is Program Director for the MBA program. He holds a PhD in Strategic Management from the Terry School of Business at the University of Georgia. He has published in the *Journal of Knowledge Management, Business Horizons*, and the *Journal of e-Business and IT*.

Detlef Schoder was recently appointed Professor at the University of Cologne, after serving as Professor and Chair at the Otto-Beisheim Graduate School of Management (WHU), Germany. His research and teaching focus on electronic commerce/electronic business, mass customization, peer-to-peer, ubiquitous computing, and media management. Dr. Schoder lists more than 130 reviewed publications, including articles in leading international and German journals. He also acts as a reviewer for several international journals and conferences, and is a member of numerous program committees and editorial boards. He holds an MBA degree and a doctorate degree in Business Administration, and has gained working experience in Germany, the USA, the Republic of Kazakhstan, and Japan.

Alan D. Smith is Professor of Operations Management at Robert Morris University, Pittsburgh, Pennsylvania (USA). Previously he was Chair of the Department of Quantitative and Natural Sciences and Coordinator of Engineering Programs at the same institution, as well as Associate Professor of Business Administration at Eastern Kentucky University. Previously employed by the Kentucky Geological Survey in rock mechanics and roof fall studies, he holds a PhD in Engineering Systems/Education from the University of Akron, and is currently ABD in the PhD program in Management Systems at Kent State University. He is the author and/or coauthor of numerous conference proceedings, articles, and chapters in books in the engineering and management disciplines.

Philip Sotiriades was born in Athens, Greece, in 1974. He received the diploma in Physics and a PhD in Electrical & Computer Engineering from the University of Patras, Greece, in 1998 and 2003 respectively. Since 1998, Dr. Sotiriades has been involved as a researcher in various programs funded by the Greek Government, the European Union, the Greek Telecommunications Organization, and major Greek Telecommunication industries. His research interests include data transmission, ISDN networks, ATM transmission, broadband communications, multimedia services, data management in group-working applications, teleworking middleware platforms, cellular mobile radio communication systems, and radio interference problems. He has published more than eight articles in international journals and conferences, and more than 20 technical papers and reports.

David C. Yen is a Professor of MIS and Chair of the Department of Decision Sciences and Management Information Systems at Miami University (USA). He received a PhD in MIS and a Master's of Science in Computer Science from the University of Nebraska. Dr. Yen is active in research: he has published two books and more that 100 articles that have appeared in *Communications of the ACM, Decision Support Systems, Information & Management, International Journal of Information Management, Information Sciences, Journal of Computer Information Systems, Interfaces, Telematics and Informatics, Computer Standards and Interfaces, Information Society,* and *Internet Research,* among others. He was also one of the co-recipients for a number of grants such as Cleveland Foundation (1987-1988), GE Foundation (1989), and Microsoft Foundation (1996-1997).

Dale Young is an Associate Professor of Information Systems at Georgia College and State University (USA). His research includes electronic commerce, and using IT in the supply chain, with publications on corporate usage of the Web for trading partner interactions. His most recent research focuses on how the Fortune 500 interact with suppliers using their public Web sites. Along with 14 years in academia, he's had 12 years of industry experience in information systems, direct sales, and retail management. This is Dr. Young's second book chapter with Idea Group Publishing. He is a member of the editorial advisory board for the *Journal of Organizational and End User Computing.*

Index

A

action agenda 168
aggregation of survey data 12
aggressive Internet strategy 274
Alaska 163
Alaska context 164, 166
Alaska's online operations 171
analytical CRM products 28
application (ASPs) 317
area networks 104
artist subscriptions 201
assumption list module 292, 312
authoring technology 165
automated campaign management
    applications 30
automation of routine 114
automobile industry 86, 88, 89, 90,
    92
automotive network exchange (ANX) 89
average variance extract (AVE) 220

B

B2B commerce 102, 103, 115
B2B commerce streamlining 109
B2B e-business 90

B2B network infrastructure 89
back-end processes 75
backbone information system (BBIS)
    75
banking and lending industry 254
bidding procedures 146
bottleneck items 130
bottom-line benefits 276
brick-and-mortar 236
brick-and-mortar buying motivator 236
brokerage effect 90
budgetary control 54
bulk bundles 203
"bull-whip" effect 89, 95
bundling 203
business continuity (BC) 79
business environment 79
business intelligence (BI) 79
business lifetime of the customer 33
business network redesign (BNR) 117
business process re-engineering (BPR)
    117
business relationship 1, 149, 154
business strategy 79
business-to-business (B2B)
    89, 102, 103

business-to-business (B2B) commerce 145
business-to-business environment 103, 112
business-to-business intermediary 107
business-to-consumer business model 112
buyer-oriented marketplace 107
buyer-supplier interface 102, 103, 114
buyer-supplier relationship 106, 111
buying firms 146
buying-firm participation in trade fairs 146

C

call centers 70
campaign management software 39
catalog sales venues 236
certification 156
certified minority supplier 153
Chartered Institute of Purchasing and Supply (CIPS) 116
chat-like conferences 331
clerical tasks 114
click-stream data 62
click-to-buy 128
co-engineering effect 86
collaboration 112
collaborative buyer-supplier relations 118
collaborative CRM products 28
collaborative relationships 111
collecting customer information 30
combination 90, 93
commercial agreements 131
commodity-like markets 112
community formation 174
community usage of the Internet 176
company-customer interaction 30
compelling forms 190
competitive advantage 51, 102, 198
competitive environment 272
competitive performance 268
competitors 188
computer networking 105
computer telephony integration (CTI) 52

connection management set-up 324
consolidation 111
consumer buying practices 236
consumer risk 235, 237, 240
contact management 78
continuous improvement 155
corporate success 9
corporate trading partner 147
corporate value 10
corporate Websites 147
COSMOS 67
cost ledgers 288
cost reduction 9
cost-prohibitive infrastructure 119
covariance structure model 11
CPR model 50, 58, 75
CRM processes 38
CRM system 21, 23, 27, 29
CRM/eCRM initiative 54
CRM/eCRM integration 65
CRM/eCRM-related technologies 65
CROSIT 58, 77
CROSIT model 50
customer billing 78
customer data 51, 55
customer drivers 52
customer information 53
customer intelligence 52
customer interaction 4
customer lifetime value (CLV) 30, 31, 41
customer management applications 27
customer management operations 27
customer process reference (CPR) 75
customer relationship management (CRM) 1, 2, 21, 22, 23, 105
customer requirements 110
customer service 145, 235, 237, 239
customer services and support (CSS) 70, 78
customer-centric approach 23
customer-centric corporate culture 21, 37
customer-centric culture 27
customer-centric Internet strategies 21
customer-centric organization 21, 23, 41

customer-centric procedures 29
customer-centric values 23
customer-company interaction 39
customer-driven markets 51
customer-focused enterprise 23
customer-oriented strategy 22
customer-service provider relationship 25
customer-supplier life cycle (C-SLC) 108
customer's profile 30
customization 87, 90
customized investments 92

D

data aggregation 4
data analysis 288
data and voice networks 317
data center (DCSPs) 317
data collection 4, 96, 241
data exchange 87, 92
data mining 39
database systems 51
dataflow simulation module 294
defensive strategies 274
derivation of model hypotheses 7
descriptive analysis 12
design specifications 288
diffusion of innovations theory 276
digital integration 166
digital markets 21
digital opportunities 163, 164, 181
Digital Opportunities Task Force (DOT Force) 168
digital platform 164
digital transactions 166
digitizing technology 165
diverse suppliers 143
"dynamic capability" 88
"dynamic learning capability" 94

E

e-banking 261
e-banking/e-lending 254, 272, 278, 279
e-banking/e-lending industry 254, 276

e-banking/e-lending services 265
e-borrowing 266
e-business environment 73, 77, 312
e-business InfoNet 51
e-business infrastructure 53, 165
e-business management 165
e-business strategy 143
e-business system development 286
e-business systems 68
e-businesses 51, 62
e-commerce 163, 209
e-commerce (eCSPs) 317
e-commerce aspects 254
e-commerce development 126
e-commerce environment 255
e-commerce purchase perceptions 241
e-commerce service providers (eCSP's) 329
e-commerce solutions 126, 130
e-commerce strategy 158, 159
e-commerce survey 127
e-commerce systems 235
e-commerce vendors 211
e-lending institutions 269
e-lending/e-banking industry 255
e-marketplaces 134
e-procurement 125, 128
e-procurement Dynamics 139
e-procurement initiatives 131, 136, 138
e-procurement solution 125, 126, 130, 137
e-procurement system 131
easy-to-buy 128
(EC)CRM process 5
ECCRM system 5
ECCRM-capability 6
economic information 302
eCRM and alignment 73
eCRM component technologies 80
eCRM implementation 56
eCRM industry 27
eCRM integration 50
eCRM solutions 29
eCRM success 57
eCRM system 27, 50
eCRM workflow 73

eCRM/CRM and integration 66
eCRM/CRM and market developments 59
eCRM/CRM implementation 55, 69, 75
eCRM/CRM integrated technologies 70
eCRM/CRM programs 52
eCRM/CRM system 75
eCRM/CRM system interactions 51
eCustomer relationship management 61
eCustomers' relationships 62
EDI transactions 111
electronic brokerage effect 93
electronic business (e-business) 89
electronic business-to-business commerce 104
electronic commerce 1, 7, 9, 109, 111, 114, 119, 257
electronic commerce customer relationship management 1, 2
electronic commerce technologies 102, 114
electronic communication effect 93
electronic data interchange (EDI) 103, 104, 148
electronic forms 156
electronic funds transfer 114
electronic integration effect 93
electronic linkage effect 86
electronic markets 51
electronic payments 166
electronic retailing 235
electronic supply chain (eSC) 87
electronic supply chain design (eSCD) 86, 87
electronic supply chain network 89
electronic trading partner systems 148
elicitation survey 218
eLoyalty matrix 25, 26
email/messaging (eMSPs) 317
emergent nature of e-commerce 255
end-user activities 27
enterprise application integration (EAI) 65, 80
enterprise information systems (EISs) 80

enterprise resource planning (ERP) 105
entity relationship simulation module 294
equity matrix 34
European automobile component industry 112
evolution of B2B commerce 104
evolution of the banking 254
exclusivity 201
exponential regression 308
extensible markup language (XML) 119
externalization 90, 93, 94

F

factory network 113
Federal Deposit Insurance Corporation (FDIC) 255
federal government expenditure 163
financial constraints 53
financial risks 270
financial stability 157
financial supermarkets. 273
financial transactions 145
financial Web-enabled strategy 259
first-tier suppliers 111
front-end systems 73
function decompositions 288
functional logic module 295

G

global ANX (GNX) 89
global Internet market 59
globalization 166
gross state product (GSP) 167

H

habit formation 215
hardware, software, and interfaces (HSIs) 288
hierarchical supply chain 88
Homo Contentus 189
horizontal organization 66
hosting (HSPs) 317
hosting service provider (HSP) 323
human capital 53

hypothesis development 212

I

immediate feedback 260
industrial markets 125
industrial procurement 132
information and communication technology (ICT) 163
information brokerage 94
information exchange 87, 93
information integration 94
information integration effect 94
information publishing 145
information sharing 109
information sharing/integration 93
information systems (ISs) 51
information technology (IT) 86, 87, 110, 111, 286, 287
information-based paradigm 165
innovation 10
integrating eCRM 65
integration 79
integration effect 90
inter-organizational information systems (IOSs) 103
inter-organizational networks 102
inter-organizational relationships 111
inter-organizational systems (IOSs) 58, 81
interactive voice response system (IVRS) 317, 319
interface documentation module 293
interface specific modules 293
intermediaries 113, 116
internal customers 146
internalization 93, 94
internalization/socialization 90
Internet as a change agent 255
Internet buying 235
Internet communication 188
Internet delivery 272
Internet infrastructure 105
Internet usage of government agencies 170
Internet-based forecasting module (IFM) 292, 307

Internet-empowered consumers 259
Internet-enabled communications 105
Internet-only banks 272
interpersonal relationships 131
interrelated systems 79
intranet usage 174
investment returns 143
involvement of suppliers 92
IT platform 106
IVRS provider (IVRSP) 326

K

knowledge creation 92
knowledge creation cycle 93
knowledge creation processes 90
knowledge-sharing network 87, 94
Korea 87
Kraljic classification scheme 129
Kraljic's matrix 128

L

least square or linear regression 307
lending industry 254
linkage effect 90
linkage effect of eSCD 91
LISREL model 11
load balancing 325
local area network (LAN) 323
location independence 324
logarithmic regression 308
logic specifications 288
logical access path module 296
logical data dictionary module 295
logistic channels 86
logistical arrangements 131
long-term relationships 131
loyalty programs 78

M

majority suppliers 147
majority/primary suppliers 152
management (MSPs) 317
management service provider (MSP) 326
materials management 136

media companies 188
message list module 297
minority business 154
minority supplier programs 146
minority supplier spending targets 146
minority suppliers 143, 157
minority-owned firms 144
mixing digital and physical 201
mobile communication 188
model for e-procurement 135
models of B2B commerce 106
modernization model 286
modularization 98
multi-functional interactions 111
multi-point control unit (MCU) 329
multi-step discounts 203
MWBE content placement 149
MWBE Web pages 156
"MWBE" 148

N

National Minority Supplier Development
    Council (NMSDC) 150
network (NSPs) 317
network publishing 165
network service provider (NSP) 326
networking technology 165

O

offline communication 330
old economy 188
on-time delivery 157
online business activities 22
online businesses 27
online communication 331
"online competition" 130
online content 190
online customer systems 54
online customers 51, 73
online leading problems 271
online management 78
online markets 23
online purchasing behavior 209
online retail businesses 23
online shopping 210
online/offline customer interaction 73

"open" market 139
operational CRM products 28
operational effectiveness 29, 268
operational requirements 155
order management process 109, 116
organizational boundaries 114
organizational culture 23
organizational infrastructure 105
organizational re-structuring 21
outsourcing procurement activities 114

P

past behavior 215
past purchasing behavior 209
perceived behavioral control 209, 214,
    219, 230
performance metrics 146
personality traits 110
personalization technologies 62, 65
Pipe-Chain 128
polynomial regression 308
portals 188
post, telephone, and telegraph (PTT)
    enterprises 317
power regression 308
premature failure 301
"premium content" 188
price customization 203
price structure 195
pricing strategy 194
private firms 170
probability of failure 301
process and e-procurement 132
process documentation module 294
process specific modules 294
procurement 126
procurement and e-commerce 127
product perception 235, 237
product suggestion 114
product 'systemization' 98
product-focused business 21
profit maximization 35
profitability of investment decisions 286
programming environment 289
prototype modules 296
provisioning module 292

publishing houses 188
purchase perceptions 235, 237
purchasing cards 114
purchasing clout 126
purchasing department 114
purchasing strategy 125, 126

R

rationalization 111
real-time collaborative conferences 331
relationship-based behavioral model 27
requests for quotation (RFQs) 107
requirement analysis module 291, 312
requirement specification 288
requirements analysis 288
research approach 6
resulting model structure 11
retail industry information technologies
    110
return on investment (ROI) 54
role of intermediaries 112
role of past behavior 215

S

sales force automation (SFA) 69, 78,
    80
seamless integration 115
second-tier suppliers 111
segmentation 33
sellability of content 190
selling content online 189
selling music online 189, 198
service prices 157
service providers (SPs) 317, 318
shared resources 78
shopping experience 235, 237, 238
shopping habits 110
simple infrastructure 87
site asset specification 92
small business administration (SBA)
    150
small minority firms 146
small to mid-sized minority firms 159
SMM added value 298
SMM algorithms 303
SMM analysis 300

SMM decision-making process 299
SMM operation 301
socialization 93, 94
software utility components re-use 324
sourcing management 136
spatial customer information (SCI) 63
statistical analysis 13
storage (SSPs) 317
storage service provider (SSP) 328
strategic alignment model 58
strategic planning process 29
strategic success factors 187
stretch discounts 203
structural equation model (SEM) 11
sub-assemblers 112
sub-suppliers 112
subjective norm 209, 214, 230
successful electronic retailers 235
supplier communications 155
supplier development 146
supplier diversity 146, 147, 154
supplier diversity content 149
supplier diversity programs 155
supplier network 112
supplier relationships 139
supplier-oriented marketplace 107
supply chain 90
supply chain coordination 87, 94
supply chain coordination effect 86
supply chain design (SCD) 88
supply chain management (SCM) 65,
    86, 105, 132
supply chain members 102, 111
supply chain performance 97
supply chain relationships 143, 144
supply chains 93
supply management 136
survey instrument 241
system designers and developers
    (SD&Ds) 286, 287
system development lifecycle 287
system functionality 56
system model module 296
system modernization module (SMM)
    288, 297
systems development and moderniza-
    tion model (SDMM) 287

T

taste matching 201
technical information 302
technological capabilities 157
technology providers' online operations 171
tele-working platform (TWP) 317, 318
tele-working platform services operational modes 330
theory of planned behavior 209, 212
time savings 260
time-to-customer (TTC) 128
time-to-market (TTM) 128
top management support 146
total financial contribution 31
trading relationship 154
traditional marketing 125
transaction costs 94
transmission control/Internet protocol (TCP/IP) 105

U

usage of government Websites 175
usage of the Internet 172
usage of the Internet in Alaska 164
user logic modules 297, 313
user profile module 292
user specification module 297
user-friendly environment 156

V

value added networks 104
value adding activities 114
value chain 103, 126
value destruction of the business 33
value segmentation 33
value-added network connections 148
value-added networks (VANs) 111
value-added services 109
vendor knowledge 239
vendor managed inventory (VMI) 128
vertical integration 166
"virtual environment" 270
virtual markets 105
virtual server (VS) 328

virtuality 166

W

Web strategies 159
Web-based B2B forms 145
Web-based B2B marketplace 145
Web-based extranets 148
Web-based information systems (WBIS) 75
Web-based links 157
Web-based minority supplier communication 148, 154, 157
Web-based MWBE 158
Web-based MWBE programs 159
Web-based programs 154
Web-based supplier communications 143
Web-based supplier diversity 155, 156
Web-based supplier diversity initiatives 159
wide area network (WAN) 323
women-owned businesses 146
women-owned firms 146
women-owned trading partners 144
Women's Business Enterprise National Council (WBENC) 150
World Wide Web (WWW) 51

X

x-service provider 325
x-service providers (x-SPs) 317